THE INDIAN MINORITY
OF ZAMBIA, RHODESIA,
AND MALAWI

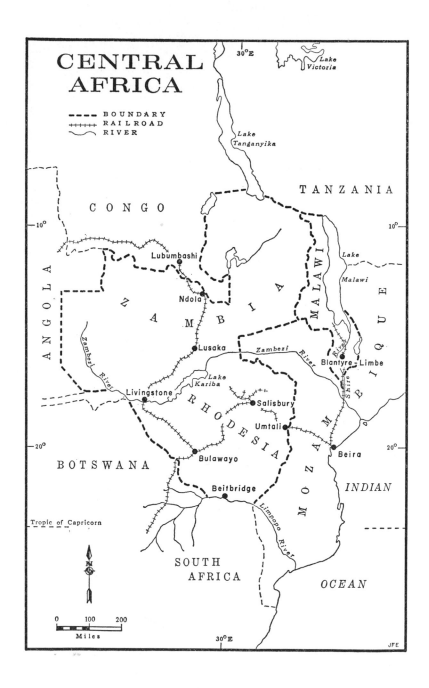

CENTRAL
AFRICA

━ ━ ━ BOUNDARY
┼┼┼┼┼ RAILROAD
〜〜〜 RIVER

Lake
Victoria

30°E

Lake
Tanganyika

CONGO

TANZANIA

10°

10°

Lubumbashi

Lake
Malawi

ZAMBIA

MALAWI

Ndola

ANGOLA

Zambezi River

Lusaka

Zambezi River

Blantyre Limbe

Shire River

Livingstone

Lake
Kariba

RHODESIA

Salisbury

Umtali

MOZAMBIQUE

Beira

20°

20°

BOTSWANA

Bulawayo

Beitbridge

INDIAN

Tropic of Capricorn

Limpopo River

SOUTH
AFRICA

OCEAN

N

0   100   200
Miles

30°E

JFE

THE INDIAN MINORITY
OF ZAMBIA, RHODESIA,
AND MALAWI

by Floyd Dotson
and Lillian O. Dotson

YALE UNIVERSITY PRESS
NEW HAVEN AND LONDON
1968

Dedicated to
Sheila

PREFACE

When first proposed in 1957, this study of the Indian minority of Central Africa was conceived as part of a series then being planned by the Rhodes-Livingstone Institute in Lusaka. Each project within this series would center upon one of the component ethnic groups—African, European, Indian, or Coloured —of what at that time was typically described as the emerging plural society of Central Africa.

It seems generally agreed that we owe the term "plural society" to J. S. Furnivall, a scholarly civil servant and banker who lived and worked for many years in British colonial Asia. Among his numerous works, Furnivall made a comparative study of administration in Burma and the Dutch East Indies, and his ideas concerning the nature of plural society are perhaps most fully developed in that setting.[1] Such societies, Furnivall contended, have a basically similar social structure, the generic characteristics of which could be found in any tropical dependency. Above all, these societies are racially and culturally heterogeneous, being composed of a "medley of peoples," each with "its own religion, its own culture and language, its own ideas and ways." The overall result is "a many coloured pattern [in] the population." Social contacts and relations between and among these disparate groups are highly impersonal. What integration is achieved is solely economic and political; and political order is imposed from the outside. "As individuals [the members of the plural society] meet, but only in the market place, in buying and selling." Relations are therefore governed upon extreme laissez-faire principles but without the uncon-

1. J. S. Furnivall, *Colonial Policy and Practice: A Comparative Study of Burma and Netherlands India* (New York, New York University Press, 1956).

scious guidance and control of a common cultural tradition which made classical laissez-faire principles in Europe tolerable.

A very large part of the colonial world as it had developed up to World War II seemed to fit Furnivall's description extraordinarily well. The concept of plural society caught on, particularly among British scholars.[2] Yet curiously enough there was only a limited effort to examine more systematically what plural society might imply in terms of established sociological theory.[3] An attempt to do so, as we originally conceived it, would constitute the theoretical contribution of this book.

As we worked in Africa, however, we became increasingly skeptical of the potentialities of plural society as an analytical concept in formal theory. Society in Central Africa is indeed objectively and vividly "plural" in that it is composed of radically different ethnic groups; *descriptively*, therefore, the term has a certain justification.[4] But as an *analytical* concept, plural society is both misleading and wrongheaded in our opinion. It is misleading in that it posits as its logical opposite a unitary society which no longer exists—if indeed it ever did. It is wrongheaded in that it focuses attention upon the largely historical differences among the various ethnic groups rather than where the emphasis belongs if we are to understand them in terms of dynamic development: upon the processes and circumstances which have brought them into interaction. These

2. To liberal intellectuals in the British Colonial Office and Central Africa during the early 1950s, "plural society" rather obviously contained a fervent implicit hope: namely, that peoples of widely different cultures and social status *could* live amiably together, each in its own sphere, each pursuing its peculiar values and following its own mode of life without painful encroachment upon others. See below, pp. 304–09, where we discuss the liberal "ideal" federation.

3. This statement is now less true than when it was originally drafted. For bibliography and a critical discussion of "plural society," see Appendix, pp. 390–95 and in particular, n. 15.

4. Significantly, this is the way in which the term has been most often used. For example, one will look in vain for a formal definition, let alone an extended theoretical discussion, in L. H. Gann's fine book, *The Birth of a Plural Society: The Development of Northern Rhodesia under the British South Africa Company 1894–1914* (Manchester, Manchester University Press, 1958). For his purposes, Gann obviously felt that the meaning of "plural society" was self-evident, as indeed it is when used descriptively.

processes are highly colored and dramatic in Central Africa, but there is nothing fundamentally particular or peculiar about them. What we find when we look at Central Africa is not a form of society so unusual that it deserves a special name. What we find, unless we err, is modern society in an admittedly somewhat exotic setting.

The unity of modern society should of course not be exaggerated. But it cannot be ignored either. Nor, surely, is there any great mystery as to where the unity that is empirically apparent comes. It is ultimately derived from (or at the very least it is intimately related to) the socio-cultural processes of europeanization.

With the end of imperialism in its classic colonial form, the dominant cultural influence of Europeans remains and is progressively extended. But socially and politically the situation in the old tropical dependency described by Furnivall has radically altered as hitherto submerged base populations have assumed political power. One of the facets of these new orders which has changed most drastically is the status of the advanced immigrant minorities enclaved within them. Caught as they are at the center of the portentous shift in cultural influence and political power now taking place in Central Africa, Indians provide an ideal pivot for the study of a new kind of minority status, its meaning and significance. It is to this task that our efforts are directed in this book.

That portion of the history of Central Africa in which Indians have participated begins with European administration and settlement; details of the story are set forth as they bear upon the Indian community and its economic role. We then examine in some considerable detail how the Central African social milieu has either forced or encouraged adaptive changes in indigenous Indian institutions: religion, caste, family, and community organization. From here we turn our attention outward once more to treat systematically some typical social roles within which Indians interact with members of other ethnic groups, and their reaction to the political changes which brought independence and African governments to present day Zambia and Malawi.

In conclusion, the salient features of the new states of this region are outlined as these bear upon ethnic relations and the future of the Indians.

To more than any other single individual, we are indebted to Henry A. Fosbrooke, former Director of the Rhodes-Livingstone Institute (now Institute for Social Research, the University of Zambia). It was he who suggested the possibility of the project to us originally, and his efforts were instrumental in bringing it into being. To other members of the Institute staff at the time of our affiliation we are similarly indebted for assistance, encouragement, and intellectual stimulation; among these people are Raymond J. Apthorpe, Charles M. N. White, Allie A. Dubb, and George G. Murrell, but the list could be greatly extended. At home base, in the Department of Sociology and Anthropology at the University of Connecticut, the senior author's colleagues bore graciously with the extra duties and inconveniences imposed by his extended absence; in particular, this observation applies to James H. Barnett, then department head. When the manuscript neared completion, it was read by Albert K. Cohen and Seth Leacock; for their constructive criticisms we are duly grateful. Michael Gordon, then a graduate student in the department, also read and commented upon the work. For help of this nature, we owe a very special debt to Chagan Lalloo of the University of Lund in Sweden who read those chapters dealing with Indian institutions; it will be seen that we have used his comments liberally and that we have also drawn upon one of Mr. Lalloo's unpublished papers which he generously made available to us.

Finally, we come to the most important debt of all, which by the established conventions of social science we cannot acknowledge directly. We refer of course to the anonymous and patiently enduring subjects of our often awkward attempts at investigation. These persons include people of all races in Central Africa, but by the nature of the study they are in the main Indians. Many of these people became in the course of time personal friends. We wish them well and will always remember them with profound respect and deep affection.

Our original fieldwork was financed by a research fellowship under the Fulbright program and was carried out in Central Africa from September 1959 through August 1961. At that time the three territories of British Central Africa (the common designation during the colonial era) were politically organized into a semi-autonomous state, the Federation of Rhodesia and Nyasaland.[5] During the summer of 1966, a National Science Foundation grant supported a return visit of two months by the senior author in order to verify our observations and conclusions in the now independent states of Zambia, Rhodesia, and Malawi.

FLOYD DOTSON

LILLIAN O. DOTSON

Storrs, Connecticut

May 1, 1967

---

5. The breakup of the federation after our initial fieldwork was completed imposes some terminological difficulties. For the sake of consistency, we will use "Central Africa" when referring to the area encompassed by the former federation; when it is desirable to include the Republic of South Africa in the discussion, we use the term "southern Africa" for the entire socio-geographic region. When referring to the Central African territories, as we constantly must, our self-imposed rule will be to use "Nyasaland," "Northern Rhodesia," and "Southern Rhodesia" when the time period of reference is *before* independence. "Malawi" and "Zambia" will be used when speaking of the first two territories *after* they achieved the status of sovereign nations, or when the statement applies to the present as well as to the past. In a similar manner, "Rhodesia" will be used instead of "Southern Rhodesia" when the rule is appropriate.

CONTENTS

TABLES

Chapter One

ETHNIC GROUP AND SOCIETY

Ethnic minorities are a common phenomenon in the modern world. As such they have perhaps received their fair share of sociological attention. Social scientists nonetheless widely recognize that this important field of interest and effort is poorly developed theoretically and suffers from a certain parochialism in terms of problems and focus.[1] What theory exists is heavily psychological in orientation, the origins, functions, and distribution of prejudiced attitudes being the perennially popular subject of investigation.

Is it too much to suggest that this predominant emphasis upon psychology is a kind of luxury, reflecting the fact that most of the research in ethnic and race relations has been done in the advanced countries, notably in the United States?[2] In such societies the minority group may very well constitute a serious social and moral problem; but its functional role is

1. Cf. Frank R. Westie, "Race and Ethnic Relations," in Robert E. L. Faris, ed., *Handbook of Modern Sociology* (Chicago, Rand McNally, 1964), pp. 576–618.

2. The sociological literature on ethnic and race relations is mainly American for the simple reason that empirical sociology is so largely an American product. What, we might profitably ask, would a theory of ethnic relations look like if it were derived not from the Old South and the Chicago of Robert E. Park but from Central and Eastern Europe, which is *terra incognita* to the vast majority of American sociologists? Intriguing hints of what some of these differences in emphasis might be are suggested in L. H. Gann, "Liberal Interpretations of South African History," *Human Problems in British Central Africa, Rhodes-Livingstone Journal,* No. 25 (1959), pp. 40–58. But, significantly, Gann is a historian rather than a sociologist.

1

unlikely to be truly critical. Minorities are marginal to the main structure of the advanced society. Practically, this marginality is seen and emphasized as their essential problem: they stand to one side and remain unintegrated into the major currents of national life. When integrated, they are absorbed and disappear.

In that considerable proportion of the world commonly called underdeveloped, the role of the ethnic minority is typically very different.[3] Superficially, minorities may seem here to be even less integrated with the other components of the population than they are in the advanced countries—an impression so strong that the resulting social structure is described by many scholars as "plural society." Their political and economic functions nonetheless loom very large indeed, belying in this respect the uncritical impression derived from vivid differences in custom and styles of life. The ethnic dimension may thus be fundamental to the existing constitution of such societies, not marginal and insignificant. The base population is by definition backward economically and culturally; in blunter terms than is usually considered polite, this is what underdeveloped means. By contrast, the immigrant ethnic minority almost always represents an advanced group; if it did not, it would never have been attracted into the area. The structural significance of such groups may therefore be utterly disproportionate to their numbers. The Europeans of East and Central Africa, to cite an admittedly extreme example, must now with the coming of African governments to these regions be counted as simply one minority among others in the population. But they more than any other group have been responsible for the shape and direction of society there in modern times.

This basic difference in the functional role of the immigrant

---

3. More specifically, perhaps we should say the role of the *immigrant* minority. While advanced immigrants are a feature of "developing" societies, marginal indigenous groups even more backward than the local base population also may be present in such societies. The numerous hill tribes of Burma would be examples of such indigenous minorities, as would the primitive peoples on the margins of Indonesia. Sociologically, the position of such groups is an entirely different phenomenon than that of the advanced immigrant minority.

minority makes it hazardous to compare ethnic or race relations in the new states recently carved out of the old colonial
territories of Asia and Africa with those characteristic of the
advanced industrial society. Similarities and parallels may be
instructively drawn. But differences in context and content are
so great that the assumption that one is talking about the same
thing because one uses the same terms may be nullified.

THE MIDDLEMAN TRADERS
OF CENTRAL AFRICA

Descriptively, this volume is a kind of sociological ethnography of the Indian people of Central Africa, a small minority
caught up in revolutionary processes which they neither created
nor control. Gujarati-speaking like their counterparts in South
and East Africa, they now number about 30,000 out of a total
regional population of perhaps 11 million. Originally, they
came to Africa under the umbrella of European power. In
independent Zambia and Malawi, they stay to make what peace
they can with the now dominant African group.

Functionally, within this fairly typical example of plural
society, Indians play the middleman trader's role. Small as
their numbers are in proportion to the total population, they
control something like 75 percent of the retail business in
Malawi, and they are correspondingly important in the African
trade of Zambia and Rhodesia.

"Foreigners" like these Indians of Central Africa are most
commonly found in the merchant's role in regions with a
developing—but still not developed—economy. In such societies, trade is expanding; there is an increasing demand for
goods, but the goods in demand are not produced locally. Up to
the point in history at which the immigrant group puts in its
appearance, the base population of such societies has been
composed in the typical case of self-sufficient peasant farmers.
As a class, these peasants possess neither the knowledge nor
the capital necessary to conduct long-distance trading operations. This function therefore must be performed—if it is in

fact performed at all—by outsiders. Middleman trading groups of foreign origin, mediating between relatively developed areas producing manufactured goods and less developed ones which constitute a market, are a far older and far more widespread phenomenon than is generally recognized.

In the best review of the subject known to the authors, Howard Becker takes as his first example the ancient Milesians of classical Mediterranean civilization, a footloose people of vaguely Greek origin who by the time they appear in history were already established "international" traders, scattered from the Black Sea to Egypt.[4] Modern Greeks, as Becker goes on to point out, have played the middleman trader's role for centuries throughout the Middle East and North Africa; representatives of this ancient lineage are still present in Central Africa. Parsees, people of the Zoroastrian religion and Persian origin, have long traded in the cities and towns of western India; there can be little doubt that the originally agricultural Gujarati Indians who are the subjects of the present study learned something from their example. Chinese, on the other hand, have been the typical commercial group throughout Southeast Asia with the exception of Burma, where Indians roughly similar to those of East and Central Africa until recently controlled most of the retail trade.[5]

Of whatever ethnic origin in whatever time and place, relations between "guest" trading peoples (as Max Weber so aptly called them) and their hosts have had remarkably similar characteristics.[6] Relations tend not only to be impersonal (as trade relations between members of the same ethnic group also typically are), but they are apt to be somewhat antagonistic as well. More sophisticated in the ways of the larger world than their hosts, guests tend to be seen by

4. Howard Becker, *Man in Reciprocity: Introductory Lectures on Culture, Society, and Personality* (New York, Praeger, 1956), pp. 225–37.

5. The position of these two minorities in the new states of Southeast Asia closely parallels in certain respects that of the Indians in East and Central Africa. See below, p. 365, nn. 27, 28, and also pp. 374–76.

6. See Max Weber, *General Economic History* (New York, Collier Books, 1961), pp. 151, 166, 263–64; and also his *Ancient Judaism* (Glencoe, Ill., Free Press, 1952), passim.

the hosts as cunning and devious. On the other hand, from the standpoint of the guest, the host is an outsider who at best tolerates you and at worst hates you. In business relations, therefore, he is fair game and must watch out for himself. *Caveat emptor*. Within your own ethnic group, however, the *Gemeinschaft* morality of kinsman and neighbor prevails.[7]

THE THEORETICAL PERSPECTIVE [8]

Theoretically, we see our work primarily as a contribution to the study of power: to the meaning and processes of ethnic dominance and subordination.

Ethnic relations in modern southern Africa, we maintain, cannot be meaningfully understood apart from the evolutionary forces which brought them into being. Like all problems of societal evolution and change, this involves an appreciation of the dialectical relationship which exists between "society" on the one hand and "culture" on the other. A clear separation of the "social" components of the problem from the "cultural" ones must be made at the *conceptual* level so that the two can be correctly related at the empirically observed level of concrete behavior, where of course they are inseparable. This has not always been done with the requisite rigor and consistency.

An all too common approach to social structures like those of southern Africa overemphasizes the cultural components at the expense of the social—most often, it must be added, quite unintentionally since no clear distinction is made between them in the first place. Sensitive to the basic lesson taught by modern anthropology, the observer sees the pluralistic nature of such social systems as their overridingly significant characteristic. Attention is called to the great variety and depth of the cultural differences which mark and divide the various ethnic groups, and a plea is made (implicitly or explicitly) for a

7. In the context cited, the nature of this "dual ethic" with its implications for "race" relations is Becker's main interest in the middleman trader's role. Becker, p. 237.

8. Readers primarily interested in theory will find in the appendix a much fuller version of this statement, complete with documentation.

5

proper appreciation of their intrinsic worth and value. Peace and harmony all around, it is rather naively hoped, will prevail once the intellectual foundations are laid for mutual tolerance based on sympathetic understanding. Thinking along such lines—it should be pointed out since it is not entirely irrelevant —is congenial with the political liberalism of most social scientists.

We have no quarrel whatsoever with these sentiments at the level of abstract desirability; they are in fact our own. Our work in Africa nonetheless gradually convinced us that a pluralistic emphasis upon the culturally unique does less than adequate justice to the observable facts of social power and tends to confuse the intimate relationship inherent between the two. Cultural differences in such situations as those of southern Africa do not simply and neutrally exist as innocent variations in folkways and customs. In actuality, they are socially and politically organized into hierarchies of power, prestige, and privilege. To our minds, it is precisely this *social projection of culture* which is most commonly neglected in sociological analyses of society in modern Africa.

In order to make the separation of "society" from "culture" which we believe requisite to an analysis of social structures of the kind treated in this study, we have found it heuristically useful to resurrect and refurbish a pair of concepts originally advanced by Park in his attempt to comprehend the organization and integration of urban communities: his distinction between *ecological* and *moral* order.

To understand Park, we must appreciate that he wrote prior to the establishment of the modern cultural or, alternatively, normative-functionalist conception of social organization and behavior.[9] Instead, his sociology reflected his reading in the just emerging science of plant ecology. Park had a concept of culture to be sure, since he constantly used the term, but it was the older, premodern folkloristic one which had prevailed up to that time. Culture to Park was that body of distinctive

9. The development of the normative-functionalist conception of society is treated extensively in the appendix.

traits—language, customs, manners, and morals—which sets one ethnic group off from another; it was not the all-inclusive determinant of behavior which it has since become to modern students. In order to understand relations between or among ethnic groups, he believed it necessary to postulate a substratum of essentially biological organization similar to, if not quite identical with, that which prevails in the plant and animal kingdoms. To this ecological order founded in impersonal competition and blind cooperation, Park attributed most of the overall unity which he saw in the diversity of Chicago and other large American cities. Opposed to this unconscious and largely unrecognized ecological order is a moral order, based in the customs and traditions of a group. Unlike the ecological order, which man shares with all other living organisms, the moral order is a strictly human phenomenon, made possible by man's capacity for language and normative consensus.

The notion that any very large proportion of human social behavior can be reduced to biological principles is now rejected by all modern social scientists. Nonetheless, as sociologists have become increasingly aware, a normative interpretation of social behavior based upon the concept of culture presents serious problems. Such theory presumes a degree of consensus which is difficult to observe in modern, heterogeneous societies, divided as these almost invariably are into diverse class, ethnic, and other groupings. Thus the theoretical issue which Park raised and so forcefully stated in his ecological theory—namely, the basis, character, and mechanisms of that portion of social integration which lies outside of normative awareness and control—remains with us and is curiously neglected in current sociological theory. In particular, as a number of critics have recently pointed out, normative-functionalist theory is ill-equipped to handle the pervasive problems of power, conflict, and change which loom so large as obvious characteristics of almost any contemporary social scene.

The reader will not find in this volume a definitive solution to these fundamental problems of contemporary sociological theory. But he will find, we believe, that we have worked in awareness of them, that our empirical data substantiate their relevance, and that we do have some ideas with respect to the direction from which the needed correction must come.

Briefly, our theoretical guideline for this study is a modernized process, or interactional, conception of society, the roots of which lie mainly in the older, pre-normative conflict school of sociology. Such a view must take culture as it is now understood fully into account; culture, we assume as do other sociologists and anthropologists, is the major determinant of human mentality. At a given level of development, culture thus sets within very narrow limits the potentialities of action, both social and non-social. But unlike normative-functionalist theory in which "society" tends to be assimilated to "culture," attention is focused upon group interaction, not upon its defining norms. From this perspective, *culture appears as an ever-emergent evolutionary product and emphasis falls upon its instrumental quality.* Culture, as is constantly illustrated in the empirical data of this volume, provides the means for group conflict.

In this perspective, socio-cultural change is made far more intelligible than it is in normative-functionalist theory. Again, as illustrated in our research materials, its dynamics are to be sought in the interplay between social and cultural elements, between concrete groups of living individuals on the one hand and the institutional forms which guide their behavior on the other. The same perspective also provides insight into the nature and functions of power. Dominant groups, we now see clearly, are not dominant by accident or through moral aberration; they are dominant because they possess superior means to power. Power as a social phenomenon is thus removed from the intellectual vacuum where cultural relativism has left it and is made intelligible in terms of cultural evolution and group processes.

In the immediate past in Central Africa, it is clear beyond quibble who has exercised both social and cultural power. For this reason, in a book focused primarily upon the Indian, a good deal of attention must be occupied by the European, his behavior and his culture. By contrast, less attention needs to be devoted to the African until the post-independence period when he assumes political (but not cultural) dominance.

Power, its source and direction, is thus a crucial element in our analysis. Yet it is one of the fascinating paradoxes of human interaction that powerful as any one group is in a given social situation, its power is never absolute, short of physical annihilation of the subordinate. Unequal as the forces may be, interaction between dominant and subordinate is never a one-way street. The dominant exercises the most power, but he no more than the subordinate enjoys complete control of the situation. Precisely because interaction between dominant and subordinate occurs, new and hitherto unmanifested socio-cultural forms continually emerge, unanticipated and unforeseen by the participating members. Since mentality in human beings is cultural, man can only think in terms of norms established in the groups of which he is a member; to conceive of that which is not yet an existing cultural reality is for him a psychological impossibility. Yet the norms which guide and determine man's thought are constantly changing through the operation of the group processes. It follows from this argument that an important part of the ultimate product of group interaction lies in the beginning beyond the conscious awareness of its collective creators and is not recognized until it becomes manifested in action. In essence, this assumption underlies our interpretation of both the imperialistic past of European dominance in Central Africa and the rise of African nationalism. Within the new African state, ethnic conflict continues but necessarily assumes different forms.

Shorn of all biological connotations, the primary referent for the term ecological intended in this volume is this unconscious, non-normative portion of the continuously emergent socio-historical process. Different in ultimate interpretation, use of the term helps to retain the valuable part of Park's original insight: namely, that social relations (and, in particular, ethnic relations) do have an unplanned and therefore uncontrolled dimension as well as a normative moral order. As in all sociological analysis, the moral order of cultural definition and institutionalized value that makes social relations possible and gives them their form and structure will receive most of the attention in this study; the emphasis given in the above discussion to the ecological factor arises more from its relative neglect in previous work than from its inherent weight. Seen in its relation to the ecological order, however, the moral order appears not as an a priori Kantian entity outside of time and history, but as a structure continuously created and recreated out of the ongoing social process.

METHODOLOGY AND FIELDWORK TECHNIQUES

Field research always involves a decision concerning the geographic boundaries within which data will be gathered. Three alternatives appeared to present themselves when field-work was initiated in the fall of 1959: (1) to collect data more or less randomly from all three territories of the then existing Federation of Rhodesia and Nyasaland, upon the assumption that this would be the best way to sample a variegated and widely scattered population; (2) to study a single community intensively, with the assumption that its similarities to others elsewhere override obvious differences; or (3) to try to combine in some manner the advantages of both (1) and (2).

In view of the fact that the initial grant was only for a ten-month period, the first of these alternatives was quickly rejected; it would, we felt, spread our efforts much too thinly. Instead, it was decided to concentrate mainly upon a single, fairly large urban community in Northern Rhodesia in which both Hindus and Muslims were represented in approximately equal proportions, paying only cursory attention to neighboring communities in the same territory or to those in Nyasaland and Southern Rhodesia.

10

As work proceeded certain disadvantages attendant upon this choice became apparent. If we were to speak meaningfully of the Indians of Central Africa, a sampling problem presented itself which could not be completely ignored. The history, populations, and problems of Indians in each of the three territories are different enough to make certain kinds of generalizations hazardous without some knowledge of the territorial variations. In the second place, we encountered resistance to certain lines of inquiry in our community of major concentration; it became apparent that information on such matters would have to be sought elsewhere. For these reasons we decided, when our grant was extended for an additional year, to include in the fieldwork program fairly extended visits to all three territories. Accordingly, the senior author (who was responsible throughout the study for the main burden of the interviewing) spent a total of five months in Nyasaland and about two in Southern Rhodesia. The rest of our time—out of a total of twenty-three months—was spent in the community of intensive study.

Apart from this not very important qualification, data for this study were collected and interpreted within the framework of the classical community-study method.[10] In keeping with this well established methodology, we used a variety of data-gathering techniques and sources, including direct and

10. Few people have written more cogently upon the theoretical rationale of the community study than Conrad Arensberg: "Community study is that method in which a problem (or problems) in the nature, interconnections, or dynamics of behavior and attitudes is explored against or within the surround of other behavior and attitudes. . . . It is a naturalistic, comparative method. It is aimed at studying behavior . . . *in vivo* through observation rather than *in vitro* through isolation and abstraction . . . [by] statistical or experimental means. . . . Of course . . . its canons of control, verification, and reliability are quite different from those, say, of attitude study or small-group experiment. Many social scientists seem confused about this difference." "The Community Study Method," *American Journal of Sociology, 60* (1954), pp. 109–24; reprinted in C. M. Arensberg and S. T. Kimball, *Culture and Community* (New York, Harcourt, Brace, and World, 1965). In the course of a well-placed jibe at the excessive abstraction and logical aridity reigning in much large-scale sample-survey research, Arthur Vidich describes community studies as representing "the eyes-ears-and-brain approach to sociology." Arthur J. Vidich, Joseph Bensman, and Maurice R. Stein, *Reflections on Community Studies* (New York, John Wiley, 1964), p. xi.

participant observation, census statistics, newspaper accounts, current government reports, and some archival materials. The bulk of the field data upon which this book empirically rests, however, consists of some 350 protocols produced from semi-structured interviews.[11]

We tried to talk to as wide a variety of people as possible: our informants include some Africans, Europeans, and Coloureds, as well as Indians; and we tried to include Indians from all the important religious and status groupings. Interviews followed a general pattern with respect to main topics which were determined by the focus of the study. Specific content, however, differed widely from interview to interview. We did not hesitate to adapt questions and probing efforts to special opportunities afforded by either the informant or the situation. Inevitably, for this reason, we talked more with knowledgeable, articulate, and cooperative informants than with others. Inevitably, too, we talked more and longer with leaders than with followers, with the intelligent more than with the dully ordinary, with the westernized and secularized more than with the traditionalists.[12] All interviews were conducted in English rather than in Gujarati, the native tongue of virtually all Indians in Central Africa.[13]

11. Relevant content was dictated into recording equipment as nearly verbatim as possible immediately after each interview; direct recording would have been totally impracticable under the fieldwork conditions. In typescript, the resulting protocols constitute about 3,200 pages of English foolscap paper.

12. In defense of whatever sins thus committed against "scientific" methodology, we plead with Homans that methodological decisions lie in the area of strategy, not in morals. George C. Homans, "The Strategy of Industrial Sociology," *American Journal of Sociology*, 54 (1949), pp. 330–38. As a matter of strategy, we sought information where and when we could get it rather than conformity to a statistical ideal, and information of the kind we needed most was not always easy to come by. By our assessment of the nature of our problem this seemed the most fruitful course. Other sociologists in the same situation would have perhaps worked differently. In that case, they would have produced a very different study, with different strengths and weaknesses from ours.

13. We originally planned, as indicated, in terms of a ten-month project. If we had been able to think in terms of a two-year project from the beginning, we would certainly have attempted to learn some Gujarati, mainly for the sake of better rapport. Some competence in English is universal among Indian men in the Rhodesias, although there is considerable range in fluency. Few women of the immigrant generation speak English, and consequently all but a

In analysis, the sociologist using data of this kind necessarily works much as a historian or anthropologist would.
Guided by his initial theoretical definition of what he is doing,
he seeks the patterns of meaning and significance that emerge
as his material accumulates in quantity and through time.
He "sees" these patterns more and more clearly as his material grows; and he probes constantly into those areas which
remain cloudy, hoping that with more data they will become
clearer. Often a single piece of information—either sought by
laborious effort or picked up at random—will clarify greatly
an entire region of the pattern. This method is not statistical.[14]
It is nonetheless something of a distortion to label it "quali-
tative" as opposed to "quantitative," as the cliché has it in
the literature. Insights derived in this manner are ultimately

---

few of our informants were male. Owing to the fact that immigrants were
admitted to Nyasaland without passing a test in English, we found the
language barrier in that territory to be considerable, even among men.

14. Persons obsessed with the incontrovertible virtues of statistical analysis
frequently overlook the fact that statistical methods simply do not apply (or
are inappropriate even if they can be applied) to a great deal of sociological
research. These methods are appropriate and necessary where questions of
distribution and *quantitative differences* are critical for accurate generalization,
in short, for the testing of many hypotheses. But a great many of the
problems of research—and this applies particularly to cross-cultural research
—are not primarily questions of distribution at all. Rather, from the standpoint of the investigator, they are simply a matter of acquiring control over a
body of cultural materials which he did not possess previously. In this case,
the parsimonious and efficient mode of procedure is often learning from an
informant who can through a combination of his expert knowledge and communication skills provide the necessary instruction. One does not learn a
foreign language for instance by sample-survey techniques; one seeks instruction from a competent informant. What is true of language applies to many
socio-cultural norms in a "foreign" culture—kinship, modes of economic
organization, policies for political action, and philosophies of religion, for
example. Assuming prior ignorance upon such matters, instruction from one
intelligent, articulate and, above all, knowledgeable informant may be infinitely more enlightening than confused responses from a hundred dull and
inarticulate ones. Cf. the excellent discussion of this point within a quite
different context by Margaret Mead, "National Character," in *Anthropology
Today,* prepared under A. L. Kroeber (Chicago, University of Chicago Press,
1953), pp. 642–67.
But let us not be misunderstood. Problems of distribution and critical difference constantly presented themselves in this study, and if they could have
been handled more adequately, our generalizations would have been enormously
strengthened. In some cases, undoubtedly, they would not have been made at
all since they would have been proved invalid.

founded upon a mass of empirical evidence, just as statistical insights are. Nor, perhaps it is unnecessary to add, is there anything new in these procedures. They are simply an application of the classical methodology in sociology, anthropology, history, and the other social sciences, in contrast to the sample-survey methods so widely adopted in modern sociology and psychology.[15]

The formal choice of a methodology—a plan of attack— is an inescapable beginning for a study of this kind. But it is only a beginning. Practically, the method must be applied.

In many respects we found Indians easy to work with, easier on the whole, for example, than Mexicans, with whom we have had a good deal of experience. Few refused to talk to us when we requested interviews, although that number would have certainly risen sharply if we had pushed without care some of the more sensitive lines of inquiry. Furthermore, we found most Indians surprisingly articulate, considering that their first language was not English. Occupational selection doubtlessly is a factor here; Indians in Central Africa are mainly in business and are thus trained in the overt social skills. When we found them inarticulate and uncommunicative, it could usually be explained as a lack of competence in English, but language was not a major obstacle.

Our problems of rapport were thus neither those of accessibility nor of communication. Rather they arose from what, following Goffman, we may call measures of information-control. Goffman points out that *any* organized group has a problem of "foreign relations," a critical aspect of which is the creation and maintenance of a group-image in the outside world which will further its interests and allow it to play its allotted role. This necessity imposes a task of information-control upon loyal "team" members. Universally, the governing rule is simple and straightforward: favorable information

---

15. The influence of C. Wright Mills in the phrasing of these matters should be fairly obvious to readers in the recent sociological literature. Cf. C. Wright Mills, *The Sociological Imagination* (New York, Grove Press, 1961).

is to be promoted, unfavorable information is to be suppressed or suitably distorted.[16]

While almost certainly a true organizational universal, information-control is, like other aspects of social behavior, subject in practice to great variation. Techniques vary widely, and of course some individuals and groups are much more skilled and disciplined in applying them than are others. Everything else being equal, we might expect conscious demands for information-control to be greatest in situations of marked conflict where the stakes are highest. Speaking upon the basis of considerable experience, we have no hesitation in rating Indians extremely high with respect to this skill, and the objective demands of their situation at the time we were in Africa provided plenty of motivation for its exercise.

Indians do not lack pride in their cultural and social heritage; they do not apologize either to themselves or to others for their existence. Still, they know by long experience that Europeans are apt to be extremely critical—and from their point of view uncomprehending—of a good many of their traditional practices and values. These negative criticisms extend also in Central Africa to the Indians' present mode of life and ways of doing business. They tend therefore to be sensitive to a surprisingly long list of subjects. A direct request for information in one of these areas is invariably met, initially at least, by a standardized defense, developed and polished to shunt off hostile or potentially harmful inquiries.

Some basic knowledge in sensitive areas is nonetheless imperative if we are to understand Indians sociologically. These include such matters as certain (but by no means all) details of socio-economic organization, factionalism within the community, caste, some aspects of religious belief and practice, and (under some circumstances) political conviction and commitment. On the other hand, getting certain kinds of data (e.g. discriminatory practices by Europeans) was extraordinarily easy.

16. Erving Goffman, *The Presentation of the Self in Everyday Life* (New York, Doubleday Anchor, 1959), particularly pp. 77–105.

What we learned in the sensitive areas—and we do not flatter ourselves by pretending that we learned everything—was usually obtained by one or more of the following techniques: (1) by letting people talk freely and naturally at length in an informal setting, thus giving them an opportunity to commit "indiscretions" which they would not have made under direct questioning; (2) through inductive conclusions arrived at after an accumulation of inconsistencies between spoken norms and known practices; (3) by talking to dissidents or opponents in conflict situations; and finally, (4) by close and persistent questioning of selected informants whose confidence had previously been gained for confirmation or correction of what we had decided were the essential facts. Here we heavily worked an ancient investigative strategy: since we often knew much more than we were supposed to know, informants often concluded that we knew more than we actually did and thus talked more freely than they otherwise would have.

The fact that we sought, and on occasion got, information which at least some members of the Indian community would have preferred that we never learn brings up the ethical issue which plagues all community studies. To the extent that community research is accurate in detail, the results are certain to prove unflattering to some people. This is bad enough. But the "truth" is also often perceived by the people whom it concerns most intimately as positively dangerous if it should come into the possession of their enemies. Where conflict and tension are high, this danger is not always entirely imaginary, despite the fact that people tend to exaggerate the audience which sociological reports enjoy.

Indians did not spontaneously welcome this study, for this and other reasons. We were sometimes asked point-blank by prospective informants: What good will this do the Indian community? [17] When so questioned, we tried to be honest. In

17. Cf. Hilda Kuper, *Indian People in Natal* (Natal, University Press, 1960), p. xx.

essence we said that it was highly unlikely that it would profit Indians much directly, but that a good many people, among them university students in the United States, would be interested in a realistic and objective assessment of their position in Africa and their problems. We tried to emphasize our professional role as social scientists who were interested in the "truth" for its own sake—as a contribution to knowledge. We are confident that most of our informants understood and appreciated the logic of this position, however reluctant they might have been on occasion to contribute to it. Yet when and if our Indian friends read this book, we are uncomfortably certain that some of them will feel that we have abused confidences—not of individuals, since individuals are never identified directly, but of the community as a whole. It may also be said that some will feel strongly on this point, believing that the "truth" is distorted in these pages or that, even when it is admitted as the truth, it should have been left unsaid, considering the circumstances of the Indian's position in Central African society.

This easily predictable reaction troubles us as, ideally, we would have preferred to say nothing which could possibly offend or disturb anyone. But to do this and to do a scientific community study is unfortunately a contradiction in terms. At the very least, we hope our Indian friends can take consolation in the fact that we have been no easier on Europeans, Africans, or Coloureds than we have been with them.

Chapter Two

HISTORY AND SETTLEMENT

It is inescapable from the perspective assumed in this volume that a history of the Indians of Central Africa should begin with the Europeans. With respect to these Europeans, however, it is necessary to see their presence in Central Africa as but a tiny ripple in the historic imperialistic expansion of European peoples and culture—a movement beginning with the great voyages of Vasco da Gama and Columbus and the conquests of Hernan Cortés. Since this book concerns southern Africa, shall we exaggerate slightly and say that it ended with Cecil Rhodes? In the years that separate the representative figures of Cortés and Rhodes, the European had roamed the world, carried where he wanted to go by ever increasingly efficient means of transportation and maintained where he chose to stop by his always superior military technology. His motives were richly mixed and not simple: he searched for opportunities to loot, to mine, to trade, to plant, and to settle. Whatever else he was doing, he also tried to convert the natives to his religion and his mode of life.

It is in the nature of human society that behavior should be continuously evaluated and reevaluated in moral terms, and the domination of weaker peoples by Europeans has not escaped such review. Much of the history of imperialism has been written to reveal its terrors or to defend the "inevitable" march of progress and civilization. It is not our intention to enter into these interminable polemics. The subject is brought up to make one significant point: until the twentieth century the moral assumptions underlying imperialism were never seriously questioned. There was criticism of *means* from the beginning; Cortés did have his Las Casas. But the broad *goals* to which imperialism was directed were not brought into really serious question until the "europeanization-of-the-world" was completed. Ex post facto, it is doubtful whether they could have been.

To have questioned the ultimate goal of the europeanization-of-the-world—and thus by implication the inherent superiority of European civilization—would have seemed ridiculous to those actively engaged in the process. Were not Europeans obviously superior in power, in knowledge, and in morals? Were they not then inherently fitted—if not indeed divinely appointed as many believed—to direct and rule the less privileged? By what moral right should a handful of naked savages at the lowest rungs of human evolution continue to occupy undisturbed vast areas incredibly rich in natural resources (North America, Australia, South Africa, the Argentine)? Who could argue that the inhabitants of those regions containing large primitive populations as well as rich resources (Mexico, Peru, West Africa, the Congo) would not benefit morally and materially from rational rule and management by Europeans? The civilized but hopelessly inept, corrupt, and pagan peoples of India, Southeast Asia, China, and the Middle East were admittedly in a somewhat different category, but not enough to radically change the imperial perspective. To raise the question of whether or not one and all would benefit from European rule and tutelage would have seemed ridiculous in the imperial age. And to repeat: *significantly, the question was not asked.*

Remote and inaccessible, Central Africa was one of the last areas to arouse European imperialistic interest and cupidity. Discovery of gold in unprecedented quantities on the Rand in the 1880s, however, spotlighted the region and set off fevered

19

speculation as to what might lay to the north. Some believed, judging from the amount of gold known to have been taken from primitive diggings by Africans, that what is now Rhodesia would prove richer than the Transvaal itself.[1]

But nonmaterialistic motives also impelled exploration and occupation. Central Africa, unhealthy and foreboding in so many respects at the time, was one of the last strongholds of a large-scale trade in slaves. The suppression of the slave trade and the conversion to Christianity of the natives who had suffered this grievous evil gripped the imaginations of many in the Victorian age. Livingstone's exploits received wide publicity. Amid the dull and uninspiring conditions of the early industrial age, his example pointed the way to escape from a life of routine into high-minded adventure.

Imperial politics offered a third and equally powerful motivation to restless men of action like Cecil Rhodes and Harry Johnston. Suddenly conscious in the late 1880s of Africa's existence, the major European powers were busy staking out hitherto vague and hypothetical claims to territory. Self-appointed guardians of British interests like Rhodes and Johnston saw that action was necessary if Britain was to get what they conceived of as her share.

No one will comprehend the social evolution of Central Africa who does not appreciate that its occupation and exploitation was in an important sense a failure—or, if failure seems too strong a word, then perhaps a highly qualified success. Gold was indeed found in Southern Rhodesia as expected; and to exploit it and to consolidate political claims, railroads were extended up from the south immediately after occupation. In quantity, however, the gold proved disappointing. To recoup something from their heavy investments, Rhodes' British South Africa Company encouraged individual Europeans to come in and farm, and a few thousand did so. But farming in tropical Africa is always hazardous and agricultural develop-

1. A. J. Hanna, *The Story of the Rhodesias and Nyasaland* (London, Faber and Faber, 1960), pp. 84–85.

ment was slow. Clearly, it was not in the cards of destiny that Central Africa should become another South Africa.

Nyasaland was a somewhat different case from the Rhodesias since initial expectations were different. A major goal in Nyasaland—abolition of the slave trade—was achieved; the task of turning pagan savages into Christian gentlemen proceeded fairly satisfactorily. But economic opportunities for European exploitation were exceedingly limited. There were no precious metals of any kind in the territory and no large areas seemed suitable to European agriculture.

The European presence in Central Africa nonetheless remained and slowly increased. Administrators and officials extended and consolidated their effective control over tribal areas. Missionaries gained converts and established schools and hospitals. The entire region was thoroughly prospected; and while no second Rand was uncovered, mining operations were begun at various sites in both the Rhodesias. Mining populations provided a market for European farms; and after considerable and costly experimentation, export crops and produce were raised in some quantity—meat, tobacco, and tea proving to be the most profitable. With these developments there grew up simultaneously a proportionate amount of service industry and trade.

Indians appeared in trade fairly early in all three territories. But trade was initiated in Central Africa by Europeans, and largely remained in their hands for a long time. Early commercial activity falls fairly clearly into two basic patterns, the trading company and the isolated adventurer.

In Nyasaland and Northeastern Rhodesia early trade was dominated by the large company, as it involved costly transportation by water beyond the means of the small individual entrepreneur. The first to appear, the historic African Lakes Company (commonly known to this day as the Mandala Company), was established in 1878 by a group of Scottish businessmen at the behest of the missionaries. In time, this quasi-missionary endeavor was supplemented by several strictly com-

21

mercial enterprises such as Sharrer's and Kahn and Company.[2] But whatever their auspices, all of these companies were bureaucratic in concept and practice.

A European informant in his seventies provided a description of the operations of a company doing business in the Northern Province of Northern Rhodesia in the 1920s. The company maintained at least one store at all district headquarters, and it had others in any area with enough population and resources to justify it. The resident agent—a Scot like his employers—did not own the shop; he literally traded for the company.[3] Native produce in this area then consisted of some grain and a good deal of dried fish from the lakes, and when collected by the company, these foodstuffs found an ultimate market in the emerging Copperbelt. Otter and leopard skins were acquired for export out of the country; now insignificant, the trade in otter skins was then apparently quite substantial.

While the company's total volume of business must have been fairly large, that of any given station was usually very small. In order to illustrate this point, our informant said that the company's manager in the province complained bitterly to him that they would be ruined when the annual licensing fee for each store was raised from five shillings to one pound.

Most of these bush stations were of simple pole-and-dagga (mud and wattle) construction. Speaking of the same company, an African informant now in late middle age described its shops as much inferior in stock and appointments to those operated in the same region by Indians today. The agent could not have been paid much, and he certainly did not live very luxuriously. On the other hand, food was cheap, he paid nothing for rent, and virtually all his income could be saved.

In Southern and Northwestern Rhodesia, the earliest trader

2. Harry H. Johnston, *British Central Africa: An Attempt to Give Some Account of a Portion of the Territories under British Influence North of the Zambezi* (London, Methuen, 1897), pp. 181–82.

3. While not commonly thought of in this role, Scots, as Becker points out, have often been middleman traders. In British North America, they typically manned the outposts of the fur trade. Previously, in the sixteenth century, they were found as roving pack-peddlers in "underdeveloped" Central Europe and Scandinavia. Becker, *Man in Reciprocity*, pp. 234–36.

was an individual adventurer who often combined hunting with trading on what was basically an established South African pattern. He made periodic forays by ox wagon or donkey train into native areas far from European settlements. There he exchanged calico, cups, saucers, spoons, blankets, beads, gunpowder, percussion caps, cheap muzzle-loading guns, salt, and fresh game meat killed on the spot for ivory (by far the most valuable and most sought-after item to be obtained from the natives), hides, cattle, grain, and wild rubber. Ethnically, the earliest of these trader-adventurers were typically Anglo-Saxons or Boers. But Russian Jews, cattle traders in their land of origin, participated in the cattle, grain, and hides trade virtually from the beginning.[4]

Both types of trade were *trade* in the literal sense of the term, in that they involved an exchange of natural and local produce for manufactured goods. The possibilities for expansion inherent in such business, however, were limited as the African possessed little of interest to the European aside from his land and his labor. But once introduced to European goods, the African avidly sought them. A major hazard of the missionaries' existence—and this appears vividly in the records —was the importunate and continual begging by Africans of all classes for a share in their scanty worldly possessions. To free themselves from this nuisance, the missionaries were most anxious to have trade established upon a regular, commercial basis. The hunger for European goods also helps to explain why both missionaries and early administrators like Johnston saw the establishment of trade as a major factor in the task of bringing the primitive African into the fold of civilization.

The scarcity of native products meant that sustained trade on any large-scale basis awaited the induction of Africans into a money economy. This was not long in coming for two reasons: the need for labor in the mines and on the farms, and the need for revenue by the colonial administration.

Head taxes are interpreted in the critical literature on imperialism as a cooperative gesture by sympathetic and com-

4. Gann, *The Birth of a Plural Society,* pp. 150–52.

23

pliant administrators to the needs of rapacious, private en-
trepreneurs. Reluctant natives, it is pointed out, were forced
by this highly effective mechanism into European employment
in order to earn money to meet their taxes.

Certainly head taxes performed this function, as they were
intended to. Yet an exaggerated emphasis upon this function
ignores the pressing need of early administrators for revenue.
It is not as widely recognized as it might be that the vicarious
joys of imperialism far outran the ordinary British taxpayer's
willingness to underwrite its costs. Johnston's administration
in Nyasaland provides a nearly incredible example of niggardly
treatment. It is a poor and backward American community indeed that does not spend far more each year on its local school
than Johnston had at his disposal for the whole of Nyasaland in
the first years of his administration.[5] Admittedly, this is an extreme case; but in essentials, the situation elsewhere was much
the same. In the Rhodesias, where the early administration was
the responsibility of the British South Africa Company, the
company paid out far more than it took in for years on end. Its
harassed officials thus welcomed the revenue brought in by
the head tax, small as this was in absolute terms. The fact is
that they depended upon it to defray a large part of the costs
of day-to-day administration. To those responsible for the creation and maintenance of the head tax, its moral justification
was patent: it seemed only right that the natives should bear
their fair share of the costs inseparable from the blessings of
civilization.

The lure of the trader's merchandise supplemented, if it did
not supplant, the goad of the administrator's need for revenue
in motivating the African to seek European employment, thus
giving his labor a more voluntary cast. In time, these sheerly
economic motivations came to greatly overshadow the socio-
political ones. Today Africans work for wages primarily to earn
money to buy goods rather than to pay taxes, and the goods

5. Johnston set up and ran the Nyasaland administration for the first six
months on a sum of £15,000. For a discussion of his continued financial
problems, see Johnston, pp. 80–154; A. J. Hanna, *The Beginnings of Nyasaland
and North-eastern Rhodesia, 1859–95* (Oxford, Clarendon Press, 1956), pp.
245–65.

which they have come to want and need are defined by a radically different standard of living than the primitive one of seventy years ago.[6]

No one planned it that way. Yet one of the somewhat incidental effects of a bit of excess money in the hands of Africans was the creation of an economic niche that Indians could occupy in the emerging "plural society" of Central Africa.

PATTERNS OF INDIAN EMIGRATION

British Africa and British India were far more intimately related than is generally recognized. India, the really valuable

6. The ethnography of Central Africa is complicated by a considerable variety of distinctive cultural groups and a somewhat tortuous pre-European history. For a very brief overview which provides some feeling for the situation as it existed throughout the entire region at the time the Europeans arrived, see Hanna, *Rhodesias and Nyasaland,* pp. 23–40.

Specialized studies, mainly by scholars associated in one capacity or another with the Rhodes-Livingstone Institute, are more plentiful for Zambia than for either Rhodesia or Malawi. A convenient summary collection of much of this work is contained in Elizabeth Colson and Max Gluckman, eds., *Seven Tribes of British Central Africa* (Manchester, Manchester University Press, 1951); this volume contains chapters on the Barotse (Gluckman), Plateau Tonga (Colson), Bemba (Richards), Ngoni (Barnes), Nyakyusa [in this case, of Southwestern Tanzania] (Wilson), Yao [Malawi] (Mitchell), and the "Shona" [Rhodesia] (Holleman).

For Zambia, a short list of specialized studies might include as representative works: Audrey I. Richards' widely known account of the Bemba, *Land, Labour, and Diet in Northern Rhodesia* (London, Oxford University Press, 1939); Max Gluckman, *The Judicial Process among the Barotse of Northern Rhodesia* (Manchester, Manchester University Press, 1955); and J. A. Barnes, *Politics in a Changing Society: The Political History of the Fort Jameson Ngoni* (London, Oxford University Press, 1954).

For Malawi, such a list would include: J. C. Mitchell's *The Yao Village: A Study in the Social Structure of a Nyasaland Tribe* (Manchester, Manchester University Press, 1956); Margaret Read, *Children of Their Fathers: Growing up among the Ngoni of Nyasaland* (New Haven, Yale University Press, 1960); J. van Velsen, *The Politics of Kinship: A Study in Social Manipulation among the Lakeside Tonga* (Manchester, Manchester University Press, 1964).

For Rhodesia, the existing literature is rather skimpy. Charles Bullock, *The Mashona and the Matabele* (Cape Town, Juta, 1950 [1st ed., 1927]), is the commonly cited, standard "premodern" source. See also J. F. Holleman, *Shona Customary Law* (London, Oxford University Press, 1952); H. Kuper, A. J. B. Hughes, J. van Velsen, *The Shona and Ndebele of Southern Rhodesia* (London, Oxford University Press, 1954); William Rayner, *The Tribe and Its Successors: An Account of African Traditional Life and European Settlement in Southern Rhodesia* (New York, Praeger, 1962).

part of the empire to which all else was secondary, had long served as a proving ground for colonial policy, administrative techniques, and organization. When confronted with a problem, administrative officers elsewhere sought a solution in terms of an Indian precedent or Indian resources. When Johnston wanted soldiers for his pocket-sized wars with the Yao and the Arab slavers, he got Sikhs through contacts within the India Office.[7] When the British decided to build the East African railway, the necessary labor was brought from India.

Precedent was not lacking either for a movement of Indians out of India into other British-held territories in response to economic opportunities created by European initiative. Although not widely appreciated for what it was, Indian emigration of this kind constitutes in sheer numbers one of the great population shifts in modern times.[8] Most Indians, it is true, went to such nearby areas as Malaya, Burma, and Ceylon. A great many, however, were transported much longer distances for plantation labor—to Mauritius, to Fiji, to British Guiana, and to the West Indies.

A good deal of the movement to nearby areas, particularly Burma and Ceylon, was temporary and/or cyclical; labor was typically recruited on short-term contracts and returned home once these were completed. For the more distant colonies, an indenture system was commonly used. Indentured labor is a kind of half-way house between free labor and slavery in the history of modern plantation agriculture. After 1834, when slavery was abolished in the British colonies, owners of tropical plantations producing commercial crops such as sugar turned to this solution for their labor problem.

An aggregation of indentured Indians in any given area cre-

7. Johnston, *British Central Africa*, pp. 97 ff., 117 ff., 129, 152–53.

8. Cf. Kingsley Davis, *The Population of India and Pakistan* (Princeton, Princeton University Press, 1951), pp. 98–106; C. Kondapi, *Indians Overseas 1838–1949* (New Delhi, Indian Council of World Affairs, 1951), pp. 1–7; Bruno Lasker, *Asia on the Move: Population Pressure, Migration, and Resettlement in Eastern Asia under the Influence of Want and War* (New York, H. Holt, 1945), pp. 58–63, 191–96; Donald R. Taft and Richard Robbins, *International Migrations: The Immigrant in the Modern World* (New York, Ronald Press, 1955), passim.

ated the economic base for a certain amount of free immigration. Attracted by the commercial potentialities inherent in the needs of their fellow countrymen, Indians of the business classes followed indentured immigration. And given any encouragement by circumstances or policy, these businessmen quickly expanded their operations to non-Indians in the territories in which they settled. In South Africa, for example, traders who came at first to trade with fellow Indians quickly extended out into the African trade and, to a much lesser degree, into the European trade as well.

The difference in origin between the indentured laboring class and the free business class provides the basis for an enduring social distinction of great importance in understanding the overseas Indian communities. "Passenger" and "indentured" carry to this day heavily freighted status connotations.

Indentured Indians were without exception miserably poor in India. Otherwise, they would never have been tempted into signing a long contract promising little but subsistence and hard labor far from home. The conditions under which they lived and worked while in service were demoralizing and degrading, particularly when judged by Indian values. Upon arrival at the plantations, persons of the most diverse regional and caste origins were forced to live together in quite un-Indian promiscuity. Some women were always included in indentured shipments but never in equal proportions. In any case, a normal family life was scarcely possible while the indentured worker was still under contract, forced as he was to live in barracks and to do gang labor under highly regimented conditions.

The free immigrant avoided these degradations even if his standard of living was very low, and he prided himself accordingly. Being able to arrange his own time schedule and living quarters, the "passenger" Indian could adhere much closer to Indian norms and values in his personal and family life than could his indentured countryman. Furthermore, having paid his own fare, he had thereby proven for all time that he could not have come from the very bottom of Indian society, as did

27

most indentured workers. Some of the indentured came from perfectly respectable castes, but their original sin was that they were poor. Any claims that they or their descendants might make to inherited status thereafter were always under suspicion simply because they bore the indentured label.[9]

East and Central Africa stand out from virtually all other areas of Indian overseas settlement in that they completely lack the ex-indentured class. Here Indians have always been traders, never laborers in significant numbers.[10] Broadly speaking, the Indians of East and Central Africa are from exactly the same middle socio-economic strata which furnished the "passenger" immigration to such colonies as Mauritius and Natal. The similarity of origin goes even further: "passenger" Indians of Mauritius and South Africa, like the immigrants to East and Central Africa, are predominantly from the Gujarat cultural region of western India. It is scarcely accidental, therefore, that many Indians in Central Africa have direct ties of kinship, friendship, or personal history to those living in East and South Africa.

Throughout any discussion of Indians in Central Africa, one fact of overriding importance must be kept in mind: Indians settled much earlier in South and East Africa than they did in Central Africa, and the former territories therefore set a socio-cultural precedent for the latter. Basic administrative and legislative policies bearing upon Indians, for example, have their direct ancestry in South Africa. But the relationship goes

9. On the distinction between indentured and passenger Indians, see Kuper, *Indian People in Natal,* pp. 1–79. For a vivid account of the living conditions of the indentured, see Morton Klass, *East Indians in Trinidad: A Study of Cultural Persistence* (New York, Columbia University Press, 1961), pp. 8–20, and of the influence of indentured status upon caste, pp. 55–64.

10. Over 32,000 Indian coolies were imported at the turn of the century to build the railway connecting the coast at Mombasa with Lake Victoria. Most of this contingent returned to India when the railway was completed, and only 6,000 (or about one-fifth of the total) elected to stay in East Africa. See George Delf, *Asians in East Africa* (London, Oxford University Press, 1963), pp. 11–14. About the same time 500 Indian laborers were imported to construct the railroad from Beira in Portuguese Africa to Southern Rhodesia. The tropical sun, mosquitoes, and lions took their toll and practically all of the workers died. See Hanna, *Rhodesias and Nyasaland,* pp. 147–48.

deeper than this, since there exists at the level of popular culture a whole complex of anti-Indian sentiment which must be seen as simply a cultural import from South or East Africa. When Europeans in Central Africa say that Indians are "just about the dirtiest people on earth," they are patently not making a judgment based in any way upon current firsthand knowledge of the local Indian community; if they were, they could not make this statement. They are repeating what they have learned to say about Indians, not what they themselves know from direct experience. Like most ethnic stereotypes, the observation may have originally had a fairly solid empirical basis in South or East Africa, but the link between verbalization and empirical reality has now been lost in time and history.

The strength and prevalence of anti-Indian sentiment everywhere among Europeans pose a question of primary importance. Why were Indians allowed to settle anywhere in Africa where Europeans were in control? Indian immigration into East and Central Africa must be seen—viewing the matter from the standpoint of the dominant Europeans—as a kind of ecological accident over which they had no control. Indians owe their presence in these territories to a long-established British imperial policy that had little direct connection with either Indians or Africa. Until the passage of the Commonwealth Immigrants Act of 1962, the British proudly maintained a rule that the citizens of one British territory should not be categorically excluded from any other territory administered by the Crown. This guarantee of free movement was originally established with considerations of empire-wide politics in mind. Citizenship in modern democratic countries means, among other things, free and unimpeded internal migration; and the British have always liked to think of the empire as potentially a single political community. The rule was abrogated, it is worth noting, only after the colonies had ceased to be colonies and had become independent countries.

This fundamental immigration principle was applied throughout the empire. The fact that a few thousand Indians were allowed to enter British African dependencies was at best, we may be sure, a tangential matter in the minds of the responsible officials in London who upheld it. Ultimately, this rule is the only explanation for the continued Indian immigration into East and Central Africa, given the local anti-Indian sentiment.

The presence of Indians in South Africa poses a somewhat different problem. Indians there are not an ecological accident in the same sense that they are in East and Central Africa. Their importation into South Africa was a deliberate, rational act of the Europeans themselves. Why then are Indians so heartily unwelcome there? The answer illustrates the fallacy of assuming universal consensus in complex societies. It was the large plantation owners, not Europeans in the generic sense, who promoted Indian immigration into Natal, and this small but influential group continued to do so long after opposition from the settlers had proved vehement and vocal.

Indian labor would have also been imported into Central Africa over settler opposition if the officials of the British South Africa Company had had their way in the matter. A file of correspondence from 1901 to 1905 in the archives of Salisbury shows that officials of the company negotiated for Indian labor for their mines in South Africa and Southern Rhodesia.[11] In the same period, at least one of the company's officials, Wilson Fox, seriously broached a scheme to settle Indians in the Zambezi Valley to operate sugar plantations there.[12] Both of these schemes foundered upon a combination of strong anti-Indian sentiment among the settlers and lack of cooperation from the Indian government.

The small and middling settler could never view with equanimity the potential competition for place and position offered by the Indian anywhere in Africa. Towards the African, the

---

11. This point will be elaborated upon below, pp. 40–41.

12. Wilson Fox, *Memorandum on Problems of Development and Policy,* printed for the use of the Directors, British South Africa Company (London, 1910), Chapter 4, "The Problem of Indian Immigration"; copy in Central African Archives Library in Salisbury. See also L. H. Gann, *A History of Northern Rhodesia: Early Days to 1953* (London, Chatto and Windus, 1964), p. 147.

settler could take an utterly complacent view. Insofar as he could see, the African was doomed by God and Nature to remain a helpless and hopeless savage. The Indian, on the other hand, was in an entirely different category. He soon proved in practice that he could work as hard and with as much foresight as could the European, and in the meantime he lived on a fraction of what the European considered necessary for existence. He also soon revealed an even more disturbing trait: namely, a disposition to demand political rights equal to those of the European, and he agitated and maneuvered skillfully to that end.

Consequently, the European artisan, farmer, and small merchant perceived the Indian as an immediate and dangerous threat. Lord Delamere, spokesman for the Kenya settlers, put the case vis-à-vis the Indian as follows early in the twentieth century:

> In all new countries, the backbone of the country is the small man, the white colonist with small means, but there is no place for him in a country when once the Asiatic is there. I have some years experience myself with the newest of the colonies in Africa, and I know from personal observation and knowledge, that every two or three Indians in the country means the loss of a white colonist. There is no place for the small white man arising in the country. All the vegetable-growing for the towns is done by Indians, all the butchers with one or two exceptions are Indians, all the small country stores are kept by Indians, and most of the town shops, all of the lower-grade clerks are Indians, nearly all the carpentry and building is done by Indians. They thus fill all the occupations and trades which would give employment to the poor white colonist, especially those arriving new in the country. That is what Indian immigration means in the early days of a very new country in Africa. It means that if open competition is allowed, the small white colonist must go to the wall.[13]

13. Elspeth Huxley, *White Man's Country: Lord Delamere and the Making of Kenya* (London, Macmillan, 1935), *1*, 206–07.

Not exactly a small settler himself, Lord Delamere represented the substantial, gentlemanly farmer-adventurer type that was attracted to Kenya—and, to a much lesser extent, to Southern Rhodesia as well. To these people the economic competition offered by Indians was remote. But the political threat was real even to this type of settler and was realistically perceived. In Kenya the Indians made a strong bid for political and social equality as early as the 1920s.[14]

It is not necessary here to retell the detailed story of the agitation over the "Coolie Question" in South and East Africa. The essentials of this history will suffice as they bear upon developments in Central Africa with respect to administrative policy and legislation. Wherever Europeans and Indians competed, actually or potentially, Europeans were invariably anti-Indian in sentiment and they constantly pressed for controlling legislation. Yet at the same time, wherever the Colonial Office retained authority, Indians were never categorically excluded, despite settler pressure. Just as soon, however, as settlers were given sufficient home-rule authority to control immigration, Indians were denied further entry.

The prototypical pattern was set in South Africa shortly after the formation of the self-governing Union. Here the Immigrants Regulation Act of 1913 gave the Minister of Interior the right to "deem" certain persons as undesirable on economic or social grounds; and the Minister thereby promptly deemed undesirable all Asians except wives and dependents of existing residents.[15] Southern Rhodesia followed with an act based di-

14. See below, p. 301 and n. 4. Winston Churchill took note of the essential facts of the relationship between Indian and settler while traveling through East Africa as early as 1907. The gentleman-farmer, he pointed out, had come to East Africa to relax and enjoy the benefits of cheap labor in beautiful and exotic surroundings. He quite patently had not come, if he had any say in the matter, to enter into a hard and grubby struggle for survival with such obviously well-equipped opponents as the Indians. This is what the Coolie Question came to, as Churchill saw and stated clearly enough. Winston S. Churchill, *My African Journey* (London, Hodder and Stoughton, 1908), pp. 45–55.

15. Cf. Robert A. Huttenback, "Indians in South Africa, 1860–1914: The British Imperial Philosophy on Trial," *English Historical Review, 81* (1966), 273–91, for a convenient summary of the history of the disabilities of Indians in South Africa.

rectly upon this prototype in 1924, the year after it became a self-governing colony. Finally, one of the first deeds of the Federation of Rhodesia and Nyasaland was the passage of an immigration bill (1954) in which the provision for the exclusion of Indians was modeled directly upon that adopted in Southern Rhodesia a generation before.

When compared to either South or East Africa, the Indian population of Central Africa is relatively homogeneous. All Indians in Central Africa, with few and unimportant exceptions, are Gujarati-speaking and come from a narrow strip of western India lying between Bombay and Ahmedabad, a distance of only three hundred miles. All come from a fairly narrow sector of the total spectrum of class and caste represented even in this small region. Broadly speaking, neither the very top nor the very bottom emigrated. Occupationally, virtually all Indians in Central Africa are in commerce, and the general level of education and sophistication is fairly high.

By contrast, the typical Indian in South Africa is a proletarian, whether urban or rural. A great many are still rural sugar workers, with a rather unsophisticated peasant culture.[16] The general level of both income and education is very low in South Africa, in spite of the fact that South Africa also possesses a substantial elite class, higher in these respects than all but a few isolated individuals in Central Africa. It is nonetheless to this South African elite, rather than to the general population, that the Indians of Central Africa must be compared.

Indians of East and Central Africa have a great deal more in common generally than either do with those of South Africa. In both of these regions they are basically Gujarati. They are "passenger" in origin and make their living principally by trade. But beyond these similarities emerge differences of considerable importance. A large part of the East African Indian

16. Cf. Kuper, pp. 57–64 and passim, and Pierre L. van den Berghe, *Caneville: The Social Structure of a South African Town* (Middletown, Conn., Wesleyan University Press, 1964), pp. 34–46, 121–50, and passim.

population is composed of Shia Ismaeli "Khojas" and Shia Boh-ras, two distinctive Muslim sects completely absent in Central Africa. In addition, other differences in the size of the total populations involved and in settlement history are important. The East African population is much larger (about 350,000 in 1960), and it is considerably more differentiated internally by class and occupation than that of Central Africa.[17] While most East African Indians are in trade, a good many are also arti-sans, civil servants, and professionals—occupational categories only minimally represented in Central Africa. History, too, makes for some basic differences. Most Indians in both regions are quite recent immigrants, but those of East Africa are never-theless more firmly rooted in the area historically. Conven-tional commentary always makes a good deal out of the in-disputable fact that Indians have been a part of the East African scene as long as reliable history remembers.[18]

Homogeneous as the Central African population is com-pared to those either north or south, within it there are still important differences by territory that should be sketched. Southern Rhodesia, Northern Rhodesia, and Nyasaland all had rather different histories, the development of which bears directly upon the fortunes of their Indian communities.

SOUTHERN RHODESIA

An air traveler arriving over modern Salisbury after an over-night flight from London must exercise considerable imagina-tion to appreciate how remote and isolated Southern Rhodesia was within the memory of people now living. The distance from Cape Town to Bulawayo is 1,200 miles—a long way by horseback and ox wagon—and prior to the last decade of the

17. This estimate includes Kenya, Tanzania, and Uganda. See Delf, *Asians in East Africa.*

18. See, for example, the convenient short summary in L. W. Hollingsworth, *The Asians of East Africa* (London, Macmillan, 1960). The relevance of this history in understanding the present-day Indians of East Africa can be (and usually is) greatly exaggerated. Nonetheless, it does give them a claim to legitimate residence which the Indians of Central Africa envy.

nineteenth century few indeed were motivated to undertake the journey.[19] But sheer geography was not the only factor creating isolation: at what is now Bulawayo, the traveler reached the kraal of the Matabele king whose word determined whether he passed beyond or not. A handful of hunters like Selous were admitted; so too, but more grudgingly, were a few missionaries like Moffat and Coillard. Mining prospectors or potential settlers, however, were rigidly excluded by royal order.

In 1890 the dam broke and a flood of Europeans swept in, spearheaded by the Pioneer Column dear to white Rhodesians' memory. More prospectors and settlers immediately followed, despite the temporary lull occasioned by the Matabele Rebellion of 1896–97. By 1901, an informal census in Southern Rhodesia showed 11,032 Europeans and about a thousand "Asiatics." [20]

The Indian immigration in Southern Rhodesia at the turn of the century must be placed in proper perspective as a tiny wavelet of the considerable passenger immigration out of India that followed Indian indentured labor around the world. In good part, this particular wavelet was simply a deflection from South Africa. Many, if not most, of the Indians who came to Southern Rhodesia were motivated and assisted in this decision by kinsmen already established in South Africa, and in all likelihood most of them would have gone to South Africa to join these kinsmen if they had been permitted to do so. As a second best, they were persuaded to try their fortunes in Southern Rhodesia, a wild and inhospitable country but still open to

19. By 1891 when Southern Rhodesia was opened for settlement, the railway had reached Vryburg, north of Kimberley; but this still meant for the earliest settlers a grueling 700 miles by ox wagon to Bulawayo across Bechuanaland. The line from Vryburg to Bulawayo was completed in 1897. Eric A. Walker, *A History of Southern Africa* (London, Longmans, 1959), p. 424; Hanna, *Rhodesias and Nyasaland,* p. 148.

20. The figure of 1,093 Asiatics given in the 1901 census is certainly too high. The 1911 census shows 870 Asiatics, with a decrease in the number of females from 300 to 102. This makes no sense by known patterns of Indian immigration. Putting the evidence together, we suspect that the error lies in a careless switching of a component figure reported for "Colonial Natives" with that for the "Asiatics" in the town of Bulawayo.

them. Exactly the same pattern of deflected immigration was repeated a generation later in Northern Rhodesia, after entry into Southern Rhodesia had become impossible.

The 1901 count gives only gross numbers. It is therefore impossible to say exactly who the few hundred Indians were in Southern Rhodesia as of that date. Judging from the census of 1921, when more details become available, the population of the early period must have been a good deal more heterogeneous in origin and occupation than it is now. Of those born in India, nearly one-third were then non-Gujarati. Occupationally, only about one-third of the economically active were listed as being in commerce; on the other hand, such categories as market gardeners and domestic servants, which have long since disappeared among the Indians, were then prominent.[21] These facts suggest that much of the early immigration was temporary and that the growth of the Indian community over time represents selection and adaptation.

Selection must have favored Gujaratis and traders, since they make up the population today. This is not of course to say that all those who eventually entered trade began there. "My father came to Bulawayo by ox wagon before the railway was built," one middle-aged Indian lady told us proudly. To appreciate the significance of this remark, one must understand that the ox wagon is the *Mayflower* of Southern Rhodesia, a symbol of primacy and lineage. She did not add, as we learned from a European contemporary who grew up in Bulawayo at the same time, that the father had at first earned his living by going from door to door mending shoes.

The settlers, both Indian and European, who poured into

21. The major categories of the economically active males may be summarized for 1921 as:

Agriculture (chiefly market gardeners)	184
Industry (tailors, cobblers, construction, mechanics)	129
Commerce	264
Commercial service (hotels, transport, laundries, barbers, etc.)	251
Domestic duties	117
All others	28
Total	973

Southern Rhodesia came with highly inflated expectations as to what they would find, and inevitably optimism soured in the face of some uncomfortably harsh economic realities. The civil commissioner in Bulawayo at the turn of the century reported that in 1899 free meals and special work-relief projects, such as road repairing and fencing, had to be provided for many Europeans who drifted up from the south and found no employment. His successor added that in 1902 relief projects were no longer necessary, but he casually mentioned a fair demand for *white* domestic servants. Business was generally depressed, or perhaps more accurately—to use the idiom still current in Central Africa—"overtraded." The completion of the railway to Bulawayo in 1897 had brought an influx of hopefuls ranging, in the commissioner's words, "from the small Jewish pedlar to the [large] Johannesburg and colonial merchant." In sharp contrast to the chronic scarcities of the ox-wagon days, more goods were suddenly available than the demand justified, and many small shopkeepers and traders found themselves facing bankruptcy.[22] It was within this context of diminished hopes and stringent circumstances that the earliest Indian pioneers in Rhodesia competed with the European settlers for a niche within the developing economy.

Market gardeners and cobblers were perhaps not particularly objectionable to Europeans. But as traders Indians came directly into competition with Europeans. In contrast to the two northern territories, the "Kaffir truck trade" (to use the then common but by now somewhat disreputable terminology) has always been an important part of European business in Southern Rhodesia. Undoubtedly, this was even more the case in the early period than now, as the economic alternatives then open to Europeans were fewer. There is little doubt, however, that the threat posed by Indian competition was felt keenly and resisted vigorously.

In 1905, the commissioner for the Fort Victoria District ad-

22. Extracts of reports of the civil commissioner of Bulawayo quoted in British South Africa Company, *Reports on the Administration of Rhodesia, 1897–1898* (n.p., 1899), pp. 269–74; *Reports, 1898–1900*, p. 300; *Reports, 1900–1902*, p. 297.

dressed a confidential report to his superiors in Salisbury entitled "Undesireable Traders." [23] The report had to be confidential as, in theory at least, the British South Africa Company was committed to fair treatment for all British subjects, Indians included, in keeping with overall imperial policy. Yet like most local administrators he had come to share the settlers' point of view, and he undertook to argue their case.

> I am strongly of the opinion that the holding of licenses by Indians or any Asiatic does, to a certain extent, seriously affect the welfare of Europeans resident in this District, and that on no grounds can the holding of trading licenses by Asiatics or other Coloured foreigners be accounted beneficial to the community.

The sixteen licenses held by Indians in his district represented "a considerable number in proportion to the number of Europeans settled here." Furthermore, each license-holder had "three or four hangers-on" living and working with him, and thus the commissioner had little doubt that a single license actually covered "a sort of joint stock business." Then he arrived at the crux of his argument, asserting that the Indian's standard of living and his business ethics made it impossible for the European to compete with him.

> He [the Indian] is no customer of the local European storekeeper; he spends little on his diet, which consists, for the most part, of fowls, rice and oil or fat; he likewise spends little on dress and nothing else, but he hoards up his money which he eventually takes out of the country. If he can find any business man foolish enough to give him credit and to entrust him with goods, he not infrequently decamps and is lost to sight for all time; he is otherwise law-abiding and, generally speaking, does no harm, but I am of the opinion that his presence is a distinct disadvantage for, owing to the reasons stated above, the Asiatic is in a position to supplant and drive out the

23. Central African Archives (Salisbury), Item T 2/2/18.

white trader, who is, from every point of view, of so much greater value to the country.

The commissioner recommended a gradual but progressive restriction upon trading licenses to Indians. Soon thereafter all the rural areas of Southern Rhodesia were effectively closed to Indians, thus forcing them into the towns, where they have remained to this day.

This did not mean that permission to trade even in the towns was easy to obtain. The Estates Office of the British South Africa Company instructed local officials to refuse applications from Indians for trading stands in the townships, except where they could be supported by the local authority or responsible British residents. Stands were to be rented to Indians on an explicit year-to-year basis, contrary to usual practice of indefinite tenure.[24]

At Umtali, on January 4, 1899, a group of about 150 Europeans led by prominent merchants set out "to run the Banyans out of town."[25] They broke into two Indian shops and manhandled the owners; the police were able to disperse the crowd and restore order before any one was seriously hurt. The next day the crowd formed and broke into another shop before they could be brought under control. Nevertheless, the Europeans accomplished their original purpose. After negotiations with the Indians, the acting civil commissioner at Umtali telegraphed his superiors in Salisbury: "They [i.e. the Indians] are quite agreeable to clear out if store and stock are taken over. No more Banyans likely to open in Umtali."[26]

Outright exclusion would have of course allayed settler anxieties, but this was impossible under official imperial policy. The formation of a legislative council for Southern Rhodesia soon provided the basis for a compromise solution that proved highly effective. Composed of representatives of the settlers and nom-

24. Central African Archives, Item L 2/2/81/2.
25. "Banyan" was the commonly used generic term for Indians in this period. It apparently derives, via Swahili, from the Hindustani word *bunia* for trader. Cf. Hollingsworth, p. 127.
26. Central African Archives, Item AC 3/5/23.

inees of the British South Africa Company in equal proportions, this council imposed an immigration ordinance in 1904. The imperial principle of free movement for all British subjects was never interpreted to mean that immigration could not be regulated; it simply guaranteed that those regulations adopted should apply equally to all persons holding a British passport. For this reason, Southern Rhodesia's immigration ordinance did not specifically mention Indians. It directed that no person would henceforth be admitted who was unable "by reason of deficient education to write out and sign with his own hand in the character of any European language an application to the satisfaction of the Administrator."

This was not an outright exclusion act. Indians who could pass the test by showing command of written English continued to be admitted into Southern Rhodesia until 1924. But few prospective Indian immigrants to Africa at the turn of the century possessed sufficient education to pass a literacy test. Between 1911 (the first reliable census) and 1926, the "Asian" population increased by only 584.[27]

If the Ordinance of 1904 represented a partial victory for the settlers, it was a victory at the expense of the British South Africa Company. Plagued by labor problems in the mines, as the yet completely undisciplined African was not a satisfactory worker, the company's officials tried to obtain Oriental labor on a contract basis. They were prevented from doing so, as already noted above, by a combination of anti-Indian sentiment among the settlers and a lack of cooperation from the Indian government—meaning of course, given the period, other English colonials in the Indian Service.

The treatment being meted out to Indians in South Africa was then beginning to feed the fires of nationalism in India, and from the standpoint of the Indian Service a further em-

27. "Asian" (or earlier, "Asiatic") is the standard term of reference for Indians in official documents in Central Africa. The term "Indian" is rarely used, although all Asians in Central Africa, with the exception of a bare handful of Chinese, in fact are Indians. "Indians and Pakistanis" is sometimes used by journalists to describe the Asians of Central Africa, but this phrase is inaccurate since the Muslims come from the same Gujarati area of India that the Hindus do.

ployment of Indians in Africa promised nothing but unwelcome trouble. They were willing to oblige the British South Africa Company, but only if they could be convinced that Indians in Africa would be given fair treatment not only in the mines, but everywhere in the country.

Despite their best efforts to varnish the truth a bit, the company officials found it difficult to provide the requested assurance. In particular, as the relevant correspondence shows, the India Office objected to the discriminatory features in the Ordinance of 1904. The main bone of contention was thus an indirect one, in that the real issue concerned free immigration rather than contract labor. Settler sentiment being what it was —and now legally embodied in the immigration ordinance—a compulsory repatriation clause would be necessary if any labor was to be imported. This the Indian government did not object to in principle. What they did find objectionable were the discriminatory features in the Ordinance of 1904 as it applied to free immigration, which stood as an affront to all Indians, regardless of whether they wished to immigrate or not.[28]

After several years of negotiations, the idea of importing Indian labor was finally dropped. Time alone helped to solve this issue, as it so often does in matters of social conflict. Since the mining potential in Southern Rhodesia failed to live up to expectations, the need for such labor shrank in importance as a company preoccupation. But for exactly the same reason, the company shifted its efforts toward encouraging European settlement and thus put itself in a position of increasing concessions to settler views.

If the Ordinance of 1904 was a compromise victory for the settlers in opposition to the British South Africa Company and established imperial policy, full victory in Southern Rhodesia came with the achievement of self-governing status in 1923. By principles agreed to at the Imperial Conference of 1918, the colony automatically gained complete powers of deter-

28. Central African Archives, Item A 11/2/8/8. A broader background to this labor problem is provided in L. H. Gann, *A History of Southern Rhodesia: Early Days to 1934* (London, Chatto and Windus, 1965), pp. 175–82.

mination over immigration. As one of its first legislative acts, the new self-governing colony rigidly excluded further immigration of adult male Indians. Following closely the precedent already set in South Africa, only wives and dependent children of those in residence were henceforth to be admitted.

Bolstered by continued immigration of women and children and a high rate of natural increase, the Asian community in Southern Rhodesia grew, as shown in Table 1, from 1,450 in

TABLE 1. EUROPEANS AND ASIANS
IN SOUTHERN RHODESIA, 1911–1961

Year	Number of Europeans	Number of Asians	Ratio (Asians per 100 Europeans)
1911	23,606	870	3.7
1921	33,620	1,250	3.7
1926	39,174	1,454	3.7
1931	49,910	1,700	3.4
1936	55,408	2,180	3.9
1941	68,954	2,547	3.7
1946	82,386	2,911	3.5
1951	135,596	4,292	3.2
1956	177,124	5,127	2.9
1961	221,504	7,253	3.3

Sources: Federation of Rhodesia and Nyasaland, *Census of Population: 1956,* p. 3; Rhodesia, *1961 Census of the European, Asian and Coloured Population,* p. 3.

1926 to 7,253 in 1961. In the same period, however, the European population increased from about 40,000 to nearly a quarter of a million.

NYASALAND

In the early days Nyasaland was somewhat easier to get to than Southern Rhodesia since most of the distance could be traveled by water. Entering at the mouth of the Zambezi, the traveler journeyed up the river to the confluence of the Shire, then proceeded up the Shire to the gorge at Chikwawa. From

Chikwawa, it was only a matter of twenty-five miles by foot, horseback, or *machilla*[29] up the escarpment to Blantyre and the Highlands, which was the destination of most people. Once down to the lake on the other side of the Highlands, one could again travel up and down the several hundred miles of shore-line by water. The only catch to the relatively easy access was this: provided the traveler was neither missionary nor administrator, there was not much to interest him in Nyasaland after he got there.

The first missionaries arrived in Nyasaland in the 1860s, virtually on the heels of Livingstone, and by the mid-1870s a mission station was established at Blantyre. Missionaries were followed by a few adventurers of the hunter-trader-prospector type (a species, incidentally, which the missionaries grudgingly tolerated rather than welcomed into the country) and an occasional wealthy sportsman came out from England to shoot game and see the sights. A handful of planters were already starting coffee estates when Johnston arrived in 1891 to set up the British administration. The first Indian trader, a Muslim by the name of Osman, arrived in 1885, according to his family's reckoning. Insofar as it concerns us, however, the real history of modern Nyasaland begins with the Johnston administration.

Johnston believed from the beginning that it was not Nyasaland's destiny to become white man's country "in the sense that all Africa south of the Zambezi, and all Africa north of the Sahara will eventually become." [30] But for exactly this reason, he did foresee an important role for the Indian in Nyasaland. "I am all for Indianizing Central Africa and making these great waste lands the seats of thriving Indian colonies where something better than the rude agriculture of Africa can be practiced, and where the Negro can be improved by a mixture of Indian thrift and industry," he wrote in a private letter to

29. Adopted as the name indicates from the Portuguese, the *machilla* was a hammock-like contrivance, slung from a long pole and carried by native bearers. See Johnston, *British Central Africa*, p. 91.
30. Johnston, p. 182.

India.[31] Needless to say, it scarcely follows from this remark that Johnston thought Central Africa should be turned over to Indians politically; at that time no British colonial officer seriously believed that Indians, let alone Africans, would soon be capable of governing themselves. For as long as anyone could then imagine, Nyasaland would necessarily be "administered under the benevolent despotism of the Imperial Government." [32] But a few European settlers could not develop the country by themselves, and Johnston believed that the Africans were far too primitive to do so either. What he thus envisaged was a multiracial society "ruled by whites, developed by Indians, and worked by blacks." [33]

With such enthusiastic support from its chief architect, why was Nyasaland not turned into another Fiji, so heavily populated by Indians? [34] Doubtlessly, the main factor was a lack of capital—or, perhaps more correctly, the entrepreneurial package of capital-plus-knowledge-plus-experience-plus-motivation. Plantation labor might have been found in India in abundance, but not the amount of money necessary to finance large-scale agricultural enterprise in the wilds of Nyasaland. To those few Indians with money to invest in agriculture, Nyasaland might

31. British Foreign Office (London), Item 6337, No. 145, Inclosure 5, courtesy of Dr. Raymond Apthorpe who provided us with a copy of his notes and the citation. In keeping with his times, Johnston conceived of "Negro improvement" in both cultural and biological terms. If Africans should be "dashed by the blood of a superior race" in the course of Indian colonization, well and good. Europeans he thought "too superior" for this task of up-breeding; Indians, on the other hand, were suitably intermediate in biological characteristics. Hanna, *Nyasaland and North-eastern Rhodesia*, pp. 226–27.

32. Johnston, p. 183.

33. Hanna, p. 227. An imaginative man, Johnston gave his dominating idea several symbolic representations (ibid., p. 228). Thus his book on Central Africa was bound in black, yellow, and white colors, and the same theme appears in the coat-of-arms that he designed for the new protectorate. It consists of a coffee tree, the motto "Light in Darkness," and two Africans holding a shield on a map of Africa. The background of the shield is black to represent the masses of Africa, but into this black is driven a yellow wedge. Superimposed over the black and yellow of the shield is a white cross. Significantly, one of the Africans is seen grasping a pick, the other a shovel!

34. On Indians in Fiji, see Adrian C. Mayer, *Peasants in the Pacific: A Study of Fiji Indian Rural Society*, Berkeley, University of California Press, 1961.

as well have been the North Pole. Many more attractive alternatives existed at home.[35]

No one after Johnston has dreamed of turning Nyasaland
into an Indian colony. But the Indians' positive, if somewhat
minor role, in the development of the economy was recognized
at an early date and remained a part of official thinking. Acting Commissioner Major F. B. Pearce discussed the Indians in
his annual report for the year 1902–03:

> There are now eighty-three Bunia stores actually open for
> the sale of goods in the Protectorate. The natives deal
> largely with these Indian traders, as the purchaser feels
> more at home in the less elaborate building than that gen-
> erally used by the European traders; and the method of
> bargaining is more in accordance with the native liking.
> The native can also take plenty of time over his decision,
> the Indian trader having the necessary stock of patience,
> and being content with a small profit, lays himself out to
> accommodate the native mind. The Indian trader gives
> each native purchaser a small present after the completion
> of the bargain; this may be only a few matches or a small
> piece of soap or a needle or two, but the native goes away
> very contentedly with the impression that he has been
> liberally treated. At the same time, it must be stated that
> the African native, if allowed to purchase in his own way
> and time, is by no means a fool.

He went on to say:

> Had there been no Indian traders, there is no doubt that
> many thousand natives would never have ventured into a

35. It probably should be noted that Johnston eventually modified his position and came to view as undesirable any indiscriminate settlement of the
"riff-raff" from India in Africa. Roland Oliver, *Sir Harry Johnston and the
Scramble for Africa* (London, Chatto and Windus, 1957), p. 258. The idea of
attracting Indian peasants to Africa occurred to a number of other officials of
the period; we have already seen an example in Southern Rhodesia (p. 30
above). In 1906, efforts were made to recruit Punjabi families to settle in
East Africa. The peasants were willing to come but only if they could bring
their entire village with them. No funds were available to carry out such an
expensive project. Hollingsworth, *The Asians of East Africa*, p. 59.

European store for the purpose of making purchases. It must also be remembered that as much of the merchandise Indian traders retail is purchased from local European firms in the country, there is profit to both parties.[36]

As already noted, commercial business was dominated in Nyasaland and Northeastern Rhodesia throughout the early period by large trading firms, but the attitude of these companies toward Indians is not known precisely. Perhaps they did not unduly begrudge the Indian his small takings, and it may be that they welcomed the wholesale business as Major Pearce suggests.

Johnston had believed that the Indian would act as a petty middleman in a produce trade with the natives, serving to collect native products into large enough quantities to be profitably handled by the European trading firm, which could supply the necessary transportation facilities for export.[37] But such trade never developed. Once his small stocks of ivory and wild rubber were exhausted, the African had little to interest the European except his labor.

Some African labor was employed locally by European-initiated enterprise—planting estates, missions, and government—but the total economic base thus provided remained small. The Highlands area, suited by climate for European occupation, was limited in extent and a profitable export crop was developed only after long and costly experimentation. Coffee looked promising at first but was disastrously attacked by disease. Cotton was tried next, then tobacco, and finally tea, which proved the most successful.[38]

These obstacles to European settlement are reflected demographically in the census figures. In 1921, there were 399 European males engaged as planters and agriculturists in Nyasa-

36. F. B. Pearce, "Report on the trade and general conditions of the British Central African Protectorate for the year 1902–1903," Central African Archives.
37. Johnston, pp. 177–78.
38. Hanna, *Rhodesias and Nyasaland*, p. 207; Richard Gray, *The Two Nations: Aspects of the Development of Race Relations in the Rhodesias and Nyasaland* (London, Oxford University Press, 1960), pp. 82–83. Considerable quantities of tobacco and cotton are still produced by African farmers.

land, whereas by 1931 this number had fallen to 290; by 1945, it had shrunk to 225. In the meantime, however, cotton and tobacco had been established among African farmers as commercial crops on a very minor scale.

Nyasaland's money economy—in the aggregate a tiny affair at best—would have been even more restricted if it had not been for the considerable export of the one product which the Africans possessed in abundance: their labor. For half a century at least, Nyasalanders have sought work outside the territory, mainly in the Rhodesias and South Africa but also in the Congo and both British and Portuguese East Africa. An estimated 30,000 workers, for example, were absent from the country as early as 1926.[39] Remittances of these workers have been (and remain today in modern Malawi) a major factor in the country's economy.[40]

Supported by these very modest developments toward a money economy, the Indian population increased from about 100 at the turn of the century to nearly 3,000 in 1945. A doubling of the population between 1931 and 1945—when Nyasaland like the rest of the world suffered through a decade of depression—may be accounted for almost entirely by increasing numbers of women and children. A close look at the figures shows little or no apparent increase in the number of gainfully occupied males during this period.[41]

Beginning in 1945, Nyasaland boomed economically with the rest of Central Africa. But compared with the truly spectacular upsurge in the Rhodesias, the territory's development remained on a minor scale. Much of this unwonted prosperity was in fact an indirect result of economic growth in the Northern Rhodesian Copperbelt and in Southern Rhodesia. In 1954, for example, it is estimated that no less than one-tenth of the personal income in the hands of Africans came from remittances of emigrant workers employed mainly in these two

39. Nyasaland, *Report on the Census of 1926*, p. xxviii.
40. See below, p. 354 and n. 14.
41. The number of economically active males among the Asians of Nyasaland was 1,256 in 1931 and 1,229 in 1945.

areas.[42] Much of the new money can also be traced to expenditures by the government for hospitals, roads, and schools. The Colonial Development and Welfare Acts passed in London during World War II provided some of the necessary funds, and programs under their auspices stimulated the further development of a trend among African peasant farmers toward the growing of cash crops.

The demographic effect of these stirrings in the economy was a near quadrupling of both the European and the Asian population within a decade or so, as can be seen in Table 2.

TABLE 2. EUROPEANS AND ASIANS
IN NYASALAND, 1901–1961

Year	Number of Europeans	Number of Asians	Ratio (Asians per 100 Europeans)
1901	314	115	37
1911	766	481	63
1921	1,486	563	38
1926	1,656	850	51
1931	1,975	1,591	81
1945	1,948	2,804	144
1956	6,732	8,504	126
1961*	8,750	10,630	121

* Preliminary census figures.

Sources: Central African Statistical Office, *Statistical Handbook of Nyasaland, 1949*, pp. 2–3; Federation of Rhodesia and Nyasaland, *Census of Population: 1956*, p. 3; Federation of Rhodesia and Nyasaland, *Preliminary Results of the Federal Census of Population and of Employees: (2) Detailed Geographical Distribution of the Non-African Population*, p. 27.

A comparatively heavy Indian immigration between 1945 and 1953 was of course only possible because Nyasaland remained under the "benevolent despotism of the Imperial Government." The European settler's view of the Indians in Nyasaland was essentially no different than it was elsewhere. Indians were passively accepted as a part of the local scene only because

42. Federation of Rhodesia and Nyasaland, *Report on an Economic Survey of Nyasaland, 1958–1959* [Jack Report], C. Fed. 132 (Salisbury, 1959), p. 53.

the territory's settlers had little to say in the matter. Significantly, not a single European representative from Nyasaland voiced real objection to Indian exclusion when the Federal Assembly debated the immigration bill in 1954.[43]

NORTHERN RHODESIA

Until the development of the Copperbelt, Northern Rhodesia was a poor and backward country with few attractions for settlers, European or Indian. Wealth from copper after 1945 radically altered this picture. Measured by almost any index one chooses—population growth, urbanization, income, or the value of production—Northern Rhodesia's development between 1945 and 1960 was phenomenal. For example, the gross domestic product rose from £15 million in 1945 to £187.6 million in 1960.[44]

But all this affluence is very recent. For a considerable period after the coming of the Europeans, Northern Rhodesia represented little more than two huge blocks of malaria- and tsetse-ridden country marginal to Nyasaland and Southern Rhodesia respectively. Until 1911, there were two separate administrations. Northeastern Rhodesia was administered from Blantyre until 1899, when headquarters for it were established at Fort Jameson. The capital of Northwestern Rhodesia was Livingstone, the port of entry by rail from Southern Rhodesia.[45] The eastern part of Northern Rhodesia is thus an offshoot from Nyasaland; "the-line-of-rail" or developed strip up through the center of the country is essentially a projection of Southern Rhodesia's development.

The area around Fort Jameson retains to this day a distinctly Nyasaland-like flavor, and this impression must have been even more pronounced originally. The Europeans who settled

43. Federal *Hansard* (July 21–August 19, 1954).
44. Southern Rhodesia, Central Statistical Office, *National Accounts and Balance of Payments of Northern Rhodesia, Nyasaland and Southern Rhodesia 1954–1963* (Salisbury, Central Statistical Office, 1964), p. 49.
45. The headquarters of Northwestern Rhodesia was at nearby Kalomo until 1907.

in the Fort Jameson region after the final pacification of the Ngoni were planters of the Nyasaland type. Trade followed the Nyasaland pattern and the bulk of it was in the hands of the African Lakes Company.

Like the Europeans, the first Indians to settle in this region came from Nyasaland in 1905, and they came and remained under a Nyasaland-like official tolerance for their presence. Codrington, the Administrator of Northeastern Rhodesia at the time, had served in Nyasaland. Indians relish telling and re-telling a story of how the first contingent of Indian traders—the Khamisa brothers and their retainers—were escorted into town upon their arrival by a brass band sent out by the "Governor," and they say that these pioneers came specifically at his invitation. The brass band is possibly apocryphal, but the official tolerance shown the Indians is not. When the European trading firms protested the presence of the Indians, the administration chose to ignore these objections.[46]

In the west, things were radically different. Here the European population contained many Afrikaner farmers, Jewish traders, and a sizable working class made up of railway men and miners. Such people inevitably brought with them the anti-Indian prejudices common to South Africa at the time. Older informants who grew up in Livingstone remember that Indians were expected to get off the sidewalk at the approach of a European. Letters opposing Indian immigration appeared periodically in the *Livingstone Mail*.[47]

In 1915 Lawrence A. Wallace, the first Administrator of the newly combined territory, by executive proclamation extended to Northern Rhodesia the principle contained in the Southern Rhodesian Immigration Ordinance of 1904 of a literacy test in English. Before taking this action, Wallace had been in consultation with the European Farmers' Association on the matter of settler representation.[48] What was discussed in de-

---

46. Gann, *Birth of a Plural Society*, p. 154; see also Gann, *A History of Northern Rhodesia*, pp. 146–47.
47. Gann, *Birth of a Plural Society*, p. 155.
48. Ibid., pp. 167–68.

tail is not known but it can be easily conjectured that the desirability of restrictions upon Indians was brought up and that Wallace, a South African from Natal, responded sympathetically.

The literacy test, combined with a lack of much economic opportunity, held the flow of Indians into Northern Rhodesia down to a trickle until the end of World War II.

TABLE 3. EUROPEANS AND ASIANS
IN NORTHERN RHODESIA, 1911–1961

Year	Number of Europeans	Number of Asians	Ratio (Asians per 100 Europeans)
1911	1,497	39	2.6
1921	3,634	56	1.5
1931	13,846	176	1.3
1946	21,907	1,117	5.1
1951	37,079	2,524	6.8
1956	65,277	5,450	8.3
1961	74,549	7,790	10.4

Sources: Federation of Rhodesia and Nyasaland, *Census of Population: 1956*, p. 3; Zambia, *Final Report of the September 1961 Censuses of Non-Africans and Employees*, p. 45.

Table 3 clearly shows the extent to which the Indian population of present-day Zambia owes its origin to the brief period of relatively heavy immigration between the end of the war and the coming of federation. By the middle 1940s, the literacy test was less of an obstacle than it had been earlier, owing to the development of education in India, and Northern Rhodesia's booming economy easily absorbed all Indians who came.

Needless to say, this rapid increase in the Indian population was viewed with some disquietude by Europeans. It was, however, an extraordinarily prosperous period for everyone; and by this time the Europeans in Northern Rhodesia had lost interest in the African trade to which most Indians were confined. The two groups were thus not directly competitive, and for this reason the influx of Indians was tolerated if not exactly welcomed.

It was in this context that a new note was struck in public discussion: the potential threat of increasing numbers of Indians upon the future welfare of *Africans* rather than of Europeans. In 1945, Sir Stewart Gore-Browne, the nominated "unofficial" representative of native interests, rose in the Legislative Council and delivered himself thusly:

> I must say here . . . that Africans, and Europeans, too, do view with a great deal of apprehension the number of Indians who are now coming into the country. Trade is more and more passing into their hands, and we do feel, we African representatives, that something (I am not prepared to say what) will have to be done to ensure our own indigenous people a fair share of the trade, certainly in their own reserves, and also in the rest of the country.[49]

Establishment of the Federation offered the solution to the Indian problem that all European settlers wanted but which was impossible as long as Northern Rhodesia retained its protectorate status. The European representatives from Northern Rhodesia, like their colleagues from Nyasaland, offered no fundamental objections to exclusion when the immigration bill was debated in the Federal Assembly. A few liberals went out of their way to put on record some kindly but innocuous remarks about the Indians.[50] But Transvaal-born G. W. R. L'Ange undoubtedly summed up prevailing sentiment—liberal, moderate, and conservative alike—when he observed: "We are not divided on [this] subject. . . . If there is one thing that we are united on it is on the restriction on Asian immigration into Northern Rhodesia."[51]

49. Northern Rhodesia *Hansard* (July 3, 1945). Similar comments were made by T. S. Page, member for the Northeastern Electoral Area, ibid. (December 10, 1946); and G. W. R. L'Ange, member for the Nkana Electoral Area, ibid. (March 29, 1949).

50. A heckler impatiently cut into one such speech, that of Dr. Alexander Scott whose Lusaka constituency included substantial numbers of Indians. "Do you want unrestricted Asian immigration?" he demanded. Dr. Scott quickly admitted that he did not: "I think it would be a great mistake to have it." Federal *Hansard* (July 21, 1954), col. 1632.

51. Federal *Hansard* (July 22, 1954), col. 1682.

SOCIO-DEMOGRAPHIC VARIATIONS

In conclusion, emphasis should be placed upon the major socio-demographic variations territorially that resulted from the settlement history sketched in this chapter.

The Indian population of present-day Rhodesia is unusual in a number of respects when compared to that of either Malawi or Zambia. By virtue of the early closure of Indian immigration into Southern Rhodesia, there have been no recent adult male immigrants. Any Indian male under forty is almost certainly either African-born or African-reared. Young and old alike are more thoroughly acculturated to European norms and values than in the north; and whether first or second generation, the Indians of Rhodesia are apt to be literate and fluent in English. The Indian community here is highly urbanized: 85 percent of the Asians live in the main towns, according to the 1961 census —in fact, two-thirds of the total number live in either Salisbury or Bulawayo. Nearly one-half (45.4 percent) of Southern Rhodesia's Asians in 1961 were Hindus; over a third (37.3 percent) were Muslims; and 11.2 percent were said to be Catholics.[52]

Malawi, by virtue of less restrictive policies during the colonial period, has the largest Indian population in Central Africa and Indians slightly outnumber Europeans. But both populations remain tiny minorities compared to the African population—about one-half of one percent of the total. In the absence of a literacy test, a great many Indians entered the territory without knowing English. Indians here also have less day-to-day contact with Europeans than in Rhodesia or Zambia. The result has been an Indian population that is on the whole less literate and less acculturated.

Other basic facts should be noted. Malawi's Asian population is predominantly Muslim (63 percent according to the 1956 census, the latest for which such figures are available). It differs importantly from that of the other countries, too, in that it

52. Rhodesia contains a small Goan community, and it has a handful of non-Indian Asians, most of whom are Chinese. Still, a figure of 11.2 percent for the Roman Catholics seems difficult to account for, unless some Indo-African Coloureds are included.

is much more rural.[53] While overwhelmingly Gujarati in origin like the others, Malawi's Indian population contains most of the non-Gujaratis to be found in Central Africa; there are small communities—from a few dozen to a few hundred each—of Sikhs, Goans, and Magalorian Christians, as well as a few Punjabis, Sindis, Konkanis, and others.

In Zambia the adult Indian population is made up almost entirely of fairly recent immigrants. All men, however, came into the country under the literacy test; in consequence they speak English, and in most cases they have had at least a primary school education. A fair number—far more than the average European has any inkling of—have university degrees.

Zambia has a larger proportion of Hindus than the other countries (70.1 percent of the Asians in 1961); in origin, many of these Hindus have close ties to the early settlers of Southern Rhodesia. Most Muslims in Zambia came into the country either through Nyasaland or by contacts ultimately traceable to Nyasaland. In consequence, Zambian Muslims tend to have characteristics roughly similar to those in Malawi. They are somewhat more rural and are on the whole less sophisticated than the Hindus.

53. No rural-urban breakdown is provided in the available 1961 census data, but 50 percent of the territory's Asian population live in places other than the three main towns of Blantyre-Limbe, Zomba, and Lilongwe.

Chapter Three

THE ECONOMIC ROLE OF THE INDIAN

Drive along a main road in present-day Malawi or Zambia and stop at one of the small trading centers located anywhere between the larger towns. It consists of half a dozen Indian shops clustered to one side of the graveled highway. Pick out the middle-sized shop and enter.

Stepping through the open door, the traveler finds himself in a rectangular room, perhaps 25 feet wide and 35 feet long. The building of which this room is the larger part is itself a simply constructed affair. The walls are made of crude local brick, plastered and whitewashed. The floor is of concrete, none too smoothly finished. The roof is corrugated metal, held in place by pole rafters and is not ceiled; light shows between the roof and the walls in many places. The floor is raised well off the ground, and there is a narrow roofed porch in front. Here an African tailor sits in the open air and works at a battered sewing machine. Two smallish and stoutly barred windows on each side of the doorway let some light into the interior, but most of it is provided by the open door.

From the doorway, the view directly in front is of a counter running across the room at the back, and perhaps part way up its two sides as well. Out here in the "bush" this counter is commonly constructed of unfinished lumber; in the poorer shops it is made from packing cases. The top surface is perhaps covered by cardboard from a large carton. The space below the counter is not boarded up; instead it is left open and screened with chicken wire. On a shelf here are displayed pots and pans, enameled dishes, small items of hardware, and bicycle parts. Within easy reach on shelves immediately behind the counter are bolts and bolts of dress material—the major item of trade—carefully selected by color and pattern to fit the peculiar taste of the region.

On the highest shelves up near the roof are piles of blankets and cheap suitcases of reinforced paper and plastic construction. On a bottom shelf, at counter-level, are opened boxes of manufactured men's shirts in cellophane wrappings; they are stacked at a forty-five-degree angle for display. To one side are other boxes which contain men's shorts and trousers; representative samples of these have been opened; the cuffs and an inch or so of the leg are pulled out over the end of the box, and the lid is replaced. Near the trousers are a few brightly colored ties and socks, and high up on the shelves wedged somewhere between the blankets and the suitcases are a few men's felt hats, all black or brown in color. From a floor rack in a nearby corner hang several suit-type coats and sport jackets; some of these are possibly secondhand from the United States. Shelves along one side of the room contain several dozen boxes of shoes, virtually all of which are of canvas-and-rubber construction. Tucked in somewhere are a few packages of patent medicines, vaseline, hair oil, and hotel-size bars of face soap. Matches, cigarettes, writing paper, and envelopes are available if one asks.

Up front near the doorway are wooden cases of soft drinks and empty bottles. Close by are bulk containers of sugar, salt, beans, and mealie meal (ground maize), with a set of scales to weigh these items. There is also a small drum of paraffin oil (kerosene to Americans) set up on blocks with a tap at the bottom, and nearby a couple of cases of coarse, yellow-and-blue laundry soap. A floor rack on this side of the room contains half a dozen new bicycles, all with their tires deflated to show that they have never been used. Hanging from the roof by a wire are a dozen or so new tires.

Across the room from the bicycle rack are strung several

overhead wires from which hang two or three dozen women's dresses. Some of these are factory-made; others are products of the shop's tailor working in his spare time. These dresses are for sale, but their main function is to serve as models of what is available on order. It is customary for a woman to select the material for her dress and then have it made up by the shop's tailor. There is no separate charge for this service; his labor is considered a part of the overhead of the business.

Details of construction and arrangement vary, but the basic pattern of the Indian shop is monotonously standard everywhere in the rural areas and in the small towns. Variation comes mainly in the amount and variety of the goods offered for sale, not in their kind or arrangement. Nor is there any great difference between the moderately well-stocked bush store and the one which we find in the "secondary trading area" of the larger towns, i.e. a portion of the town originally set apart from the European shopping center in the days of the colonial administration. The urban shop is a unit of a well-constructed building; it has plate-glass windows at the entrance and possesses (except for the very poorest) at least one interior glass showcase. Still, the basic stock carried and its arrangement for sale falls into the familiar pattern described for the rural shop. Perhaps the biggest difference is that no food is sold in the urban shop—a rule laid down by town ordinances. Consequently, the sale of food in town is a function of a specialized establishment, the so-called "tea-room." A shop in town may also try to achieve a reputation as a good place to buy blankets or shoes, for example, and is therefore comparatively well stocked with them. Some shops, too, are more self-consciously modern in their appointments than others. But after all of these qualifications are dutifully entered, the overriding impression remains one of a lack of specialization and monotonous similarity.

Economically, the shop described represents the Indians' toe-hold in Africa. It is behind the counter of such an establishment that the typical adult Indian male in Central Africa spends the greater part of his waking hours. Taking the three territories of the ex-federation together, the 1956 census shows no less than four-fifths of the Asian male labor force engaged in trade, either as shop owners or employees.[1]

TABLE 4. DISTRIBUTION BY INDUSTRY OF ECONOMI-
CALLY ACTIVE ASIAN MALES IN SOUTHERN RHODESIA,
NORTHERN RHODESIA, AND NYASALAND,
1956 AND 1961

	Southern Rhodesia		Northern Rhodesia		Nyasaland*
Industry	*1956*	*1961*	*1956*	*1961*	*1956*
Commerce	67.1%	63.9%	86.0%	87.0%	79.4%
Manufacturing and repairing	15.5	14.7	5.0	6.0	6.3
Services	9.0	8.5	4.2	3.9	4.4
Transport and communications	2.2	3.9	1.3	.6	5.5
Agriculture, forestry, etc.	1.2	1.4	1.0	.2	1.6
Miscellaneous	5.0	7.6	2.5	2.3	2.8
Total	100.0%	100.0%	100.0%	100.0%	100.0%
Total numbers	1,382	1,772	2,049	2,049	2,346

* 1961 figures not available.

Sources: Federation of Rhodesia and Nyasaland, *Census of Population: 1956*, Tables 32–34; Rhodesia, *1961 Census of the European, Asian and Coloured Population*, Table 23; Zambia, *Final Report of the September 1961 Censuses of Non-Africans and Employees*, Table 7.

Sociologically, the shop described above represents the single most important mediating point in Indian-African relations. The vignettes from our field notes presented below illustrate some typical behavior within this arena.

This twelve- or thirteen-year-old boy was very poorly dressed. The ragged shirt which he had on was tied at the front with a piece of bias tape since all the buttons were long since gone. He walked up to the counter rather

1. Economically active females were omitted from Table 4 because of their relatively insignificant numbers. Southern Rhodesia had much the largest contingent—229 and 341 in 1956 and 1961 respectively, with nearly two-thirds in commerce.

hesitatingly and asked for a postage stamp. P [the Indian shopkeeper] looked at him quizzically and then said, in English, "You mean an envelope?" The boy nodded his head, as if he wasn't sure whether or not that was what he really meant, and P then asked, "How many?" He said, "Two." So from the pile of rather dusty and dirty stationery on the shelf behind the counter, P extracted a couple of light pastel-green envelopes and handed them to the boy, quoting as he did so the price of one penny. A half hour later the same boy returned with the envelopes, which he handed back to P and asked for his money. Without comment, P went to the cash drawer, took out a penny, and handed it to the boy in exchange for the envelopes.

A young African woman came in and asked to see a boy's khaki shirt of the standard type. G went and got it, slapping it down on the counter in front of her with the characteristic gesture Indians habitually use. He said, "Six bob!" Then they talked for a moment in Kitchen Kaffir [the trade language of the area], and I caught the word, "four." There was more exchange in Kitchen Kaffir, and then G said, "Five-and-six." The woman then turned away from the counter and began to look idly at something else. Turning to me, G said in English, "You see how it is. In this business every transaction is an auction sale. These people expect to bargain, and you have to bargain with them. That shirt cost me four-and-six; I should get six shillings for it. But she wants it for four." Dotson: "Will she eventually buy the shirt at five-and-six?" Answer: "Yes, she will buy it all right; she needs the shirt." She hadn't yet bought it when I left the shop some time later.

I spent nearly two and a half hours in the shop. During this time there were a variety of customers. N was in fact fairly busy, but certainly the total take must have been very small. Some came in and simply asked the prices of goods on display; for example, a man in a very ragged pair of trousers, which had been patched frequently but somewhat ineffectively, came to admire a new pair of trousers. However, he left without buying them. Another customer was a middle-aged woman in very rough clothes. She had on a dress of sorts, a wrap-around arrangement consisting of a single piece of unshaped cloth. [This used to be common; now African women usually wear tailored dresses.] She approached N rather coyly and there issued a long exchange in Chinyanja [the local language]. When the woman left, I asked what she had wanted. "She wanted sugar," he said, "but she wanted it on credit."

After this followed a series of sales, some of sugar. There were three of these, two to children. There is a box on the counter which contains brown sugar and a small scoop. Taking a piece of newspaper, N scoops out a portion of sugar and puts it on the paper. He charged a penny a portion. One customer came in with a Coke bottle which N filled from the five-gallon container of paraffin oil in the corner. There were several soap customers; most of these bought one bar at a time [the small kind used by hotels], but one customer actually bought three bars. Several bought matches. One woman, after duly opening and sniffing all the bottles on the shelf, bought a vaseline preparation for her hair.

Most of the stock in this shop is of course—as always —piece goods and clothing. Noting that there hadn't been a single textile sale all morning, I asked N when cloth was sold. Answer: "We don't sell much now. People don't have any money. It's just the small things now, like matches and soap. The textiles move only in the season." [By the "season," he means when the African-grown cotton in this Nyasaland region is gathered and sold.]

As a market, the African trade consists of a large volume of low-income customers, with only a few pence, shillings, or pounds to spend at any one time. By European standards, per capita income is extremely low, although the amount of money in African hands has in recent years increased steadily and substantially. Table 5 compares average annual earnings of

TABLE 5. AVERAGE ANNUAL EARNINGS OF AFRICAN
AND EUROPEAN EMPLOYEES IN SOUTHERN RHODESIA,
NORTHERN RHODESIA, AND NYASALAND,
1954 AND 1960

	Southern Rhodesia		Northern Rhodesia		Nyasaland	
	1954	*1960*	*1954*	*1960*	*1954*	*1960*
African	£ 56	£ 84	£ 71	£ 119	£ 34	£ 51
European	875	1,117	1,162	1,464	922	1,185

Source: Federation of Rhodesia and Nyasaland, *Economic Report: 1961,* p. 25.

African and European employees in the three territories of the federation for 1954 and 1960.[2] Table 6 shows typical earnings of African employees at the more recent date of 1964, together with comparable figures for 1960. When assessing

TABLE 6. AVERAGE ANNUAL EARNINGS OF AFRICAN
EMPLOYEES IN SELECTED INDUSTRIAL SECTORS
IN ZAMBIA, RHODESIA, AND MALAWI,
1960 AND 1964

	Zambia		Rhodesia		Malawi	
	1960	*1964*	*1960*	*1964*	*1960*	*1964*
Manufacturing	£118	£203	£125	£198	£ 64	£ 87
Construction	118	143	106	162	51	62
Commerce	116	194	120	180	49	63
Services (excluding domestic)	128	196	124	180	94	116
Domestic service	81	98	94	110	56	72

Sources: Zambia, *Monthly Digest of Statistics,* August 1966; Rhodesia, *Monthly Digest of Statistics,* February 1966; Malawi, *Quarterly Digest of Statistics,* April 1966; Malawi, *Budget 1966: Background Information,* Treasury Document No. 5 (Zomba, Government Press).

2. Cash income may be somewhat less than the figures in Table 5 as they often include income in kind and, for large-scale employers, various fringe benefits.

61

these statistics, it must be kept in mind that *paid* employment of any kind is largely an urban phenomenon throughout Africa and that even in the cities regular employment has historically been (and continues to be) a relatively rare privilege.[3] Modern Africans, both rural and urban, do nonetheless have access to some money income, little as this may be in comparative terms, and on this basis they have established a level of living that now includes a considerable variety of manufactured goods. Demand is fairly stable and is sufficiently standardized to be highly predictable.

We have seen many of the common items of trade on the shelves of the Indian shop. But let us now look at them again in the somewhat different context of the purchasing habits of urban Africans, including judgments as to quantity, quality, and pattern of change; rural Africans buy most of the same goods but in significantly smaller quantities.

First and foremost, the African now living in town needs mealie meal in large quantities. His staff of life, this is what he mainly eats. In addition he must have sugar, salt, perhaps some tea, and paraffin oil for light. His wife and daughters must have dresses of cotton prints, and brightly colored kerchiefs to cover their clipped heads. Increasingly, African women are also buying slips and other items of intimate feminine wear, but this trend is only beginning and is as yet not common. Boys and men must also be clothed. They ordinarily wear shorts and shirts; these constitute the male uniform in Central Africa and are sold in huge quantities. The style is a direct imitation of the clothing Europeans wear out in the bush and on the farm, but there is a marked difference in the quality of the cloth. Africans use a distinctive stout khaki, which, because it is worn by Africans, is avoided by Europeans. Assuming they can afford them, men wear long trousers, odd or sport jackets, sweaters, and hats for dress-up occasions and for street wear in town.[4] Shoes for both sexes are becoming

3. See below, p. 347 and n. 8, and p. 350, n. 12.
4. This describes dress as of 1959–61. By 1966, styles had changed considerably. See below, p. 346, n. 4.

the rule; the larger part of the adult urban African population in the Rhodesias and Nyasaland never go barefoot any more. Rural Africans may also own a pair of shoes, even if they do not ordinarily wear them.

Household items of manufactured origin include quantities of long-handled enameled pots in a variety of sizes suitable for open-fire cooking, pocket knives, pails, tubs, and tin lanterns. Inexpensive cotton blankets are sold in enormous quantities. They do not last long under the usage they receive and must be constantly replaced; the demand naturally rises with the onset of the coldest period of the year which begins in May. Suitcases of paper and plastic construction are widely used and sold; their popularity reflects the greatly increased geographical mobility of the population. Matches, soap, candles, and locally-made cigarettes have become necessities everywhere. Minor luxuries such as hair oil and a few popular patent medicines (such as aspirin) are taken for granted. Since bicycle ownership has become all but universal among urban male Africans, the commoner spare parts (such as new tires and wheel spokes) are found in even the most skimpily furnished Indian shop. Reflecting a rising standard of living among the better-paid Africans is a considerable sale of iron bed springs and mattresses (most Africans, however, continue to sleep on the floor), inexpensive wristwatches (it is a poor urban African male indeed who does not own one), radios and gramophones, musical instruments (the guitar being the favorite), and canned foods and bottled European-type beer.

The typical Indian shop is planned to meet the demands of this fairly stable market. Each shop tries to carry all the common items in order to make sure that a customer will be accommodated, thus the marked lack of specialization that we have noted. Even such things as bicycles are usually stocked, a few to each shop.

The major exception to this rule is the "tea-room" of the larger towns. The main business of this establishment is not, as the uninitiated American might assume, the serving of food and drink on the premises, although this is indeed done. Soft drinks, fresh milk, tea with lots of sugar, and bread and jam are the standard offerings and are served at two or three tables set aside in the corner. The chief business of the tea-room, however, consists of the sale of staple food in small quantities: sugar in sixpence packets, vegetable and paraffin oil in Coke bottles, beans, bakery bread (which is constantly becoming more popular), jam, packaged tea, and fresh milk in bottles. Mealie meal is sold in hundred-pound jute bags for two or three days at the beginning of the month, when African wage earners are paid, and in three- and five-pound paper bags after the middle of the month when these same employees are reduced to living upon their weekly cash "ration" money.[5]

Nonfood items sold in tea-rooms consist of such things as matches and cigarettes (a large demand, since locally-made cigarettes are very cheap), soap, and stationery. A variety of canned foods are always carried, but the demand for these is not large; perhaps their main function is to decorate the shelf area behind the counter. Such items as pocket knives (Hong Kong-made and selling for two shillings and sixpence), ball-point pens, and wristwatches are also often stocked in tea-rooms.

With the legalization of the sale of European wines and beer to Africans in Northern Rhodesia, Indian-owned bottle shops quickly appeared. The main business in these shops was beer, but they otherwise functioned very much like tea-rooms and were stocked accordingly. In Nyasaland, where the legal restrictions upon alcohol had always been less severe, bars and bottle shops for the African trade were generally in the hands of Africans.

SOCIO-CULTURAL PREREQUISITES FOR THE AFRICAN TRADE

Since the African market consists as it does of a great multiplicity of low-income customers of restricted physical

5. Traditionally, Africans throughout southern and East Africa have been paid a monthly wage, supplemented by a small cash allowance (commonly five to eight shillings).

mobility, it follows that shops must be distributed widely in space and kept individually small. There is simply no great concentration of money in any given area. The same characteristics mean that the profit from any one transaction may approach the infinitesimal. After serving four African children from a sweets jar in the course of half an hour, a shopkeeper once said: "You see, at this rate I need a dozen customers to take in a shilling!"

This in turn means that the productivity of the labor spent behind the counter in the African trade is low, far lower than that which is generally taken for granted in the advanced industrial countries. Yet the skills and personality characteristics prerequisite for such business are considerable. These, it is safe to say, cannot be attained without rigorous socialization and experience.

For survival—to say nothing of success—the following preconditions must be satisfied. The owner must first of all possess sufficient capital, small as that amount may be in absolute terms; historically this has been a serious hurdle in Central Africa as elsewhere. Capital, however, is but the beginning: to use capital effectively he must be able to see clearly the conceptual distinction between gross and net profit and have the will and resolution to act in terms of this distinction. In other words, he must avoid eating into his capital for ordinary consumer expenditures at all costs—a very difficult requirement for people living close to the margins of economic existence. Psychologically, this means that the small shopkeeper must have a highly trained capacity to defer gratification; he must be able to put off and to look to the future. He must also be highly self-disciplined in work habits; methodical, patient, and enduring. But all this is still not quite enough. To achieve a small modicum of success, he must have a measure of business sense. At the most immediate level, this means a firm and objective knowledge of what his clientele will buy and what they will not; and at a broader and more inclusive level, it means judgment and foresight to appreciate general economic trends of relevance to his business. Finally, with all these skills in hand, he must be motivated by the objective circumstances of his life situation to apply them.

With respect to both cultural background and historical situation, the Gujarati Indians who perform the middleman trader's role in Central Africa today seem to an extraordinary degree preadapted to it. Europeans speak of them as "born businessmen," and Indians themselves often explain their success by reference to a presumed inherited capacity for business not shared by most other people—Jews (and perhaps Chinese) excepted. These beliefs of course represent the common tendency of people everywhere to interpret and justify a given division of labor in terms of supposedly innate racial characteristics. This tendency is greatly exaggerated in the plural society where functional differences in the social division of labor do coincide with obvious physical differences.

As will be seen when caste origins are discussed below, few of the Indians who engage in trade so successfully in Africa were actually traders in India. Most of them came from farm families, but from groups whose relatively prosperous circumstances have for a long time encouraged some members to enter into business and the professions. This has been particularly true of the Patidar, a dominant caste of small landowners in the Gujarat region. By extension, the stereotype derived from the Patidar is applied to everyone from this subcultural area. Indians from other parts of India tend to see the Gujaratis stereotypically as "businessmen." This view is internalized by the Gujaratis themselves, with profound influences upon their behavior.

Beyond this quite specific orientation of the Gujaratis, the sociologist has little difficulty in seeing how Indian culture generally is conducive to success in trade. Indians are, with few exceptions, ascetic and self-denying; at the same time, they are disciplined to hard and persistent effort toward future goals. The same culture provides them with the normative basis for effective social cooperation in small, tightly knit kinship, caste, and locality groups. The historical accident of their earlier contact with Europeans (in contrast to Africans) has made them literate—but not *too* literate to disdain the humble tasks of shopkeeping. Their middling social placement in India guaranteed that they would be poor but ambitious and therefore appreciative of the potentialities unwittingly opened up to them in Africa by the action of their conquerors, the Europeans. In Africa itself, circumstances decreed that they exercise these talents rather than any others they might have. Like Jews over so much of the world since the Diaspora, Indians in Central Africa have been tolerated in trade, but they have not been welcomed in other sectors of the economy.

BUSINESS CAREERS

Through this happy combination of socially inherited capacity and the fortunes of history, Indians in Central Africa have on the whole done very well economically. This does not mean, however, that they have done so uniformly (not *every* Indian is a super-businessman) nor that even the most fortunate are to be compared with really rich Americans or Englishmen.

Because most Indians are relatively poor while at the same time some are known to be rich, Indian wealth tends to be either greatly exaggerated or greatly underestimated by Europeans. The average net return from a small Indian shop is probably something like fifty pounds a month—a little less than a European woman would earn as a secretary and not much more than half the wage that an experienced European automobile mechanic would command. Such an income by itself is scarcely sufficient to turn a poor man into a rich one, no matter how rigorously managed. Nevertheless, a few Indians have acquired real wealth judged by any standard. Twenty families in a major Northern Rhodesian town, for example, owned in 1960 real property assessed at nearly a million and a quarter pounds.[6] Considering the limitations inherent in the small shop, how has the accumulation of such substantial fortunes in a single generation been possible? An examination of

6. Based on figures taken from Lusaka, Municipal Council, *Valuation Roll* (December 1958).

the typical career-history of successful Indians will show the following sequence:

1. A chain of shops operated by assistants. If he came to Africa as a young man without capital, as in most cases he did, the Indian pioneer served an apprenticeship of about five years behind the counter of a shop belonging to his patron—a relationship which will be examined more fully in a later chapter.[7] He then acquired, with his patron's help, a shop of his own. His next step—and relatively few advanced so far—was to acquire a chain of several such shops which he in turn operated with the help of young assistants recruited from India. Income from any one shop was small, but that from several combined might be quite substantial. An operation of this kind, however, was possible only as long as a continuous supply of new assistants could be had from India.

2. Wholesale trade in African goods. The next step of a rising Indian businessman was to enter the wholesale trade, a niche in the total economic system hitherto occupied almost exclusively by Jews in the Rhodesias and by the trading companies in Nyasaland.

Currently, a wholesale trade in goods destined for the African market is the economic mainstay of most well-to-do and wealthy Indian families in all three countries. It is a vigorously—if not to say viciously—competitive business. Virtually all sales must be made on credit, and the chances for serious losses are high. Yet everything else being equal, no one is better equipped for the business than the Indian with a long and rigorous apprenticeship in the retail side of the trade. Kinship ties and other contacts within his community give him a margin of advantage; often enough, a wholesale business is simply the economic facet of a highly ramified patron-client system.

3. Real estate. Wholesale is more profitable than retail. But opportune investments in real estate have been the principal basis for truly spectacular gains among the Indians of Central Africa, as such investments have been for other people elsewhere since time immemorial. Too late to cash in on op-

7. See below, pp. 198–210.

portunities that had made several of his older compatriots rich, a well-to-do younger man once remarked to us rather bitterly:

> Originally, they [i.e. the Indians just referred to] were all in the African trade. When they made a bit of money, they would buy a stand [a "lot" to Americans]. And those stands for which they originally paid two or three hundred pounds now sell for ten, twenty, thirty, or even fifty times what they paid. You can operate a grocery business [the informant is in the grocery business] for a hundred years and not make that much money.[8]

Few Indians, however, are engaged exclusively in real estate. They invest in real estate, but such investments tend to be relatively inactive for long periods of time. A businessman needs a day-to-day operation to provide a steady and reliable income, and for this reason even the heaviest investors in real estate are also generally in other types of business.

The African trade provides, as it always has, the basic economic niche for Indians in Central Africa. But not all Indians are engaged in it. To varying degrees, three economic alternatives have been available.

1. European retail trade. If an Indian is not in the African trade, at either the retail or the wholesale level, the most likely alternative is trade directed to a European clientele. Given sufficient capital, social skills, and experience, this kind of business may be highly profitable. Europeans are everywhere small in number compared to Africans; yet the European market accounts for a very large proportion of the total retail business done in Central Africa. As Table 5 (p. 61) indicates, the average European enjoys an income about twelve times as high as the average African.

The degree to which Indians have been able to penetrate into the European market varies by country. In Rhodesia, the

---

8. By 1966, this particular informant had moved out of the retail grocery business into real estate and wholesale food lines. To all appearances, he was rapidly becoming wealthy.

needs of the large white population are met almost exclusively by European-owned business; the racial division of the market there is greatly reinforced by urban segregation. In Malawi, on the other hand, the European population is small; furthermore, it is served fairly adequately by the large trading companies which have long had general or department stores in the main areas of European settlement. Only in Zambia has the Indian acquired a very sizable share of the European retail trade.

In the capital city of Lusaka, for example, a reasonable estimate would put something like three-fourths of the grocery business in Indian hands. Half or more of the retail trade in manufactured clothing for European men is done by Indians, and they enjoy a complete monopoly of the custom tailoring business. Indians are not so important in women's wear, but one large and popular shop in this line is Indian-owned. Indians do perhaps half of the European dry-goods trade. Shoe repairing is also an Indian monopoly in Lusaka; incidental to this business is a certain amount of trade in new shoes, but European-owned specialty shops get the bulk of it. A large proportion of the camera and commercial (portrait) photography business is in Indian hands. Indians also do a certain amount of the hardware and appliance business, but at present the major portion of this trade is still in European hands.

2. Industry. The potentialities of small industries producing goods for the African market have not escaped the attention of Indians; it is in fact a subject of constant discussion among them. Yet prior to 1961, there were only a few tentative moves in this direction.[9] A really substantial industrial enterprise—a cotton mill to be located at Salisbury—was being promoted during our period of fieldwork but had not yet materialized when we left Central Africa in 1961. That Indian-owned industry which exists is confined in the main to the manufacture of clothing, sweets, biscuits, and candles. Indians also do a fair amount of service business, particularly

9. See below, pp. 352–53, n. 13, and p. 363, for more recent developments.

tailoring and shoe repairing, and these show up under "manufacturing" in the official statistics.

The most important factor inhibiting ventures into production industries seems to be a lack of experience. It is one thing to see potentialities in the abstract; it is another to turn vague perceptions of possibilities into an operating plant producing goods. For very simple and straightforward operations, such as the manufacture of clothing or biscuits, a lack of experience is not too great a problem. But for anything more complicated it is an all-important barrier.

Capital too is a factor which cannot be ignored. Well-to-do Indians typically have all their money—and all they can borrow—invested in commercial business or real estate, and they are not actively searching for additional opportunities. Furthermore, industrial capital must be available in very considerable quantities even for a modest plant; and it must be obtained on a long-term rather than a short-term basis.[10] The poor man with only a few hundred pounds at his disposal cannot realistically think of going into industry.

In addition to these economic barriers, the strictly sociological one of racial discrimination was always mentioned by Indians when industry was discussed. A small manufacturer stated:

> The government here does not give any encouragement to industries, particularly if they are Asian-inspired. The government does not mind seeing Asians as traders; they have decided that is inevitable. But they don't like to see them branching out into industry.

He then went on to illustrate with a concrete example:

> Take the matter of electricity. You would think that the government would give some encouragement on the elec-

10. For example, we were told that a biscuit plant demands something like £80,000 to start—£50,000 for plant and equipment, £10,000 for working capital, and £20,000 to cover the value of the product placed initially on the market on the usual terms of 90 days credit.

tricity, but they charge us a ridiculous sum. We have to pay five hundred pounds a month for our electricity here. We would like to put in our own electric plant; this would cost us something like five thousand pounds, but we could pay for it in less than a year. But the municipal electrical authority won't let us. It's the same way with the water. We would like to drill our own borehole and use our own water. But again, we are forced to use the municipal water supply, even if we have to pay dearly for it.

It is difficult for the outsider to disentangle the element of prejudice from legitimate adhesion to a reasonable bureaucratic rule: what Indians perceive as prejudice may in the concrete case be really nothing of the kind. We can, nevertheless, simply state as a fieldwork fact that we never encountered among European officials anything which looked to us like a positive encouragement to Indian enterprise of any kind, industrial or otherwise. Officials share the widespread fear among Europeans generally that if Indians are allowed to expand freely, they will soon acquire, it is said, a "stranglehold" on the economy.

3. Employment in European-owned enterprises and the civil service. The economic alternatives to the African retail trade just discussed require capital and business experience. They are consequently not real alternatives for a very large proportion of the Indian population. For the shop assistant or the boy just leaving school who has nothing to offer except his labor, the only alternative to employment by fellow Indians is a job in European-owned business or the government bureaucracy. But with insignificant exceptions these have been closed to Indians.

A few Indians work for European firms, but their number is infinitesimally small. In one of the largest Indian communities in Northern Rhodesia, for example, barely a dozen Indians worked for Europeans during the period of our original fieldwork. In the same community only two Indians were in the civil service, not counting teachers in the segregated schools.

Indian business differs sharply from European business in the degree to which its social organization uses the status ties of kinship, caste, and religion rather than the impersonal bonds of rational contract. But like the rest of culture, such status ties are instrumental in character; they must be *used* and used intelligently if they are to be ultimately manifested in behavior.

The Indian businessman who has achieved unusual success in Central Africa is typically a self-made man in that he and he alone is primarily responsible for the difference in wealth which sets him off from his fellows. He certainly made use of the kinship, caste, and religious ties which he possessed, and at critical points these were doubtlessly important. Yet the fact remains that the wealth which he has was accumulated by him, not inherited. He, like his less successful countrymen, arrived in Africa initially with nothing much more tangible than bare hands and large hopes; but in his case luck and sharp wits gave him the advantage that ultimately made most of the difference.

A moderately well-to-do pioneer now in late middle age illustrates the typical successful career. He came to Nyasaland in 1927, where he put in the usual five years of service for the patron who had "called" him from India. He started as a shop assistant, earning in the first year one pound and ten shillings a month. All that he earned, however, he saved, since his employer did not give him the money but kept it according to the custom as an account to be paid in a lump sum at the end of his service. Being literate and quick witted, he soon advanced over his fellow assistants; for the last two years of service he worked as a bookkeeper, keeping the accounts for all of his employer's chain of stores. For this he was paid £9 a month (actually a very sizable salary considering the time and place). The experience gained in this position must have been much more valuable than the actual money earned.

By 1932 he had scraped together £325 and was ready to launch himself as an independent entrepreneur. With this capital he went to Northern Rhodesia and set up a shop, paying the Jew who had previously owned it several times what it was worth in order to get the trading license.[11] For the next few years he made a living and gradually acquired other shops, each of which he stocked and staffed with a relative "called" from India. These shops, it must be appreciated, were small and simple affairs, each bringing in only a few pounds a year; their owner would certainly never have become rich from them alone.[12] Nonetheless, they were the key to his eventual success, and when war came in 1939 he was in a position to take advantage of the unusual opportunities suddenly available. Goods became scarce, while at the same time war-inspired expenditures by the government placed unprecedented amounts of cash in the hands of the Africans.[13] He thus made money rapidly, expanded his retail operations greatly, and bought real estate.

With the coming of federation and the restriction on Indian immigration which followed, this informant, like all others who operated chains of shops, had to retrench and realign drastically—a necessity which he still bitterly resents. Raw and un-

---

11. Another pioneer described how this was done: "Let us say that the Jew had £300 worth of stock. We would offer to buy it at £300 and in addition to give him £500 for goodwill. All together this made the price £800—far more than a little business like that was actually worth. So he would be very anxious to close the deal, and he would say, "How much can you pay in cash?" and much to his surprise we would lay down the £800 on his desk.

"Now where did that £800 come from? Of course none of us had £800 alone, but we would collect it from the other Indians in the community, borrowing £50 here and £50 there until we had the £800. What we were really interested in was the trading license and not the existing business which the Jew had. That was how both Mr. B [the subject of the biographical sketch above] and I got established in this town. But after we got in, we really gave the European traders some competition."

12. An informant who came in 1945, after both prices and wages had risen considerably over the level of the 1930s, explains the economics of a typical shop during his service: "My first employer paid me £10 a month. He couldn't have paid me much more than that. The shop only had a turnover of £125 a month. On that turnover, let's say, there was a gross profit of 33⅓ percent, or £40. From that £40, I got £10 in salary. He had to pay the rent—say £15. And then on top of that, he had to give me board and lodging and free laundry."

13. A comment from another informant: "In those days there was lots of money around. All you had to do was to pick it off of them [i.e. the Africans]."

sophisticated assistants being impossible to get, he sold most of his shops to his erstwhile employees. Now he lives in semi-retirement on income derived from the two large shops in town which he kept, his wholesale business, his rents, and interest on the credit which he extends to a considerable circle of client-dependents.

This man represents a typical case of ascent from nothing but bare hands and sharp wits to a modest fortune. In other cases, the initial advantage of existing status ties were more important. A few Indians were able to bring several hundred pounds with them from India or, more commonly still, were able to acquire a like amount from relatives already established somewhere in Africa. When used intelligently, initial help of this kind proved to be a great advantage.

The career of a business and social rival of the man cited above offers a concrete example. He came to the same Northern Rhodesian town several years later, but he arrived as the local representative of a well-established family in Southern Rhodesia. Yet he too began in a small way. But because he had the resources of his Southern Rhodesian relatives behind him, he was able to take advantage of the war situation on an even larger scale than our friend above. Rather than petty profiteering in the African trade, he was able to obtain several large Army contracts for supplying clothing and other textiles. Using his profits and his abundant family credit, he was able to buy real estate at the very beginning of the postwar expansion. These investments have now multiplied many times in value and currently constitute the main foundation of his very considerable fortune.

To the individuals concerned, the small amounts of capital brought with them from India or obtained elsewhere in Africa may have made the difference between years of abstemious saving and a modest competence from the start. Nevertheless, the amounts imported should not be exaggerated. As a fraction of the total foreign investment in Central Africa, the capital brought into the country by Indians must approach the infinitesimal. The point is worth stressing, since a common myth exists among Europeans that mysterious "Bombay investment companies" are behind local Indian business.

The myth of the Bombay investment company which spreads its sinister tentacles throughout the business world of Africa is held simultaneously with a firm conviction that Indians drain wealth out of the country by sending everything they make back to India. Indians do of course send some money to India, but most of it is for strictly social expenditures to maintain kinship and local ties in India, which means support for certain kinds of obligations. An aged parent needs a small regular sum. They are asked to contribute toward the dowry of a poorer relative's daughter or to the education of a brother's son. Some money goes to priests for horoscopic readings or as payments in the fulfillment of a vow undertaken when the family was afflicted with great trouble. They contribute to the cost of constructing a new house on the family property or to the boring of a well. Taken all together, however, the amount sent to India must be rather small.

The stereotyped notion that Indians send all they make out of the country is completely inconsistent with a fact which soon impresses itself upon the objective observer: the constant hunger for capital in the Indian community. As businessmen Indians are interested in making money, not hoarding it. To make money one must have capital—and no one ever seems to have enough of it. The richer an Indian is (and thus by definition the more successful and experienced he is), the more heavily he is in debt. A judicious manipulation in the past of all the credit which he could get is the chief explanation for his present wealth.[14]

Significantly, bankers flatly reject the notion that Indians export any great amount of money, whatever other stereotypes

14. A well-to-do informant had spoken to us several times of retiring to India; it became obvious that he was much preoccupied with this possibility. Finally, a younger mutual friend was asked if the old man was really serious. The friend snorted at the idea: "He can't go back to India! He owes too much to the building society to get away." Banks, building societies, and insurance companies are in this area all firmly in European hands.

they may hold concerning Indians. Rather, to the banker's mind, the Indian appears as a tenacious and importunate beggar of credit, bent on ruining himself by willingness to assume debt. This version of what the typical Indian business-man is like is very different from the usual European stereo-type of an excessively mean-minded individual who has labori-ously collected a meager hoard from which he only reluctantly spends an occasional penny.

Yet paradoxically both views have an observable basis in empirical reality. The inherently petty nature of the African trade supports the latter image. But this common stereotype leaves no room for what the banker sees. The Indian business-man is also willing to gamble years of effort and thousands of pounds on some exceedingly risky venture without batting an eye, given what he perceives as a reasonable opportunity. A banker with many years of experience with Indians commented upon this characteristic:

> Indians are very different from Europeans. They think differently, they live differently, and they do business differently. In business, the Indian is shrewd and ruthless, but he is also much more willing to take a chance than the average European. He is much more willing to plunge than we are.

A tiny shopkeeper in the African trade with a net income ap-proaching zero for long periods of time has no choice except to play the miser if he hopes to survive. But Indian behavior is not—any more than that of other people—immutably fixed in one pattern. Fifteen years later, when he has collected a bit of capital and sees what looks to him like a surefire gilt-edged opportunity, the erstwhile miser turns into a reckless plunger, willing to risk his all in one fell swoop. He knows very well from the example of successful compatriots that real money is not made quickly in any other way. He acts according to the demands of the situation as he perceives it, not in terms of some presumably permanent character structure.

Indian economic behavior is nonetheless "premodern" in an

important sense. The Indian shopkeeper in Central Africa is a closer counterpart in many respects to the European business-man of the seventeenth century than he is to the salaried bureaucrats who run the modern corporate European enterprise in the same town. Like his historic counterpart, the Indian shopkeeper is an independent entrepreneur, intent upon accumulating capital by the classic pattern of restricted personal consumption.[15] Furthermore, even the largest Indian business in Central Africa is still a family rather than an impersonal corporate concern, and its members think in precorporate, prebureaucratic terms.

ETHNIC SUCCESSION IN THE AFRICAN TRADE

It has been emphasized throughout this chapter that Indians are well fitted, psychologically and culturally, for the special role which they play in the economy of modern Central Africa. Europeans of any extraction are too advanced, economically and socially, for the African trade; given current conditions, they find other activities—including commercial ones—more rewarding. Africans, for reasons presently to be explored, are not yet ready for commercial enterprise on a substantial scale. The African trade has thus gone by default, so to speak, to the Indians as the one group in the total social order both willing and able to accept its rather onerous conditions. Still, this observation is not quite the equivalent of saying that Indians and only Indians could perform this function or that they will continue to do so indefinitely. Elsewhere in Africa, the middleman trader's role has been very successfully performed by ethnic groups other than Indians, by Lebanese and Syrians in West Africa, by Greeks in the Sudan and the Congo, or by advanced African groups like the southern Ibo who traded in the Muslim north of Nigeria.

15. Cf. Floyd Dotson and Lillian Dotson, "Cultural Values and Housing Needs," in Raymond Apthorpe, ed., *Social Research and Community Development, Based on the Fifteenth Conference of the Rhodes-Livingstone Institute for Social Research* (Lusaka, Northern Rhodesia, Rhodes-Livingstone Institute, 1961), pp. 58–66.

Even in Central Africa itself, it must be remembered, Indians
are relatively late-comers to the dominant position which they
now hold in the African trade. Examined historically, there
has been a well-marked ethnic succession. One group has
followed another as socio-economic conditions within the region
have changed. In the days of the large trading company, the
agent was usually a Scot, poor enough in his homeland to
appreciate the small salary that he was paid in Africa.[16] The
trader-adventurers characteristic of the Rhodesias were most
likely in the beginning to be British or Boers, but they were
quickly replaced by Russian Jews throughout Southern Rhodesia and up through the Northern Rhodesian line-of-rail.
Jews were soon forced in turn to compete with Greeks and
Indians. North of the Zambezi, it was the Indians who won out
in this struggle, but Greeks have held their own fairly well
to the present day in the south, where Indians have been
restricted in the main to the larger towns.

It is worth noting, however, that Europeans everywhere
tended to hold on indefinitely to that portion of the African
trade which was really profitable. Trade in cattle, for example,
has always been in European hands; the same was generally
true of the lucrative trade in grain before the establishment of
the government marketing boards.[17] And it was only during
the period of this study that Indians began replacing Jews and
Greeks in the so-called "closed" townships of the Copperbelt,
where a heavy concentration of relatively well-paid Africans
constituted an exceptional market.[18]

16. The trading company described above, p. 22, illustrates ethnic succession:
the Scots sold out to a Polish Jew around 1930, he in turn gradually sold
his chain of shops to Indians during the 1940s and 1950s.

17. Indians managed to do some trading in grain in the two northern territories; they were apparently still doing so illegally on a very small scale up
to the time of our study. In Nyasaland, Indians used to do some trading in
cotton. It is also true that Indians traded in cattle in Southern Rhodesia in
the very earliest period, but they were soon forced out of this business by the
Europeans; see above, pp. 37–39.

18. Kitwe, Mufulira, and Chingola, sites of important mines, were established as "closed" townships in 1935, 1938, and 1945 respectively. By agreement between the Northern Rhodesian government and a small handful of
European businessmen, the latter were given trading monopolies in return for
the financing of essential urban services. See Northern Rhodesia, Commission

The next step in this ethnic succession is now at hand: Indians take it for granted that a large proportion of the most localized African trade will inevitably be taken over by Africans. An analysis of why this has been slow in coming and why it cannot materialize immediately constitutes an essential element in an intellectual comprehension of the ethnic division of labor in Central Africa.

Statistically, the number of Africans holding retail licenses is impressive even now. A study of the distributive trade made in Nyasaland for 1952–53 showed that 70 percent of the retail shops in that territory were owned by Africans. Between that period and 1956–57 (one of very rapid economic growth in Nyasaland) the number of retail businesses increased from about 7,000 to more than 11,000 and of this increase all but 200 was among Africans.[19] A tally made by us for the year 1959 shows that 85 percent of the applications for trading licenses were filed by Africans.[20] The same general trend could certainly have been found in Northern Rhodesia and perhaps in Southern Rhodesia as well.

Considered in terms of the volume of business done, however, the African share is exceedingly small.[21] Most African-

---

of Inquiry into the Closed Townships, *Report,* 1948. After the agreements had expired in the mid-1950s, however, Indian businessmen continued to be excluded through one device or another until the general relaxation of the color bar during the late federation period. Early in 1959 there was not a single Indian shop in Mufulira; by October of that year there were more than twenty. Likewise during the same short period, Indians acquired several shops in Kitwe and Chingola. *Northern News* (Ndola, October 30, 1959). The "open" townships of Luanshya and Ndola had Indian traders from the beginning.

19. Federation of Rhodesia and Nyasaland, *Report on Economic Survey* [Jack Report], p. 279.

20. The actual figures and percentages are African: 2,846 (85.1%); Muslim: 291 (8.7%); Indian: 120 (3.6%); and European: 86 (2.6%). Ethnicity had to be judged from the name; since Muslim names may be either Indian or African, they had to be counted separately. This means in effect that both Indian and African percentages are somewhat higher than as given.

21. Judging by national income account statistics for the late 1950s, Indians earned about 75 percent of the total income derived from unincorporated distributive enterprise in Nyasaland, around 60 percent in Northern Rhodesia, and only about 25 percent in Southern Rhodesia. The African share was about 23, 22, and 11 percent respectively in the same territories. Probably these figures reflect with reasonable accuracy the proportionate shares of Indians and

owned shops are tiny affairs. Few indeed have goods worth more than £150 and the great majority have much less. By contrast, an Indian assumes that he needs a minimum of £1,500 worth of stock just to stay in business.

But capital alone is clearly not the critical difference between African- and Indian-owned enterprise. Sufficient capital on credit to set up shop has been easy to obtain in recent years by any one capable of convincing wholesalers that he could operate a shop successfully. The critical factors are education, experience, and a set of socio-cultural conditions and values compatible with business activity. After noting that many African shopkeepers are shrewd and can handle a small-scale operation very well, an Indian informant from Nyasaland added:

> The biggest difficulty is that most of them are completely uneducated. In order to operate a business of any size, you need a certain amount of education. You don't need much, but you need some. For example, a store of this size [£10,000 worth of stock] demands a knowledge of arithmetic and bookkeeping which would be completely beyond the average African retailer. He just couldn't keep track of the goods in a shop of this size.

Sufficient education, however, is not in itself enough to turn an African into a successful shopkeeper. An African business-man of our acquaintance—a small operator but one generally considered an outstanding success by African standards—touched upon some of the other factors in a long and unusually fruitful interview. The African, this informant pointed out, has no tradition of doing business in a money economy. When he considers setting up a shop, he moves mentally (more likely than not) into an area completely new to his experience. He

Africans. Since European commercial business outside of Southern Rhodesia tends to be mainly corporate, the European share in the retail trade was far greater than the figures for unincorporated enterprise (2.5, 18 and 74 percent respectively) would indicate. See Federation of Rhodesia and Nyasaland, *National Accounts of the Federation of Rhodesia and Nyasaland, 1954-1959* (Salisbury, Central Statistical Office, 1960).

does not know prices or where to buy stock advantageously. (Indian suppliers consequently often sell him goods at retail rather than wholesale prices, and they sometimes use the occasion to unload dead stock.) Nor does the African shopkeeper know in detail what each item costs him, and he doesn't bother to figure out a fixed markup item by item. For this reason, he often sells at a loss without realizing what he is doing. Furthermore, he typically makes no distinction between capital and income. When business has been brisk and he finds himself with an unusual amount of money, he is under the impression that he is rich. He does not fully realize that the larger proportion of what he has in hand is capital, not profit, and that it must be reinvested if he is to stay in business.

The informant then went on to give us a very helpful analysis of the socio-cultural factors which impede the development in Africans of a character structure conducive to successful business operations.

> When the African businessman makes a bit of money, he begins to think of himself as a big man. First of all, this leads to drink, since he is in a position, he thinks, to afford it. Secondly, he thinks of an additional wife or, if he is really making money, two or three.

The matter of wives illustrates the socio-cultural complexities involved in a single-generation leap from tribal society to a social order based upon *Gesellschaft* principles. Throughout much of Africa, an important man traditionally symbolized a rise in status by the acquisition of more wives than he already had. In a subsistence agricultural economy, these wives were in fact a good investment: they were economically productive. But for a tiny shopkeeper who is trying desperately to accumulate a surplus from which he can expand his business, additional wives can only serve to multiply the nonproductive economic demands made upon him. Necessitous kin understand even less well than he that capital must be reinvested rather than spent. Even if the shopkeeper himself understands this principle fairly well and acts successfully upon it for a time, the demands made upon him to spend are hard to resist because of a subtle change wrought in his own personality by unwonted prosperity. According to the informant, "he begins to think of himself as being above the human level. He lives up in the clouds, and he tends to let his humanitarian impulses get the better of him. I know, because that happened to me!"

Culture and character structure have, in short, prevented the African up to the present from offering the Indian serious competition in the African retail trade. But culture and character are subject to change, and the pace of change in Central Africa proceeds with breathtaking speed. What has been is a very unsure guide to what will be.

Consider, for example, the most easily measurable index of change, that of education. The spread of education among Africans in recent years has reached truly impressive proportions. The total enrollment of African children in the primary schools of Southern Rhodesia tripled between 1948 and 1964; as of the latter date, the government claimed that about 80 percent of the children in the lower primary age group were in school attendance.[22] The present government of Zambia foresees that by 1970 all children of primary school age in that country will be in school.[23] Much of this recent education, it is true, is superficial; critics point out that the official statistics tend to gloss over an extremely high dropout rate after the first year or two—in short, before functional literacy can be achieved.[24] Yet, however interpreted, the general

22. In absolute figures, the total primary school enrollment of African children in Southern Rhodesia increased from 203,800 to 610,300 between 1948 and 1964, or by 199 percent. Comparable statistics for Northern Rhodesia show an increase from 134,400 to 365,400, or 172 percent. No statistics are available for Nyasaland as of 1948, but the total enrollment as of 1964 was about 367,300, the same as that of Northern Rhodesia. Very roughly speaking, the populations of Zambia and Malawi are similar in size, although it seems clear that Malawi's is somewhat larger. Actually, no one knows with any precision what the African population really is in any of these territories. The Central Statistical Office at Salisbury recently discounted all previous estimates and moved them upward, particularly for Malawi.

23. See below, p. 348.

24. For a discussion of African education, see "Literate Masses or Educated Few: How the Territories Differ in Policy," *Central African Examiner* (January 1962), pp. 14–15, and "Enlightened Educators: Edwin Towsend-Coles Re-

meaning of these statistics with respect to the point in question is patently clear: the number of Africans with the minimum education necessary to handle a small business is steadily and rapidly rising.

Increasing education is but symptomatic of the total pattern of socio-cultural change taking place in Africa. The much commented upon trends toward urbanization and "detribalization" are certain, whatever their other effects, to undermine traditional barriers to entrepreneurial behavior. Indians are very much aware of the ultimate significance of these trends, and they take what steps they can in preparation for the inevitably greater competition from Africans.

Many substantial shopkeepers see their salvation in a wholesale trade which will service the emerging African retailer. Many are even now trying rather desperately to get in on the ground swell of this business.[25] Indians complain bitterly that extending credit to African retailers is utterly ruinous; but they go ahead and do it anyway, hoping that the numbers of those who prove reliable will increase. After making this point, a member of an old Nyasaland firm added: "It is only a few years ago that there weren't any African traders at all, but there are a great many now. Within five years we expect them to have most of the retail business in their hands. That is what we are expecting, and we are planning accordingly."

Others believe that a move into manufacturing, producing goods for the expected expansion in the African market, is a better answer.

A lot of people are afraid to invest money in industry at the present time, given the political situation. And in fact one has to think carefully about it. We thought about it too, but decided to go ahead. We decided that no matter what the political situation would turn out to be in the future—that even if an African government comes into

views the De Kiewiet Report," *Central African Examiner* (February 1963), pp. 18–19.
25. But see below, pp. 362–63.

power—there will still be a need for our products. So how can we go wrong?

Whatever else they do, those who can afford the heavy expenditure try to educate some of their children for professional careers, knowing that the demand for professional services will be inexhaustible in Central Africa for any foreseeable time to come.

This perception of the best way Indians can meet the inevitable threat of greater economic competition from Africans is so radically different from that of the Europeans that it deserves comment. The idea that appreciable numbers of Indians should ever become professionals—and thus compete with them precisely where they have always felt most secure—is naturally not one which would spontaneously occur to Europeans. Indicative of their view of the ideal ethnic order is the fixed notion among Europeans that Indians should be turned into skilled artisans. The influential Jack Report, a socioeconomic plan for Nyasaland, contains the following passage— which, just incidentally, represents virtually all the attention given to Indians in this 300-page document:

> Unlike the Europeans, the type of technical training they [Asians and Coloureds] require can be provided comparatively easily and cheaply. It seems possible that if more attention had been paid to the provision of educational facilities for Asians and Coloureds in the past they would now be filling a gap in the economy which Africans have not yet demonstrated their ability to fill. . . . In spite of its shortage of reliable foremen and skilled artisans, the Government has made very few openings for Asians and Coloureds. This is an avenue which we think might be explored.[26]

The comment of a liberal European businessman, knowledgeable far above the average with respect to the Indians, reveals the same widespread idea.

26. Jack Report, p. 186.

I have always wondered why there weren't more Asian artisans than there are. Nearly all of the artisan-type work in East Africa is done by Asians. Why couldn't it be done here? It will be a long time before a class of African artisans are developed, and it would seem to me that it is here that one of the big opportunities for the Asians lie. *But for some reason or other, they don't seem to go in for that kind of work.*

To a sociologist, at least, the reasons are hardly obscure. Many Indians are from castes which have traditionally shunned manual labor of any description. But caste aside, it is as unrealistic to expect Indians in Central Africa to think spontaneously in terms of manual labor as it would be to expect white-collar Europeans to do so. By psycho-cultural orientation, the poorest Indian shop assistant is a businessman, not a laborer.

It is to the most significant aspects of this psycho-cultural orientation that our attention is now turned. Comprehensively understood, ethnic relations must be seen as a two-way interchange between an ingroup and an outgroup; analysis therefore must have both an inside and an outside focus, and dynamic interpretation will seek the interplay between the two in terms of process and change. Historical and economic matters have an outside character. In the next chapters on religion, caste, family, and community organization, the focus will be turned inward. How are these inherited, indigenous institutions related to and how have they been affected by the plural society in which Indians now live? Since mentality is cultural in content, this examination should provide a glimpse of the ever-shifting ground upon which Indians stand as they look out and perceive the world about them—to borrow the suggestive phraseology of Kurt Lewin.[27] The focus in later chapters turns outward once more in a consideration of the social and political roles which Indians play vis-à-vis the other ethnic groups.

27. Kurt Lewin, *Resolving Social Conflicts: Selected Papers on Group Dynamics* (New York, Harper, 1948), particularly pp. 84–89.

Chapter Four

THE TRADITIONS OF RELIGION

The existence of two very different and yet very highly elaborated religious traditions among the Indians of Central Africa requires that each be discussed separately before conclusions are reached concerning the role of this institution in general.

THE HINDUS

Hinduism in India is notable for its richly profuse mythology, the philosophical subtlety of its doctrines, and the tremendous variety in its ritualistic practice. Something of this complexity has come to Africa. But fortunately for us, the ordinary Hindu in Central Africa is as little instructed in his religious heritage as is his Christian counterpart in European societies. His basic beliefs, therefore, are neither numerous nor unduly complicated. Assuming the risk of some distortion through oversimplification, these may be previewed as follows:

1. Most Hindus in Central Africa still believe that supernatural powers are ultimately (but not very immediately) in control of the affairs of men. Inevitably, these are conceived intellectually (to the extent that they are) in the cognitive forms inherited by and carried within the group. As will be shortly seen, however, the great multitude of deities worshipped in traditional Hinduism constitutes a social embarrassment to modern, educated, urban men. Even the ordinary Hindu, therefore, now sees the supernatural beings of his re-

ligious tradition as essentially mythological symbols, to be taken metaphorically rather than literally. With some exaggeration, we can thus say that he has achieved by ecological accident a level of interpretative sophistication in regard to the supernatural comparable to that of the most advanced Christian theology. If hard pressed upon this point by a European, a Hindu will soon say that he *really* only believes in one God—a God which has taken many diverse forms in presenting himself concretely to human experience. God, nonetheless, remains vague and inexactly defined. But this vagueness is not sheer intellectual fuzziness; it is consistent with what is one of the Hindu's most fundamental tenets: namely, that it is ultimately not very important what particular form of God a person recognizes and worships as long as he recognizes and respects the existence of the supernatural.

2. From the premise that it is unimportant as to what form of God is worshipped flows another of the Hindu's strongest convictions. Religion in and of itself is a "good thing," whether one is a Hindu, a Muslim, or a Christian, and all religions possess an element of truth. Upon this point, as in many others, the Hinduism of Central Africa parallels to a remarkable degree the "progressive" Christianity of the American suburb.[1]

3. Moreover, the import of these direct parallels between Hinduism and modern Christianity is not lost upon even the ordinary Hindu. He is exceedingly proud of his religion's "advanced" and "progressive" relativism, and he takes the respect accorded it by outsiders as proof of Hinduism's superior philosophical insights. Whether he himself is religious or not in any meaningful personal sense, the Hindu never seriously questions that Hindu philosophy has attained a profounder and truer version of the ultimate mysteries of existence than any other system of thought in the world, religious or scientific. He is accordingly proud of being a Hindu, and it never occurs to him that he might "be" anything else.

1. The literature upon the modern secular Christianity of American suburbia, the kind referred to here, has grown enormously in recent years. The uninitiated may still safely begin with Will Herberg, *Protestant-Catholic-Jew* (Garden City, N. Y., Doubleday, 1955).

4. In keeping with these basic tenets, conformity to the socially accepted Hindu way of life in concrete behavior is far more important than cognitive doctrine. It is by conformity to the rules governing diet, marriage, and (in a much looser sense) general behavior and attitude, rather than by any given test of doctrine, that "good" Hindus are differentiated from "bad" Hindus in the community.

Despite a fair number of outright nonbelievers, it is still undoubtedly true that the average Hindu in Central Africa is a good deal more religious than the average European, in the sense that he habitually interprets more of his experience in terms of supernatural forces.

Every minute, every hour of our lives is determined. What we do is not our will; what we do is God's will. He is the one who decides. I had planned to go to India in 1958, but God decided otherwise. I wanted to go, but He said, "No, I'm sorry!" So—finished! Our life is a roll [*karma*]. Now we are up, now we are down. We never know which it will be. But whether we are up or whether we are down, we know that it is God's will and not ours. What we have to do is to pass through.

[After the visit of a respected *swami* (a religious teacher), a schoolteacher told this story of his telepathic powers] As you know, the swami has been living in East Africa. While there he came to know a very pious and holy man in Nairobi. Now a curious thing happened. When the swami was in Bulawayo he was very tired and was coming down with a bad cold. So on this afternoon he was resting and took a nap. When he awoke—which was about three-thirty—he immediately called in the two people who had been traveling with him and said to them: "So-and-so [the pious and holy man of Nairobi] has just died. We must get in touch with his family and offer them our condolences." The swami knew he was right, but his friends thought it would be best to be sure, so one of them telephoned to Nairobi. He discovered that the man had died at the very moment the swami woke up from his nap. Imagine what a wide and deep soul a man like that must have in order to be in contact with a soul as far away as Nairobi is from Bulawayo! Just as soon as the soul of the man in Nairobi underwent the transformation of death, the swami knew it because he was in contact with it.

[On the supernatural in folk medicine] In India there are people who are especially trained to extract ghosts from people. Women are particularly apt to have ghosts which are making them ill. In such cases, the person who extracts the ghosts is called in and he gives her a regular treatment. He gathers up the hair at the back of her head in his fist and pulls it very tight and hits her on the forehead [i.e. he strikes the patient's head against a wall or the floor]. Sometimes he burns the arms. When the ghost leaves the body he catches it and puts it in a bottle. Often the ghost is in the form of a little insect, like a fly or something. That's the form it takes when it leaves the body. Then he goes and buries the bottle in a safe place, and the person gets well. When you go and dig up the bottle after a long time, you find a piece of bone in it. That shows the ghost has been there.

Practice and Belief

When his religious sentiments are translated into a concrete act of worship, the Hindu in Central Africa usually addresses one of the traditional deities of the Hindu pantheon, with others perhaps then following in turn. Which deity is chosen for veneration depends upon cult affiliation, and cult affiliation is usually but not necessarily determined by family and group tradition. The individual is formally free to choose, but voluntarism is countered by a strong conviction of the "rightness" of that person's inherited cult by primary social identity.

With the exception of the few Brahman families, most

Hindus in Central Africa associate themselves with cults in the Vishnuite tradition. Ram and Krishna, together with their respective spouses, are accordingly among the most popular deities.[2] Brightly colored lithographic representations of these reincarnations of Vishnu compete with pictures of Gandhi and Nehru and the family photographs for space on the crowded walls of most Hindu homes. Typically, the representations follow modern rather than traditional artistic conventions. The god and his female consort appear in idealized human forms. Lightly clad and smoothly handsome, they are provided with a romantic natural setting *à la* western neoclassicism; only relatively inconspicuous traditional symbols denote their divinity. Not surprisingly, pictures in this style provide popular subjects for the calendars put out by Hindu commercial firms.

As in India, most actual worship is in the home and consists in the main of ritually prescribed prayers. The deity (or "saint") addressed is usually represented by a postcard-sized lithographic picture (or more rarely by a little statuette) placed on a box or low table before which the worshiper kneels. Alternatively, one may pray before a larger picture hung on the wall. Ideally, by most cult rules, one should pray at least twice daily, before the morning and the evening meal. But for children, especially, it now seems more common to have them follow the Christian practice of praying just before going to bed.

If he is pious enough to worship regularly—an assumption which can scarcely be taken for granted—the Hindu in Central Africa addresses not God in the abstract but a traditional Hindu deity. By this act, he presumably makes an *implicit* affirmation in the deity's reality as a discrete and distinctive spiritual personality, capable of responding to the human appeal directed to him. Thus the mother of a sick child, when she prayerfully makes a vow to the goddess Amba Mata to carry through an expensive haircutting ceremony in India if

2. "Rama" is standard Anglicization, but "Ram" pronounced without the final vowel is the form used by the Indians of Central Africa. "Rama" came to sound as strange to us as it doubtlessly does to them, although they are familiar with it.

the goddess will spare the child's life, presumably believes (and *wants* to believe) in both the goddess' existence and the special powers attributed to her by tradition.

But as soon as religion is self-consciously examined in intellectual terms, the lush polytheism of Hindu tradition is turned into a vague monotheism indistinguishable from that of many contemporary Christians, Jews, and Muslims who also believe in God but are not particularly interested in God's characteristics. We never met a Hindu believer during the period of our fieldwork who did not quickly assure us in the course of a religious discussion that he actually only believes in one God. Polytheism is clearly not socially respectable, and Hindus tend to be sensitive upon this point, fearing that they will be misunderstood.

Of course, it is quite true, an assertion of respectable monotheism is made easy and plausible by selective emphasis upon certain long-standing theological doctrines in traditional Indian philosophy. Thus a Brahman who, as good Brahmans are, is in practice a devotee of Siva, habitually spoke to us of God in the singular. When pressed to comment upon this apparent contradiction, he said:

> I have difficulty sometimes in explaining to Europeans why there are so many deities in Hindu religion. There are a total of 33 million. . . . The reason there are so many deities is this. People are not all alike in their attributes. So neither are the deities. With so many deities to choose from people can find one who corresponds to their own attributes. With 33 million to choose from, everyone can be taken care of.

A much less sophisticated but unusually pious informant who worships Ganeshi, the popular elephant-headed god of good luck and good fortune, had this to say:

> A long time ago, our ancestors told many stories about the different gods and goddesses—Shri Krishna, for example, and Ganeshi and Hanuman and many others. But all of

92

these separate and distinct deities are directed and controlled by the Super Soul. Thus they are really only one.

Still another explained it somewhat more technically: "All Hindus worship the same God in different forms. Or perhaps it would be more correct to say that God does not have a form. In His formless state He is called *Aum*. *Aum* is what I myself really believe in."

Socio-cultural reality is multifaceted and all too easily distorted by sheer emphasis alone. Inevitably, through description of what Hindus in Central Africa believe and practice—*if* they believe and practice—an exaggerated impression may have been inadvertently given of the actual extent of either. Religion is socially respectable among these people in much the same way (and for essentially the same reasons) that it is in an American middle-class suburb; conventionally, it is a good thing, and everyone is supposed to have it. But we strongly suspect that disbelief is much more common than is openly acknowledged.

Not everyone by any means would talk freely about religion, and we assume that one good reason (aside from sheer ignorance and lack of interest) was a reluctance to admit disbelief. Still, flat statements of disbelief do appear in the interview protocols. For instance, one young man, when pressed persistently for his family's cult affiliation, finally burst out, "Oh, we just worship God!" Having said this, he seemed somewhat embarrassed and went on to explain, with the air of making an unwelcome confession: "Personally, I don't believe in this religious stuff at all. But the rest of my family are very religious—my wife and my mother in particular. But if you are asking me what I believe, then I have to say that I don't believe in anything."

On occasion, the denial is simple and straightforward. When asked what cult he worshiped, another young man told us matter-of-factly: "That question is really quite difficult to answer. You see, I don't believe in any of those deities."

Yet much more common than outright and self-conscious

93

rejection is a twilight state familiar enough to the American observer since it parallels so closely what he is used to in his own culture. People profess religious belief verbally but show clearly enough in their overt behavior that their belief, whatever it ultimately comes to in the cognitive or affective sense, is too weak to matter much in the course of everyday life. Like the present-day American, the ordinary Hindu in Central Africa lives in a highly secularized world, a world in which the traditional deities of the Indian village must appear as slightly fantastic or, at best, as only remotely relevant to his real interests and concerns.

The relevance which the traditional religion has in such a context is almost entirely social. Professed belief ties one comfortably to one's ethnic group and its past; for the sake of group continuity the individual feels very strongly that the traditional religion, suitably modernized to make it intellectually respectable, *ought* to be believed in. But in fact Hinduism in Central Africa is woefully lacking in effective communal and institutional supports. The individual believer is typically left with no very effective or satisfying way of expressing concretely the sentiments that he may feel. The result is widespread apathy and indifference—which may, however, hide a good deal of vaguely perceived guilt. These observations apply with particular force to the younger generation growing up in Africa.

One of our most intimate informants will serve as a convenient illustration. This young man had always professed himself to be quite religious. Yet when he served as our escort to a Hindu temple, he admitted—appearing quite nonplussed for the moment—that he had never been there before although he had lived in the town for nearly a year.

When we first became acquainted, our friend was already married but his wife was still in India. Once during this period (in which he naturally talked about his wife a good deal) he remarked that he and she were of "different religions," i.e. affiliates of different cults. In explanation, he said:

94

I didn't think to ask her what her religion was during the interview. [The marriage had been arranged, but following modern practice, the young people were allowed to meet for mutual approval.]

Dotson: Would you have married her if you had known that you were of different religions?

[With an emphatic shake of the head] No, probably not. In my family we have always been of the same religion, and I would have liked to have kept it that way. Now, it doesn't make so much difference.

We were curious at this reply and wondered what to make of it. Sometime later when we had the opportunity of discussing religion at length with a swami visiting from India, we reported the substance of this conversation to him. Before we had quite finished, he interrupted and said with considerable heat:

The fact is that neither of them worships and neither of them has any religion! They tell you this because they would like you to believe that they did. You are a stranger and you don't know any differently. But I know my people and I know that they don't.

With respect to this particular case, the swami was not entirely correct, although he was fairly close in principle. When the wife finally arrived in Africa, the young couple set up housekeeping in the usual manner in a single room at the rear of their shop. An early morning visitor there—a nosy sociologist, let us say—might find in the corner of the room opposite the bed a wooden apple box spread with a little white cloth. Upon it would be two or three small religious pictures and a tiny lamp filled with ghee. The wife, it would be explained, had just finished her prayers and had not yet had time to put the paraphernalia away. When pressed as to whether he had joined her, the young husband would sheepishly admit that

95

he had not. He was tired, he would say, and had taken the occasion to catch a few more winks of sleep before breakfast. But he had, he would assert, taken care of his religious duties. Just before going to sleep at night he had closed his eyes and repeated to himself the name of God (Ram).

Generalizing beyond this particular couple to the local community as a whole, the visiting swami explained:

> People here would like to be good Hindus, and they think of themselves as being Hindus. But in fact they are uninstructed. When I ask them to come and pray with me, they don't come. Why? Because they are ashamed. They don't know the prayers, and they are ashamed to admit it to me. In India I can talk to an audience of a thousand people with confidence that when I make a point with respect to doctrine or a reference to the sacred literature, I will be understood. In my lectures here in Africa I can't make that assumption. I have to begin with the alphabet—with the ABC's.

Our theoretical argument holds that it is a mistake to view social institutions as a structure of norms and values erected apart from the process of interaction. Insofar as society has a structure, that structure is created and re-created daily in concrete acts of social significance by living persons. The listless state of Hindu religious life in Central Africa can be partly explained by the virtual absence of any community-wide organization to reinforce the faith and encourage ritual practice.

Ritualistically, Hinduism as it is practiced in India is essentially a family and individual responsibility; in traditional Hinduism there is no organized congregation at the local community level comparable to that of either Christianity or Islam. Temples exist in India in great profusion, but they are essentially sacred places, the local abode of the deities symbolically represented there. They are, by virtue of their sanctity and the paraphernalia which they provide, convenient and efficacious places to carry out certain religious acts. But they are not the exclusive property of a socially organized group, nor are they ultimately necessary for worship in the way a church or mosque is for a Christian or a Muslim.

Hindus have not therefore felt the urgency to build temples in Africa that other immigrant groups have. Every town in Central Africa where Indian Muslims reside in any appreciable numbers has a mosque or a prayer-house. But there are only two real Hindu temples in the whole of Central Africa, one in Salisbury and the other in Blantyre. What community religious activity there is in the other towns takes place in a Hindu Hall. These halls, however, are not primarily religious establishments; the motivation for their construction was mainly political, if we use the term broadly rather than narrowly. The need was strongly felt for a general meeting place where issues affecting community welfare could be thrashed out and where visiting dignitaries could be heard. In the minds of most people, the Hindu Hall is doubtlessly more directly associated with their chief recreation than with religion. This is the place where Indian-language films are shown, and the revenue from these constitutes the primary basis of its financing.

Still, the Hindu Hall does have some religious functions. On one or two days a week, mats may be laid down in place of chairs for a session of community prayers sung or chanted in unison. Participants are mainly women and children (the adult male assumes that religion is good for the children), and ordinarily attendance is not impressive. In a community of seven or eight hundred Hindus, a turnout of thirty-five or forty is considered excellent. Interest in communal prayers typically follows well-defined cycles. It is generated to a high point of enthusiasm by the visit of a swami. It then dwindles down, often to a vanishing point, until charged again by another visit.[3]

It is highly significant from our point of view that the two temples which do exist veer sharply from the most common

3. In some communities, prayer sessions are organized by a Hindu women's association (*Mahila Mandal*). Here the organizational pattern is borrowed from the European women's clubs: meetings are held in the homes of the members in rotation, with refreshments being prepared and served by the hostess. Enthusiasm for these associations is also highly variable.

Indian norms in both architectural conception and function. The one at Salisbury might be taken from the outside for a small Christian church except for a few inconspicuous decorative symbols. Its public part consists of a single bare rectangular room, not very large. At the farther end of this room is the single object of worship: a piece of stone, about the size and the proportion of a modest grave marker, encased in an electrically lighted glass framework. Upon a smoothed-off face of this stone is engraved the symbol for the sacred word *Aum*.

Such a severely simple and thoroughly modernized temple —without idols, flickering open lights, incense, or soot-covered attendant priest—seems well suited to the highly selective emphasis given traditional Hindu doctrine in Central Africa. And so perhaps it is. Yet the modernistic character of the temple is ecological, that is, more the result of a peculiar set of social circumstances than self-conscious planning. A Brahman explains:

> The reason why there are no images in the Salisbury temple is simple. Since the community is a heterogeneous one and most people are Sudras, they worship a great variety of deities. They couldn't possibly agree which deities should be represented by idols, so if there was to be a temple, this seemed to be the only solution. People of different cults can all worship the symbol *Aum*.

In South Africa most temples are close copies of those in India, despite the fact that the people there are further separated from their historical origins than those of Central Africa. But in South Africa the Indian population is large and variegated enough to support specialized temples for separate cults. Each temple has idols representing a particular set of deities, and it attracts those people out of the total community who associate themselves with that cult. A temple can be built in Central Africa only through community-wide participation, and this can be achieved only if cult and caste differences are submerged rather than emphasized.

Still, it is doubtful that this is quite the whole story. Sudras or not, the Indians of Central Africa tend to be solidly middle-class in aspirations and values. In keeping with this orientation, they are upwardly mobile, not only with respect to their status in the Indian community but in the total community of this plural society as well. Most of them—especially the younger and the better-educated—would be distinctly ill at ease in a traditional Indian temple. Nor, it is certain, would they care to be associated in the European or African mind with such a hopelessly "outdated" and "unprogressive" place.[4]

Rituals and Rules

Traditional Hinduism elaborated an extended series of life-cycle ceremonies— the *sanskara*—which began with rituals to promote conception and ended with postmortem rites. Counts of these vary; a fairly exhaustive statement lists seventeen, but many of these were never commonly practiced even in India.[5] In Central Africa, where there is a pronounced tendency to select and attenuate all ritual, the number is reduced to a minimum of two or three which are universally practiced, together with a few others that appear fairly frequently.

Conception and growth-promoting rituals in the early months of pregnancy, for example, have completely disappeared in Central Africa. The only prenatal *sanskara* at all commonly followed is the eighth-month ceremony, and this has lost most of its spiritual significance. Traditionally presents were offered to the mother as well as prayers for the welfare of both her and the child. In Central Africa the presents have all but supplanted the prayers, turning the occasion into a "baby shower."

4. Well-educated Hindus, we discovered, are more than a little embarrassed in South Africa by the gory ritual and carnival atmosphere at a popular place of worship such as the Mariamma temple at Isipingo, near Durban. The complete absence in Central Africa of the trance cults and animal sacrifices which flourish in South Africa is to be explained in good part as a difference between North Indian and South Indian Hinduism. But an important class difference also has to be taken into account. These vivid South African practices appeal to a largely illiterate and severely suppressed (and repressed) population. They demonstrably have little or no appeal to the westernized middle-class, irrespective of origin. For a description of these cults, see Kuper, *Indian People in Natal*, pp. 217–35.

5. Cf. Kuper, pp. 140–85.

Traditional birth rituals are now obviously complicated by the fact that babies are born in hospitals. Being out of the family's hands, the newborn's natal cord cannot be burned after it is cut by the prescribed bit of lighted ghee mixed with herbs, even if the parents should feel the obligation. But horoscopic readings, now amalgamated with the naming ceremonies, are obtained by all believers. Only outright skeptics neglect them.[6]

Boys' haircutting ceremonies, often connected with vows taken under distressful circumstances to the goddess Amba Mata or a similar deity, are fairly common. Since these must normally be performed in India, they provide the occasion for a family trip that might not otherwise be taken.

The *sanskara* prescribing betrothal and marriage are universally followed, even by the avowed skeptics. The day when any Hindu will be satisfied with a civil ceremony at the local *Boma* (district headquarters) has not yet arrived. Marriage and betrothal forms are still traditional, but they have undergone considerable modernization through drastic cutting.

Certain of the *sanskara,* such as the assumption of the sacred thread by the "twice-born" castes, were by their nature never universal. Others of strictly Brahmanic origin have been democratized by "sanskritization," a process characteristic of modern India but perhaps somewhat speeded up and extended in Africa.[7] The *sanskara* prescribing retirement from active eco-

6. Naming the African-born generation of a well-known Mochi family, a Brahman informant made this comment on horoscopes: "They have never had horoscopes taken for any of their children. They say that since they don't believe in all that stuff, why go to the trouble?" But he emphatically disagreed and went on to discuss the charge of determinism implicit in horoscopic readings: "There are some things which are going to happen and there is nothing you can do about it. But there are other things which you can do something about, if you have a strong enough will. This is the thing about horoscopic readings which people forget. The only time that everything which is going to happen to you actually happens is when you are afraid of the horoscope. But if you accept the challenge to your will, then you discover there are many things in your horoscope which you can avoid. In my own case, for example, my horoscope said that I was going to become a cook. Of course, I didn't become a cook, but that is because I had a strong enough will to avoid it."

7. Once the sole prerogative of the literate Brahman caste, Vedantic concepts and practices have progressively spread both geographically and socially to lower castes and to people originally non-Hindu. Modern anthropologists see this process of "sanskritization" as still very active and as yet uncom-

nomic life in late middle age (presumably for study and meditation) is an example. This norm has no formal ceremonial
recognition in Central Africa that we could discover. Yet, as
a widely accepted ideal, it exercises a good deal of influence
upon the attitudes and behavior of the older generation.

Funerals, like the rest of the *sanskara* in Central Africa,
take traditional forms but are subject to important modifications. As with marriage, there is a marked tendency to shorten
the ritual. As one informant explained:

> In India when somebody dies, everyone in the family has
> to go through a long elaborate ritual. To someone who
> has lived in Africa, it seems like a lot of unnecessary fuss
> and bother. It's a lot different here than in India. Here we
> just try to get down to the essentials.

Bodies are cremated and the ashes are carried by a member of
the family (or the extended family) to India, as soon thereafter as possible, to be cast into one of the sacred rivers.
There has never yet been an exception to this rule insofar as
could be determined. But certain strictly European practices
have nonetheless crept into Hindu funerals. Coffins, for example, are bought from a European undertaker for the corpse
which is taken to the cremation area in a hearse. Mourners and
participants follow in automobiles.[8]

---

pleted. See M. N. Srinivas, *Religion and Society among the Coorgs of South
India* (Oxford, Clarendon Press, 1952), pp. 30–31, and McKim Marriott, "Little
Communities in an Indigenous Civilization," in McKim Marriott, ed., *Village
India: Studies in the Little Community* (American Anthropological Associa-
tion Memoir No. 83, 1955), pp. 171–222.

8. Like most of our generalizations with respect to religious practice, this
statement is based upon our original fieldwork in what is now Zambia. As of
1966, Chagan Lalloo notes in a personal communication: "It is becoming common practice in Rhodesia *not* to have the ashes taken to India. The corpse is
carried instead in a basket to the crematorium where with the accompanying
ritual it is cremated, and ashes, collected after the lapse of some days, are
buried into a tiny piece of land measuring about 12 by 18 inches. Placed on
this burial ground is a canopy-like structure made of copper and glass to
facilitate the lighting of the traditional ghee lamp required in the offering of
prayers to the dead. These usages are for the moment confined to Salisbury and
came into practice only about three years ago. The change-over from the use
of coffins to that of baskets was motivated chiefly by economic reasons—a
former president of the Hindu Society originated the idea."

As we have already said in our categorical statement, "good" Hindus are differentiated from "bad" Hindus by neither ritual nor doctrine but by the degree to which daily life conforms to the principal rules of behavior (*dharma*). Diet is the major symbol of conformity; but at the subtler levels this complex ethic also includes "right" attitudes and appropriate habits not only with respect to food and drink but also to work, sex, and the material things of this world. In a word, the ideal in all these matters is given an ascetic and self-denying cast. Food and drink, however, stand symbolically in the Indian mind for the whole, and in the last analysis it is mainly upon conformity to the dietary rules that the public reputation of a Hindu rests.

By this single test, most Hindus in Central Africa are reasonably good Hindus. And in all truth, the powerful informal sanctions which have up to this point operated within the community scarcely allow them to be otherwise. People who by any test of ritual or doctrine would have to be defined as irreligious may nonetheless conform to the most important of these rules—the abstention from meat—and are accepted as good Hindus accordingly. What is involved in terms of ideal behavior is perhaps suggested in the following statement:

We are completely nonviolent in our household. [He really means that they hold to the rule of *ahimsa,* the prohibition against taking life.] I myself do not eat any living thing—no meat and not even eggs. I have never drunk beer nor do I take tea. I don't even smoke. Some people say that you have to have animal food in order to live. That's nonsense. One can get enough protein from milk and butter. Look at me. Although I am nearly 60 years old, I am perfectly healthy.

Tobacco, alcohol, and tea of course do not literally violate *ahimsa,* but they are added to meat as dispensable vices signifying self-indulgence. One is better off without them. The negative reaction to tobacco and alcohol is not as strong as that toward meat, but it is nonetheless sufficient to arouse guilt feelings in those who indulge in them. One middle-aged informant told us sadly: "Smoking is the only bad thing I do. I tell you that for a fact. I was 16 years old before I even tasted tea, and I didn't take up smoking until I was 25."

Still, the ultimate test is meat. A Coloured friend and the senior author were enjoying a chicken sandwich in a Nyasaland cafe when a mutual Hindu acquaintance stopped in. He sat down opposite us and watched for a moment in disgusted fascination. Then unable to contain himself, he burst out: "How *can* you eat it! A chicken is alive; it has blood in it, just as we have. If you cut it, it bleeds. It has eyes and sees as we do. It has a brain, and it even talks. To eat a living thing like that is almost like eating another person!"

The prohibition is stronger against beef than it is against other meat, but the distinction (at least among the Gujaratis) is not as great as we had supposed it would be. A Gujarati Hindu who will eat meat of any kind is not apt to draw the line at beef, although he may feel somewhat less guilty while eating chicken or lamb. A young English-educated Hindu professional remarked while devouring some fried chicken in the company of a Muslim friend, "I am the only one in my family who eats meat." Seizing the opportunity, we asked if he would eat beef. He replied: "No, I won't eat beef unless I can't avoid it. If I were invited some place and I were served beef, then I would eat it rather than make an issue of it. But if the man to whose house I were going asked me beforehand whether or not I eat beef, then I would say quite flatly that I do not."

Hinduism and Change

No discussion of modern Hinduism—certainly no discussion of the Hinduism of the Gujaratis—would be complete without some attention to the enormous influence of Gandhi upon religious attitudes and practices.

Gandhi was himself a Gujarati, and whether or not this revered figure is appreciated in quite the same way among the non-Gujaratis is a question which we cannot answer. In any case, it is a fact that Gandhi stands among the Gujarati Hindus of Central Africa as the pure Hindu ideal incarnate. He is infinitely more real than any of the shadowy supernaturals of the traditional pantheon. Pictures of Gandhi are found in every house. And while he is not literally worshiped—as he certainly would be if he himself had not strenuously opposed the idea—attitudes toward him are nonetheless specifically religious.[9] An articulate young schoolteacher is explicit with respect to Gandhi's religious significance in a way that few of our informants could be, but most would certainly accept his sentiments as their own:

> I believe in Gandhi even more than in Lord Krishna. Of course, I believe in both, but I think that I believe in Gandhi even more. His teaching is more pertinent to our times. In some ways Gandhi was very orthodox, in some ways very radical. There were a good many bad things in the old Hinduism as it came down to us before Gandhi— untouchability and the whole caste system, for example. Gandhi showed us that these were not necessary in order for us to be good Hindus.

In this statement, we see the key to much of Gandhi's great influence. Religiously he *did* consider himself an orthodox Hindu; he was not a self-conscious reformer and modernizer. Significantly "reformed" Hinduism is virtually absent from Central Africa.[10] Still, Gandhi preached accommodation and change under the influence of western concepts and values and thus sanctioned the attempt to sift the "good" from the "bad" in the "old" Hinduism. His authoritative example can therefore be used to legitimate change in inherited concepts and practices while at the same time allowing the retention of one's

9. Worshiping Gandhi would be entirely consistent with orthodox Hinduism. The human founders of a great many cults (*Rishis* or "saints") are regularly worshiped as divine reincarnations.

10. We met only one person who claimed membership in a reformed sect, in this case the Arya Samaj. The Arya Samaj and other reformed sects seem very popular among most overseas Indian groups. See, in particular, the excellent discussion by a young Indian anthropologist, Chandra Jayawardena, "Religious Belief and Social Change: Aspects of the Development of Hinduism in British Guiana," *Comparative Studies in Society and History, 8* (1966), 211–40.

self-image as a good, even orthodox, Hindu (often, it need hardly be added, with results in the specific instance from which Gandhi himself would have recoiled in horror). Thus we constantly hear statements like this from a young Brahman: "The Hindu religion teaches that everyone is equal before God." Or to cite a cliché popular among the younger people: "Hinduism is a religion, and there is nothing religious about caste. It is just a social custom." These sentiments are expressed in all seriousness. It is certain, however, that Abbé Dubois never heard them—but Abbé Dubois lived a hundred and fifty years before Gandhi's time.[11]

Hindus in Central Africa strike us as remarkably complacent about the prospects for survival of their religion, despite the fact that many of them appreciate very well the extent to which it has already been affected by recent changes. A Brahman remarked, with no evident concern: "Things change, and we must accept it. My own children know their prayers, but they just pray. They don't really understand what they are doing. If they grow up here in Africa, then maybe they never will."

Insofar as this complacency has an intellectual basis distinguishable from sheer indifference engendered by secularization, it seems to rest upon two postulates, one logical, the other historical:

1. Since Hinduism is not identified with any specific doctrine or ritual practice, Hindus are not particularly worried about change in the ideological content of their religion. Such change they take for granted. It is accepted by everyone as axiomatic that a person can believe almost anything and still be a good Hindu, as long as he thinks and lives like a Hindu. The unspoken assumption here is: if one is born a Hindu, how can he think and live like anyone else?

2. Hindus also know that Hinduism in India has success-

11. This keenly observant French missionary, who spent thirty years in India at the end of the eighteenth century, provides an invaluable account of the Hindus before they were much influenced by European civilization. Abbé J. A. Dubois, *Hindu Manners, Customs and Ceremonies, Translated from the Author's Later French Ms. and Edited with Notes, Corrections, and Biography,* by Henry K. Beauchamp (Oxford, Clarendon Press, 1906).

fully managed to survive centuries of foreign invasions, both social and ideological, and they all too easily conclude from this knowledge that what has been true in the past will always continue to be so. A comment from a community leader who holds a post-graduate degree in science exemplifies this attitude: "Hinduism has existed for centuries. It has withstood the onslaught of Buddhism, Islam, Christianity, and modern science. There is no doubt that it will continue to exist. We are sure of that." Then, as a qualification, he went on to add: "We are sure, that is, as long as we keep our language. As long as we maintain our language, then there won't be any danger of losing our religion."

Taking this judgment at its face value for a moment, we might then ask what the outlook for the retention of the language is. From what we could assess of the rather haphazard state of vernacular teaching in Africa and extrapolating from similar experience with ethnic language schools in the United States, we would guess that complacency in this respect is indeed ill-founded. Among the African-born generation, real competency in written Gujarati already verges upon the nil.[12] Spoken Gujarati, with a vocabulary adjusted to the needs of a commercial community, might conceivably be retained almost indefinitely. But with all systematic formal education being confined to English, it is quite unlikely that any more than an occasional student will be motivated to acquire enough written Gujarati to carry him through a moderately difficult religio-philosophical text.

But the retention of a religion is a far more complicated matter sociologically than the retention of a language. Insofar as we can see, the mechanisms for an effective transmission of traditional Hinduism are simply not present in Africa and can hardly be created. While it is true that the practice of Hinduism in India is mainly an individual and family matter, the assumption that religion in Africa can therefore be safely left to the family is certainly erroneous. In India the family

12. Parents of young people in school elsewhere commonly write to them in Gujarati, only to receive letters in turn written in English.

suffices since the necessary elements for socialization in the religious culture are numerous in the general social milieu. There are sacred rivers and holy places. There are temples and shrines, and holy practitioners of innumerable varieties who provide vivid examples in the flesh of the ideal religious life. There are festivals and devotional pilgrimages. But how, cut off entirely from this diffuse yet elaborate institutional context, can the family transmit this complicated and subtle cultural pattern? The answer, obviously, is that it cannot.

A few Hindus appreciate the nature of this problem and in a vague way would like to do something about it.[13] Yet any attempt to create community-wide support for religious practice immediately runs into sectarianism. Given a large population, as large as that of South Africa, for example, sectarianism need not be disruptive; in fact it may be adaptive, since it provides people sharply divided by caste, class, and other social dimensions with religious concepts and practices suited to their needs. But in a small population such as that of any Central African town, sectarianism is hopelessly divisive. But it also follows that any truly integrative effort which would embrace all Hindus in one place could not be by definition traditional Hinduism. It might be religion and it might be called Hinduism, but it most assuredly would be neither of these as they have been historically understood in India.

13. In a personal communication, Chagan Lalloo provides this significant observation: "In an effort to inculcate a sense of religious responsibility, the Hindus of Salisbury have been trying for the past several years to introduce the practice of *regular Sunday worship* in the temple. This attempt has not measured up to expectations—in fact the usual 'apathy' prevails." [Emphasis added.] In his general comments upon this chapter, Mr. Lalloo points out the masculine bias inherent in our material. If we had paid more attention to women, he suggests, we would have received a rather different impression of religion among the Hindus than we did: "There is a fairly sharp dichotomy between males and females in their respective roles regarding religion. Broadly categorized, the men tend more toward the philosophical, abstract nature of religion—acting, it seems, as the custodians, the interpreters—while women tend to view religion much more from the ritualistic, "practical," and functional point of view. Their total orientation, i.e. patterns of belief, perceptions, etc., is decidedly more internalized and functionally more meaningful than for men. Their religious roles are manifestly more varied and the positions they occupy in the rituals and ceremonies clearly demonstrate the relative importance assumed by them and conceded to them in these matters."

At an immediate and practical level, it should be noted finally that Hinduism in Central Africa suffers from an absence of professional specialists. The few priestly Brahman families came to Africa because they wished to earn their livelihood in another occupation; routine priestly functions are poorly rewarded in terms of income and prestige even in India. There are only one or two full-time Brahman priests in the whole of Central Africa (the number fluctuates); several others who grew to adulthood in India and know the *mantras* (prayers) will pinch-hit somewhat grudgingly on special occasions such as a wedding. Nearly all astrological readings are done in India by mail.

Some sporadic leadership of an inspirational character is provided by a constant (if somewhat thin) stream of visiting swamis from India. These are of great variety. Some are purely sectarian and meet only with devotees of their cult. Others, such as an Indian Buddhist monk (and former journalist) who toured the country early in the period of fieldwork, address the entire Indian community including Muslims as well. In such cases, the religious message is marginal at best. Their appeal is essentially a nationalistic one. They have one theme which their audience would be sorely disappointed not to hear. They reiterate the ancient past and the great accomplishments of Indian civilization and exhort the gathered community to remain faithful to this heritage despite all temptations to the contrary in the midst of alien Africa.

THE MUSLIMS

In an evolutionary perspective, Hinduism contrasts with Islam in much the same way and for the same reasons that Judaism contrasts with Christianity. Like Judaism, Hinduism is an ancient, particularistic, people- and place-oriented way of life rather than a self-conscious religion in the modern theological sense. As the last of the great universalistic and evangelical religions to appear in history, Islam is fundamentally a modern religion in a way that Hinduism is not.

An important fact for the sociology of ethnic relations follows from this somewhat formal distinction. The religion of the Hindu or the Jew is an indivisible part of his ethnic heritage and current social identity; an avowed atheist can still feel emotionally and socially a "good" Hindu or Jew, since religion is something which one *has* rather than acquires. But in the formal sense a person is not born a Muslim or a Christian; he becomes one, in theory, only through a self-conscious spiritual commitment.

In practice, the results of these differences are somewhat paradoxical in Central Africa. In spite of (or perhaps because of) their ancient religion, Hindus tend to want to be more modern than Muslims and to acculturate more readily to urban secularism. Muslims, to whom the act of faith looms larger in personal experience, find the path to the modern secular world more strenuous. But by the same token Muslims when secularized are more likely to drop any pretense of piety.

Organization and Belief

The Indian Muslims of Central Africa are orthodox Sunni theologically, and Hanfi in ritual practice. In these important respects they resemble the Gujarati Muslims of South Africa and Mauritius to whom they are closely related by origin. They thereby contrast sharply with most of the Indian Muslims of East Africa, where Ismaeli "Khojas" and Shia Bohras are in the majority. Apparently, only three or four Ismaelis live in the whole of Central Africa. There are, it is true, several hundred non-Gujarati Muslims in Central Africa, mainly Punjabis and Konkanis, but these are also Sunni by sect affiliation.

The organizational structure and doctrine of Sunni Islamism show marked parallels to Protestant Christianity, particularly Protestant Christianity of the fundamentalist varieties. In orthodox Islamic theory, religious authority ultimately rests upon holy scripture and holy scripture alone; between the individual worshiper and his God stands only the human agent of divine instruction: Muhammad, the Messenger of God. It follows that within the Sunni communities, as among Protestant Christians, the learned and pious who know the scripture intimately are recognized religious leaders. But leadership in both cases rests upon learning and piety, not upon ultramundane qualities of lineage or ordination.[14]

Dependence upon scripture as the sole sacred authority leads, as among Protestant Christians, to a decentralized church organization within which each local congregation has complete autonomy. Where enough Muslims reside to make it financially feasible, the faith demands a mosque, constructed and maintained by the congregation (the *jamat*) to which all local believers belong. In theory, as it is explained to the inquisitive outsider, the *jamat* has a set of officers freely elected by the members. In fact, these offices in Central Africa are filled more or less informally by recognized community leaders. The priest (*imam* or, more commonly, *maulvi*) is very much a servant of the congregation, being hired and fired at its will, exactly as is a minister in those Protestant Christian churches with a congregational type of organization.

The uncompromising monotheism of Islam makes matters of fundamental theology infinitely easier for Muslims than for Hindus—or for Christians too, for that matter. All Muslims know and at some level understand the often repeated essentials: God, who is the *only* God, created and rules the world; Muhammad was the last of His many Messengers; and the holy Koran contains in wonderful and majestic totality the sum of His Message to mankind. Beyond these simple articles of faith, few Muslims in Central Africa show much intellectual interest in theological questions.[15]

14. It is here, incidentally, that Shia sects depart generally from Sunnis. Shias believe that the descendants of Ali, the Prophet's son-in-law, do have a divinely appointed role in the leadership of both sacred and secular Islam. Ismaeli Shias carry this doctrine a step further. They see in the person of the Aga Khan the current representative on earth of this sacred lineage and divine authority. Cf. H. S. Morris, "The Divine Kingship of the Aga Khan: A Study of Theocracy in East Africa," *Southwestern Journal of Anthropology, 14* (1958), 454–72.

15. We were astonished when a university-educated but unusually pious Muslim friend stumbled over a statement in English of the five pillars of Islam. Only slightly embarrassed at his ineptitude, he added apologetically, "I don't pretend to know much about my religion. I have never studied it in a

No one, therefore, worries self-consciously over God's precise characteristics; but in practice, God's relationship to man is seen in a markedly Calvinistic manner. His will is His pleasure, and the bases of His decisions are in the last analysis inscrutable. Man therefore has no recourse except to worship this omnipotent and omniscient autocrat unreservedly. If he faithfully does so by the minute formula laid down in the Koran, God has indicated that He will be duly pleased, and insignificant man will consequently escape the punishment of hell which otherwise surely awaits him. On this earth, man is promised nothing. The faithful can simply hope with some justification that they will receive a little consideration.

Since God made the world, it is His and He can do with it what He likes. That was shown up in Morocco just the other day [after the major earthquake there in late 1959]. Some people up there had been millionaires one day; the next day, after the disaster struck, they were beggars. That should be a lesson to us: it shows that everything we have is not in our hands but is in God's hands.

Suppose you had a group of a dozen ants who lived in an area about the size of that bed over there [pointing across the room]. There they live and build their homes and get what they can to eat. There they have their families and get old and die. Well, a human being might come along and he would look at them and think, "Their lives don't mean very much, do they? They are really pretty insignificant little things, those ants!"

Well, on this globe of ours which is covered with people, maybe that's the way we look to God. Nobody, not even the richest man [the informant, incidentally, *is* a rich man], ever really has anything. What he has God gave to him and eventually God will take it away. Even the life which we have belongs to God. The bodies which we have

scholarly way." Yet at the time this informant was rigorously adhering to the prescribed five daily prayers, a sure test that he takes his religion with unusual seriousness.

111

belong to the earth. Maybe in this wall, for example, [and here he patted the brick wall behind him with his hand for emphasis] there is a body of some long dead human being. There probably is. But the life it had went back to God.

General observations on the state of the world are therefore apt to end on an apocalyptic note, similar in tone to fundamentalist Christianity:

Personally, I believe that this internal dissension which we have here within the Muslim community is a sign that the end of the world is near. All Muslims, according to our religion, should be brothers, and when they disagree over something like this [a local community squabble between two powerful patrons], then that is very bad indeed. It has been foretold that there would be signs of the end when it came, and one of the signs would be "when brother will rise up against brother," even within the Muslim community. Personally, I see this as a sign that we are in our last days here on earth.

As I said before, I think that some day God will say, "I've had enough!" And when God says that—finished! Everywhere you look, you see sin and injustice, and I don't believe God is going to put up with it much longer.

What practical significance do such sentiments have? They are in the first place highly stereotyped verbal conventions, expected upon appropriate occasions. But it does not necessarily follow that they are hypocritical or insincere. In fact, they seem to reflect what the speaker *thinks* when he is in a philosophical mood. But no Muslim known to us really *acts* as if he believes the end of the world is at hand. The faith is one thing; the business of day-to-day living in a thoroughly secularized urban world is another.

The Ritual Obligations

The first of the "five pillars" of Islam states the faith, and a wholehearted acceptance of this ringing declaration that God is God and that Muhammad is His Messenger makes one a Muslim. In essence, the ritual duties spelled out in the other four pillars are designed to keep the faith constantly before the mind of the Muslim—literally, the "true believer," "the acceptor." In practice, if the Muslim actually follows his ritual obligations rigorously, he can scarcely forget the faith more than an hour or two at a time.

The most basic of these ritual duties is the five daily prayers. Their performance is the ultimate test of conformity to the straight and narrow path of Islamic virtue. It is a rigorous test indeed and it is therefore not surprising that people who otherwise consider themselves good Muslims should often fail to meet it.

No attempt was made to determine adherence to the prayer regime statistically; direct questioning on such a matter would not, in our opinion, be very profitable. Estimates obtained from Muslim informants vary widely, anywhere from five to sixty percent. Part of this exceedingly wide variation is to be accounted for by the individuals doing the judging: the most pious and rigid are harshest on their fellows. But a good deal of it comes from a great difference among the Muslim communities, some being markedly more pious than others. All we can say with the certainty of personal knowledge is that some Muslims maintain the regimen rigorously. Others do not, although many of these claim they do. The number who do not is certainly larger than the number who do.

To follow the prayer regimen faithfully in Central Africa means rising before five in the morning. One prays in the middle of the day, again at about four-thirty, and again at about six. The final prayer comes at about eight in the evening. Informants often commented upon the difficulties inherent in this schedule.

It's the prayers at five in the morning and four-thirty in the afternoon which are the hardest for us. In the morning, particularly when it is cold, we hate to get up and take a bath and make the preparation for the prayers.

113

And then for business people, four-thirty in the afternoon is a very difficult time because it means that one must close one's shop at that hour or leave it in the hands of someone else. But it is just for this reason that these times are of most benefit to us. These are the times when God would most like us to pray because they are the hardest. Most people find the other hours easy enough. Here, in this area, it isn't much of a problem to close one's shop at one o'clock and then go to the mosque for prayer before eating lunch. Nor is it very difficult to pray at home at six and at eight since one is free at these times.

The observation that God is particularly pleased with prayers at times when physical comfort and financial gain must be sacrificed is entirely consistent with the ascetic values at the core of Indian Islam. The speaker quoted below was the secretary of a Young Men's Muslim Association (note the westernized titles). He was formally addressing a meeting to which the senior author had been specifically invited, and enlightenment for the foreign visitor was doubtlessly foremost in his mind. Still the thought and the sentiments are common enough:

> The goal of religion is to conquer the animal in man. The body is unruly; it has its needs and desires which if we let them will dominate our lives. But the spiritual part of man must rule the body. The spirit must say to the body, "I will rein you, I will curb you; I will make you do God's will, not what you will." In the morning when it is time to say our prayers, the tired and sleepy body says, "I don't want to get up; I want to sleep some more." But we must get up. During the fast, the thirsty body cries out for a cool drink, but we say to it, "You must wait." . . . Islam builds character. That is the great thing about our religion. It builds character. I don't think you can say the same thing about any other religion in the world.

Being public and thus more subject to overt social control, prayers at the mosque on Fridays are more commonly adhered to than the daily prayers, most of which are said at home. A drive through a large town between the hours of one and two on a Friday afternoon quickly shows by the closed doors and shutters the Muslim-owned businesses. The Hindu shops, of course, are open to take advantage of the temporary lack of competition—except in those towns where they too must be closed by local ordinance.

Ramadan is kept by most Muslims, although this practice is also subject to considerable local and regional variation. In a smallish Malawian town, adherence will approach 100 percent. In Salisbury or Bulawayo, perhaps 50 percent would be a closer estimate. In all communities, however, Ramadan greatly intensifies religious interest. Even those who have wavered in their everyday religious duties are caught up in the communal enthusiasm and are thus induced to make this dramatic symbolic reaffirmation of their Muslimhood. As one informant commented: "It's something which you have to experience in order to understand. When the month of Ramadan comes around, the whole atmosphere in the Muslim community changes. People suddenly become interested in religion, where they may have been indifferent before."

Public enthusiasm, with its inherent social pressures, becomes so strong that people explicitly exempt from the fast—children, pregnant women, and sick people—often keep it along with the others. A doctor in Nyasaland complained to us of the number of sick children (some as young as five or six) whose ailments during Ramadan were complicated by weakness brought on by sheer hunger. Commenting upon this observation, a Muslim said:

> I am sure that no child is compelled to fast against his will. But the child sees all the other members of the family fasting and he wants to try it. If he wants to try it, I see no harm in it myself. Let him try. Let him find out for himself what the fast means. If he tries it and finds he can't maintain it, then it is all right for him to break the fast and nothing is lost because he is not required to fast anyway. But if he attempts to fast, then he will know, in

a way in which he couldn't possibly otherwise understand, what the fast means.

What the fast "means" was often explained to us, but not always in exactly the same terms. After commenting that charity was one of the primary virtues of Islam, an informant went on to say:

> The idea is that if one is hungry, then one appreciates the position of people who are so poor that they don't have enough to eat all the time. It is one thing to have the idea of charity as an abstract ideal; it is another to put it into actual practice. By the fast of Ramadan, we are reminded, rich and poor alike, of how it is to be poor. Consequently, we are more apt to feel charitable toward the poor because we feel it in our stomachs.

More commonly, it is explained that Ramadan purifies the mind and trains the character. The following statement of this theme by a young informant is unusual only in its explicit reference to sex, not normally a subject of polite conversation among Indians, either Hindu or Muslim:

> One of the things which the fast does for us is to take our minds off sex. If you are not married and you see a woman—any woman—then your passions are going to be aroused. I will be frank with you. I was not myself married until I was twenty-five. Before then, whenever I saw a woman I wanted to have intercourse with her. But of course our passions must be controlled. The rules of our society must be maintained or there wouldn't be any society. The fast of Ramadan helps to train one to control one's passions. When you are really hungry or thirsty—I mean when you are hungry and thirsty enough—then you forget all about women. All you want is something to drink and something to eat. Or maybe what you want more than anything else in this world is a cigarette.

The two other obligations of the five pillars appear to be only weakly institutionalized among the Indian Muslims in

Central Africa. These are the *jacat* (the compulsory tax upon personal income for almsgiving and supporting religious institutions) and the pilgrimage to Mecca.

In Muslim countries, as one of our better-educated informants pointed out, the *jacat* used to be collected by the state without differentiation from other taxes. Muslims living in non-Muslim states are apt to feel (like everyone else) that they pay more than enough in taxes; they are thus in no mood to make a sizable additional payment. No pressing need is felt for the *jacat* since the traditional Islamic public institutions which would be supported by it in a Muslim state are lacking.[16] The mosque and the *madresa* (the Arabic school) are the sole representatives. It seems safe to say that no reasonably well-to-do Muslim in Central Africa gives anything like the ideal two and one-half percent of his income.

There is nonetheless a well-defined pattern of collections based upon voluntary offerings, and by always giving something to each of these when asked, Muslims feel that they are meeting the *jacat* obligation. One man stated this rather peevishly: "There isn't a week that we don't get a request for money somewhere! Yet we always give something. That is our duty." Demands for a contribution may arise from anywhere in the Muslim world. Considerable sums, for example, were collected in Central Africa for the relief of the victims of the Moroccan earthquake previously mentioned. But most of the demands actually come from nearby communities. A community building a mosque or a school may typically collect as much as half or more of the required capital outside its own town.

There are remarkably few individuals who have made the pilgrimage to Mecca, considering the relatively short distance involved and the cheapness of present-day air travel. In one of the largest Muslim communities in Northern Rhodesia, for example, only four individuals had made the pilgrimage, and of these four, only one is a rich community leader. By con-

16. See, for example, Carleton S. Coon, *Caravan: The Story of the Middle East* (New York, Henry Holt, 1951), especially pp. 109–12, 258–59.

trast, virtually all of the adult men have been back to India at least once, and most have gone many times—a journey which involves considerably more time and money than the pilgrimage would. The only conclusion to be drawn is that the pilgrimage is not in fact very high in the typical Muslim's hierarchy of values.

The obligation to make the pilgrimage is of course not absolute. The Koran explicitly reserves this obligation to those who can afford it, and it specifically cautions against borrowing money to make the journey. Furthermore, there is no fixed time in life when one should go. A great many probably intend in a vague way to make the pilgrimage but keep putting it off, only to find in the end that they never go.

Islam and Change

If being religious means more than simply an attitude, if it means a translation of belief into some kind of overt action, then the Indian Muslims in Central Africa are a good deal more religious than Hindus are. They certainly participate more in ritualistic activity, and by virtue of their more coherent communal organization, they are better able to control behavior in the name of religious principles.

For example, during the period of our fieldwork the number of Indian Muslims throughout Central Africa who held licenses to sell beer and liquor could literally be counted on the fingers of one hand. And it is a rare Muslim indeed who himself uses alcohol. By contrast, although Hindus in theory also abhor alcohol, many deal in liquor, and of those who do, a fair number on occasion sample their own wares. The liquor business is tempting; it is profitable not only for itself but as an additional attraction to a man's other business. Many Muslims would certainly sell liquor without any serious twinges of conscience if they could do so without incurring the wrath of their fellows, and the fact that they do not constitutes an impressive demonstration of communal control. How is this considerable difference between the groups in degree of religiosity to be accounted for?

Muslims, it will be recalled, are statistically more rural than Hindus; and, everything else being equal, urbanization is universally correlated with secularization. More pointedly, most Muslims in Central Africa reside in what is now Malawi, to which they were drawn by the accidents of immigration history. The literacy test applied in the Rhodesias had the practical effect of screening out the less educated and diverting them to Nyasaland. As a result of this selective process, the Indian populations of Rhodesia and Zambia—which happen also by historical accident to be predominantly Hindu—are much more sophisticated (judged by the standards of cosmopolitan culture) than the predominantly Muslim population of Malawi.

Aside from these extrinsic historical factors, there are also intrinsic differences between Hinduism and Islam which up to a point make it easier to retain a world view cast in traditional Islamic terms than in traditional Hindu ones. These differences are in the effective *ideological content* and not simply group identification.

Intellectually, the Muslim clearly escapes a number of embarrassments which are inherent in Hinduism as an ancient religion. He can, for example, say simply and straightforwardly without apology or tortuous argument that he believes in one God—not gods—and he thus places himself firmly and unambiguously in the mainstream of modern religio-philosophical thought. Monotheism quite clearly is the only socially respectable conception of personal deity permitted by modern cosmopolitan society.

But if Hindus are socially embarrassed—as they demonstrably are—over Hinduism's heritage of popular pantheism, this embarrassment is mild compared to that of caste. Caste clearly discredits Hinduism's respectability, not only in the minds of non-Hindus but also within the less traditional part of the Hindu community itself. By contrast, Muslims can and do stress the democratic and egalitarian aspects of formal Islam, and this is a very considerable intellectual advantage in the modern world.

119

Yet, as suggested above, the intrinsic advantages which Islam enjoys over Hinduism hold only up to a point. Religious concepts and practices still have to contend with the overwhelmingly secular character of contemporary life everywhere, and Islam, which is indubitably modern and progressive in certain important respects, can be no exception. The logical end to secularization is complete disenchantment with the world view provided by any traditional religion, and such disenchantment comes to Muslims as well as to people reared in other traditions. A young Muslim professional stated, with a note of impatience in his voice: "Frankly, I think that this business of religion is something which should have been long since forgotten. It's essentially a carry-over from the Middle Ages and doesn't fit into the modern world."

Outright and overt rejection such as this, however, is rare, and it is rarer among Muslims than among Hindus. The far more common stance is the one familiar to Christians, Jews, and Hindus: it is to call oneself a believer while at the same time revealing by one's overt behavior that the professed faith is almost entirely verbal and barely touches daily life. A young Muslim who had just returned from a long sojourn in England provides a convenient illustration. Having quizzed him closely as to the effects of an English education upon his religion, we were assured at great length that it had only strengthened it. All men, we were told somewhat pedantically, need "roots." He was a Muslim, he said, and he was proud of it. He would rear his children in the faith and remain a Muslim until he died.

Shortly after this lecture, we visited in his company a local Muslim businessman. As a matter of course—such gestures of hospitality being invariable in the local Indian culture—we were offered a refreshment. However, it was Ramadan, and our host, who had not served himself, looked at our friend expectantly. Would he have a soda also? The reply: "What do you think! I have been too long in England to pay much attention to that!" And, it being a hot day, he reached out eagerly for the cold bottle offered him.

In matters of organization and ritual practice, again Muslims have certain intrinsic advantages and disadvantages vis-à-vis Hindus and other religious groups when confronting the forces of secularization. The greatest of these is their effective communal organization at the local level for maintaining and transmitting the religious heritage. However, this undoubted advantage is seriously offset by certain highly unadaptive features of the inherited religious culture and social organization.

The extreme sex segregation traditional in Islam is a good example of customs that are unadaptive. All Muslims in Central Africa have relaxed their inherited practices in this respect a good deal in recent years, but enough segregation still exists to provide an embarrassment to young people. The trend here (described in somewhat more detail in the family chapter below) is clear and inevitable. It is toward an early end to this distinctive Islamic symbol.

In one Rhodesian community, unusual in the extent of both its religious enthusiasm and its religious modernism, plans are being made by the youthful leadership to provide a place for women within the new mosque which they hope to build. Such an innovation will certainly mortify the older conservatives in the other communities when they hear of it. In their defense one of these young leaders explained:

> In some of these other communities the women now attend the cinema. Yet the men would be horrified if they should go to the mosque. This is ridiculous, of course, and it is a wrong interpretation of Islam. The best Islamic authorities agree that women should go to the mosque. And in some countries they do—in a special balcony provided for them. That is the arrangement we may adopt. We haven't made up our minds yet.

By ending the remaining restrictions on women's participation in religious activities, these young leaders hope to strengthen interest in religion among women, where apathy is a serious problem. Making it possible for women to take an active role in communal religious affairs will certainly increase their interest, but sheer social activity will not necessarily lead to a greater *intellectual* interest in religion. Muslim Ladies' Aid Societies and Sewing Circles will only help to make Islam simply another "church," indistinguishable in any important way from Christian and Jewish congregations.

Formidable problems of adaptation also exist in the areas of ritual, indoctrination, and leadership, all of which can be traced in good part to the problem of language. For the Sunni Muslim, it is an absolute necessity that prayers be said in Arabic; the holy word is inviolate, and to translate the Koran is to change it.[17] In non-Arabic speaking countries, therefore, the Muslim priest's main function is to lead the communal prayers in Arabic and to teach the children these prayers in the religious school.

Yet to find a qualified *maulvi* for this job is not easy in Central Africa. There are no local Islamic seminaries, and the authorities have been most niggardly in allowing priests to be imported from India or Pakistan. Under federal immigration policy, priests had to come on a strictly temporary visa and without their families. Furthermore, the pay is low; a common salary is £20 a month, slightly less than the lowest rate for teachers in a government-operated Indian public school. These conditions make recruiting of desirable people difficult. Plenty of eager applicants can be found in India, but upon investigation it is often found that few of these are qualified—and many are downright fraudulent.[18]

If a community is lucky enough to get a qualified *maulvi,* it is still most unlikely that he knows English. By the nature

17. Pious Muslims of a scholarly bent may study an English translation for the simple reason that this is what they *understand* best. Such translations, however, are considered only an aid to comprehension. No orthodox Sunni Muslim would accept them as authoritative, and the better editions always contain the original Arabic on the opposite page.

18. According to one informant: "Anybody can get a certificate in India for almost anything if you have enough money. And some of these people get a certificate which says they are a *maulvi* and they come into this country on that basis. I have in mind one man whom we had here. He called himself a *maulvi* and he didn't even know how to pray correctly. How can you teach people to pray if you don't know how yourself?"

of his professional training, he has attended a university in which the instruction is given in Urdu, Arabic, and Persian rather than in English. The fact that the *maulvi* speaks no English is of course no handicap for the immigrant generation who can communicate with him in Gujarati. But it must be remembered that one of his primary duties is to teach the children Arabic, and the children's Gujarati is elementary. Hindu children may be taught Gujarati in the Hindu "afternoon school" which helps to reinforce its maintenance among the Hindus as a home-and-community language. Muslim children, however, are taught Arabic in the afternoon school, and thus have a greater tendency to use English among themselves and in their families. In Rhodesia, the family tongue may very well be English, or mostly English.

As a result, a *maulvi* who does not know English must teach Arabic almost entirely by rote. He cannot explain adequately as he goes along what the words mean. Religious instruction becomes uphill work indeed and must be imparted at a very superficial level. Used to a modern approach to education in the public school, children get discouraged and rebel against learning something that they do not comprehend. Religion, it is safe to say, thus gets associated with a highly boring and unpleasant experience which must inevitably color a person's perception of it throughout life.[19]

But if somehow enough Arabic is learned to say the prayers, the faithful then have the task of actually putting the prayer schedule into concrete act. And here, upon analysis, the obstacles look formidable indeed. In simple cultures with very low standards of living and few competing interests, an active religious life composed mainly of verbal formulas learned and repeated by rote may be maintained indefinitely. The ethnographic literature provides a wealth of examples. Under harsh

19. We were told, for example, of the enthusiastic interest which an English-speaking *sheikh* from South Africa aroused upon a visit to one Southern Rhodesian Muslim community: "They leaned forward in their seats, as if waiting for his next word. They were so interested. For a great many of them, this was the first time that they had ever heard any discussion of their religious principles in a language which they could understand."

life-threatening conditions—and we need occasionally to remind ourselves how directly life-threatening existence has typically been for most preindustrial peoples in the past—extensive prayers of a formulaic type had functional meaning, even if their intrinsic meaning was obscure. Prayer and other ritual performed with meticulous detail warded off God's wrath for yet another day—one fervently hoped. The time was thus well spent, especially when attractive alternative uses for one's time were not plentiful.

But what modern urban middle-class people, living in comfortable economic circumstances, can be expected to assume the heavy burden of an empty ritual, the intrinsic meaning of which they do not even understand? Their most pressing needs are of a different kind, and the means to fulfill them are perceived very differently than by their progenitors in the folk village.

Chapter Five

THE HERITAGE OF CASTE

The word *caste* perhaps epitomizes better than almost any other the vision which the sociologist or anthropologist has in the back of his mind when he uses the term *social structure* as a set of ideal cultural norms so closely adhered to in practice that overt behavior and norm in the concrete instance seem essentially one. Although normative interpretations standard in textbook treatments surely exaggerate the tight congruence between norm and behavior even in the case of caste, we must accept the essential facts supported by the ethnographic evidence: caste in traditional India controlled a large part of the ordinary Indian's behavior in daily life, and it did so, everything considered, with extraordinary predictability and rigidity of pattern.

But caste in traditional India and caste among the Indians in modern Central Africa are very different phenomena. The difference provides an exceedingly interesting and significant study in the processes of socio-cultural change. Society and culture, sufficiently intermeshed in India to provide a fairly smoothly working system of social relations, are in Africa sundered apart. The former caste culture applies only to restricted facets of the Indian's social experience, and even where it does apply, the fit between norm and behavior is apt to be grindingly discordant. Radical shifts in both the normative complex defining caste and in concrete social relations are accordingly being made.

The first fact impressed upon the fieldworker's attention with respect to caste in Central Africa is that it is a subject of considerable delicacy and embarrassment. The most immediate reason for embarrassment is the peculiar meaning which caste assumes in this particular social situation. No Indian can protest to a European against the discrimination imposed upon him without meeting an automatic response: "But what about your own caste system in India?" [1] This stereotyped retort is blunt, cruel, and effective. Indians know from ample experience what to expect, and they not unnaturally want to avoid the encounter.

But caste would not be as effective an ideological weapon in an ongoing process of ethnic conflict if the democratic and egalitarian values which lie behind the Europeans' disparagement of it were not thoroughly internalized by the Indians themselves. Well aware of the degree to which they in fact have departed in thought and deed from traditional caste norms, Indians deeply resent the implicit assumption made by Europeans that they are undemocratic and unprogressive.

Furthermore, given the existing political situation, Indians perceive the dissemination of "false" information concerning this part of their socio-cultural heritage as positively dangerous. To the extent that Africans come to believe, as many Europeans do, that Indians are inherently fated by this heritage to remain undemocratic, their relations with Africans and an African government are adversely affected.

It is little wonder, then, that Indians should resist sociological inquiry into this area, or that when forced to talk about caste they should universally deny and decry it. We did not encounter a single informant throughout our period of fieldwork who would give us a straightforward and unqualified defense

1. Two English anthropologists were kind enough to take us around for initial introductions to the Indian community. On the very first visit, our Indian host protested the injustices of discrimination. He had barely opened his mouth on the subject, however, before one of our companions hurled this heavily loaded question at him. Given appropriate circumstances, the question is as predictable as "Would you want your daughter . . . ?" in the United States.

of caste as traditionally conceived of in Indian culture, that, as a direct result of an individual's spiritual purity and consequent standing within the reincarnation cycle. The accepted public stance is to deny its validity, to deny that one ever individually accepted it, and to decry any concrete application of it (beyond marital choice) within the Indian community at the present time. Statements like the following preface virtually all discussions of the subject:

A Brahman: Here in Africa caste doesn't mean a thing. A Brahman will sit down and eat with a shoemaker or with anyone else. Everybody is treated exactly alike. There are no caste discriminations here. That, too, is the way it is in modern India. Personally, I like it that way, and that is the way I think it should be.

An Anavil: When I say untouchable, I am of course referring to the way it was in India a long time ago, not now. Now, there isn't such a thing as being an untouchable. [Correcting himself] There is in just this one sense. You wouldn't invite an untouchable to your home or you wouldn't allow your daughter to marry an untouchable. But the untouchables can go to the theatre, or the park, or any other public place. The discrimination against the untouchables in India isn't like the racial discrimination here. It's what you might call a social discrimination. Of course the untouchables used to be discriminated against even in public places. It used to be that they couldn't even go to the temple. Can you imagine that? But now they can go any place.

Another Anavil: Caste doesn't mean a thing out here in Africa, but it still means something in India, particularly among the people of my parents' generation. Here, people of different castes eat together and think nothing about it. But at home my mother wouldn't think of serving someone of the Sudra caste. Personally, I don't consider myself any

127

better than anybody else; having an untouchable in my house wouldn't mean anything to me. But at home, I couldn't invite such a person into my house. My mother wouldn't understand, and I couldn't do it.

A Khumbhar: We have forgotten all that nonsense over here—all that caste stuff, I mean.

Yet the fact remains that those Indians not born in Africa grew up, typically, in a rural village in India where caste still governed a great deal of social behavior and where deeply cherished values of family, religion, and status were intrinsically interwoven with it. Such a heritage so deeply internalized during the socialization process is not easily exorcised by mere intellectual rejection or by practical convenience. Despite verbalized claims, the evidence indicates that caste remains a determinant of behavior which must be reckoned with, despite the fact that relevant norms and their application are rapidly and drastically changing.

CASTE ORIGINS

A commonly repeated stereotype among Europeans in Central Africa holds that the members of the local Hindu community are low caste, much lower than the average in India. For example, a lawyer who claimed exceptional knowledge of the local community told us: "One of the basic facts which you have to understand about the Indians here is that they are a pretty poor lot to begin with. With very few exceptions they are untouchables swept out of the gutters of Bombay. You can't really expect very much from such people."

Where such notions originally came from is difficult to say, although the reasons for their maintenance and perpetuation are easily understood in terms of the social psychology of prejudice. In good part it is perhaps nothing more than sheer imaginative invention, given the basic motivation to denigrate Indians. It is possible, however, that the Europeans' conviction that local Indians are peculiarly low in the caste hierarchy might owe something to defensive remarks made by Indians themselves: "I must warn you, you won't find what we might call 'the cream of Indian society' out here in Africa. The Indians here are frankly not the best. Here, most of the people are Sudras." Factually, this informant is not incorrect. Most Indians in Central Africa *are* Sudras, as indeed are most people in India. But the way he puts it could easily lead to misinterpretation.

Actually neither the top nor the bottom of Indian society is proportionately represented in Central Africa. The African-bound immigrant typically came from a broad middle stratum of Indian rural village society: farmers, artisans, petty businessmen, professionals, and officials. In this respect, the pattern is perfectly consistent with what is known of voluntary human immigration in general. The wealthiest, the best educated, and the most securely established did not emigrate. They had little motive to do so. The very poor, the outcaste, and the hopelessly illiterate did not emigrate either. In the first place, they lacked either the financial means or the social connections to make possible such an expensive undertaking. Furthermore, for entrance into the Rhodesias, the literacy test in English was an obstacle in and of itself sufficient to prevent something like two-thirds of the typical Indian villagers from even thinking of emigrating.

Considering the extreme sensitivity surrounding the whole question of caste, a direct census-type approach to the question of representation and distribution would have been worse than futile. Even an indirect approach had its pitfalls, as the following example shows. Soon after we started fieldwork, a seemingly candid informant remarked in the context of an unrelated conversation that his family were "carpenter people" in India, and we carefully tucked this bit of information into our notes, confident that given the circumstances it was an accurate designation of caste status. When later checking our information with a higher caste informant, we asked for the Gujarati term for carpenter and he gave us the word *Suthar*. Then, much to our surprise, he added, "But there are no carpenters here." Naming the family whom we had hitherto assumed to be carpenters, we asked if he could not be in error. At this he laughed and replied:

> No, I am sure they are potters [Khumbhar]. To the best of my knowledge, there are no carpenters here at all. You see, some of these people are ashamed to admit that they come from a caste as low as the Khumbhar. They wanted you to believe that they came from a higher caste, even if it were only carpenters.

Fortunately, the higher castes do not hesitate to identify themselves, and they will normally discuss freely enough the more innocuous aspects of their caste customs, such as those bearing upon ritual and marriage. Higher castes will also often discuss lower castes in the community (as the example cited above shows) if they can do so naturally in a gossipy way within a safe context that does not imply discriminatory attitudes. Thus if he is patient the fieldworker can in time learn the essentials in such a situation, even if he is denied a good many of the details.

In the case of the Hindus, there is also an objective index of caste status of considerable usefulness, although it has serious limitations. The surname adopted by Hindus in Africa reflects caste origin in most cases, but certainly not always. The very common name Patel, for example, is associated with the numerous Patidar caste; Naik or Desai indicate with very few exceptions a family of Anavils; Parmar and such names as Solanki are used by the Mochis; and if a family calls itself Khatri, we can be reasonably sure that they belong to a common caste of cloth merchants (or weavers) of the same name. When we apply this index to the surnames of Hindu males in the voters' registry for a large Northern Rhodesian town, we get the distribution shown in Table 7. A similar table for other communities in the Rhodesias would show most of the same castes, but in differing proportions.

TABLE 7. CASTE ORIGINS BY SURNAMES OF ADULT
HINDU MALES IN A NORTHERN RHODESIAN TOWN

Caste	Number
Patidar and other Patels*	187
Anavil	39
Khumbhar	22
Mochi	22
Khatri	16
Brahman	3
Unknown and others**	29
Total	318

* "Other Patels" include mainly those of the Koli caste but in unknown proportion.

** "Others" include Bania, Nai, Sonar, Dhobi, etc.

By a wide margin the largest Hindu caste in Central Africa
is Patidar. As peasant farmers, whatever they are called locally, they constitute a broad and basic middle stratum in village society throughout the Indian subcontinent. In Gujarat,
the Patidars are a dominant peasant caste, as Srinivas uses this
term.[2] But local conditions have given them a somewhat higher
position socially and economically than many of their counterparts elsewhere in India enjoy. Land tenure in western and
northern India followed the *ryot* rather than the *zamindar* pattern, with the result that the higher caste agriculturists in this
area are small landowners rather than tenants.[3] Furthermore,
since a good deal of the land in Gujarat is exceptionally fer-
tile, it has for a long time been devoted in good part to such
commercial crops as tobacco and cotton, and landowners in

2. M. N. Srinivas, "The Social System of a Mysore Village," in Marriott,
Village India, pp. 17–19.

3. In pre-British India, no modern concept of land ownership existed. In
some sections, the British settled upon the *zamindars* (high officials in the
existing native states) permanent rights of tenure to the large tracts from
which they had previously claimed tax revenues. Under such an arrangement,
the actual cultivators were turned into tenants. In other sections, permanent
tenure was settled upon the *ryots* (the peasant cultivators themselves), thus
creating small peasant proprietorships. Among numerous other standard
sources, see L. S. S. O'Malley, *Modern India and the West: A Study of the
Interaction of Their Civilizations* (London, Oxford University Press, 1941), pp.
278–90.

this area have prospered in modern times well beyond the norm for Indian farmers as a whole.[4]

The relative prosperity of this group laid the economic foundation for considerable upward mobility by providing capital for business ventures and education. These facts also help to explain an apparent paradox. One is constantly told that the Gujaratis (and typically it is the Patidars whom the speaker has in mind when he says "Gujaratis") are a commercial people. Yet upon persistent inquiry, it is discovered that virtually all of the Patidars in Central Africa came from farming families. The seeming paradox is resolved when it is understood that as a landholding group, the Patidars might not work their land themselves, preferring to spend their time and capital in a variety of business ventures. The same set of facts goes a long way toward explaining why the members of this caste are relatively well educated.[5]

The upward mobility characteristic of this group has created some interesting complications within and without the caste. Given the nature of Indian social structure, a caste can only achieve a higher status vis-à-vis other castes as a unit; movement, therefore, is a cooperative enterprise—a group effort—and it necessarily takes time. In a bid for higher status, the culturally standardized technique is to adopt and practice ever more stringent behavioral norms according to the ascetic brahmanic ideal. This, hopefully, proves that the group is spiritually purer than its competitors and thus in time establishes its claim to a superior status.

The Gujarati Patidars represent a good example of this peculiarly Indian form of social mobility. They are known throughout India as a distinctly ascetic lot and are widely disliked because of their superior claims and airs. In particular, the Patidars of the old Charotar (or Kaira) district stand out in this respect. Among them a complicated hypergamous system

4. David F. Pocock, "Inclusion and Exclusion: A Process in the Caste System of Gujerat," *Southwestern Journal of Anthropology, 13* (1957), 21.

5. Cf. Rashmi Desai, *Indian Immigrants in Britain* (London, Oxford University Press, 1963), p. 8.

of marriage circles prevails, a system which epitomizes their mobility strivings in intent and organization.[6]

Upward mobility strivings within this group have led to another typically Indian result: namely, a great deal of bitter factionalism within the caste as a whole and the formation of well-marked endogamous subcastes. The Charotar Patidars, for example, do not recognize the Patidars from Surat as equals and try to assert this claim to superiority by stricter adherence to brahmanic behavior. These claims to superior status were carried by the Charotar Patidars to Central Africa, where they have confronted the rapidly developing modern egalitarian norms from the cosmopolitan culture, sparking a considerable degree of intracommunity conflict.

When using the family surname assumed by Indians in Africa as an index to caste status, we were careful to qualify this procedure by stating that it was subject to some serious limitations. The most important of these qualifications concerns the exceedingly common surname of Patel, about 60 percent of the people in Table 7. Most persons who bear the name Patel (if they are not Muslims) are probably Patidars by origin. But because the name is so common, members of other and lower castes have adopted it, taking advantage of the relative anonymity of Indian community life in Africa to promote themselves (verbally) into a higher status.

In particular, a large but unknown number of Kolis have assumed the surname Patel. In origin, the Kolis are a numerous landless laboring caste in western India; originally agricultural laborers, many of them have in modern times become seamen, fishermen, and dockworkers. House servants in Gujarat are also apt to be Kolis. (One hypothesis holds that the English word "coolie" is a corruption of Koli.) In the overall caste hierarchy, they are usually counted as clean, but they are certainly at the very bottom of respectability. Even the Dhobis (washermen) are higher, and the only castes which are unambiguously lower are the universally recognized untouchables,

6. Pocock, pp. 21–23.

notably the Bhangis (sweepers) and the Chamars (skinners and removers of dead animals).

That such a lowly caste as this should have the temerity to adopt the surname which the Patidars consider theirs is almost more than these proud and highly status-conscious people can bear. Early in our fieldwork we were warned by a young Leva, a high-ranking subcaste of the Patidars: "Many of these Patels are not real Patels. They weren't Patels in India. But since it is a good name, they pinched it out here in Africa." Much later, after we had inadvertently learned that a well-known pioneer and minor community leader was a Koli instead of being a Patidar as we had assumed, an older Leva explained:

> In India there were no surnames. A man had his own name and his father's name, and it was only when our people came to Africa that they adopted a surname. If you looked on old B's passport, you would find that he didn't call himself Patel when he came here. Two-thirds of the Patels are not Patels at all. But what can you do? In India they wouldn't be allowed to call themselves Patels. But here, they do what they like. I have tried to do something about this, but I've never gotten any support.

It seems to be mainly Kolis who masquerade under the name Patel or an equivalent; significantly there are no Kolis known to us who use, as the artisan castes generally do, names consistent with their origins. There are instances, however, of persons from other castes besides the Kolis who have adopted the name Patel. We were told of a Mochi, for example, who suddenly changed his name from Parmar to Patel when he sold his shoe store and went into the grocery business because, as he said, "the name Patel is easy for Europeans to pronounce."

In any case, it is quite clear that an accurate accounting of Patels by caste origin would reveal a goodly number who are not Patidars. But that these would add up to anything like the "two-thirds" stated by the informant quoted above can be confidently discounted. A Brahman whom we queried on this point, replied with un-brahmanic heat: "No! That isn't true!

That is just a prejudice on the part of these people who are trying to set themselves off from everybody else."

Among the artisan castes, the Mochis (shoemakers) are well represented in Central Africa, particularly in the Rhodesias. Several important pioneers were of this caste, and they prospered and "called" others from India. Potters and tailors are fairly well represented, and there are a few others such as goldsmiths, barbers and washermen. None of these castes had a very high standing in traditional Indian society, but none of them fall below the clean or touchable line as it is usually determined by most authorities. There is only one family of clear-cut untouchables (Bhangi) in the whole of Central Africa. At the other extreme, there were only seven or eight families of "true" Brahmans (i.e. those of the priestly subcastes) in the whole of Northern Rhodesia at the time of our original field work.

The Anavils, who are quite numerous and tend to be influential in the community beyond their numbers, claim to be Brahmans; but this claim is typically disputed. In any case, Anavils have never been priests by occupation, a fact of which they are very proud. Instead, they have traditionally functioned as officials, landowners, and civil servants. The caste furnished the government even in Mogul times with high-ranking civil and military officials; hence, the common surnames of this group—Desai, Naik, and Mehta— were originally the titles given to such positions. Officials in the pre-European period were not paid in money; they were given instead the income from designated plots of land. Under the British, these rights were turned into freehold, and the tradition of using Anavils in governmental service continued. Any listing of the membership of a governmental bureaucracy or the legislature of the state of Gujarat will quickly show a great many Anavils, although the caste as a whole is small in number.

The distribution of castes within the Hindu community of Malawi is different enough from that of Zambia or Rhodesia to warrant a brief comment. Here again the Patidars are the largest single component of the Hindu population. But the second largest is the Lohanas, a group virtually absent elsewhere in Central Africa. Traditionally a caste of traders and merchants in India, the Lohanas are also one of the more numerous castes in East Africa.[7] Malawi differs too from Zambia and Rhodesia in the scarcity of Anavils and in the presence of small communities of non-Gujarati Hindus such as Magalorians, Konkanis, and Punjabis. We have already pointed out that Malawi has the only sizable Sikh community and shares with Rhodesia the small Goan population of Central Africa. Here too are a few Syrian Christians and a handful of Christian Indians of other origins.

A very distinctive group, represented by only a few families in each of the three territories, are the Sindhis. The Sindhis are cosmopolitan, well-to-do businessmen, typically fluent in English and yet suavely oriental in manner, who are always found in the European trade. They specialize as silk merchants and handle fine quality textiles, draperies, and decorative art objects. As a group which has been in the international trade since time immemorial, they were among the first Indians to come to Central Africa. But they did not typically enter the African trade and consequently have remained few in number. Nor have they become leaders in the general Indian community. Their relationship with the Gujaratis seems to be one of amiable mutual tolerance given the best of circumstances, but always underlaid with a strong current of latent antagonism. Some Sindhis have attempted on occasion to identify with Europeans—a tactic hardly designed to increase their popularity with other Indians.

MUSLIMS AND CASTE

In our discussion of theory, emphasis was laid upon the instrumental and adaptive nature of culture. The applicability of

7. David F. Pocock, " 'Difference' in East Africa: A Study of Caste and Religion in Modern Indian Society," *Southwestern Journal of Anthropology, 13* (1957), 291–92.

this principle becomes quickly apparent in situations of ethnic conflict. The ethnic group is defined by its distinctive cultural heritage; but culture in this case, as always, is subject to change and modification. The actual behavior of such groups reveals that they actively *use* their received culture, selecting out those traits or characteristics which give them an advantage while trying as best they can to suppress those traits which prove damaging or punishing.

This simple formula is unpretentious as sociological theory goes. But it is perfectly consistent theoretically with modern behavioral psychology, and it has the great virtue of being directly applicable to concrete behavior.[8] Selective emphasis and de-emphasis from a body of traditional culture are nicely illustrated in a contrast between the Hindu and the Muslim reactions to their heritage of caste in Central Africa.

Since caste is so thoroughly and so widely identified with Hinduism in India, Hindus cannot deny it as a historical fact, although they (as we have seen) vigorously deny its current relevance to existing community social structure. In an encounter with members of other ethnic groups upon the subject, the Hindu reaction is defensive, with avoidance as the basic tactic.

Muslims are more fortunate in this respect. They can accent the positive and actively take the offensive. A European fieldworker is continuously reminded of the egalitarian and democratic doctrine taught in the Koran. Those Muslims who are interested in scoring off Hindus may invariably be counted upon to derogate caste, using it as a club with which to beat their rivals.

The Hindus here complain about the Land Apportionment Act down in Southern Rhodesia. The fact is, however, that every village in India is divided up by a land apportionment act of its own. The Brahmans live in one section. Each of the other castes live in their separate section. And

8. Cf. George Caspar Homans, *Social Behavior: Its Elementary Forms* (New York, Harcourt, Brace and World, 1961), particularly pp. 17–29.

the outcastes are not even allowed to live in the village at all.

Sometimes we were given a personal experience to illustrate the "evil" system. While still in India, an informant and his companion were walking down a railway track one evening. They were wearing the distinctive Muslim cap, he explained, and consequently were easily identifiable:

> Since it was near sunset our shadows were very long. Suddenly, we met a shepherd woman who was coming along toward us on the other side of the track. When she looked up and saw us, she called out, "Please! Please! Stop and move back! I don't want to lose my food!" If we had kept on walking toward her, our shadows would have fallen on her, and then she would have had to throw away her dinner which she was carrying since we would have polluted it. Not only would she have lost her dinner, but she would have had to have gone and taken a bath and changed her clothes completely. Knowing this, we stopped and went around her. Silly, isn't it? But that's the way those Hindus are.

Given this stance of outraged innocence with respect to caste, it is understandable that Muslims should be—as indeed they are—even more reluctant than Hindus to discuss any application of it among themselves. The standardized response considered appropriate for European ears is: "We Muslims don't have castes; we can marry anybody, even an African." We knew of course, from the literature on caste, that this could not be quite true. Nonetheless, the statement was heard so often that we were momentarily startled when a Muslim in Nyasaland replied (surely without thinking of what he was doing) to a question concerning a Muslim community in Northern Rhodesia: "Yes, they are mostly from Surat, and that is where we come from too. But they are of a different caste."

Yet, the point having been made, it must be acknowledged that caste certainly does not have the same subjective meaning and public significance for Muslims that it does for Hindus.

Whether the endogamous groups which Muslims recognize are called castes or not is a matter of taste in terminology. The observable facts are: (1) that Muslims themselves do on occasion call these groups castes when their guard is down; (2) that these groupings have their historical origin in the Hindu system; and (3) that caste determines behavior among Muslims in Central Africa about as much as it does among the Hindus.

Since Muslim names are typically adopted from the Arabic, they normally give no hint of caste origin. There are exceptions: if a family calls itself Shaik, Sayed, Quereshi, Khatri, or Meman, then we know that it is their intention to make public their origin—or, as the case may actually be, the origin which they would *like* to have publicly accepted. This qualification is in practice much more important than it is among Hindus. Claims to being a Sayed or Quereshi, for example, are regularly discounted by Muslim Indians themselves. When a mutual acquaintance was asked if an informant who regularly used the name Quereshi in addition to his other surname was actually a Quereshi by caste, he laughed uproariously at the suggestion: "The only Quereshis are people of pure Arabian blood. It's just a name that some Muslims have adopted because they think it sounds nice. It's the same with those who call themselves Sayed."

The use of surnames in the modern European fashion is a very recent innovation among Indians, both Hindu and Muslim, in Central Africa. As indicated, some Muslims use an existing group identification such as caste (e.g. Meman) or regional origin (e.g. Surti). A more common solution, however, was to adopt one's father's name, and therefore most Muslim families use Mohammed, Ibrahim, Ahmed, or Musa as surnames. For this reason the surname cannot be even an approximate index of caste origin as in the case of the Hindus, and any statement of distribution must be highly generalized.

In Malawi, the home of most Indian Muslims in Central Africa, the two major caste groupings are the Memans and the Khatris; most of the rest are Sunni Vahoras (Bohras) from

Surat. A good many other castes are marginally represented, but these three are the main ones.

The Memans were traditionally itinerant traders in India. Their status apparently never amounted to much in the overall hierarchy. Nevertheless, they have a stereotyped reputation for great shrewdness. An improvident informant of a higher caste commented musingly: "A Meman can leave India with only a penny in his pocket and go anywhere in the world and eventually become a millionaire." They are considered uncouth in their personal habits and unlettered by the standardized stereotype; to the extent that the latter characterization is accurate, it may help to explain the virtual absence of Memans outside of Malawi. The caste, we have been told, were originally Lohanas before their conversion to Islam. All Memans in Central Africa are from Saurashtra.

The Khatris, on the other hand, come from Kathiawar and speak Kutchi as a home dialect. Khatri literally means "dyer"; they like their Hindu counterparts of the same name were known as cloth merchants (or weavers) in India. A good deal of status rivalry exists between the Khatris and the Memans in Malawi, and the two groups conventionally dislike and denigrate each other.

Sunni Vahoras (Bohras) are the third most important group in Malawi, and they are the largest component of the Muslim population in Zambia and Rhodesia.[9] Unlike the Memans and the Khatris, the Vahoras were commonly independent farmers and landowners in India. In terms of socio-economic status, they were thus essentially equivalent to the Hindu Patidars. In fact quite a number of this group use the surname Patel; and, significantly enough, the legitimacy of this usage is not questioned in principle by the Hindu Patidars. Patel literally means "village headman," and village headmen in the Gujarat area under British rule were often Muslim as well as Hindu.

With the exception of a few Khatris and scattered representatives from other castes, Sunni Vahoras from Surat and

9. The Muslims of Zambia and Rhodesia originate for the most part from a very restricted area of a few villages in Surat. See below, p. 197.

Broach make up most of the Muslim population in both Zambia and Rhodesia. But in the area around Bulawayo and elsewhere in Rhodesia there are a fair number of Konkani Muslims who were brought in via South Africa as mine workers in the very earliest period of settlement. As members of a humble, landless laboring caste in India, the Konkanis are socially the equivalent of the Hindu Kolis, and they are looked down upon by the Surti Vahoras wherever the two groups are represented in any appreciable number. This difference in caste thus constitutes a divisive factor in the community.

This general sketch of the major Muslim castes has not taken into account the subcastes and endogamous "marriage circles" which are apparently numerous within them. These distinctions are known to exist, but accurate and reliable information on such matters as the details of their operation is very difficult to obtain.

After learning (significantly enough, outside this particular community) that the Broach Vahoras wouldn't think of marrying into the local Surti Vahoras, we asked a trusted informant from the former group if this were true. With obvious reluctance, he replied:

No, it isn't customary. A Muslim can marry any other Muslim, but it isn't customary.

Dotson: But you are all Vahoras?

Yes, we are all Vahoras. But [very aggressively] even these Surtis here [motioning with a wave of his arm to take in the surrounding neighborhood] wouldn't marry freely with each other. They have their own groups within which it is customary to marry.

The informant would not elaborate on this statement. But it is clear from other sources that perhaps even his statement that "we are all Vahoras" needs to be taken with a grain of salt: in at least some instances the distinctions drawn are more fundamental than this suggests. Speaking of a well-known Khatri family in another community, a higher caste informant added with unusual candor: "They call themselves Khatris. Actually, they are Khumbhars—you know, the people who make bricks and tiles."

VARNA, REGION, AND CASTE

Two social categories are closely related to caste in the Indian mind but not identical with it: the classical varnas and the socio-cultural evaluations made in terms of regional or territorial origin.

The Varnas

Articulate Hindu informants of some education and sophistication almost invariably begin a serious discussion of caste by reference to the classical fourfold division of Vedantic Indian society: Brahman, Kshatriya, Vaishya, and Sudra. As often as not the informant may insist that this *is* the Hindu caste system. If the questioner calls attention to concrete groupings, such as the Anavils, the Patidars, the Kolis, etc., it is reluctantly conceded that these exist, but he is assured that they are unfortunate aberrations which in the last analysis have no sanction in the *real* system, meaning the varna categories.

Two points are commonly made with respect to the varnas. First, they correspond to a natural and inevitable division of labor, which in its original and unpolluted form was ethically free of discriminatory features. And second, the varnas represent ideals or grades of purity and virtuous behavior rather than actual groups of people. Early in the fieldwork, a Brahman patiently explained, using the first argument, what the caste system was all about:

> Really, this matter of caste simply comes down to a division of labor. Everyone can't do the same thing; otherwise, there wouldn't be an organized community. There must be teachers because not everybody can be expected to have specialized knowledge. There must be workers to do all the other trades—shoemakers, carpenters, and farm-

ers. So, in India, it worked out that some people became teachers: those were the Brahmans. Others became warriors: those were the Kshatriya. Others were traders: those were the Vaishya. A great many people—those not so intelligent—became ordinary workers, the Sudra. They couldn't do the Brahman's job, but they could do other things. And all the things they could do contributed to the life of the community.

But unfortunately people were not content simply to let this be a division of labor. They began to make all kinds of distinctions among these various groups and to divide them up, so finally there were hundreds of them. Some people were not even recognized as belonging to any of the four groups I just mentioned. These became the untouchables. With all the distinctions and discriminations that developed, things eventually got to be almost as bad as they are in South Africa! But now there aren't any untouchables any more. Caste is now a thing of the past, in India as it is here in Africa.

A remark by an unusually pious Patidar illustrates the second common interpretation of the varna system. He characteristically referred to a clique of local young people as Sudras. When we at last protested that some of these people were certainly not Sudras by caste, since the clique included a Brahman and an Anavil, he replied heatedly: "What I mean is that they live for the belly, and anyone who lives for the belly is a Sudra in my opinion, no matter what his caste is!"

The same informant would admit when pressed that his own caste, the Patidar, were Sudras. But the tenor of his thinking is apparent. Despite the theoretical rigidity of caste status philosophically defined, Indians tend to believe in practice that if a person strives hard to maintain rigorously the brahmanic prescriptions for spiritual purity, he will surely rise above the status of his birth to a higher level of existence. If this were not true, attempts at caste mobility of the sort characteristic of the Patidars would have no validity. By the same token, persons from reputedly higher castes who drink and otherwise "live for the belly" *ought* to be considered for what their behavior in fact proclaims them to be.

In the fieldwork context, when details on caste membership and behavior were sought, these continual references to the varnas were exceedingly frustrating. Initially, therefore, we were inclined to interpret this automatic response to the subject of caste as a protective smokescreen. In a good many cases, this interpretation was surely not entirely wrong, it being quite clear from the context that this was exactly the intention. In time, however, it also became clear that this explanation was too simple to cover all the facts adequately. Indians, we gradually came to recognize, really do think in terms of the varna categories when they are forced to reflect abstractly upon caste.

A study by D. F. Pocock places the matter of caste in a quite meaningful perspective.[10] The caste system, he points out, is often described as if it were common to the whole of India; and at a suitably high level of abstraction, this is perhaps correct enough. Yet the fact is that in the concrete instance caste is experienced and perceived primarily as a strictly *local* matter. A given Indian knows that the castes recognized in his village have their counterparts elsewhere, perhaps over all of India. Nonetheless, the claims to prestige and position which are made concretely against other persons in the name of caste must be made locally, for the simple reason that face-to-face relations with others do not extend beyond the village and its immediate region.

It follows that claims validated in one region are not necessarily negotiable in another and that in the last analysis no universally agreed-upon hierarchy of rank order for the various groups really exists. The empirical observation is that some groups everywhere claim a higher status than others are willing to accord them and that conflict over such claims and counterclaims is the rule rather than the exception.

The neat arrangement and universal consensus implied in

10. Pocock, "Inclusion and Exclusion," pp. 19–31.

many of the standard sources and textbook discussions simply do not exist. Reality is better described as a complex of claims and counterclaims to hereditary status which must be validated—if they are—by social power and persuasion. And it is within this context of loosely organized chaos that the classical varna system finds its function for the Indians themselves. It provides a set of highly generalized criteria for rank, together with the requisite authority in history and tradition to apply them. But the gain is mainly intellectual rather than social; it seems generally agreed among competent ethnographers that the classical varnas have little direct connection with the caste system as it operates on a day-to-day basis in the Indian village. What the varnas do help to do is to translate the concrete complexities of caste into a statement intellectually comprehensible to Indians as well as to non-Indians.

Status Based upon Territorial Origin

The preeminently local character of caste at the operating level of the Indian village helps to explain not only the retention of the varna categories, but also why regional distinctions assume so much importance to Indians. Subcultural differences originating in regional variation inevitably acquire caste connotations in a culture in which caste is a primary criterion for status evaluation. Strangers are not only viewed with the initial ethnocentric suspicion and hostility normal in any society, they are in India at the same time automatically assimilated conceptually into an appropriate slot in the caste hierarchy since Indians think in these terms.

Territorial and regional differences therefore become confused with other caste criteria so that regional labels are often substituted for (and become virtually synonymous with) caste names in the social placement of people. For example, if you are a Patidar in Central Africa or East Africa, and you meet a stranger Patidar, it is not sufficient to determine that you both belong to the Leva subcaste. It still makes a lot of difference whether you come from the Charotar or the Surat district. To the Charotars the Surtis are an inferior grade, although naturally enough, the Surti Levas refuse to accept this evaluation of themselves. Among the Muslims, the Broach Vahoras look down upon the Surti Vahoras and both patronize the Khatris and the Memans from what they consider the culturally backward Kathiawar and Saurashtra regions.

Both Hindus and Muslims, as these examples show, use regional origin to determine status, but the criteria of regional origin plays a larger role for Muslims than it does for Hindus. The difference is important, since it reveals something of the meaning and significance which caste has in the two groups respectively. Muslims tend to see the caste distinctions which they make among themselves as differences in subculture, Hindus as differences in spiritual purity. Among Muslims, "tribe" is the euphemistic English synonym for "caste"; Hindus, on the other hand, commonly use the word "community." These English terms probably reflect fairly accurately an actual perceptual and conceptual difference, an inference reinforced by the fact that historically the relationship between caste status and ethnic origin is more clearly marked in the north and west of India than in the south and east.[11] A group like the Memans, to take that example, do objectively possess "tribal" features, being set off from fellow Muslims by a distinctive dialect and noticeable differences in diet and social custom.

In the plural society of Central Africa, however, the Muslim concept of tribe, like the Hindu concept of varna, takes on new and highly convenient functions, thereby illustrating once again the principle of selective instrumentalism which we have ascribed to culture. When put on the defensive by harshly critical outgroup inquiry, Hindus find the obscurities of the varna categories exceedingly useful in forestalling painful probing. Muslims, on the other hand, have long since discovered that "tribe" sounds much nicer to non-Indian ears than "caste." After all, do not all other people—most notably, in this social

11. Cf. McKim Marriott, "Caste and Ranking and Community Structure in Five Regions of India and Pakistan," *Bulletin of the Deccan College Research Institute, 19,* no. 1–2 (1958), particularly 73 and 96.

context, the Africans and the Europeans—make distinctions based ultimately upon tribal origins?

CASTE AND BEHAVIOR

Caste functioned in traditional India as a major (if not *the* major) determinant of: (1) occupation; (2) formal education; (3) socialization into an appropriate subculture; (4) rank in a community-wide structure of prestige and social honor; (5) religious practices; (6) marital choice; and (7) strictly voluntary associations. A convenient way of summarizing the present meaning and significance of caste in Central Africa is to examine each one of these in turn, and to seek the degree to which the relevant traditional norms still control concrete behavior. After having stressed as strongly as possible the observation that caste norms and values are neither uniform nor stable, it is perhaps needless to add that these brief obiter dicta roughly approximate the prevailing situation rather than describe it with complete accuracy.

1. Occupation. Some continuing relationship between caste origin and occupation in Africa can be discerned, but not in the usual or typical case. Immigrants, whether Hindus or Muslims, came mostly from rural villages in India. In Africa they engage predominantly in the African trade—a business which has no very close counterpart in India. The most direct relationship between caste and occupation can be seen in those businesses which combine a craft skill with retail sales—barbering, tailoring, shoe repairing, and watch repairing are examples. In these instances, the owners and assistants are often, if not invariably, members of the castes traditionally associated with these trades. The correlation does not hold in the inverse direction, however. Not all members of these castes necessarily follow the traditional trade or trades prescribed for their caste. Some natural extensions can be noted; a Mochi shoemaker, for example, may specialize in auto upholstering.

It is also true that the strongly negative evaluation placed traditionally upon some types of occupations helps to steer

147

higher castes away from them in Africa. When we asked a Leva Patidar whether a certain Patel was a Mochi or a Patidar, he grinned broadly and replied that he was a Mochi: "I know, although I don't know him personally. He has a shoe store and a shoe repair business. No Patidar could be in that kind of business!"

Laundry and dry cleaning establishments illustrate some of the ambivalences which inevitably crop up in an attempt to apply the traditional criteria to modern situations. "Laundry and dry cleaning people" is used on occasion as a derogatory epithet, but such businesses are also modern and profitable. Insofar as we know, no such establishment in Central Africa is owned and operated by other than an appropriately low caste family. But we do know of one case in which a modern laundry is owned (not necessarily operated) by a Leva Patidar family in the city of Bombay.

Not surprisingly, the relationship between caste and occupation is strongest in the intimate professional and personal services. No one, needless to say, can chant the *mantras* at a wedding except a Brahman, even in Africa. All of the larger communities have a Nai barber whose monopoly on the Indian haircutting business was assured up until the time of our fieldwork by the color bar enforced in European barber shops.

2. Formal education. A statistical relationship between caste rank and the amount and kind of formal education could certainly be shown within the Indian community in Central Africa. Yet formal education has long since ceased, even in India, to be an exclusive prerogative of the higher castes; and in modern India as elsewhere, education is commonly used as the principal mechanism for socio-economic mobility. With few exceptions, children of the generation growing up in Africa all go to elementary school, irrespective of caste origin. How far beyond elementary school they continue depends more upon the economic status of the family than upon caste origin per se; but since caste and socio-economic status are related to some extent, there is unquestionably *some* relationship between education and caste status.

Older members of the higher castes demonstrably still have difficulty in disassociating the privileges of higher education from caste position. A young Patidar told us that a well-known Anavil leader in his community was "not happy" when he learned that the former planned to proceed with professional training. Most of the young men in the Anavil's family are— or are in the process of becoming—professionals; this of course is "right" and appropriate. Presumably the Anavil is even less happy to see Mochis and Khumbhars becoming professionals.[12] Yet the fact is that they are doing so in ever-increasing numbers.

3. *Subcultural perspectives and values.* Here we can comment only in a most tentative fashion. To do so with any claim to precision would demand nothing less than a definition of a modal personality structure for each caste. This would constitute a carefully designed and executed research project in itself—if in fact it could be done, given the methodological obstacles such a task would confront.

In our own minds we are nonetheless convinced that something approaching a distinctive subculture and correlated social personality exists for the major caste groupings. Indians themselves characteristically think in these terms. A Patidar relates a story illustrative of the point. While working as a commercial traveler a few years ago, he befriended a Mochi woman on a train by helping her to handle the several young children she had with her. In gratitude, the woman invited him to "come and stay with us anytime you like." On his next trip through the woman's town he presented himself at her house:

> When I came in she said, "Are you going to have lunch here?" That's what they always say. But we [i.e. the Patidars] never say that. If a person is with us, then we simply go ahead and cook lunch; if they want to eat, all right; if they don't, all right. But it is there if they want it. We don't insult them by asking ahead of time if they are going to eat.

12. It need hardly be added, we suppose, that this self-same community leader always emphasized his complete severance from the outmoded norms of caste thinking.

149

The assumption that there exists for each caste a distinctive subculture, together with a correlated social personality, is perfectly consistent with all that we know about the relationships between social structure, culture, and personality. Yet if our assessment of the trends now present with respect to caste are correct, it logically follows that the influence of caste upon cultural values and personality is declining rapidly and will continue to do so until it shortly all but disappears.

4. Prestige and social honor. As in the case of occupation and education, there is no doubt that a statistical relationship could be shown to exist between general community prestige and caste rank if one set out to make the demonstration. Taking each group as a whole, the Anavils would certainly appear high in both, the Patidars would unquestionably have a quantitative edge over the Khumbhars, and the Khumbhars would outrank the Mochis, and these in turn the Kolis. Still, the more significant thing is that the higher castes no longer have a monopoly upon either wealth or positions of leadership and that this will soon be even less true than it is now, given a straight-line projection of existing trends. By informal reckoning, the wealthiest family in Zambia is Mochi; and Mochis, Khumbhars, Kolis, and Nais are acknowledged leaders in several communities.

These discrepancies between caste status, leadership, and social honor indicate quite clearly that the really dynamic factors at work here must be sought in *achieved* rather than *ascribed* characteristics, despite the fact that caste still retains some influence as a determinant. This point will be discussed in further detail in the chapter on community organization.

5. Religious practices. In India, cult affiliation and its related practices are strongly influenced by caste. Among the Hindus of Central Africa the relationship between religious practice and caste does not loom very large, for the simple reason that religion plays such a small role in ordinary daily life. Here the most clearly demarcated trend is negative: the tendency is, particularly among young people and the more progressive of all ages, to disassociate religion and caste conceptually.

6. Marital choice. Here is the one area of overt behavior which is still unambiguously controlled by caste norms and values.[13] Even here, however, a drastic shift in the covert (or thought) pattern is plainly evident, and the control which caste now exercises over marital choice will certainly not last much longer. The evidence will be treated more comprehensively in the next chapter.

7. Voluntary associations. Nothing short of a special study very carefully done could determine with precision the extent to which friendship groupings are influenced by caste. That such a relationship exists can scarcely be doubted: it is what one would expect upon the basis of general sociological principles. An Indian sociologist-in-training from the area writes as follows with respect to a Rhodesian community:

> Each caste has its own special values and norms, and members insist on their preservation. . . . [Yet] there is more or less wide freedom in inter-caste associations and contacts. No restrictions of the kind which existed between different castes in ancient India find operation among the Hindus in Salisbury. . . . However, there are certain limitations but no restrictions. Families in the lower rungs of the caste-ladder do not interact so frequently with those in the upper echelons and vice versa. Hence, in family visits, caste is a fairly important determining factor when deciding which family to visit. Consciously or unconsciously, caste comes into the picture and indiscriminate visiting is the exception rather than the rule.[14]

But here again the existing statistical norm is much less significant than the trend away from it. Observation quickly

13. This sentence remains essentially correct, but see below, p. 359.
14. Chagan Lalloo, "The Hindu Family in S. Rhodesia—Traditional versus Modern" (Department of Sociology, University of Lund, Sweden, mimeo., December 1963), p. 25.

reveals friendship circles and clique groups radically mixed by caste: a clique of young men thoroughly familiar to us included a Brahman, a Bania, a couple of Patidars, and a Koli.[15] In one town, the community leadership positions at the time of our fieldwork were firmly occupied by a small and intimate clique of middle-aged men composed of a Khatri Muslim, a Sikh, a Patidar, and a Syrian Christian.

With the traditional barrier against commensality down, common interests and congeniality based in modern cultural values may be more important in determining friendships than caste origins. The determining role which remains to caste in these matters seems to be secondary. Intimate friends may happen to be predominantly of the same caste simply because they are also relatives within the extended family or associates at work.

Formally organized voluntary associations do not play a very important role in the community life of the Indians of Central Africa.[16] A Hindu Association and a Muslim Society (the terminology varies) exist in all the larger towns. In a few instances, there is an Asian Association or Asian Convention which claims to combine both Hindus and Muslims. Sports clubs affiliated with European and African organized athletics are usual. Anything else beyond these predictables is probably a strictly local phenomenon.

Whatever their announced nature or public purpose, formal organizations among the Indians have one outstanding characteristic in common: beneath the facade of formal offices and membership, they tend almost without exception to be highly *informal* in character. In most instances, no dues are collected, no meetings are regularly scheduled, and the officers are self-designated from the little clique who originated the

15. This group has already been mentioned in a different connection. See above, p. 143.

16. As one might expect, voluntary associations are much more important in the larger, more heterogeneous populations of East and South Africa. See Kuper, *Indian People in Natal*, pp. 80–94, and H. S. Morris, "Factions in Indian and Overseas Indian Societies: III. Communal Rivalry among Indians in Uganda," *British Journal of Sociology*, 8 (1957), 306–17.

idea of the club or the convention. The line between the presumptive association and the general community structure is consequently thin indeed, and the organization's meaning and function must therefore be sought in the context of the broader community. Chapter 7 on the community will discuss the role which caste has played in the formation and internal dynamics of such groupings.

Chapter Six

FAMILY AND THE HOUSEHOLD

In no other institutional area does the quality of being Indian impress itself more forcibly upon the observer than in the family and its associated values. Originally organized upon principles radically different from those of western industrial societies, the Indian family still retains enough distinctive qualities in Africa to make it a very different institution from the European family—or, it seems hardly necessary to add, from the African family. Yet increasingly, Indian family behavior is becoming motivated and constrained by norms and values whose origins lie outside the Indian cultural tradition, and the direction taken by these modifications is quite clear. The trend is toward the small nuclear family characteristic of cosmopolitan society and culture: a family in which the marital bond is formed by free choice, in which the internal structure of roles and authority is egalitarian, in which economic rights and obligations do not extend beyond parents and children, and finally in which a severely restricted group of recognized kin is reckoned bilaterally.

True, these generalizations must be made in full awareness of the considerable range of variation applicable in the concrete case. No family in our sample now exhibits all of these cosmopolitan characteristics, and some families seem far removed from them. Yet all show some signs of change in this direction; and some, as we might expect, have changed much

154

more than others. By the convenient ideal-type construction—
beloved by sociologists to whom greater precision is denied—
we have a continuum lying between traditional and modern,
with no family actually conforming to either of the pure types.
In actuality, we also have a fairly wide range of diversity
within families with respect to the members' normative conceptions as to how this unit should be organized.

Indian kinship, like the rest of Indian society and culture,
presents in the concrete a highly complex and greatly elaborated
pattern, with many strictly localized peculiarities of usage and
terminology. The Charotar Patidars, so liberally represented in
our population, may be offered as an illustration. A specialized
feature of their caste subculture is the terminology with which
they refer to the patrilineal lineage, a social and kinship unit
which they share with all other Indians but which, in the course
of their own historical development, they have come to give
distinctive functions. We found, for instance, that the Patidar
terms *khadiki* and *thadiyu* for this patrilineage meant nothing
to a Surti Brahman. "They must be," he said, "local terms of
some non-Hindu tribe or some people like that." But underneath such localized elaborations, specialists assure us, lie
basic principles shared by virtually all the non-tribal peoples of
India, Hindu and Muslim alike.

The most fundamental of these principles is that of unilineal descent in the male line. Unilineal descent is reinforced
by village exogamy, which under premodern conditions effectively prevented much contact with relatives in the female
line. As usual, unilineal descent is expressed in classificatory
terminology; anthropologically unsophisticated Europeans in
Africa are constantly surprised at the number of "brothers"
Indians commonly have. Extended indefinitely into the past,
the entire group of relatives aggregated by this rule of descent
constitutes one's *kul*. However, the known living members of
such a lineage, together with the adult women brought into it
affinally by marriage, constitutes the *khutumb*.[1]

1. Or, alternatively, the *khutumb-kabila*. Muslims, in particular, often drop
the first term and use the second—*kabila*—alone.

155

H. S. Morris points out that Indian terminology shares the ambiguity generally characteristic of kinship systems.[2] Thus we find that in practice the word *ghar* (which narrowly construed means "house" or "house and furnishings") is used more or less interchangeably with *khutumb* and that both are normally translated by informants speaking English into "family" or "joint family." This terminological confusion adds considerably to the "real" socio-cultural confusion created by westernization. We found, for example, that Indian informants seem incapable of making (at least in English) a clear-cut distinction between *khutumb* and *kul,* except that they all recognize that the *kul* assumes a much longer time perspective and constitutes a larger, more abstractly conceived group. When the Brahman referred to above was asked what he understands by *kul* he replied: "Take my case. My family descended from a Brahman ascetic who lived two or three centuries ago. [Note the indefinite 'two or three.'] All of his descendants since that time make up my *kul.*"

Yet when pressed, this comparatively sophisticated informant seemed unsure as to whether or not his *kul* included all his consanguineal relatives or only those in the male line, and this ambiguity is apparently typical. Of course, he knows very well who belongs to his *kul* and who does not, but he cannot state the abstract principle by which membership is determined unambiguously.[3]

2. H. S. Morris, "The Indian Family in Uganda," *American Anthropologist* *61* (1959), 779–89.

3. Women, who in practice are brought into their husband's lineage group by marriage, of course retain the *kul* membership that they acquired at birth. Significantly, therefore, a Patidar informant sees the *kul* as primarily a woman's term; and given the built-in status inequality inherent in the hypergamous system characteristic of his caste, he sees the *kul* as primarily a basis for invidious status comparisons: "The *kul* is your grade-family. For example, my brother's wife has a lower grade than ours. Consequently, when we speak of them, we speak of their *kul.* When two women have an argument or a little quarrel in the house, the first thing which is always brought up is the differences in their respective *kul.* One will immediately say to the other, 'You come from a lower *kul* than I do,' or 'Your *kul* is worse than my *kul.*' In other words, the *khutumb* means the family, but *kul* means the grade."

This of course should not really be surprising. It is axiomatic among sociologists and anthropologists that people take the underlying principles of their social structure for granted, as they do the grammar of their language, and they cannot ordinarily discuss these principles analytically. Still, we are inclined to see more in this particular ambiguity than ordinary confusion. The point is highly relevant to a basic argument.

Informants such as the one just cited have difficulty in recognizing the unilineal character of the underlying principle by which descent is traced, and for good reasons. Since he does, in the concrete instance, recognize his mother's relatives as relatives, what the ethnologist abstractly describes as a "unilineal" descent principle is lost upon him. He lives his kinship system rather than analyzes it, and this much is as true of the Indian village as it is of the Central African town. But at the level of face-to-face social experience and its associated perceptions, a major difference appears in the two situations. Village exogamy means (or, perhaps more correctly, meant prior to modern communications) that one had little contact with the mother's relatives. Under these circumstances, the *khutumb* was perceived in concrete experience as it appears in ethnological analysis, namely, as a localized group of paternal relatives. And it was these relatives in the male line who constituted one's family in practice.

In Africa, however, the exigencies of immigration may mean that the mother's relatives are equally or even more prominent in one's actual social experience than the father's relatives. The same exigencies may also mean that no relatives outside the nuclear family are very important to one immediately and directly. To the extent that either of these possibilities occur, we might expect logically that an interpretation of kinship by the bilateral norms of the non-Indian cosmopolitan culture would be encouraged. We believe on the basis of the evidence which we collected that this is exactly what has happened. But first the *joint family* must be described as an abstract concept and as an existing reality.

THE JOINT FAMILY: IDEAL AND REALITY

While often used and translated as equivalents, a clear-cut distinction between *khutumb* and *joint family* is necessary for sociological analysis. A localized group of relatives aggregated by the traditional kinship principles remains a primary unit of Indian social organization in both India and Africa, despite observable tendencies toward a dilution of its strictly unilineal character. Yet the degree to which the *khutumb* constitutes a joint family in anything like the original sense of the term is quite another matter.

Ideally, the joint family was, as Morris puts it, joint in residence, in worship, and in property.[4] Ideally, again, all members of the *khutumb* in any given village would constitute a concretely organized group and live together in a common household. Actually, the ideal in India was always more of an ideal than a social reality. Being a lawyer as well as an anthropologist, Morris suggests very pertinently that discussions of the Indian joint family in the standard literature have usually been excessively legalistic, thus emphasizing the ideal norm at the expense of the concrete social reality. A great many Indian families—perhaps the majority—have always lived for one reason or another in what were essentially independent nuclear units. Existing joint family households were constantly being divided by internal dissension in prosperity as well as being constantly broken up by disaster and poverty. Traditional Hindu law, simply codifying the mores in these matters, made formal provision for the division of the joint family every third generation. In modern times its property could always be legally divided by common agreement among its constituent adult male members.

Some approximation of the joint family arrangement was nonetheless the cultural ideal; and among those of substance and status in the community, the ideal was regularly put into practice. It is important to recognize in this connection that

4. Morris, p. 780.

even an isolated nuclear family of husband, wife, and dependent children was still perceived as "joint" legally and culturally, the presumption always being that it contained the nucleus out of which hopefully a large and thriving joint family organization would emerge in the future.

Economically, the joint family was in theory a cooperative and communal enterprise in which all adult male members had an equal share. With respect to work and consumption the reigning rule was "from each according to his ability, to each according to his need." In power and authority, however, the joint family was anything but egalitarian, in either theory or practice. It constituted in this respect a pyramid of age and sex, the ultimate power of decision-making being lodged in the oldest male: grandfather, father, or eldest brother. Formal authority was minutely graded in definition and supported symbolically by kinship terminology and customary behavior. A younger brother, for example, indicated subordination to an older brother—real or classificatory—by attaching the suffix *–bhai* to his name when addressing him. Moreover, he was supposed to show proper respect by certain symbolic avoidances, such as not smoking or using undignified language in the older brother's presence. On the other hand, the head of the family was expected to give equal treatment to everyone in any given sex-and-generation status. In particular, he was supposed to treat all of his brother's sons with the same consideration that he would his own.

The ideal norms defining authority, responsibilities, and obligations within the extended family were of course applicable in theory whether or not the *khutumb* actually constituted a co-residential unit. Naturally, they were much easier to apply in practice if the *khutumb* did live in a common household.

Immigration to Africa bifurcated the *khutumb* geographically, thus preventing it from constituting a joint family in the literal sense of co-residence. But in theory and in hope, as Indians themselves saw these matters, the emigration of some of its members did not destroy or even weaken the *khutumb* as a tightly knit, cooperative social unit. On the contrary, in-

159

sofar as the emigrants prospered in Africa, the assumption was that the *khutumb* as a whole would be strengthened by a broadening of its economic base.

Furthermore, there was originally no anticipation that the physical separation imposed by emigration would be either permanent or continuous. When he came to Africa, the Indian pioneer had no intention whatsoever of remaining there. Exactly how long he was to stay was left indeterminate, but in any case, his purpose in coming to Africa was to make money, not to make a home. Like the modern suburban commuter, of whom it has been said that he works where he would rather not live and lives where he would rather not work, the Indian immigrant sojourned in Africa rather than lived there. Home remained in India, and he returned there as often as he could. Ideally, the immigrant stayed three years in Africa and one in India—although like all ideals, this was often compromised in practice. It was adhered to closely enough, nevertheless, so that many of the older adults in the community have spent a good part of their lives shuttling back and forth between Africa and India. When you were not on one of these prolonged visits yourself, someone close to you was, thus maintaining a constant flow of news and gossip concerning kinsmen and the affairs of the natal village back and forth across the Indian ocean.[5] By these means substance was given to the ideal of the joint family, the values of which constantly appear in the data. A Patidar pioneer commented:

My father has been dead for forty years, but the paternal property in India [consisting of a house and land] is still undivided. Both my brother [the eldest brother, who continues to head the *khutumb* there] and I still contribute to it. But it is neither my brother's nor mine. It's the family's.

5. These generalizations apply more to the two northern countries than they do to Rhodesia, where the earlier closure of immigration forced Indians to "settle down," psychologically as well as physically.

Society, nonetheless, is more than a structure of norms alone. Norms must be constantly reinforced by action, and here again is a case in point. Time and circumstances have tended to weaken the solidarity of a *khutumb* that is split between India and Africa. Very little in our material suggests that when the children of the present African-born generation reach adulthood they will identify themselves importantly with the India-based branch of the *khutumb*—and there is much that suggests they will not.

In Africa the norms and values supporting *khutumb* solidarity and the joint family are still very much alive. But they are strong and relatively undiluted only among those persons who grew to adulthood in India, and they are by no means universal even there. It is obvious when actual family behavior is examined that these older norms and values are in severe and unequal competition with newer and non-Indian conceptions from the cosmopolitan culture.

Family Organization

Family organization in the concrete case is a range of variation from units approximating fairly closely the traditional joint family principles to aggressively individualistic families, living as best they can in independent isolation. These poles constitute the extremes; most families fall somewhere in between. A fairly detailed look at some actual families lying along this continuum may help to flesh out the abstract generalization.

The A's are Anavil by caste, and they are one of the three extended families in a large Northern Rhodesian town who seem determined to live by the traditional norms. The core of this family consists of four married "brothers"—three siblings and a paternal first cousin—who range in age from the early twenties to the early forties. In keeping with joint family principles, the oldest of the four is the accepted head. Together, they operate as a firm of commercial agents, and they live together in one house, with the exception of one of the brothers who manages a branch office in a neighboring town. He is in constant communication with the others, however, and there is much visiting back and forth.

As Morris points out, English law makes no provision for joint family business arrangements in either legal organization or tax matters.[6] Legally, therefore, Indian joint family businesses are compelled to assume one of three forms in Africa: (1) they are legally held in the name of the oldest member, it simply being understood that the others have an equal share; or (2) they may be simple partnerships, as most statistically are; or (3) they may be incorporated into limited companies, as virtually all of the really large firms are, whether they make any pretense of being joint or not.

The A's business is legally of the second type. "When we are asked by the officials," the head explained to us, "we tell them that our business is a partnership by mutual consent." For the benefit of income tax collectors, profits are divided and paid as salaries to each of the members; but by family reckoning these salaries are family rather than individual property and are put into a common family account. When one of the brothers wants money for any purpose, he is required by the rules to write a check on this account so that there will be a record of exactly how much he has drawn and how the money was spent. Again, the head explains: "Nobody ever spends cash. Then one of us can't say, 'Look, so-and-so is spending more money than I am. I am working and saving, and he is spending it.' "

In describing the way in which money is allocated, he stressed that there is no attempt to regulate too closely the expenditures for strictly personal items. Really expensive things like automobiles are family matters for collective decision. But for small items and pocket money each brother is free to take what he likes, keeping only in mind that he may be called upon to justify the expenditure:

If one of us wants a fancy silk shirt or an expensive suit,

6. Morris, pp. 786–88.

then he buys it, while maybe the other one says, "I will be content with an ordinary cotton one." [The informant is wearing a cheap and ostentatiously well-worn shirt while he is speaking.] Or maybe one brother wants a piece of jewelry for his wife. If he does, he goes ahead and buys it; he doesn't have to get the consent of the others.

It is clear, nonetheless, that the head believes it is one of his duties and prerogatives to offer advice and guidance on these matters, but he points out that the authority so exercised demands great tact:

Maybe I think that a certain expenditure is not advisable at this time. Then I say, "Look, can't you put this off?" or, "Can't you do without awhile? I think that this money would be better spent on the children's education." It's the duty of the head of the family to give such advice when he thinks it is right. But he has to be careful. If he clamps down too hard, then there is a quarrel and maybe the family itself will break up.

The B family illustrates how well grounded is the fear of internal dissension expressed by the head of the A's. The B's are well-to-do Muslims who operate a combined industrial and commercial concern upon what was described as true joint family principles, i.e. joint in property and in household. The core of the family in this case consists of two middle-aged men, a paternal uncle and a nephew. The nephew is close to the uncle in age, and each man has married sons.

This family seemed so closely knit that we long took it for granted that they were one of the few families in our sample who really approximated the traditional ideal. Yet having learned in time how volatile Indian kinship relations are— which strike the westerner as being both singularly close and singularly quarrelsome—it came as no surprise to hear near the end of the original fieldwork that the uncle and nephew had quarreled bitterly, that the nephew had left the house which all had shared, and that he was seeking a lawyer to divide up the business. What did really surprise us was that it was apparently the third time this had happened, the prior difficulties having never been called to our attention.[7]

The C's represent a compromise between traditional modes of cooperative living in a single household and *unequal* private shares in a cooperative business enterprise, a pattern which is exceedingly common, with variations as to details. The C family consists of three Khumbhar brothers (siblings), all married. They own and operate a prosperous business, but there is no pretense that ownership is joint, as the traditional norms would insist. It is an unequal partnership with the eldest brother, who established the business before he "called" the younger ones to Africa, holding the largest share. Income is divided by shares, and each brother considers his income his own, to do with as he pleases without consulting the others.

The C's do live together in a single household and apparently get along without much friction. Nevertheless, while showing us around the new house which they had recently built, the eldest brother took it upon himself to point out that the house was so constructed that it could easily be divided into three completely separate units, each with its own entrance. "We wanted a house large enough so that we could all live in it," he said, "but we decided we had better fix it up this way just in case there is a quarrel."

An even more common pattern than the C's exemplify is close economic cooperation among a group of kinsmen without either common property or inclusive co-residence. The members of such a group may, significantly, sometimes refer to themselves as a joint family. The D's, well-to-do Anavils, serve nicely as an illustration.

There are five D brothers in Africa, and these in turn maintain close contact with a sixth (the eldest) who is the head of the *khutumb* in India. A son of one of the brothers, who was born in Africa and sent at an early age to his uncle's house in India for schooling, once remarked to us:

7. A check in 1966 showed this final division to be permanent.

I never felt that I was an outsider while I was in India. You see, we are used to living in a joint family. And it so happened that the headmaster of the school I attended was an uncle [classificatory] of mine, and another uncle [also classificatory] was a professor in the college which I later attended. With you Europeans, an uncle is just a relative. You are friendly, and you visit him sometimes, but it is a different relationship among us Indians. In the absence of my father these uncles of mine felt the same obligations toward me that a father would feel toward his sons, and they treated me in exactly the same way in which they would treat one of their own sons.

These remarks reveal the living reality of joint family *values;* but in fact the D's do not constitute, concretely, a joint family in Africa, even though this informant says they do. The D's property is not held in common; nor do they live together in a common household, although there is so much visiting back and forth that one might easily get this impression. "In our case," as one of the brothers himself remarked, "we fall somewhere between complete independence and the traditional joint family. As brothers, we do business together, but we live separately."

Being a scholarly man, he went on to make the familiar point that while the joint family is well suited to a subsistence agricultural economy, it is ill-adapted to modern urban conditions. He laid particular stress upon the now greater independence of women, a factor sharpened by education and urban sophistication:

Living in a joint family may become very difficult, particularly in those cases in which the women have some education. With education, your perspectives on the world broaden. You know more and you have more ideas. And when people think more, there is more room for conflict. Ordinary people never think; they just act according to custom. Having no ideas, they can live happily together. But with educated people there is bound to be friction.

165

The last family in this series is clearly atypical but not nearly so much as the first which tries so hard to maintain the traditional ideal. E is the nephew of a well-to-do Anavil merchant in a large Northern Rhodesian town, and he was brought to Africa in the usual way by his uncle to work as a shop assistant. But E, who appeared to be a rather bristly young man, soon began to feel exploited and abused. Such sentiments are usual among young shop assistants, but E's action with respect to them is not, although he had plenty of precedents. He quit his job in his uncle's shop and took up employment with a Sindhi firm, thus asserting independence not only from his uncle but from all fellow Gujaratis as well. (In similar cases, others have gained economic independence by seeking employment in the opposite religious group or with Europeans.) E and his wife and their two small children now live alone in a small modern apartment, determined, as he put it to us, to stay hereafter entirely away from relatives.

The E's behavior is certainly not typical; still, they have a fair amount of company. If we assess current trends correctly, they represent the pattern of the future. In the meantime the older values live on and die hard.

A well-to-do Mochi of humble origins shows us around the large new house which he built. He proudly points out to us that the house is so constructed that three families can live in it comfortably. One of his two sons has recently married and lives with him; the other is to be married shortly. We ask: "Then both of your sons will stay in the business and live with you?" He replies: "Yes, I hope so!" His voice wavers, thus conveying a little of how desperately he hopes and how much he fears that these hopes may be ill-grounded.

Another father of a large family of sons and daughters unfolds an elaborate scheme for the future, surely much too complicated in all its contingencies to work out as he plans it. Undaunted, the old man (a Patidar pioneer) goes ahead implementing his plan, step by step. The eldest son will take over the existing business. One son is to be a doctor. A daughter is already married to a doctor and another to a pharmacist. Contrary to traditional practice, the father half hopes that these sons-in-law can be induced to come and live with him. In any case, one of his sons will become a pharmacist and has an eye toward the development of a drug manufacturing business. Another will be trained in modern commercial and accounting methods. By and by the cogs of this machine-in-the-making will hopefully mesh to produce a flourishing medical clinic and associated drug concern, financed initially out of capital supplied by the parent enterprise in the African trade. All are to live happily together—perhaps not literally together but in the same town—in one large prosperous and thoroughly modernized joint family. Such is the stuff that an Indian father's dreams are made of.

The fact that this father dreams—however unrealistically— that his *daughters'* husbands will be incorporated into his modernized joint family illustrates how the unilineal descent principle has weakened in practice. Unilineal descent, as we have already pointed out, was reinforced in traditional India by its corollary: village exogamy. The aggregation of a closely related kin group in Africa, however, was never in practice strictly confined to the patrilineage. The result is that young Indians growing up in Africa may be as intimate with their maternal relatives as they are with those of the paternal line, and in some instances, more so.

Immigration to Africa was guided and directed to a very large extent along kinship lines, but the motivation to immigrate must be understood mainly in economic terms. A pioneer, once established, proceeded to "call" others from India. He did so in both his own interest—in order to expand his business—and in theirs—to give them economic opportunity. The first people whom he thought of were his most intimate younger brothers—real and classificatory—and their immediate offspring. Insofar as his choice was confined to these relatives, the *khutumb* was unchanged in principle from what it had been in India, except that the effective leadership of the branch based in Africa was shifted to the original settler, irrespective of his status in the lineage as constituted in India.

167

But very often the pioneer's business demanded more assistants than could be readily found within his own *khutumb*. In such circumstances, before he considered nonrelatives (and ultimately even strangers from outside his village), he turned to his wife's relatives. These clearly constituted a second choice by traditional values, but they were a *second,* not a third or fourth alternative. The reasons lie in the Indian mode of organizing and conducting business—a matter considered in more detail in the following chapter.[8]

Briefly, the reasons for preferring relatives lay in the degree to which the Indian business demands honesty and loyalty. Presumably a man might trust his own relatives more than those of his wife; but on the other hand the ties of kinship provided through the wife were that much better than none at all. Yet practically speaking, we come here to a fact of great importance. The degree to which the kinship tie to the wife's relatives could be successful economically *depended upon the degree to which these relatives were in fact treated as relatives.* In practice, it is clear, these relatives were inclined to make demands in the name of kinship not essentially different from those coming from the patrilineage.

These pressures toward bilateralism in practice are strongly reinforced by the numerous changes which have tended to equalize women's formal socio-economic and legal status with that of men. The strong-minded modern wife may insist that *her* relatives receive something like equal consideration with those of her husband. To the extent that she is successful in pressing her claims, the effect is a weakening of the unilineal principle.

The kind of strain produced in the traditional normative definition of kinship by the new social situation in Africa can be illustrated by reference once again to the "D" family discussed in the last section. The husband of a sister of one of the D wives operates a small and none-too-productive shop located in one of their buildings. He has been given his chance

8. Cf. pp. 203–05.

to make his fortune in Africa; but beyond this bit of help, the D's apparently try to hold to the traditional norms. It seems to be understood that he is now expected to go it alone. Certainly it is obvious enough that this brother-in-law is not treated in the same manner as he would be if he were one of the brothers and thus a *khutumb* member. He and his family live independently in small crowded quarters behind their shop. When they look out of their single rear window, they see across the way their brother-in-law's house, large and spacious. Their poverty stands in sharpest contrast to the affluence of the D's. Yet the wife is in close daily association with her sister's family, and so are her children. They are not tucked away, as they would be in India, by the rule of exogamy in another village.

There is no concrete evidence in this particular case that relations between the brothers-in-law are anything but amiable. Speaking generally, however, such relationships are often a source of conflict, since rights and obligations between kinsmen from different lineages are traditionally much less firmly defined than those within the *khutumb*. Charges of ingratitude on the one hand and exploitation on the other thus frequently occur when kinsmen from the paternal and maternal lineages attempt close economic cooperation. In the family of one community leader, this situation has led to great dissension and much bitterness.

Too much should not be made, however, of the presumed solidarity arising from descent reckoned by traditional principles in contrast to the difficulties of the new tendencies toward bilateralism. Now that the old rule of common shares in a joint property has been so generally abandoned, marked differences in age and affluence may create very differently perceived interests within the *khutumb*, thus producing conflict as sharp as that between maternal and paternal relatives. E, for example, is a close *khutumb* relative by the traditional principles. This does not prevent him from feeling exploited by his uncle.

THE HOUSEHOLD

Indian households are apt to give the Western observer an impression of serious crowding, regardless of the degree to which the family is actually joint or not, or whether it is rich or poor. Members of a poor family, living in nuclear isolation behind their shop, are crowded because they have so little space. But rich families living in large houses are crowded too. Indians think space exists to be used and it is. Beds typically line the walls of all the rooms except the kitchen. Dining tables are long, and one is always struck by the number of chairs.

Table 8 provides some official statistics (now unfortunately somewhat dated) on the size of Asian households as measured by number of persons. In the main cities of the Rhodesias, it will be noted, twenty percent of the Asian households consisted of nine persons or more.[9] The lower percentage in this category for Nyasaland is to be accounted for mainly by the greater tendency there for Indians to live in small, behind-the-shop quarters.

The first and most important reason for the near-universal impression of crowding is the comparatively large number of children. Some of the younger people are beginning to practice birth control, but the number of children in what demographers call "completed families" typically runs to five or six or more. This is true whether the family is rich or poor.

The second reason applies particularly to the well-to-do. Several shop assistants or employees may live with their employer, thereby extending the number in his household. This practice was more prevalent in the immediate past than it is now, although it is still common; it used to be taken for granted that a shop assistant would live with the man who had "called" him and for whom he worked. In any case, it is still true that virtually no Indian lives alone in bachelor quarters. A young assistant who is either unmarried or whose wife is

9. Figures from the 1961 census are available only for Rhodesia. When compared to those in Table 8, little overall difference appears, except that the percentage of Asian households containing nine persons and over increased from 21.5 percent to 28.8 percent.

TABLE 8. EUROPEAN AND ASIAN HOUSEHOLDS*
BY NUMBER OF PERSONS PER HOUSEHOLD
IN SELECTED URBAN AREAS
OF CENTRAL AFRICA, 1956

	Salisbury and Bulawayo Municipalities and Suburbs		Lusaka and Ndola Municipalities and Suburbs		Blantyre-Limbe Municipality	
Persons per Household	*European*	*Asian*	*European*	*Asian*	*European*	*Asian*
1–4	75.9%	30.0%	77.3%	36.6%	82.3%	55.3%
5–8	23.2	48.5	22.0	43.0	17.1	37.3
9 and over	.9	21.5	.7	20.4	.6	7.4
Total	100.0%	100.0%	100.0%	100.0%	100.0%	100.0%
Total numbers	25,877	400	4,159	216	672	405

* Household defined as (1) lodgers (not boarders) living on their own, and (2) a group of two or more persons both living and having their meals together.

Source: Federation of Rhodesia and Nyasaland, *Census of Population: 1956*, Tables 65 and 67.

still in India (a fairly common situation) lives with some family, irrespective of whether that family is his employer's or not—and it usually is.

Thirdly, there is the fact that the Indian household is constantly being swelled in number by visitors of one kind or another, some of whom stay for considerable periods of time. Visitors who present themselves are always accommodated, no matter how many other people are already present. When the available beds are taken, mattresses are borrowed from neighbors and laid on the floor. If necessary there is an extra relay or two at the table. This visiting pattern involves everyone. A well-to-do family, however, will have more visitors than a poor one, not only because their kinship circle is wider (and visitors are often kin) but also because of a constant stream of visitors on business. Some families may almost literally never eat a meal without having an outsider present. Conversely, commercial agents may travel for weeks at a time without ever paying for a meal or a hotel room. Indians were of course not allowed in the European hotels until recently. But it is safe to say that commercial transient facilities are still not used very widely by Indians even though restrictions have been lifted outside of Rhodesia.

MARRIAGE AND SEX ROLES

In or out of marriage, relationships between the sexes among the Indians are still different enough from modern European customs to offer a sharp contrast in pattern. Arranged marriage, dowries, caste endogamy, marriage circles, plural marriage, child marriage, and partial seclusion of women are phenomena well known as verbal abstractions. To meet them for the first time in the behavior of living people, however, is a different matter: unmistakably one is now confronted with real rather than hypothetical differences in culture. Yet, as elsewhere in Indian social organization, a clear-cut drift in the direction of cosmopolitan norms is easily discernible once we look beneath the exotic surface.

1. Age at marriage. Child marriage, a much publicized and much misunderstood feature of traditional Indian family organization, is now a matter of history within this population.[10] A number of informants in their late forties and fifties were nonetheless married as children.

> I was married at the age of twelve. My wife was ten. My parents had arranged the marriage and got us engaged when I was only seven. Of course we weren't really married until later. We didn't even know what to be engaged and to be married meant. After we were married we used to play together out in the yard when my wife's family visited us. It was just like two children playing together nowadays, except that in this case the other child happened to be my wife.

10. This particular custom has of course been under a long and vigorous attack by reformers. Since the passage of the Sarda Bill in 1929, it has been illegal in India. Cf. O'Malley, *Modern India and the West*, pp. 360–61, 451–52.

Age at marriage remained low by European standards after child marriage ceased to be generally practiced. A major reason is easily apparent. Heavy dowries are to this day usual in most castes. This has meant that daughters were a serious financial burden, and parents have typically sought to relieve their anxieties with respect to them by getting their marriages arranged as soon as possible. Sons brought money into the family rather than taking it out, but the pressures for an early settlement were present in their case as well. To a hard pressed father—perhaps brought to the edge of financial ruin by payments made for his daughters—the lure of a sizable dowry might become a virtual obsession. A thirty-year-old Charotar Patidar explains his case:

> I was only eighteen when I got married. But I didn't want to get married.

> Dotson: Why did you have to?

> You know in the Indian family the young people don't have any say about who they marry or when they get married. It's our parents who decide these things. From the time I was seventeen my father began to insist that I get married and he found my wife for me and made all the arrangements. In our community [i.e. his caste], a girl brings with her a payment of perhaps 30,000 rupees. That's what my wife brought. And a man may be anxious to get his hands on that money so that he can use it in his business. You should understand that I didn't get that 30,000 rupees. It was paid to my father. All of the arrangements are between fathers. So consequently if a man needs money, he forces his sons to get married sooner than they otherwise might want to.

Adequate statistics for the Indian population of Central Africa would doubtlessly show that age at marriage has tended to rise in recent years, contrary to the recent European experience. In part the change reflects a greater respect for the wishes of the young people involved—and boys in particular seem in no hurry. It also reflects the fact that young people, including girls, are getting much more education than formerly. Education is a prized asset in the marriage market for both boys and girls, and this new value tends to raise the age of marriage. A girl of eighteen or nineteen, if still unmarried, would have been getting dangerously old only a few years ago; now, if she is still in school, she is increasing her desirability. Muslims have lagged behind Hindus in this respect, but they too have changed recently. Age at marriage in both groups currently approximates the European norms rather closely.

2. Caste endogamy. Caste endogamy is still the strict rule: when we began our fieldwork, we were assured time and time again that there were only four publicly known cases of caste intermarriage among Hindus in the whole of Central Africa.[11] Owing to the ambiguity of "caste" among Muslims, it is less easy to be so categorical with respect to them; nonetheless, insofar as could be determined, there is no essential difference between the two groups. The one case of intercaste marriage within the Muslim community personally known to us aroused a great deal of highly derogatory comment—most of which, it is needless to add, was not explicitly in caste terms.

To discuss the trend with respect to caste endogamy intelligently, we need to distinguish the *thought* from the *action* (or performance) pattern. Among the progressive and "modern-minded," there is little doubt that the thought pattern has shifted radically. Yet, since the rule against intercaste marriage is all but universally respected, there is no difference at the performance level between liberals and conservatives. A young African-born Hindu radical described in detail how his younger sister had had, at his insistence, an opportunity for a "truly romantic courtship experience." But we noted that she had had it with an eligible young man from her own caste. Still, man being the symbolic animal he is, the change in the

11. "A very small number of marriages have recently taken place between members of different castes and even outside the community itself." Lalloo, "The Hindu Family in S. Rhodesia," p. 50.

thought pattern doubtlessly indicates that a change in the action pattern is not far behind. Within the next generation we predict that intercaste marriage will become common.

The very thought of intercaste marriage still brings a shudder down the spines of the traditional-minded. "Yes! They are killing themselves!" exclaimed an older informant when we brought up the subject with respect to the South African Indians. And he then added prophetically, "I am afraid that it will soon be the same here!" But to the modern-minded, the thought of intercaste marriage holds none of its traditional terrors, although the fear of adverse criticism prevents them from putting belief into action. In the following exchange, marriage plans for a son were discussed with a thoroughly secularized father who grew up in Africa.

Dotson: Would it worry you if your son married outside of your caste?

No, not at all. I wouldn't care. It wouldn't bother me a bit. I personally don't believe in this caste business at all. I think it should be done away with. And it will be in time, too. But you know as long as the law [i.e. the custom] holds, it is hard for the individual to break it. One never knows what the reaction of other people will be. Consequently, you are afraid. You hate to be the first.

3. Marriage circles. Within some communities, marriage is complicated far beyond the requirements of caste endogamy by established "marriage circles." The Charotar Patidars, for example, must not only marry another Patidar, but he must also marry into a family of suitable status and prestige from some six particular villages.[12] To the African-born Patidars these highly complicated rules may seem almost as ridiculous as they would to the ordinary European. A twenty-three-year-old young man from the caste who was born in Africa explained why he is in no hurry to get married:

You Europeans marry whom you want to, and that is all there is to it. But you know in our community you can't

12. Pocock, "Inclusion and Exclusion," pp. 19–31.

marry just anyone you want to. We have a whole series of different circles, and you have to marry into the right one. It's all very complicated and very silly. But [said with an expressive shrug of the shoulders] it's the custom and there is nothing you can do about it.

4. Marital choice.   Marriages are still universally arranged, and finding suitable mates for their young people is a task of no mean proportion for many families, considering all the contingencies involved. Assistance therefore is generally sought through whatever contacts the parents have, the most important being those within the extended family. Help is all the more necessary considering that the search must in most cases be carried outside Central Africa: in India, in the main, but increasingly also in South and East Africa. Some few marriages are now being managed locally. This is particularly true among Muslims, where the problem of finding mates is made much easier by the possibility of marriage within the extended family.

These problems become particularly acute with respect to African-born daughters. Under federal immigration law, Indian women could not find husbands in India without, in effect, losing their citizenship since they could not, like their brothers, bring their spouses to live with them in Africa.

Nor, increasingly, is marriage simply a matter of finding someone who fits the formal requirements of caste and astrological compatibility. Immigration has meant social as well as physical mobility for most families. Such qualifications as education, personality, and relative family prestige now enter into the picture along with all the traditional criteria. A family with a daughter educated beyond the elementary level, for example, must attempt to find a husband for her with comparable or superior education if the prestige it has gained by educating her is not to be lost.

In such a case, too, the daughter might very well refuse to marry an uneducated husband, which brings us to another important change. Marriages are still arranged in all of their essentials, but young people are nonetheless given veto power. The day is past when a young couple found themselves staring at each other for the first time at the wedding ceremony itself. Young people are now anxiously consulted as negotiations proceed, and alternatives are discussed.[13]

Negotiations now commonly lead ultimately to a direct "interview" (the term used by Indians when speaking English), during which the young couple are left alone together for perhaps half an hour. Alternatively, an ostensibly casual meeting or two may be arranged in someone's home so that they may look each other over. An informant says of his interview:

> I have told you that my village is not far from X [in India]. The village where my wife lived was on the other side of X. So it was agreed that we should meet at Y [i.e. in the house of an intermediary in a village half-way between the two home villages]. We went upstairs alone and sat down and talked. We talked mainly about my position in Africa and what life was like out here. She agreed to marry me. There was nothing said about love, but I liked the looks of the girl.

In other words, young people already exercise several more degrees of freedom in marital choice than traditional practice allowed. The trend is clearly in the direction of still more. A glimpse of the processes at work to enlarge choice can be seen concretely in the following case.

A prominent pioneer father has a twenty-one-year-old African-born son who is still unmarried and is without plans to do so. The father is visibly agitated over the delay. Naturally, he did not emphasize the point, but the truth is he has recently suffered business reverses, and he could use the substantial dowry which the marriage would bring. Nor is the difficulty a lack of attractive offers: the father has been approached

---

13. The groom, in particular, may come to feel that he has made a "free choice." When we asked a young man about to depart for India to get married if he had a particular young lady in mind, he replied: "No, I haven't. Not really. My mother has made up a list [after, we can be sure, a great deal of spade-work]. When I get there I will make my own choice."

several times by representatives from families anxious to contract such a desirable alliance. The difficulty simply is that
the young man drags his heels. He feels that he is being pushed,
and any attempts to get him to choose between the several
alternatives offered only increase the considerable tension
which already exists in the father-son relationship. So the old
man throws up his hands and says:

> We have to remember that we are not living in India, and
> things are done differently out here. I have told my son
> that he will have to find a wife himself. It's going to be
> his choice from now on. I don't want him saying later,
> "Look, you have ruined my life for me!" After he has
> decided who he would like, then of course we will go ahead
> and make the arrangements in the usual way. But I don't
> want to be put in a position where it looks like I am making
> up his mind for him.

More freedom in marital choice, however, has still not led
to anything remotely resembling Western dating practices.
Relationships between young unmarried people of the opposite
sex are reserved when they are not restricted, as they are apt
to be in conservative Muslim households. Significantly, there
is no pairing off by either the married or the unmarried on
public occasions. At the local cinema, for example, women,
girls, and small children sit on one side of the hall, the men
and the boys on the other. Among Hindus and among the
more modern Muslims, young people of the two sexes talk
and sit near each other casually enough in the home without
embarrassment. But there is no intimacy and there is certainly
no overt expression of sexual interest. Nor is there as yet, insofar as could be determined, any very strongly felt need
among young people themselves for greater freedom of association.[14]

It need hardly be pointed out, perhaps, that to the traditional-minded the degree of social promiscuity between the

14. These generalizations were accurate enough at the time of our original
fieldwork. But see below, p. 359.

unmarried sexes common in both European and African societies is downright repulsive. Such people say to a European
without apology, "Our culture is superior to yours in this
respect," confident that the European will acknowledge the
superiority without question. Even the more liberal Indians
tend to be conservative on this point; as a concession to the
European point of view they may simply say that Indians are
not yet ready for this degree of personal freedom. For both
progressives and conservatives in Central Africa, the Khoja
Ismaelis of East Africa—whose young women wear frocks and
cosmetics, cut their hair, date in the European fashion for the
cinema, and "get married along the road home" afterward—
serve as horrible examples of the dangers inherent in too much
westernization.

As a final word on these matters, for what it is worth, we
never heard personally of a single case of illicit relations between Indian men and Indian women in Africa throughout
the original fieldwork period. This is hardly tantamount to
saying that illicit relations never occur, but compared to most
populations, they certainly must be rare.[15]

5. Wedding ceremonies. Weddings are not yet commonly
performed in Central Africa, for the simple reason that mates
are usually found elsewhere. There are, however, some local
weddings and the number has been increasing. Both Hindus
and Muslims follow traditional forms for wedding rites, the
important modification being a radical shortening of the ritual.
Traditionally, the Hindu ceremony was often a twelve-hour
affair. By drastic excisions of everything "but the bare essentials," this has been cut down to one or two hours in Africa.[16]
Judged by the impatience of the audience, even this seems to
be more than is really wanted. Modern urban man, apparently,

15. But, again, as a significant index of change in these matters, we did
hear of one such case upon our return to Africa in 1966.
16. A young and thoroughly secularized Brahman could not resist a quip
when he recalled these twelve-hour ordeals: "At the end of that ceremony, the
bridegroom was so tired that all he could do was say to the bride, 'Sorry!
I'll see you tomorrow!'" In terms of content, Hindu wedding ritual consists
of *mantras* (i.e. chanted prayers and invocations) and a series of ritual acts
involving fire, food, ghee, flowers, and symbolic monetary exchanges.

will not tolerate the extended ritual which provided interest and drama to his forefathers in the rural village.

Well-to-do families among both Hindus and Muslims are expected to provide a feast after a wedding, although it seems clear that this expectation is more binding on the former than on the latter. Everyone within the family's religious community must be invited, and some guests from the opposite group, Hindu or Muslim, commonly attend. Food is prepared in huge pots that are made especially for this kind of occasion; the cooking is done by male volunteers over open pits dug outdoors, and the quality suffers accordingly. Special delicacies are prepared at home for several days before the wedding by the bride's female relatives. Guests are served from steaming buckets of food as they sit cross-legged in long lines upon the floor of the community hall.

Significantly, there is no attempt at caste segregation in either the preparation or the serving of the food. All eat together. Of this aspect of the Hindu wedding in Africa, a high caste individual remarked disgustedly: "In India our marriages are very simple. There, only the family and a few friends are invited. They are not the ostentatious affairs that they are here. Here, every single Hindu in the community has to be invited." That Hindu weddings in India are typically "very simple" affairs will be news to ethnographers, who have consistently reported otherwise. What this informant refers to of course is the social promiscuity forced upon the higher castes by developments in Africa, which will be explored in detail in the next chapter.

A large wedding is an expensive affair. Food alone may cost as much as a thousand pounds. For this reason, a great many of the younger people are increasingly highly critical of this part of the received culture. Expensive weddings and the even more costly dowries which normally go with them seem to these critics at best a waste of money and at worst a very serious and senseless burden upon people who can ill afford them. There is thus a strong current of sentiment in favor of change toward the infinitely less complicated European pattern, which many young people openly envy.

Still, the forces at work here are not all in the same direction. It would be rash indeed, in our opinion, to confidently predict an early end to either the dowry system or the large wedding pattern. Families complain bitterly about the cost of both dowries and weddings; yet at the same time they take obvious pride in the size of both—which, incidentally, tends to get humanly exaggerated in the telling. And the simple fact seems to be that in the immediate past both dowries and weddings have apparently grown in size rather than declined.

The reason for this is not terribly obscure. Ruinous as they may be under certain circumstances, these affairs effectively symbolize socio-economic status in an unambiguous fashion, and they do so in a culture which otherwise tends to limit conspicuous display severely. A thumping dowry for its daughter and a really bang-up wedding announce in a manner which cannot be ignored the socio-economic prowess of what is perhaps a family of quite humble origins.

For these reasons, it would seem safer to predict that both the dowry system and the large wedding pattern will continue until functional equivalents for symbolizing gains in status through social mobility are evolved and accepted. In the long run, however, both are inconsistent with the demands of a high standard of living based in a mass-consumption economy and will thus die out in time.

6. Plural marriage. Most immigrant informants can recall Hindus in their own or neighboring villages in India with more than one wife. These were nearly always, we were assured, cases in which the first wife was barren, incurably sick, or insane. Divorce being impossible, this was the only means of fulfilling the strongly-felt religious prescription that one must have progeny. It is also always pointed out by these informants that under recent legislation new plural marriages have been declared illegal in India.

To the best of our knowledge, there are no Hindus in Central

Africa with more than one recognized wife. We have been told of cases in which a Hindu married a wife in Africa in addition to the one he already had in India; but legally and socially, these cases are viewed as bigamy rather than true plural marriage, since it is apparent that the man always lied about his marital status when contracting the second.

The situation is formally different among the Muslims, where plural marriage is religiously sanctioned. Yet insofar as can be determined, it seems doubtful if plural marriage was much more common among Muslims in those areas in India from which our population was drawn than it was among Hindus.

Plural marriage exists among Indian Muslims in Central Africa, but it is exceedingly rare. We personally know of only two cases, although there are undoubtedly more. In one of these, a well-to-do man in his mid-thirties who already had six children by his first wife married a young woman and built a separate house for her in a neighboring town. Informants were reluctant to discuss this case; it seems very clear that public opinion within the community strongly condemned it. In the second instance, a middle-aged man whose wife had suffered from a long and incapacitating chronic illness married another before the first wife died. This marriage was accepted, although somewhat begrudgingly, by the man's relatives and supporters —and, not unnaturally, strongly condemned by his personal enemies, who welcomed it as ammunition to be used against him.

7. Divorce. Despite the ease with which divorce is technically possible under Koranic law, it is nearly as rare among Muslim Indians in Central Africa as it is among Hindus—a telling commentary upon the essential similarity of the family institution in the two groups. The one divorce which turned up among the families interviewed was that of a Hindu rather than a Muslim.

Since Europeans in Central Africa have one of the highest divorce rates in the world, the difference between them and the Indians in this respect is particularly striking. The official statistics, which do not do justice to the real difference, are presented in Table 9.[17] Indians are proud of this divorce record, and it is often offered to the investigator as proof of the moral superiority of their culture. Spirited support for arranged

TABLE 9. DISTRIBUTION BY MARITAL STATUS
OF EUROPEANS AND ASIANS EVER MARRIED
IN CENTRAL AFRICA, 1956

	Europeans		Asians	
Marital Status	*Males*	*Females*	*Males*	*Females*
Married	94.3%	86.8%	96.4%	92.5%
Widowed	2.3	9.9	2.5	6.9
Separated	1.2	1.2	.7	.2
Divorced	2.2	2.1	.4	.4
Total	100.0%	100.0%	100.0%	100.0%
Total numbers	64,887	66,767	4,502	3,842

Source: Federation of Rhodesia and Nyasaland, *Census of Population: 1956,* Tables 8 and 10.

marriages comes about as close to an open defense of the caste system as one will find among Indians. A youthful informant explained patiently:

> Among our people, marriages which are made by the couple themselves never work out. You take the common case where a boy meets a girl while they are both in college and marries her without his parents' permission. After two or three years they find they don't love each other as much as they thought. Then there is always a divorce.

Indians nonetheless both expect and hope to find love in marriage like people in other modern cultures. Indian films are invariably romantic in theme; and long centuries before movies were thought of, the beloved story of Lord Ram and his faithful wife Sita helped to give these deities the very special place that they occupy in the Hindu pantheon. Yet clearly in

17. Later figures are available only for Rhodesia. The 1961 statistics for both Europeans and Asians in that territory are virtually identical with those of 1956.

the priority of values laid down in the traditional culture, love is dispensable if it conflicts with duty. A sixty-year-old man once startled us by exclaiming:

> Don't ask me about love! [We in fact had *not* asked him; we were discussing the impending marriage of one of his sons.] I am not talking about love! Love has nothing to do with it. Perhaps in many cases a Hindu husband and wife don't love each other. But they stay together. The moment you are married you forget about love and from then on your only thought is duty.

But as the values sought in marriage shift under the manifold pressures for institutional change and adaptation, the old perception of "duty" becomes clouded. No Indian wants for Indians the amount of divorce that he sees in the European community. At the same time, a good many have come to question the quality of the marital relationship in the typical Indian family, judged in light of the newer values. Rightly or wrongly—and the data are too inadequate to support a judgment—some Indians believe that Indian marriages are typically unhappy.[18]

The Role of Women

By European standards, women's social participation outside the family is still notably restricted among both Hindus and Muslims in Central Africa. A marked difference between the two religious groups nonetheless exists in this respect. Within both there is a very wide range of variation when individual families are examined.

18. This statement is based primarily on the interview materials. On the same point the young Indian sociologist whom we have previously cited (Lalloo, "The Hindu Family in S. Rhodesia") writes: "This phenomenon [i.e. a low divorce rate] cannot be strictly regarded as a reflexion of widespread happy marriages. Divorce is viewed with opprobrium and social disapproval and is avoided to the extent of personal suffering." (p. 33) And again: "It would not be presumptuous to suppose that unhappy marriages do exist. The extent of these is difficult to estimate. In the case of such marriages, a semblance of unity is maintained with toleration and some measure of personal discomfort. Mutual obligations are a primary force making for family cohesion." (p. 34)

A partial seclusion of women—falling well short of traditional *purdah*—still commonly prevails among Muslims, but it is by no means universal. In such families a male visitor will not be introduced to the women of the household, although he may catch an occasional glimpse of them through an open door. Nor, if he is invited to share a meal, will the food be served by an adult woman as it would be in a Hindu household. Instead, it will be brought in by either a preadolescent girl— a fairly common practice—or by an African servant.

Still, not all Muslims follow these restrictive practices. The women of less traditional Muslim families may have as much freedom of movement as Hindu women have. The range of actual behavior in this respect is thus remarkably wide. On the one hand, a husband may become very agitated when his middle-aged wife dares in the middle of the day to go out of the house alone to buy a spool of thread. On the other, a young husband may try to get his wife to learn how to dance so that they will not be so conspicuous when invited to European social functions. These are admittedly extremes, but they perhaps illustrate the current lack of firm consensus with respect to the proper public conduct to be expected of women among Muslims.

Among Hindus, social participation outside the family seems more a matter of cultural adequacy than external social restraint: those women who are equipped by experience, education, and fluency in English to take part in general community activities do so; those who lack the necessary prerequisites do not. Within the sample of families, there are several Hindu women who play essentially cosmopolitan roles; these are intelligent, sophisticated, and forceful females who are no more subordinated to their husbands than their counterparts in suburban America.

Given this exceedingly wide range of variation and the sharp conflict in values which it reveals, the male attitude toward the female role is typically more than a little ambivalent. A man may feel very keenly his wife's lack of western sophistication —particularly if he is young and socially mobile—and thus

185

wish that she could participate more in the community. At the same time, he is apt to share something of the common tendency to see in women the ultimate repository of the ethnic virtues— and thus is happy to have her remain secluded at home.

Nor does it take any great analytical acumen to see that the male's ambivalence toward the female's role is in good part a reflection of his ambivalence toward male values. Torn between two value systems by acculturation, he has not made up his mind which he wants. Or more accurately, he wants the best of both but has difficulty in reconciling them.

A man finds himself of necessity participating a good deal in the non-Indian world. While doing so, he may consciously revel a bit in the freedom from restraints imposed by his own culture. He may—to revert to an instance previously cited— devour half a fried chicken, washed down with a couple of bottles of beer, in the company of non-Hindu friends.[19] Yet when asked point-blank whether or not he expects to eat meat in his own house after he is married, he emphatically replies: "No. Any Hindu girl whom I would marry will not eat meat. And I won't insist that she serve it in my home. If I did, she probably would cook it, but she wouldn't eat it herself. But I won't insist, so the problem will never arise."

The modernization of the female role which has occurred among the Indians of Central Africa still leaves women securely within the family. In sharp contrast to the European group, in which virtually every married woman works for pay outside the home, Indian women rarely have gainful employment, the only important exception being a very few schoolteachers. In poor families, it is true, women rather commonly assist in the family shop. But such work is still organized within the family unit.

This describes the present situation within the family. But there is no reason to believe that it will remain unchanged indefinitely. Given greatly increased cultural capacity through education and more attractive opportunities, the Indian women

19. See above, p. 103.

in Central Africa will certainly have a future of very different dimensions.[20]

20. Employment of women had already notably increased by the time of our 1966 visit.

Chapter Seven

UNITY AND DISUNITY

WITHIN THE INDIAN COMMUNITY

"Community" is a word constantly heard in Central Africa. Seldom, however, does it appear in its most common American usage as the appropriate term for the totality of social organization clustered about a central point in space. In Central Africa, "community" is essentially synonymous with the sociologist's "ethnic group."

The difference is instructive since it indicates the degree of normative integration that many Americans assume will follow from the simple fact of propinquity, that is, that enough communality to deserve the term "community" will spring up among otherwise diversified people because of common residence. There is significantly no such assumption in the plural society of Central Africa. Here, social distance overrides geographic space in people's consciousness. Indians, Africans, Europeans, and Coloureds constitute communities. Lusaka, Bulawayo, Blantyre, and Broken Hill are places on the map where people without much else in common may happen to live.

This, with the inevitable oversimplification in the telling, is the ordinary perspective. The sociologist of course can easily show that the Central African town is ecologically a community in the functional sense; functionally, it constitutes an integrated whole, diverse as its parts may be. With equal validity he might also point out that none of the presumptive ethnic communities is a "real community," if we choose to make that term mean a tight and seamless web of purposive organization and wholehearted psychological commitment. Indians sometimes conceive of themselves as constituting one community. Often they do not. The same might be said of the other ethnic groups.

In other words, we confront here again the troublesome question of degrees and modes of integration in social organization. Like Europeans and Africans, Indians constitute a fairly unified group culturally: they are a social aggregate of people capable of understanding each other's behavior and motivations in a way that outsiders cannot. If we choose to define community as that population within which such relatively intimate communication is possible, then Indians taken as a whole may be said to be one. If, on the other hand, we think in terms of an organized group headed by a legitimately established leadership speaking for and representing the group vis-à-vis other groups in collective action, then there is no Indian community. Instead, there are factional groupings based actually or ostensibly upon religion, caste, personal loyalties, or generational differences and led by leaders more often interested in their prestige vis-à-vis one another than they are in the interests or welfare of Indians as a whole. The bases, alignment, and organizational dynamics of some of the more important of these groupings provide the subject matter of this chapter.

THE RELIGIOUS DIVISION

The sharpest and most persistent line of cleavage is that ostensibly drawn by religion. As expected, the religious division is particularly marked in those large settlements where something approximating a rough balance in numbers exists between Muslims and Hindus, thus giving rivalry between them more point and meaning.[1] Significantly, Indians living in these

---

1. A formalized division into rivalrous moieties (or "half-tribes") is a common feature of social organization often noted by anthropologists. See, among

places seldom use the term "Indian community"; instead they refer to the "Hindu community" or the "Muslim community." With some few notable exceptions, there are no formal associational bonds between the two groups. In the same town there may be an Indian (i.e. Hindu) Association and a Muslim Society, an Indian (Hindu) Sports Club and a Muslim Sports Club, an Indian Chamber of Commerce and a Muslim Chamber of Commerce—the exact terminology varies from town to town. This formal division does not rule out a certain amount of friendly informal association on an individual basis. But informal contacts, too, tend in such towns to be largely confined to one's own religious group.

Religious cleavage is maintained and supported with the aid of mutually derogatory stereotypes which serve as boundary-maintaining devices. Some of the common themes are illustrated in extracts from interview protocols cited below. Hindus, for example, charge that Muslims are: (A) deliberately contrary and uncooperative; (B) "fanatical" (a constantly used expression) and thus undemocratic; (C) really disguised Hindus but of low and questionable origins. Muslims, on the other hand, see Hindus as: (X) devious and untrustworthy— a very common charge; (Y) undemocratic, the proof being the Hindu caste system; (Z) superstitious and backward by the nature of their religious beliefs.

> A. The Muslims are contrary to everything we stand for. Everything we value, they are against. We worship the cow; they kill the cow. We wash our face this way [making a downward motion over his face with his two opened hands]. They wash their faces this way [making a similar motion upward over his face].

> B. All Muslims tend to be fanatical. You will find that they are much more narrow-minded and less liberal in their approach to any problem you care to name than Hindus are. It's their religion that makes them that way. Our

---

other sources, Robert H. Lowie, *Social Organization* (New York, Rinehart, 1948), pp. 240–48.

190

religion, as you know, is not dogmatic. No Hindu ever tells another Hindu what he must believe in. We are encouraged by our religion to think for ourselves, but the Muslim is told what to believe. That is why Muslims are inherently undemocratic. They preach an egalitarian philosophy, but in fact they have a dictatorial mind. In every Muslim country in the world where there is a Muslim government you have a dictatorship, and usually it is a military dictatorship.

C. They don't like to admit it now, but all Indian Muslims were originally Hindus. You see, Indian society in the past was not as democratic as it is now. Originally, we had four distinct classes of people: priests, warriors, traders, and then the ordinary people. Below them were a fifth group, the untouchables. These untouchables were not allowed in the villages in some places, and they weren't allowed into the Hindu temples. You might say they didn't have any religion. When the Muslims came to India and conquered the country by the sword, the only Hindus they could convert were these untouchables.

X. Hindus are a very mild, soft people. The Muslims are much more independent and much more straightforward. We are also much more hot-tempered. If a Muslim disagrees with you, he says so. The Hindu, on the other hand, is very sweet-tongued. Even if you insult him to his face, he just smiles and takes it. But he doesn't forget it. He waits patiently until he finds an opportunity to hit you [figuratively], and then when you think he must have forgotten all about it, he knocks you off your feet.

Y. You know, traditionally the Brahmans and the Sudras wouldn't have anything to do with one another. Gandhi was a Vaishya; he belonged to that caste. And while he was in India he never complained about the caste system. But when he went to South Africa and saw how the British and the Dutch people treated the Indians there, then he could appreciate how it must be to be a Sudra in India. But he had to go to South Africa in order to open his eyes.[2]

Z. Hindus don't even believe in God. They claim to, but they don't. You know what a Hindu prays to? Sticks and stones! [By "sticks" he presumably means the *tulsi* and other plants sacred to the Hindus.] They say that they even drink their own urine in some of their rituals. I don't know. But that is what I have been told.

Stereotypes like these enter into but do not determine concrete social relationships, since other situational factors are always present and may be of greater importance. Relations between Hindus and Muslims living in the same settlement have in practice varied widely depending upon time and circumstances, and they still do to a very considerable extent. In some towns relations are markedly more amiable or more hostile than in others, and in the same town they may have undergone a good deal of fluctuation historically.

A generation or so ago relations were typically rather intimate in some settlements, and for quite understandable reasons. There were in the early 1930s only half a dozen Indians, for example, in what is now an important Zambian town. About equally divided between Hindus and Muslims, these were young men and most did not yet have their families with them. Looking back now, informants from this original group remember those years as a period of innocent amiability in contrast to the rancor which developed later.

This particular Indian settlement grew to over a thousand people after World War II. Growth alone would have militated against the old intimacy, but growth also happened to coincide with the partition of India and its tragic consequences. Many of the new immigrants coming to Africa at that time had been themselves directly and personally involved in partition incidents, and virtually everyone had kinsmen or friends who were, even if they themselves were not. Naturally enough, re-

2. We may note, apropos the point made in the chapter on caste (pp. 142–45), how convenient even this Muslim informant finds the classical varna system as a point of reference.

ligious conflict in India was reflected in Africa, where it enflamed and estranged local relationships. No physical violence occurred, if we except a cracked head or two at local cricket matches, but feelings ran high—high enough to effectively prevent much cooperation between the two groups during this important period when community institutions such as schools, political associations, and recreational clubs were taking initial shape.

Partition was thus an important background factor in religious cleavage. Yet essentially the same result would probably have come about without this stir and emotion in India. A small group of young men living alone in a strange and forbidding country is one thing situationally; the same men in a sizable settlement of families is quite another. As responsible leaders, they are now forced to distinguish and support group values which they as individuals perhaps happily ignored.

CASTE

Within the traditional Indian village, caste was often more important than religion as a line of cleavage. In Central Africa both religion and caste present barriers to communal unity, but with a difference of great significance. While its divisive effects are deplored, religious identification is publicly respectable but caste is not.

Since caste is now overtly rejected, details upon the way in which its deeply ingrained and widely pervasive set of norms for the identification, placement, and evaluation of others enters into community organization are difficult to come by, although the main drift seems clear. The denial of caste has in fact greatly weakened its power to determine much of the overall community structure, and the trend is constantly toward even less. Actually, as we have seen, most Indians in Central Africa neither believe in the traditional caste norms in the traditional way nor do they attempt to apply them very consistently in social relations, with the single exception of marriage. What they commonly retain of caste is some tendency to believe that people can be differentiated on the basis of certain inherent and immutable qualities of spiritual purity and worth; but if they are modern-minded and "democratic," they also believe that people should be treated equally in all strictly public matters in spite of these differences. This position manages to separate the spiritual meaning of caste from its traditional overt manifestations in ordinary day-to-day behavior.

An Indian informant can thus honestly say that he no longer believes in caste, if caste is to be equated (as he is sure it is in the European's mind) with social discrimination. A Patidar tells us in one breath that he personally doesn't believe in caste and that caste has no role in the local community. In the next, he refers with obvious disparagement to "those steam laundry people"—a Dhobi family known to eat meat and drink liquor, sufficient and obvious proof in his eyes of their inferior grade. Yet since this Patidar would not hesitate to eat or sleep in the Dhobi's house if the occasion called for it, he feels that he has transcended the objectionable features of caste as a system of public discrimination. That he would never think of allowing his son to marry the Dhobi's daughter seems to him a private and religious matter and in no sense an objectionable discriminatory one. His professed egalitarianism is thus in his own eyes perfectly sincere.

Yet in the none-too-subtle airs of superiority which the Patidar unconsciously (or perhaps not so unconsciously) assumes in interaction, the Dhobi senses the old caste attitude and bitterly resents it. In India he might have swallowed his resentment. But in Africa, where *all* Indians have had to fight down-grading by the dominant Europeans, he loudly proclaims his indignation in the name of the same egalitarian norms and values as those used in ideological battle with the Europeans. In this protest he is supported by the self-conscious liberals of the higher castes (Anavils, for example), who in turn resent what they interpret as the exaggerated claims to status by the Patidars.

The choice of the Patidars in this not-so-hypothetical example is not accidental. Intracommunity quarrels and conflicts

ultimately hinging upon the implicit question of caste suprem-
acy have been part and parcel of the history of most of the
larger Hindu settlements, and in these clashes it has in fact
been the Charotar Patidars who have typically asserted and
supported traditionalist positions. A dominant caste in the area
from which most of the Hindu immigrants were drawn, the
Patidars have tended to see themselves as naturally suited to
leadership. Owing to their own very recent ascendancy, they
have furthermore found it difficult to gracefully accept socio-
economic mobility on the part of castes traditionally much
lower than themselves. The Anavils, in contrast, are much more
relaxed on these matters of relative status—a stance doubtlessly based in their case, as with secure groups everywhere,
upon their unquestioned superiority by the established criteria.

As we have so often emphasized, no Indian in Central Africa
talks willingly about caste except to deny its relevance to the
local and current situation. Details on intracommunity conflicts of the nature just indicated were thus extraordinarily
difficult to come by. After being pressed into making a few
noncommital observations on one of the more notorious of these
affairs, an unusually cooperative informant burst out indig-
nantly: "You can write about all this in your book if you
want to. But personally I hope that you won't. There's nothing
good to be said about this dispute. And nothing good would
come from describing it."

We do know, however, that in at least two major communities
the pioneer Patidars (1) asserted their right to the leadership
of the Indian Association when it was formed, and (2) sought
in the teeth of violent resistance from most of the rest of the
Hindus to establish a caste *mandal* (literally, "association")
in order to protect the surname Patel from appropriation by
lesser castes. We also know that in at least two other communities the forms of communal religious worship were complicated by questions of caste.[3]

Still, after due recognition is given to caste as a source of

3. Cf. the interpretation of the modernistic nature of the Salisbury temple
made above, pp. 97–99.

internal dissension, the really significant fact to emerge is exactly that which suspicious informants like the one just cited always feared would be overlooked: namely, the degree of unity achieved in the Hindu community, considering the depth and pervasiveness of caste in traditional Indian society and culture. In all of the settlements large enough to support an Indian (i.e. Hindu) Association, a community hall has been built from which no one is categorically excluded. For such social events as a marriage or the entertainment of important public guests from India, it is taken for granted that everyone will be invited. In public meetings called to discuss political questions, no one is excluded by caste or religion, and no one hesitates to have his say because of his caste. Some of the most important offices of the association in several towns have in recent years been held by Mochis, Khumbhars, and Kolis, who represent the lowest castes present in Central Africa.

Viewed from the perspective of the communities in which these Indians were reared in India, the degree of caste equality thus far achieved constitutes a truly revolutionary change. Yet, like all revolutions, this one did not just happen. It came about, as socio-cultural changes of a comparable nature almost invariably do, through group conflict, made possible and encouraged by the development of a particular situation at a particular point in time.

In this instance the lower castes were provided with irresistible ideological weapons by the concurrent status battle of all Indians against the Europeans. Seeing the possibilities inherent in the situation thus happily offered them, the lower castes pressed the attack mercilessly. Furthermore, they gained enough ground so that in even the strictly private interpersonal relations, demeanor indicating any degree of caste consciousness (or "snobbery") is now defined as a serious breach of good manners.

A factor not to be overlooked in considering the rapidity and extent of these changes is undoubtedly the size of the population involved. If the Hindus in any given town in Central Africa numbered thousands instead of mere hundreds, a forcefully dissident group such as the Charotar Patidars might have been able to splinter off and successfully create viable community institutions of their own—meeting halls, for example, or perhaps a separate religious school for their children. Such attempts would certainly have been made if the number of dissidents had ever been large enough to support them ideologically and financially.

So-called "tribal" distinctions among Muslims have played a far lesser role in local community dynamics than caste has among their Hindu counterparts for two good reasons. There is, first of all, the undeniable element of truth in the proud Muslim claim to an egalitarian social polity: tribal distinctions determine social identity and control marital choice, but even in India they have never been so clearly hierarchical nor so grossly discriminatory in public practice as caste has been among the Hindus.[4] Secondly, Muslims have tended to be more widely scattered geographically in Central Africa than Hindus, and small local concentrations of Muslims are apt to be quite homogeneous in origin. The great majority of Muslims residing in Zambia, for example, are from less than a dozen villages in the Surat district of India.

Still, any difference between Hindus and Muslims in this respect is a relative one, and it would be far too much to say that tribal distinctions have never played a divisive role in community affairs. In one Muslim settlement, such differences were at least a contributory factor in a factional conflict so violent that it ultimately led to a murder and the expulsion of one entire group.

The fact remains that caste is integrated into Muslim social structure in a rather different way than it is among Hindus. Class and caste, for example, are in theory two different things among the latter. But class and caste are clearly somewhat

4. Cf. Zekiye Eglar, *A Punjabi Village in Pakistan* (New York, Columbia University Press, 1960), p. 29.

more closely related phenomena among Muslims, where status distinctions based in the last analysis upon caste are passed off as class differences, founded in wealth and prestige. (We need hardly add that the investigator who would try to separate the two is given very little assistance in the Muslim community.) It took us a long time to see that the remarkable non-involvement of a small group of Broach Vahoras from the violent dissensions which rent one Muslim community could best be interpreted as the aloof disdain of aristocrats for the petty squabbles of caste inferiors.

PATRONS AND CLIENTS

Religion and caste supply most of the symbolic content for factional identity. The patron-client system has provided the main organizational framework through which intracommunity conflict and competition has been most often expressed. The past tense in this description is appropriate because both the foundation and the mode of exercising power and authority at the local community level are currently undergoing rather drastic reorganization.

The structure of patrons and clients which exists in Central Africa is a direct adaptation of the traditional form as it is found in the Indian village. In India, the patron-client system was (and is) a primary mode for organizing and directing interpersonal relationships involving power, influence, and authority beyond the household unit. In essence, it consists of a hierarchically ordered group of individuals and families bound to a recognized leader through a network of reciprocal services and obligations. These take many different forms. Master and servant, landowner and tenant, creditor and debtor are some of the examples which Srinivas cites in his enlightening discussion of the institution as it operates in a Mysore village.[5] The well-known *jajmani* relationship of reciprocal economic and ritual obligations between members of the various castes which prevailed throughout India until recently is probably best

5. Srinivas, "The Social System of a Mysore Village," pp. 26–33.

seen as simply one manifestation of organization on this basic principle.[6]

While clearly Indian and traditional in its normative model, the organization of patrons and clients which emerged in Central Africa was necessarily new, consisting as it now did of new elements put together within a new situation. As Srinivas and others have made clear, the patron-client system in the Indian village created a functioning social unit transcending (to an important degree) kinship and caste; here, it was concerned mainly with agricultural production and village politics. In Central Africa it was used mainly (although not entirely) to organize and carry on business operations in the African trade; compared to the situation in India the field within which it could operate effectively was very restricted. Furthermore, in Africa clients were apt in the first instance to be kin and in many cases remained so.

By the nature of the situation, the system in Africa was closely tied to the peculiarities of the Indian immigration and settlement pattern. Everything else being equal, wealth, power, and influence are closely correlated with age and length of

6. Both Morris and Pocock touch upon the patron-client system as it operates in East Africa, and Morris contrasts its operation there with the even more closely knit system of the Chinese in Southeast Asia. Morris, "Communal Rivalry among Indians in Uganda," pp. 306–17; H. S. Morris, "Indians in East Africa: A Study in a Plural Society," *British Journal of Sociology, 7* (1956), 194–211; David F. Pocock, "Factions in Indian and Overseas Indian Societies: II. The Basis of Faction in Gujerat," *British Journal of Sociology, 8* (1957), especially 304–06.

Klass' treatment of the phenomenon in the West Indies is particularly interesting. The patron-client system could not operate in its pristine form among indentured laborers any more than could other traditional Indian institutions. Yet when Indian social structure was reconstituted in Trinidad in recent times the patron-client system quickly reemerged as a fundamental mode of organization. Morton Klass, *East Indians in Trinidad: A Study of Cultural Persistence* (New York, Columbia University Press, 1961), pp. 199–220.

Groups of leaders and followers bound together by reciprocal ties of loyalty and obligation are of course very common in other societies. Even in the West, where other principles of social organization have generally predominated in recent times, examples of patron-client structure might be cited from Greco-Roman times down to the big city political machines of the present. The Indian system is peculiar only in the sense that its modes and values are distinctly Indian.

residence in the country. Although pioneers are of no great antiquity—in Northern Rhodesia they came in most cases no earlier than the late 1920s or early 1930s—the fact that they were the first gave them great advantages. When the economy boomed during and after World War II, these men were on hand to exploit the opportunities offered.

As has been pointed out, until recently a man bent upon expanding his business in the African trade did so horizontally. In other words, he opened more shops rather than build larger ones, although he may have done both. In either case, expansion in the African retail trade depended primarily upon his ability to get assistants from India to handle the increased volume of business, and a continuous supply was essential. From the time they came to Africa, assistants began to look forward to the time when they too could set up a shop of their own, and they were typically impatient to take this step. After all, it was the dream of eventually becoming independent businessmen which motivated them to come to Africa.

The assistants which one personally "called" became one's clients, irrespective of other ties such as kinship that one might also have with these persons. But the total of a patron's clients did not necessarily coincide with the number of his employees. Ex-assistants who had set up independent shops typically continued to depend upon their patron for help in getting *them* assistants in turn, and this was true even if the assistants to be obtained were their own relatives.

The services which a patron could render a prospective immigrant were in the main based upon knowledge, experience, and presumptive contacts, although upon occasion an outlay of cash was also involved. Sheer knowledge of how the contemplated move to Africa was to be accomplished was perhaps the most important factor. While intrinsically simple enough, the immigration requirements and procedures presented a formidable barrier in the minds of most candidates and their families. They therefore felt a powerful need for information and guidance. And, finally, a signature guaranteeing employment or financial responsibility was an absolute necessity.

Given their cultural predispositions, Indians never viewed these matters as being simply or solely technical. Behind the bureaucratic rule Indians automatically see the *person* of the official, and this human element they firmly believe is open to a certain amount of manipulation. Whether one passed or failed the English examination, for example, was known to depend upon the judgment and discretion of the immigration inspector; perhaps when the time of decision came, he could be persuaded. The belief that he could be persuaded doubtlessly tended to be exaggerated, but it was stronger than the Indians' faith in sheer bureaucratic impersonality. It would be the patron's task, among other things, to do the persuading.[7]

Thus it was to a patron in the Indian community to whom one looked for help if one wanted to go to Africa. Some were responsible for bringing to Africa literally hundreds of their compatriots, only a fraction of whom became their own employees. A major patron told us that near the close of the immigration period he had often had as many as sixty young men staying in his house at a time, and he added that he had signed so many papers that the authorities had charged him with running a commercial immigration agency.

All human action is presumably motivated, and the patron in such instances as these had his reasons for lending a hand to the aspiring immigrant. If he personally needed assistants, then his action can be explained in direct economic terms. But in many cases he was simply interested in extending his following by putting the immigrant under obligation to him, and he often did so at an immediate cost rather than an immediate gain. Some large patrons, for example, paid out substantial sums to lawyers to get prospective immigrants another chance at the English examination; others spent money for different sorts of bribes to officials in one capacity or another; and some lent money on occasion to immigrants who found themselves without funds. While doing these things, they typically acted without any thought of immediate return.

What the patron did expect was that the young man so

7. See below, pp. 223–25, for documentation.

helped would be duly grateful and would continue to come to him for guidance and advice. The opportunity to come to Africa was impressed upon him and his family in India as a valuable favor (as it was) which could best be returned in the traditional coin of gratitude and loyalty: this much was implicit in the norms defining the relationship of patron to client which both well understood. Beyond this, the patron expected his client to support him in any position which he took in intracommunity politics. From the patron's point of view, these would be considered the minimum and binding obligations.

Implicit in all this was a wide range in degree and kind of obligation. A large patron necessarily had a considerable number of clients bound to him rather loosely by only minimal or indirect ties. The whole system was of course hierarchical, and small patrons had large patrons in turn. The core, however, of any patron's following consisted of those directly and continuously under his control. In the main these core clients were either employees or debtors.

Until recently, employees were mainly youths from eighteen to twenty years old. If possible, these young assistants lived in the employer's house; if this were not possible, then they were expected to live with a trusted lieutenant, who stood as a surrogate for the great patron. These prescribed living arrangements for shop assistants rested in part upon economic considerations. It was not customary to pay the assistant regularly; instead, a settlement was made at the end of his period of service. He therefore had no money to pay for day-to-day maintenance elsewhere than his employer's house, even if this had been considered feasible, which it was not. Delayed payment had certain advantages for both parties. The employee could always look forward to a sum large enough to launch him independently into business at the end of his service. The employer, on the other hand, could in this way use as working capital the money which he would otherwise be paying out in wages. These strictly economic advantages were important considerations. But in the balance they were small compared to the really critical issue: the intimate controls over the employee's behavior which the living-in arrangement allowed the employer to exercise.

These controls were in part benevolently paternalistic. Homesick and badly disoriented youths of eighteen or so who had always lived in a firmly ordered hierarchical family setting generally felt the need for authoritative guidance during their first years in Africa, and both they and their responsible relatives in India were generally happier knowing that they could depend upon it. Under "Uncle's" watchful eye, they were provided with a protective environment while making the inevitable adjustments to the new life of Africa. This positive function, needless to say, is the one patrons always emphasized when interpreting the system to the outsider.

A closer look, however, soon shows that the controls exercised over an assistant's behavior were not wholly benevolent in intent or operation. From the employer's point of view, assistants presented two serious problems, one immediate, the other less pressing but no less important in the long run. Immediately, there was a problem of sheer honesty and dependability in the shop. The long-range problem was one which Parsons would doubtlessly call "system maintenance."

The problem of honesty was complicated and difficult, given the manner in which the African trade was conducted. Operators of modern business establishments find the reliability of their employees something of a problem too; but in their case, petty thievery is minimized through a combination of fixed prices and modern accounting methods whereby a continuous check is possible between cash register and stock. The African trade, however, has been (and much of it still is) conducted through a bargaining process whereby one extracted whatever one could from each customer in turn.

Without fixed prices the fixed relationship between stock and cash box disappears. The competent shop assistant who manages by these rules to extract from a naive or careless customer an extra shilling or so above the minimum price is only doing his job. But what is to prevent him from pocketing the extra money—at least occasionally—since he can always say if questioned that the lesser price was all he was able to get? Nothing much, obviously, except his feeling of loyalty to his employer or his fear of getting caught. Petty thievery of this sort has apparently always been widespread.

Faced with this difficult problem, employers attempted to deal with it in two ways. First of all, they tried when possible to get close relatives as shop assistants, hoping that relatives would see the employer's interest as their own. As a second best, they tried to obtain persons as close to them as possible by caste and regional affiliation. Still the problem was not always solved. In the interview protocols several instances are recounted in which brothers bitterly accuse each other of dishonesty, and complaints concerning more distant relatives are legion.

The only other alternative was strict surveillance, and this was made much easier if the employee ate and slept in the employer's house as well as worked in his shop. The arrangement allowed for a check upon the employee's pockets occasionally and a constant overview of what he was doing and spending. Employers never hesitated to inquire directly into these matters, feeling that they were well within their prerogatives.

More generally, the living-in arrangement guaranteed against tendencies to subvert the system both at the ideological and action levels, a somewhat vaguely defined problem to which employers were nonetheless extremely sensitive. As a group, they disliked the idea of assistants getting together to compare notes on wages, working conditions, and future prospects. Above all, they did not care to have their assistants trading informed estimates of what they were taking as profit or exchanging details on other trade secrets.

Naturally, the desired goal in this case was difficult to achieve. A fairly effective technique was to keep assistants busy—twelve to fourteen hours a day, seven days a week—so that they literally did not have much time for such comparisons. When athletic clubs came into existence following World War

II, they met a good deal of sullen and disgruntled (but not very openly expressed) opposition from employers for exactly this reason. Similar motives reinforced the strongly felt need for a constant supply of new assistants fresh from India. Old ones soon learned too much to be disciplined easily. At that point, the sooner they graduated to an employer's status and point of view, the better for the "system" as a whole.

This tight relationship between employer and employee loosened considerably with the graduation of the employee into a business of his own at the end of his service. But it loosened rather than ended. In the first place, the strong sentimental tie binding the two remained. The employee was heavily obligated to his patron for the very fact that he was in Africa and could now take this step; and irrespective of how harsh his experiences with his patron as employer had been, he generally felt a deeply internalized sense of obligation. Sentiment, however, was in virtually every case wedded to some very practical matters. The ex-employee did not in fact become really independent. His relationship to his patron simply shifted from that of employee to debtor.

When the ex-assistant received his wage settlement at the end of his period of service, it was typically paid not in cash but in a stock of goods advanced by the erstwhile employer. Typically, too, the terms under which these goods were transferred were monetarily all in the employer's favor. The employee was usually required to take them at or near retail prices, thus allowing the employer to make a handsome profit on several hundred pounds' worth of goods. Obviously, this fact was not lost upon the employee, but he was in no position to complain. Until established, he would find it difficult to get credit elsewhere than from his patron; and, since his paid-up stock of goods in hand was small, he might very well need additional credit before he could stand on his own feet. Besides, credit from his patron was preferable to credit from other sources even if it were costly, since the patron would be more lenient if things did not go well. Finally, the patron would be available for business advice and counsel—an advantage which the wise client generally appreciated and the foolish one ignored at his peril.

As is the case of other traditional Indian institutions, the patron-client system in Central Africa is being steadily undermined by a combination of forces deriving from the cosmopolitan world culture and the strictly local social situation. New forms of community leadership are emerging, and once powerful patrons now find themselves with only a shadow of their former influence.

The greatest single blow was the end of immigration, but there were others. Pressures from the government labor office, applied at about the same time that immigration was cut off, encouraged the payment of regular wages, and the shortage of assistants forced these wages up to hitherto unheard of levels. The employee thus found himself with more money and far more independence than he had ever had previously. He could live where he wished or marry and set up an independent household. Credit, too, was suddenly much easier to obtain, once the postwar shortages were ended; and thus the transition from employee to independent shopkeeper depended far less on the cooperation of the all-powerful patron. Working in concert, such forces as these encouraged more impersonal relationships between the haves and the have-nots within the Indian community and contributed to a growth of individual autonomy as understood by Western norms and values.

Once equally characteristic of both religious groups, the patron-client system survives more persistently among Muslims than Hindus. Why this should be so is not entirely clear, but presumably it is related to the overall difference in sociocultural development between Hindus and Muslims which has been often mentioned. During the period of field research, the Muslim population of Northern Rhodesia could still be fairly accurately described as under the control of some five or six powerful patrons. Their influence was visibly waning; it was nonetheless strong enough to make even the more loosely affiliated clients hesitate before taking any action of which their patron was certain to disapprove.[8] By contrast, once-powerful Hindu patrons had by this time lost effective control over all but the most directly dependent core of their once-numerous client followings, and in a few cases some of these ex-patrons were subjected to criticism verging at times upon ridicule.

Examined from the standpoint of the central theme of this chapter, the patron-client system created both unity and division at the local community level, thus sharing the universal paradox of all group organization: namely, that social unity must come from social differences. Individuals and families which would otherwise have remained separate entities were brought together through the mechanisms of the patron-client system into a fairly tightly knit unit, capable, upon demand, of decisive collective action. Yet by the nature of their internal dynamics, these organizations tended to frustrate the achievement of the larger unity which most Indians passionately desire.

If an entire community was fortunate enough to be under the effective control of one great patron, then there was no division along this dimension. Some few of the smaller settlements might, by stretching the imagination a bit, be described as falling into this category. But this happy state has always been atypical, and where a multiplicity of patrons existed, intense rivalry and competition among them invariably followed.

A large patron could not by the very nature of the system cooperate very much with a rival patron without appearing to subordinate himself to the other, thus destroying his own hard-won position of power and prestige. Thus rivalry and competition was inherent in the situation so constituted. For this reason all community issues in such situations tended to be quickly reduced in practice to personal ones, although verbally presented and fought out in the name of impersonal and transcendant values: religion, caste, "the welfare of the entire Indian community," or what have you. A powerful patron could not agree and work with another who initiated some

8. Such as talking unguardedly to sociological investigators.

community-wide action, no matter what position he might have independently taken on the same issue under other circumstances. Nor could any client, no matter what he personally might be inclined to believe, support any position except that assumed by his patron. If he did, the mildest of the punishments visited upon him would be the charge of ingratitude; and if the bonds were strong enough to provide the leverage, more concrete manifestations of the patron's displeasure were certain to follow.

Detailed illustrations of the effects of such rivalry upon community unity are difficult to provide without identifying specific groups and persons, and this we are reluctant to do. Without any very great elaboration three typical cases will be cited to show the general pattern.

1. In one large town, we were initially assured by everyone that the religious division existing nearly everywhere else had been successfully bridged locally by an Asian Convention that united the hitherto separate Hindu and Muslim associations for strictly political purposes. A closer look and more persistent questioning did not bear out these optimistic interpretations, as leaders of both religious groups eventually admitted.

The inclusive association existed in theory and seemed to work for a time in practice. But the painfully constructed facade of unity which it was supposed to represent had been quietly and effectively shattered when a powerful Muslim patron, who had seemingly gone along with the original negotiations, privately let it be known that he was displeased at the enthusiasm expressed by some of his younger clients in this venture. His reasons—as explained to his clients (and doubtlessly to himself)—were cast in the stereotyped forms of traditional Hindu-Muslim conflict: the devious Hindus cannot be trusted, and since they were in this case in the numerical majority, they would certainly pervert the association to their own ends at the expense of the Muslim minority. As interpreted by the deeply chagrined young Hindu leaders, however, he was primarily motivated by a fear of loss of control over his clients if they acquired independent ideas, and this explanation seemed obviously valid to us as outside observers.

2. After a humiliating defeat at an attempt to control the community-wide Hindu Association which he was instrumental in establishing, a once-powerful but slipping patron tried to organize an innocent-looking "social club" composed of fellow caste members. If this club had in fact ever materialized, it would have functioned as a *mandal* in defense and support of caste interests.

This maneuver aroused violent reactions throughout the rest of the Hindu community, and the club was fought vigorously in the name of democracy and anti-discrimination. When the battle lines were drawn for the show-down fight, the patron responsible was able (as he had been counting upon) to draw to his side most of his "community" by the fact that they were also clients. He was responsible, directly or indirectly, for the fact that most of them were in Africa. A good many were ex-employees and debtors. But unfortunately for him, most of this support turned out to be half-hearted and unreliable. Times had changed and ties were loosened far beyond anything the old man imagined. Many of the younger clients, in particular, were embarrassed at being put into a position in which they had to support values they could not honestly defend. So they equivocated. They still hated to say no directly to "Uncle's" face and managed for the most part to avoid doing so, but when positive action was called for they dragged their heels and found excuses. The "social club" eventually came into existence in theory, but in fact it had no substance, as even its founder was finally forced to admit.

3. Our third and final illustration involves a rancorous ingroup split within a Muslim community. It was explained again and again to the fieldworker that the two vigorously embattled factions were quarrelling over the legitimacy of the mosque. A permanent and "true" mosque (as distinguished from a temporary "prayer house") must by Koranic law be built upon land owned by Muslims rather than by infidels. There is, however, no freehold land available in the townships of Northern Rhodesia and Nyasaland: all land is 99-year

leasehold. By a literal interpretation of the Koran, a true mosque would therefore be impossible anywhere in this area. Yet in fact all other communities of a comparable size have mosques, and their congregations seem to worry little about their ultimate legitimacy.

Actually, as everyone knows, this stated issue was artificial and extraneous. Rivalry for overall community leadership between the two most important Muslim patrons in town was the real issue. One of these had at his disposal the largest following of clients; the other had the most money. Clients of both leaders had to fall in line and take sides in the long-continued battle, although most of them were thoroughly sick of the whole affair. Nevertheless, as we have previously explained, the bonds between patron and client remain relatively strong among Muslims, and up until the time we left Africa in 1961, this long-standing division in this particular community still held.[9]

INTERGENERATIONAL CONFLICT

A marked line of cleavage within any rapidly changing society is that of age. Post-Freudian personality theory offers an explanation as to why this should be true. The childhood period is critical in socialization: each generation therefore absorbs as its ideal orientation the values and behavior patterns characteristic of a particular time and place. As it grows older, change proceeds apace, but regardless of the modifications forced upon an adult generation by the exigencies of later life conditions, the norms and values absorbed in childhood remain.[10] By definition, however, these norms and values cannot be those to which their children are exposed during *their* critical childhood period, if important change has indeed occurred.

9. By 1966, however, both of these patrons had apparently lost virtually all of their former influence.

10. Expressed psychologically, this is an aspect of "canalization," the process by which positive satisfying values are fixated during socialization. Gardner Murphy, *Personality: A Biosocial Approach to Origins and Structure* (New York, Harper and Bros., 1947), pp. 161–91.

Intergenerational discontinuity and conflict are therefore built into any social order subject to change. And the more drastic the change is, the greater the conflict.[11]

Intergenerational conflict seems particularly acute among the Indians of Central Africa, a fact which, by the logic just stated, would seem to stand as an index of particularly rapid change. Indians are acculturating to the dominant cosmopolitan models of behavior and values far more rapidly than almost any of them realize—or, for that matter, faster than the sociologist might, at first glance, think possible. A priori, it might reasonably be supposed (as we in fact did) that the social isolation apparently imposed upon Indians by segregation would strongly inhibit acculturation. Yet the degree to which the African-born generation has acculturated, particularly in Southern Rhodesia, is indeed remarkable. This discovery constituted one of the greatest surprises of the fieldwork. Quite obviously, a great deal of acculturation can be achieved without what the sociologist usually considers "intimate" contact.

Acculturation has nonetheless proceeded faster under some conditions than it has under others. Both Indians and Europeans constitute tiny minorities in Rhodesia when compared numerically to the African population; but the cities there are thoroughly European in character, and it is in the cities that virtually all of the Indians of Southern Rhodesia live. In Malawi, where there are more Indians than Europeans, the towns have a distinctly Indian cast. In the little trading centers scattered over the countryside there, both Indians and Europeans constitute tiny encapsulated outposts of external and foreign cultures in an otherwise overwhelmingly African milieu.

In American experience, the greatest single agency of acculturation by far is the public school. Schools seem to have played a very comparable role in the acculturation of Indians in Central Africa despite social segregation. In cultural content, the Indian school is a thoroughly European institution.

Schools for Indians were established earlier in Southern

11. Cf. Norman B. Ryder, "The Cohort as a Concept in the Study of Social Change," *American Sociological Review, 30* (1965), 843–61.

Rhodesia than they were in the north, and for a considerable period of time the only secondary schools to which Indians could go were located there. Indian children in the Southern Rhodesian school were thrown together with English-speaking Coloured children, and they were taught by European, Coloured, or South African Indian teachers. Even if the teacher were an Indian, he (or she) was thus normally not a Gujarati. These South African Indian teachers in fact presented to their charges a persuasive version of cosmopolitan rather than Indian culture, above and beyond the thoroughly European content of the formal curriculum. In Nyasaland and Northern Rhodesia, the pupils were more homogeneously Indian, and the teachers, if not European, were apt to be Gujarati immigrants like the parents. A noticeably lesser degree of acculturation among the children predictably followed from these territorial differences.

The acculturative effect of the school is even more pronounced in those few instances in which a child was sent to England for his education. The uniform result in these cases has been a profound shock to the parents, who had naively assumed that an Indian was an Indian and would remain an Indian through the long years spent away from home acquiring the coveted formal knowledge and skills of an educated person.

Still, important as it is, it would be an error to see all of the cultural differences which exist between the younger and the older generations as a product of the school. Generational differences are also pronounced—although not quite so great—between the older and younger immigrant generations. This point was driven home to the fieldworker in Northern Rhodesia where nearly all adults, whatever their age, were born in India rather than in Africa. Yet two men from the same village will differ importantly in their basic cultural orientation if they are a generation apart. If he immigrated, say, in 1923, a fifty-five-year-old man left (and remembers) an India which was certainly much closer to the traditional India of the past than that of a twenty-five-year-old who came in 1953.

So far, we have spoken of the intergenerational conflict as if it were simply a cultural phenomenon, which it is not. Differences between the generations in perspectives and values are important and basic, but like all cultural elements, they manifest themselves at the behavioral level within a socially organized situation. In the Central African Indian community context, these situational factors give generational differences a character markedly like social class.

Power, wealth, and status are so distributed and controlled in Central Africa that age alone is a primary factor in their determination, irrespective of who one is by ascribed criteria. Thus the rich man's son and the penniless shop assistant find themselves with much in common despite the fact that their ultimate destinies will presumably be very different. The work relationship particularly tends to place the younger and the older generations into much the same position vis-à-vis each other, whether the young men are sons or employees. The result is that sons feel like employees and vice versa. In either case, the younger generation tends to see itself as oppressed and overriden by the elder. Both the rich man's son and the poor employee have to work hard, and neither (for different reasons, it is true) are allowed to spend much on personal luxuries or pleasures. Both have a very limited range of personal autonomy in action. A thirty-year-old son of a moderately well-to-do father once remarked to us:

> Our fathers were the pioneers in this country. They were the ones who established the businesses, and they are the ones who run things. At least they think they should run them. You know, the Indian family is very different from the European family. In the Indian family the younger people, even those who are my age or so, are often not very independent. You might say that we are almost enslaved by our fathers. Economically, they hold the whip-hand. If we do something they don't like, then they refuse to help us.

213

Then, catching himself, he went on to add:

> But I'm afraid that I might be stretching this economic
> factor too much. The Indian family is a very tightly knit
> group too, and the ties of love and affection among the
> members are strong. Even when we disagree with our
> fathers, we don't like to do anything to hurt them.

One result of intergenerational conflict is a marked apathy
and spiritlessness in the African-born generation of some well-
to-do families. Sons in these families may show little interest
in the family business, the building up of which absorbed the
energy, the zeal, and the wholehearted devotion of their
fathers' lives. Often they are actively hostile to the idea of a
business career and daydream more or less openly of doing
something else.

This reaction appears particularly in those young men who
were given a secondary education abroad in England or India
and were then brought home to prepare for the time when they
would take over the family business. Upon returning home
from school, the young man is taken into the business but is
not given a responsible role. Fearing the disastrous errors of
inexperience—and he can always cite plenty of horrible examples to justify his caution—the wealthy Indian father tends
to keep a very tight rein upon his son's actions, leaving him
with nothing but routine chores to do.

In the traditional type of family and economic structure,
subordination of this kind would have been taken for granted
by the son and legitimized by the prevailing age-respect norms.
But the African-born son has been exposed to quite contrary
ideas, and in consequence he has a different perspective. In
some cases he has thoroughly internalized the European evaluations of Indian business as "petty," "dishonest," "mean," etc.;
and in reaction, he feels a fierce resentment toward what he
sees as a European-imposed economic role from which he cannot escape. Yet short of open rebellion, there is little he can
do about it, and apathy is the result.

For very similar situational reasons, antagonisms between employer and employee tend also to be markedly intergenerational in character. The older men—the pioneers between forty-five and sixty who are in control economically—typically came to Africa as youths of eighteen to twenty. Frugal and hard-working virtually without exception, the more intelligent and lucky of them have created fortunes. In most cases, it is true, these fortunes are modest enough; so-called "rich" Indians are for the most part only relatively well-to-do by English or American criteria, and all have many financial obligations. But a few, as has been previously pointed out, are wealthy by any standard.[12]

It seems most unlikely that similar opportunities to start with nothing and acquire comparable fortunes will ever again be so generally available, and perception of this fact sharpens the inherent conflict between the generations. Progressive step-by-step expansion from a tiny shop to the great department store of the future will not be easy, and few will make it. Whatever happens to the Indians of Central Africa politically, it is clear that many of the current shop assistants who would have become modestly well-to-do independent shopkeepers under the older system must now be content to spend their lives as employees.[13]

Accompanying this shift in career expectations is a subtle but profound change in economic perspective and life-style which as it proceeds cannot help but widen the gap between the older and the younger generations. The young shop assistant of twenty-five today earns several times what his employer did when he came to Africa. But lured by the enticements of a high standard, mass-consumption economy, he is in a growing number of cases spending what he makes rather than saving it for capital investment, or alternatively, as his employer might have done, for filial contributions to a sister's dowry in India. New and radically different expectations

---

12. See above, p. 67.
13. We have let these generalizations stand, as they were written prior to the 1966 visit. But see our observations on these matters on pp. 361–62.

leave him no real choice in the matter, as even the older generation on occasion reluctantly recognizes.

> Conditions have changed a lot since I came out here [in the late 1930s]. At that time we really didn't have any living expenses; one could sleep behind the counter in the shop, and food cost next to nothing. But you can't live in your shop now; the government won't let you. You have to get a house. And people want a car.

The pervasiveness of these new trends and the conflict which they create within the older pattern can be illustrated by the situation of one young man. Born in India, he is intelligent, aggressive, and highly ambitious. Knowing that the only way he can acquire "real" money is by working for himself rather than for others, he quit a well-paying job to become an independent shopkeeper in the traditional style, although his initial income from this venture was much less than what he had been making as an employee. He and his wife set up housekeeping in a single room at the back of their shop in the classic manner, and some three months later they still lacked a table and chairs. They could not afford these luxuries, they said, as indeed they could not. But they had bought a television set by installment payments and the young man was thinking of a car!

A big, late-model American car is a fairly standard success symbol among rich men otherwise too penurious to be tempted by most of the material baubles of mass culture. But not unnaturally they would prefer that this symbolic representation of their status and virtue should be confined to themselves and not usurped by the young and the unworthy. A disgruntled Muslim pioneer exemplifies this common attitude:

> A boy used to come out from India and he was satisfied with what he got. He could begin back in a bush shop some place and gradually work his way up, like all of us had to do. But now when he comes out to Africa, the first thing he sees is that I have a car. So he begins to ask

himself, "Why does that fellow have a car? What has he done to deserve it? Why can't I have a car too, if he has one?" He never stops to think how long I worked for that car!

This inherent economic conflict between the generations came to an open crisis in Northern Rhodesia in the early 1950s. Up to this time, relations between employer and employees had been fairly tightly controlled by the norms of the patron-client system. But the obvious disparity between what employers were taking as profits and what employees were getting as wages became increasingly apparent during this lush period of rapid economic expansion.[14] Dissatisfaction among the assistants spread. A good deal of more or less open criticism of the employers was expressed for the first time; and buoyed up by this general sentiment, a small group of dissidents decided to lodge complaints with the European labor officer. On the basis of these complaints, a full-scale investigation of the employment situation among the Indians was ordered by the government, and a commission was formed for that purpose.

Rightly perceiving this investigation as a major threat to their existing operations, the big employers organized in defense, Hindu and Muslim for once acting in concert. As a first step, the most prominent troublemakers among the assistants were fired and blacklisted—a very serious punishment, considering the fact that employees not only worked for but also lived with their employers. Without a job, the assistant had no place to live. And as a persona non grata, he could not even travel about freely in search of work, since to travel in this period Indians had no recourse but to depend upon the hospitality of other Indians.

Refusal to cooperate with the investigating commission was discussed within the employer group, but this tactic was ultimately rejected in favor of evasion and intimidation of the prospective witnesses. At the hearings, the commissioners

14. Experienced assistants' salaries, which in the late 1950s ranged to a top of around £45 a month, were no more than £12 to £15 as of 1950.

217

found only a bare handful of assistants willing to testify. Even the dissident leaders retracted many of their complaints when forced to support them in public. Most of the talking was done by the large patrons and their general stance was one of aggrieved innocence. Employer-employee relationships among Indians, they argued, were organized upon a family basis; such matters as wages and hours therefore could not be judged by impersonal European norms. When the shop assistants' union demanded by the Labor Code was formed in the wake of the investigations, large patrons appeared prominently in this union as officers!

The large patrons thus won this first open and public test of their authority. Still, the issue between the owners and the assistants had been openly posed and fought out in terms of class conflict, and so it remains defined in the minds of many of the younger generation. When we tried to get a fairly co-operative schoolteacher informant to talk about caste, he impatiently cut in with the remark: "The caste system isn't so very important here in Africa. The important thing is the division between the shop owners and the assistants."

The generational conflict posed so sharply in the family and the economic spheres inevitably appears in the broader and more impersonal arena of community affairs. Community politics everywhere have reflected this basic cleavage, along with those of religion and caste. Here the younger people have on the whole done well. Better educated on the average than their elders, they have demanded a greater voice in the establishment of publicly espoused policy and have gotten it. In community after community everywhere such offices as those of municipal councilman and the presidencies of the major community associations have passed from the old to the young leaders, despite the fact that the great weight of economic power and family influence remains firmly lodged in the hands of the older generation.

Insofar as it is based upon superior educational or sheerly technical qualifications, this generational shift in community leadership has been accepted gracefully enough by the older people. It is generally conceded, for example, that an English-trained lawyer—even if very young—is specially qualified to speak on political decisions affecting the whole community. But often the qualifications of the younger claimants to power are not so patently apparent, and the transfer is more grudgingly conceded by the older people. Speaking of the recent generational shift in the leadership of a large and important Hindu community, a spokesman for the younger generation commented:

> One of our big problems is that the old men who came out here first and made the money want to dominate things. They take the position that just because they have been here longest, they can tell the rest of us what to do. Now it would be perfectly all right with us if some of these so-called leaders would actually lead the community. But they don't. You can't lead the community by doing nothing; you have to do something for the community in order to command respect of the people you are trying to lead. These older men don't want to lead. They just want to dominate.
>
> Take X. In the years when he was at the head of things like the Indian Association, what did he do? Absolutely nothing. So what do we owe him? Nothing! Or you take Y. I have nothing against Y; he is a nice enough chap. But he thinks that just because he has been here for a long time he should be at the head of everything.
>
> If one of these old-timers decides to do something for the community, then they always want the community to accept it on their terms, or otherwise they won't play. When it was decided to build the Hindu Hall, X offered [*x* thousand pounds] as a contribution. But when he was voted out of the chair [i.e. as president of the Association], then he got cross and withdrew his money and hasn't paid a penny to this day. Y is the same way. He would like to give money to the community, but then we would have to do exactly what he wanted or he wouldn't give it.

On the other hand, a man like Z [an emerging young leader] takes an entirely different attitude. First he consults the community to find out what we want, and then that is what he suggests should be done.

NEW LEADERSHIP AND INSTITUTIONAL TRENDS

The emergence of the younger generation into the forefront of public community affairs clearly signals the profound socio-cultural reorientation among the Indians of Central Africa. What these young men are in thought and deed points clearly to the future, however unrepresentative in the purely statistical sense they may be as individuals. From the standpoint of theory, they also conveniently illustrate and exemplify the basic argument underlying the last four chapters: namely, that culture is fundamentally instrumental in character and always operates within specific historico-social contexts.

Many of these emerging young leaders were born in Africa. Already thoroughly secularized and westernized, they find little which appeals to them very strongly in the classic identities and loyalties of the Indian village of their fathers. It is remote from their world of actual experience, and for the most part these young people have little sympathy with its basic values. Insofar as the key symbols of religion and caste can be reworked to comply with their current social requirements, they are given lipservice; but those elements of the old faith and its associated values which conflict with present social realities are summarily rejected. To have a religion, for example, is still convenient and expected by the norms of the western-oriented part of modern cosmopolitan culture, and accordingly young people who lead thoroughly secularized lives in an urban milieu still label themselves as Hindu or Muslim. Yet it is illustrative of the newer search for community-wide unity that the divisive features of all traditional belief and practice are deplored and rejected as outmoded. It is indeed remarkable, for example, with what equanimity most of the younger people of both religious groups can now contemplate the passions of the partition period a short generation ago. Caste, being almost completely divisive and also called "undemocratic," is simply not respectable among the younger generation and is rejected in toto. In like manner, the powerful sentiments of identity, loyalty, and gratitude engendered in their fathers by the patron-client system leave these young people cold. Even the feeling of that solidarity founded in kinship tends more and more to be restricted, in the western manner, to the immediate nuclear family.

This scarcely means that the younger generation are an unfeeling and dispassionate lot, for exactly the opposite is probably much closer to the truth. But intelligent realists that they are, the *common* fate of Indians in Central Africa looms infinitely larger in their minds than the quarrels engendered and perpetuated in the Indian village of their fathers. What this means concretely is that survival in Africa interests the younger generation, not the perpetuation in the abstract of Indian society and culture.

Thus the foundation is increasingly laid in cognitive definition and supporting sentiment for a truly inclusive community to which all Indians belong, by the fact that they are socially identified vis-à-vis other ethnic groups in this plural society as Indians. Yet, paradoxically, when and if this inclusive community comes into existence, it will necessarily be "un-Indian" since such unity can only be achieved by the rejection and denial of what are in many respects the most distinctive features of Indian society and culture.

Chapter Eight

INTERETHNIC RELATIONS:
INDIAN AND EUROPEAN

Surely Indians are not unique in that the moral fabric of
their community is rent by the kind of dissension and discord
revealed in the last chapter. Examined in similar detail, the
gap between the moral ideal and the real in any one of the
other ethnic communities of Central Africa might appear as
wide. What is seen in the Indian case is a sociological universal: community as moral unity is always a relative matter,
imperfectly and partially achieved. Yet relative or not, people
in Central Africa do as an observational fact feel socially and
morally at home within their own ethnic group in a way they
do not in others. Imperfectly or not, the ethnic group bounds
the greater part of their expectation of moral community.

When we pass from the relationships which Indians have
with each other to those which they have with non-Indians, we
move therefore, in Park's terms, from "moral" to "ecological"
integration. Properly modernized and qualified along the lines
laid down in the theoretical discussion, this distinction can
serve a useful heuristic purpose. Yet we must understand that
it is suggestive, not absolute. So far in this volume, we have
taken considerable pains to show how Indian subculture is
permeated through and through with moral norms of European origin, and we will end on this note in the present
chapter.

222

Supported and sustained by an overwhelmingly superior culture, the European invaded Africa, established himself as the supreme political authority, and immediately began to rearrange matters systematically to conform to his vision of what they ought to be. The social order which the European imposed upon all others was a moral order as perceived within his own ethnic group. But to the African, the Indian, and the Coloured, the European-imposed social order was an impersonal set of life conditions, unmodifiable through mutual exchange of moral evaluations. It was in short "ecological," as we have defined the term.

Let us now move a step closer to empirical particulars. To do so systematically, some of the major role contexts within which Indians and Europeans interact will be examined. These include: (1) Indians and European officials; (2) Indian businessmen and European businessmen; (3) shopkeeper-customer relations; (4) employer-employee relations; (5) professional-client relations; (6) mutual participation in what we will call "ceremonial public occasions" and formally organized multi-racial voluntary associations; (7) interracial athletics; and finally (8) friendship, or informal voluntary associations.

Both the nature of the available materials and space limitations guarantee that the discussion will be at times sketchy and fragmentary. Yet if we manage through pertinent comment and illustration to suggest something of the mode, tone, and quality of interaction in these typical role-situations, the goal will have been achieved. In Chapter 9 we will apply the same pattern of analysis to the relations which Indians have to Africans and Coloureds.

The Indian and the European Official

From the Indian's point of view, the option to immigrate to Central Africa was real while it lasted; and suddenly in the immediate postwar period, this option became very attractive. But at the very door of these tempting opportunities stood a cool and impersonal white-skinned bureaucrat. Little wonder, then, that the immigration inspector stands in the Indian mind as a potent power symbol, representing in his person the main qualities and character of Europeans and their government: foreign, hostile, irrational, and arbitrary. Fortunately, however, the European was perceived as maneuverable if one were knowledgeable and skillful enough to attempt it.

A young informant living in Northern Rhodesia who was "called" by an older brother in 1951 describes his experiences in getting into the country. He came via Beira to Livingstone by train, crossing through Southern Rhodesia as usual on a temporary transit permit:

> You have probably heard how it was in those days. There was an immigration check post on the Southern Rhodesian side of the bridge and another in the Northern Rhodesian territory. To get into Northern Rhodesia you just walked across the bridge.
>
> My brother was unable to leave work to meet me, so I had to come in alone. The day I came three other Indian chaps were already there, waiting to take their [English] examinations. They were called in, one at a time, and so far as I could see they all passed without any trouble. But I was getting more and more worried; it seemed to take a long time and it was getting late in the afternoon. Sure enough, before I was called inside the doors were shut, and from where I was waiting I could see the Inspector going to his house in the back. There I was, left at the bridge, unable to go either way. I couldn't get into Northern Rhodesia, and I couldn't go back to Southern Rhodesia, since my transit permit had already expired.
>
> I was standing there on the bridge wondering what I was going to do when C [an Indian businessman] came along. He said he had come "just to look at the Falls." [Actually, he badly needed assistants and hoped to pick one up at the bridge, as he proceeded to do.] We struck up a conversation and C asked me where I was from in India. I told him I was from Charotar, and he said, "That's my district, too." [In other words, they quickly determine that they are fellow Charotar Patidars.] C said he knew

the Inspector and thought he could be persuaded to give me the examination, even if it was already after hours. We walked over to his house and called him out. He said he would.

The examination was like this: the Inspector dictated a paragraph in English and you were supposed to write it down. I couldn't understand him very well, and I asked him to repeat a word or two. But he said, "No, that's the idea of the examination." So I said, "I know English, but I can't understand the way you speak; I'm not used to your accent." It was then agreed that C should read the paragraph instead of the Inspector. I made only four mistakes in the entire paragraph, and the Inspector admitted that one of the others whom he had already passed had made sixteen. But he said, "I can't let you through. You know I can't let everybody in; we're required to fail some people, and I haven't failed anybody today." So C said, "Why not let him in and fail somebody else tomorrow and put it down as today for the record?" He said he would, and I got in.

This, however, is not quite the end of the story:

About three months later this Inspector happened to be passing through X [a line-of-rail town] and he stopped in at C's shop where I was working. They had a little chat, at the end of which the Inspector said, "By the way, what would it have cost that assistant of yours over there [pointing to me] to get back to India if I had failed him?" So C said, "What do you want?" And he said, "Well, I just wondered what it was worth to him, that's all." And so C said, "Well, I guess about £25," and he took £25 out of his wallet and gave it to him, and then the Inspector left. Of course, you understand, that £25 came out of my salary.

Given the world-wide reputation which the British civil service enjoys for incorruptibility, the number of such reports from Indians was mildly surprising. Nor, apparently, were payoffs of this sort limited to immigration officials. Other valuable official favors were—by the Indian account—commonly bought, for example, trading licenses in the tight period immediately following the war.

The actual extent to which the European civil service was thus corrupted by Indians is of course a matter for which we have no accurate and reliable data. We heard only the Indians' side of the story, with an occasional confirming hint from a European informant. What we do know is that Indians have typically assumed that officials could be corrupted, given appropriate circumstances, and that this assumption has played an important functional role in relations between them. To the Indian, the idea that the European could be successfully corrupted helped to prove what he was most eager to believe in any case: namely, that the vaunted standards by which the European sought to legitimate morally his overriding position of power and privilege were false and hypocritical and thus need not be respected. To the European, on the other hand, the frequency of Indian attempts at bribery was proof of moral and cultural inferiority. To a people as moralistic as the British, apparent willingness to resort to even the milder forms of corruption is in principle deeply offensive.

Liberals in particular, since they are even more moralistic than the average Britisher, are strongly influenced by the stereotyped belief that Indians are peculiarly susceptible to the temptation of corruption. For this reason, violent anti-Indian prejudice among the professional worriers over the sad-state-of-the-underdog is fairly common.

The wife of a European liberal politician reported to us with great indignation how she had been approached by an Indian leader who hinted—as she interpreted it—that she might find it profitable to influence her husband on a vote important to Indians:

I wanted to hit him with something—if nothing else, then with the handbag which I was carrying. But I didn't *do* anything. I just stood there and stared at him. Then

226

I said, "Mr. D, if there is anything which I hate, it is dishonesty in any form! If I thought my husband would stoop to anything dishonest, then I would immediately leave him!" Then I turned on my heel and walked away. Since then Mr. D and I have never spoken to each other. When we meet, he gives me a cool nod and I just stare at him.

Insofar as we could judge the circumstances from what she herself said, it seems quite possible that she might have mis-interpreted the man's intentions. In any case, it is clear that the established stereotype helped her to the conclusions which she made from whatever he did say.

Quite apart from outright bribery, there is an assumption among European officials that Indians attempt to cultivate them, not necessarily with a specific and immediate purpose in hand but as capital for as yet unforeseen contingencies. An important provincial administrator who had an unusual number of fairly intimate contacts within the Indian community put it this way:

Indians are great intriguers, and they are much better at it than we Europeans. They like to cultivate a high official because they are always looking for the main chance, and they don't want to miss it when it comes by. They reason that they can't go wrong with such an approach. Maybe at some time or other—and they are always looking into the future—a highly placed official will be in a position to do something for them. Their basic technique is flattery. But if they think it will work, they don't hesitate to use cruder means. Some people in government have received some very expensive gifts from Indians whom they barely know.

Empirically, this observation seems accurate to us in its essentials. Indians do take a highly self-conscious and rational attitude toward power relations. They assume that things get done through a manipulation of persons in power rather than through following impersonal bureaucratic rules and principles. To Indians the common American adage, "It ain't what you know but who you know that counts," is simply an unquestioned fact of life.

Analysis soon shows that this assumption constitutes a fundamental postulate concerning the nature of social reality which is built into the very fabric of indigenous Indian institutions. It is in good part the foundation of the patron-client relationship, to take that example. But the utilitarian and instrumental aspects of this relationship are as openly and as readily acknowledged by both parties as are the sentimental ones. Nor, significantly, do Indians themselves ordinarily try to hide the fact that they value contacts with Europeans (or anyone else) which may prove to be important, although those Indians who know European culture best realize that among Europeans a certain decent hypocrisy with regard to such motives is expected.

During the early period of federation, expensive parties at which Indians entertained Europeans as the principal guests-of-honor were very common throughout Central Africa.[1] Both the ability to support such affairs financially and sufficient social skills to deal with Europeans in this completely un-Indian atmosphere came to be considered primary prerequisites for leadership within the Indian community. A candid informant specifically pointed to these when commenting upon the shift from the older to the younger leadership which was noted in the last chapter.

> You take old J. J was head of the Indian Association for years. But he has almost no business to speak of. On the other hand, D [a young progressive leader] is a rich man. If he has to spend £500 on a party for the Europeans then he can do it. It's nothing to him.

Such parties were in fact already past history at the time this interview took place, despite the informant's present tense. Given Indian tastes, the motives on the Indian side were

1. Cf. Morris, "Indians in East Africa," pp. 209-10.

patently ulterior. When it became apparent that it was no longer profitable to cultivate Europeans, the parties suddenly ceased. Yet, surely Indians cannot be considered unique if they try on occasion to manipulate social relationships to ulterior ends. The billions of dollars spent on public relations, advertising, business entertainment, and congressional lobbying in the United States (and elsewhere) contradict any such notion. Why, then, the violently negative reaction of Europeans when confronted with this facet of Indian behavior?

The highly moralistic reaction of the European official at the Indian's attempt to cultivate him rests, it seems, less upon the behavior itself than upon its apparent crassness, coming as it does from a social inferior. Coming from social equals, flattery, gifts, and expensive entertainment can be accepted and defined as acts of "friendship" and thus morally legitimated. Manifested by a social inferior to whom the equality of true friendship is denied, the same acts can only be perceived as subversive of the "system" which defines the line between equality and inequality.[2]

Indian Businessmen–European Businessmen

Here a distinction must be made between relations of interdependence and those of competition.

1. Relations of interdependence. Business, it is commonly and rightly said, is business's best customer. A very considerable number of European firms in banking, wholesaling, manufacturing, and building and contracting, together with some in real estate and insurance, do a substantial volume of business with Indians. "I do 75 percent of my business with the Indians," a manufacturer's representative once told us. A local banker commented, "It's the business which we do with Indians which keeps our bank going."

It is simply a fact that Europeans who regularly do a substantial amount of profitable business with Indians know them better and have a greater respect for them than any other

2. See below, pp. 251–53.

group in the European community. We never heard an expression of rank anti-Indian prejudice from a European businessman involved extensively in such an interdependent relationship with Indians. On the contrary, it was noted that such people often went out of their way to attempt to correct for us some of the stereotypical notions current generally. For example, the banker just quoted above went on to say:

> I suppose by this time, Doctor, you must have learned enough to know that the common European view here of the Indian as an economic parasite is completely wrong factually. He is not a parasite. Far from it. He has contributed tremendously to the economic well-being of this country.

Business norms and values are among the most rational and universalistic in a capitalist culture. The business customer tends to be perceived and evaluated primarily in his role as a fellow businessman. Intelligence and drive, acumen, financial responsibility, and successful achievement receive recognition; other social attributes are either ignored or kept in the background. A European supplier described in awed tones an Indian family who had built, within the space of a few years, a large and flourishing business from almost nothing:

> They do a gross business of over x thousand pounds a month. I know because I have seen their balance sheet. Some months they have an overdraft at the bank of as much as x thousand. That's a lot of money. But the bank doesn't worry about that overdraft for a moment. They have utter confidence in the P's.

2. *Competitive relations.* When we turn from business relationships of mutual interdependence to those of competition, however, the scene changes drastically. If Europeans in the first category are among the least prejudiced toward Indians, those in the second category are by contrast surely among the most prejudiced. To be strictly accurate, it should

be added that this prejudice is richly reciprocated by the Indians.

Historically, it was principally Jews whom Indians faced in this competitive position: Jews were already established in the African trade when the Indians arrived. Indians, naturally, were welcomed by the Jewish traders with something less than enthusiasm. After thirty years an Indian pioneer remembers in bitterness walking (because he did not have the money to buy a ticket) up the line-of-rail from Livingstone: "When I passed through M, I stopped at a Jew-boy's shop and asked for a drink of water. They refused to give it to me." He went on:

> There was nothing but Jew-boys in business here then, and they had no competition. But we soon saw to it that they got some! They were selling blankets which cost them five shillings for a pound; we sold them for ten. They wanted a sixpence for one of these [holding up a soda bottle]. We sold 'em for four-and-a-ha'-penny.

Fortunately for them, the Jews did not suffer unduly in the long run from this economic contest with the Indians. They retired from the African trade in the face of Indian competition, but they were typically able to sell out advantageously to Indians, thus gaining the necessary initial capital for other and more profitable types of business. Some—but by no means all—moved into the European trade. In this case, they were apt to find themselves again soon confronted with stiff Indian competition. When we asked a European accountant who it was who was mainly responsible for keeping the Indians out of the local European chamber of commerce, he replied: "Oh, that's X's idea [naming the largest independent European retailer in town, a Jewish pioneer]. Of all the Europeans here, X hates the Indians the most." That this antagonism between Jew and Indian is essentially "structural" rather than "racial" can be seen when their relationship is one of interdependence rather than competition. In that case, each group perceives the other in a far more friendly light.

A certain large Jewish wholesaler, for example, is highly popular among small Indian shopowners all over Central Africa since he not only advances credit on his own goods, but is also willing to make cash loans to people who cannot get bank credit. One Indian informant observed admiringly:

> You probably know that as a general rule Indians don't like Jews. But G is different. He is one of my best friends, and there are a lot of Indians in my position who feel the same way. To get a loan from him you of course have to show how you can repay it, and you have to have two friends sign with you. The interest is plenty high, too. [It approaches a usurious 20 percent.] But I'll say this for him: G has never yet gone to court with a single Indian customer, although I'm sure that not every one manages to repay him.

Shopkeeper–Customer Relations

The large Indian businessman comes into contact with European businessmen and officials regularly in the course of his day-to-day operations. The ordinary shop assistant, however, has much less opportunity for direct contact with Europeans unless he happens to work—as most do not—in a shop with a European clientele. It is eloquent testimony of the paucity of other meaningful contacts that this role (a stock textbook example of the "secondary," "segmental," and impersonal in social organization) should loom as large as it does in the total picture of Indian-European relations. The only Indians whom most Europeans know are the young men who regularly attend their needs in the shops they patronize. For the shop assistants involved, our data suggest that the acculturative effects from such interaction may be considerable.

Assessment of these acculturative effects is complicated by the fact that the more westernized and acculturated are selected for such work: only those assistants who speak good English, who are unusually alert, and who have developed appropriate social skills can find and hold positions in the European trade. Nonetheless, it still remains true that these original foundations are extended and broadened within this situation. An opportunity to practice one's English continuously is a highly valued aspect of these positions among assistants. Language is the thing of which they themselves are self-consciously aware, but more subtle acculturative influences are also unquestionably present. One gets a hint of these in such remarks as the following:

> We have a very pleasant type of trade here since we deal mostly with Europeans. That way we learn about what's going on in town [i.e. outside the Indian community]; we get to know everything that happens through talking with them. If I had to live like some of those assistants over there in the secondary trading district, then I don't know how I would do it!

Or from another informant:

> I like to find out about any new customer who comes in —what they do for a living, what they think of this country, and how things are going with them. If they aren't going so good, then I can say, "I'm not so bad off, after all; even the Europeans have their troubles!" Sometimes, too, I learn something from them which turns out to be very useful to know.

That Indian shop assistants value their contacts with European customers is suggested in an incidental remark made by a European friend of ours:

> We used to buy at X's [a large European-owned department store]. But the service is so poor and impersonal there; they don't seem to care whether you buy anything or not.

> Dotson: Do you feel that you get more personal attention at an Indian store?

> Oh yes, definitely. Sometimes almost too much—you know how the Indians like to talk. But if I have the time, I don't mind that. And the assistants seem to enjoy it too.

Given the instrumental and manipulative view which Indians take of personal relations, it should not surprise us that attempts are occasionally made to turn contacts with Europeans toward ulterior ends. An alert young shop assistant reported what must be a fairly typical example. His brother, who had been unhappy with his job with a hard-driving and small-minded Indian employer, obtained a better one with a European. The new employer, it turned out, was a regular customer at our informant's shop where they had become good "friends." [3] When he learned that the European needed more help in his business (a small service industry), he sent his brother to apply for a job. The brother did so and was summarily refused. The next day, the European came into our informant's shop:

> As usual, Mr. W waited until I was free to wait on him, and then he said, as he always does, "How are you this morning?" I replied, "Not so good." So he said, "What's the matter?" and I said, "I don't feel so good because you didn't give my brother a job yesterday." Then he said, "What? Was that *your* brother who came to see me? I didn't know that. Tell him to come around again." So he went and got the job. You see, friendship pays off.

This informant was trying at the same time to use another contact which he had made to get himself a job in the cooperative creamery, in Central Africa a large, monopolistic, bureaucratic organization. One of his European "friends" was a woman customer who had recently lost her job with an automobile agency and had gone to work for the creamery. By using her influence, he hoped (in vain, as it turned out) to obtain a position there, although he knew that the creamery had never hired an Indian.

The evidence is abundantly clear that "friendships" of this kind rarely transcend shop boundaries. European shop "friends," Indians observe, may be less than friendly in other situations. One assistant put it this way: "It is true that some

3. See below, pp. 251–52.

Europeans are willing to be friendly and talk when they come to one's shop. Yet if you saw these same people in a cafe dining room and you went over and sat down at the same table with them to talk, then they wouldn't like it."

Some assistants reported that they never made an effort to be friendly with European customers through fear that they would be rebuffed if they tried or that their motives might be misinterpreted. Asked if he talked much with Europeans, one man replied:

I do, but some fellows in the shop don't. You know, some people are kind of funny. You never know how they are going to react. Once one of the other assistants asked a European woman where she lived, just to make conversation. She got cross and complained to the manager, "What does that fellow want with me? Why should he ask where I live?" And she closed up her account at the shop.

Employer–Employee Relations

Few Indians work for Europeans in private employment. Conversely, few Europeans work for Indians. But both types of relations do occur.

1. European employer–Indian employee. In a large Northern Rhodesian town with an Indian population of more than a thousand, a careful count revealed just a dozen Indians in private European employment. The number fluctuates, but the proportion would seem fairly representative of Northern Rhodesia as a whole at the time of the original fieldwork. More Indians worked for Europeans in Nyasaland, but even there the number of such positions was small. In Southern Rhodesia, where segregation was more pronounced, even fewer Indians worked for Europeans than in Northern Rhodesia.

A common stereotype prevails among Europeans that Indians have no interest in wage or salary positions in European firms. "All they are interested in is business," a labor officer once told us, repeating what Europeans generally say.

Like most stereotypes, this is a half-truth, but only a half-truth. Indians are oriented toward the ideal of an independent business of their own as an ultimate goal. But to start a business, one must have capital. If there is no other source, one must work for it, as Indians are prepared to do. Furthermore, our data clearly show that a good many marginal shopkeepers would close their shops if they had the alternative of steady employment at (or near) going European wages since they would raise their incomes considerably by doing so.

The reasons why more Indians are not hired by European firms are rather complex. To most Indians, the answer is simply "discrimination"—and this is undoubtedly the larger part of the story. Still, this explanation is not wholly satisfactory. The mere fact that discrimination exists does not explain why there are so few Indians in European employment. In other words, there is no inherent reason why Indians might not work for Europeans under discriminatory conditions. Coloureds work almost exclusively for Europeans and are grossly discriminated against. So are Africans. So, too, are Indians in European employment in South Africa. Europeans, it is certain, would be very happy to get Indian labor, if it could be had on *their* terms.

The Indians' refusal to work for Europeans on the Europeans' terms is thus the crux of the matter. When Indians say that they would like work in a European firm, it is clear that the kinds of position and remuneration which they envisage are those enjoyed by Europeans. With this fact in mind, we can question whether or not the European refusal to hire Indians is really, in many cases, purely discriminatory. That Indians *could*, by and large, learn to do anything which Europeans currently do is undeniable. That Indians *can* do what European employees do in many of the positions to which they abstractly aspire is an entirely different matter. The number of potentially excellent stenographers in the Indian community must be tremendous. Yet as an actual and existing resource, there are virtually none.

The view often taken by those few Indians who do work

for Europeans is instructive here. A bricklayer who learned his trade in India and who now works as a construction foreman for a politically conservative European contractor had the following comment about his employer and his job:

> You can be sure of one thing: the only reason Mr. M keeps me on is because of my ability. Why else? He isn't my relative. He isn't even my friend. He just knows I can do the job well. Sometimes there is a lot of work to do. Sometimes there is very little, like right now. When there isn't much to do, Mr. M has let other foremen go. Recently, ten South Africans [i.e. Afrikaners] lost their jobs, but he kept me on.

A university-educated manufacturer's representative who has carved out for himself an unusually successful career in a large English firm commented somewhat smugly:

> I tell the people in my community frankly that it is their own fault. Of course there is some discrimination; I'll admit that. But I don't believe discrimination is the most important element. The most important thing is the complete lack of training and capacity on the part of the Asians who apply for the jobs. How can they expect to be hired when they have no qualifications whatsoever to offer?
>
> I know a chap with an LL.B. from an Indian university. He came to this country expecting to be hired by government or some big corporation at a high salary. When he wasn't, he went around talking about discrimination. Such people have no humility. They don't ask for the kind of job which they can fill, with the qualifications which they have. What good is an Indian LL.B. in this country? It's no wonder the Europeans aren't impressed.

When asked how he had obtained his job with a large European firm a warehouse clerk replied: "I just walked in and asked Mr. B if he had a job when I was looking for work several years ago and he gave it to me. . . . Most of my people have an inferiority complex. They don't find work with Europeans because they don't go and ask for it." [4]

It has been pointed out that more Indians worked in European employment in Nyasaland than in any of the other territories, a fact which seems to have been mainly traceable to a shortage of European labor during and following World War II.[5] Most of these Indians, however, worked under discriminatory conditions. When we commented upon the difference between Nyasaland and the Rhodesias in respect to European employment for Indians, a wealthy young independent Indian businessman replied bitterly:

> Yes, there are quite a number of Indians here who work for European firms. But in those cases you will find these Indians are employed at £40 or £45 a month, although they do the same job for which a European would get £100 or £125. Furthermore, there's absolutely no hope of advancement in those jobs. All the best-paying jobs at the top are occupied by Europeans, you can be sure of that.

2. Indian employer–European employee. By actual count, the number of Europeans who work for Indians is considerably greater than the number of Indians who work for Europeans. This relationship, however, takes only one major form. Except for an occasional skilled artisan called in for a temporary job, virtually all the Europeans who work for Indians are female shop assistants, employed in the women's clothing and accessories departments of the larger European-oriented de-

4. This man is a Brahman by caste. He went on to say: "Personally, I have never had an inferiority complex. I know I don't have a very good education, but I am not afraid of a man because he has a better education than I have. Nor do I consider a European better than I am. Nor do I look up to a rich man. I respect and admire him for the abilities which gave him his wealth, but I don't admire him for his wealth alone."

5. The manager of a leading firm of estate agents and manufacturers' representatives, for example, told us how they had been induced under these circumstances to try an Indian for the first time, and he added that they were so pleased with him that they then hired more until finally all but their top staff were Indians.

partment stores. In addition, there is a rare bookkeeper or typist, but these are found only in the very largest firms. Most Indian businessmen, including those who have a volume of trade which by American standards would demand an office staff of two or three girls, do their own accounting and letter writing (usually in longhand). If they do not, then these tasks generally fall to some younger male member of the family.

Despite the fact that nearly all European women in Central Africa work, the supply seems to fall well short of the demand. The overall quality of the sales personnel available to either European or Indian firms is thus certainly not very high. After saying that he had had to discharge several European women assistants in a row, the owner of a large store commented with unusual candor upon those he currently had. Pointing to one on the floor below the office balcony where we were talking, he said:

> She's all right. At least she doesn't steal. But she's very apathetic. She refuses to learn her stock. A customer comes in and asks for something, and she says, "Wait, and I'll see if we have it." It's only a very small department, and she should know what she has and what she doesn't have. But all she can say is, "Wait, and I'll see," keeping the customer standing there. I have warned her time and time again that this will not do. But it doesn't do me any good.

Few informants were so unguarded. But we nonetheless gathered the impression that most Indians who employ European women rather resent the necessity of doing so. It is not a matter of cost; an Indian male assistant would have to be paid as much (£45 or so a month). An Indian assistant, however, would be more alert, zealous, and efficient. Young Indian women will probably be employed for this type of work just as soon as an English-speaking generation appears in sufficient quantity. Some Coloureds are already hired; but Coloureds leave much to be desired despite the fact that they can be paid much less than a European. Few Coloured women are sufficiently middle-class to be either suitable or comfortable in this position.

Where European women work for Indians, the relationship seems typically to be strictly impersonal from both sides. Only large businesses employ such help; in such a case any employer-employee relationship would tend toward the impersonal. Moreover, the sex difference guarantees—or perhaps encourages—a degree of reserve which might not exist otherwise.

Interestingly enough, the anti-Indian sentiment so widespread throughout the European population does not seem to rub off, so to speak, onto the women who work for Indians, a fact indicative of the relationship's essential impersonality. To the employee, work with an Indian firm is just a job like other jobs. The pay and working conditions are the same as they would be in a European-owned shop, and her family and friends seem to accept this employment in the same light. To the employer, if our assessment is correct, the European shop assistant is simply a reluctant necessity if he is to attract European women customers. The balance is struck at this level, and all concerned seem willing to leave it at that.

Professional–Client Relations

In South and East Africa, professional services for Indians are provided in the main by qualified members of their own ethnic group. In Central Africa, however, Indian professionals are barely beginning (as of this writing) to put in their appearance. In time they will doubtlessly be plentiful enough. Until this stage is reached, Indians will have to do what they have done in the past, that is, turn to a European when they need assistance of a professional nature.

1. Legal. As businessmen and as immigrants of insecure status, Indians have a good many occasions to seek legal advice and they appear with some regularity either as plaintiffs or defendants in civil suits. Some disputes are with Africans. Indians sue (or, far more often, threaten to sue) other Indians to collect debts, and European customers and suppliers are sometimes involved. The great majority of the resulting charges and counter-charges never reach a court. But lawyers are often consulted even if they do not.

Many of these cases strike the middle-class European as "petty" and "mean" in the extreme. Lawyers whose sole contact with Indians comes through counseling claimants in such cases inevitably get a lopsided—although vivid and realistic —view of the community. They tend therefore to be among the most prejudiced of Europeans with respect to Indians. The following illustrates, in the words of one of these lawyers, what is perhaps a fairly typical case:

This African client of mine had left his new bicycle at this Indian's shop for safekeeping while he was in town. When he came back, the bicycle was gone. The Indian said somebody had stolen it. The African knew who had stolen it, all right, and so he came to see me.

I called the Indian on the telephone and told him to produce the bicycle or £14. His answer was, "I can't do that. The bicycle was stolen! The African left it here at his own risk; I told him that. I have no legal responsibility for it." But I had plenty on him, and I knew I could cause him a lot of trouble. So I said, "How long have you been in this country?" And he said, "Seven years." And so I said, "In that case your citizenship is not yet completed. If you are convicted of a crime, then you lose your citizenship, and back to India you go—right back to the gutter! I want that bicycle or £14, and I want it in twenty-four hours!"

Later on the same day, the telephone rang. It was the Indian, who said, "What do you know? I was walking down the street and what do I see leaning against the curb but that African's bicycle, and so we have it back now." Of course, he had it all the time.

These negative attitudes are reciprocated from the Indian's side. Indians fear and distrust European lawyers, and they charge that lawyers exploit them when they can. A good many Indians, for example, reported to us that they were forced to pay a semi-legal shake-down to lawyers working in collusion with immigration officials for entry into the country. The immigration inspector would fail the Indian on his English examination; when he (or more likely his patron) protested, he would be told to see a lawyer, who was conveniently at hand. After parting with a handsome fee, he would then be allowed to re-take and pass the examination.

It hardly needs to be added, perhaps, that the Indian's characteristically instrumental view of bureaucratic rules and regulations as machinery to be manipulated encourages this kind of exploitation. On this point one of the very few Europeans whom we met in Central Africa who could reasonably be described as having intimate contacts within the Indian community commented: "Mind you, I have no illusions about the Indians! Of course, they are great bribers and corruptors. And there are plenty of shyster lawyers in this town who are willing to help them out in their schemes."

At the time of the fieldwork, Indians commonly charged that local lawyers fought and delayed acceptance of Indian legal graduates into the profession. European lawyers countered that they were only maintaining "standards." Prospective lawyers who had already qualified for the bar in England were forced to take a special examination in local law, given and graded by a local board, a requirement which Indians and Africans believed to be directed solely at them. Furthermore, they had great difficulty in getting "articled"—a form of professional internship required before one can practice independently. Despite these hurdles, three Indians were admitted to the bar while we were in Africa, and several more were in training.

2. *Accountants, architects, etc.* Relationships involving this type of professional seem generally similar to those of the interdependent businessmen described above. These professionals nevertheless find Indian ways of doing things rather different and sometimes irritating. An accountant:

Indians have their own way of doing business. They can never understand that when I set a price for a job that is the price which I expect to be paid. They agree when we first discuss it, and then when I come back to collect the fee they refuse to pay what we agreed and expect me to bargain over it. The other day I went to see the M's and they pulled this old trick on me. I got mad and called them all sorts of names, but they just stood around and laughed. Very funny! What they want you to do is to knock the price down a bit. If a job is worth £200 and they can get you to settle for £195, then they will go to bed happy that night.[6]

3. Medical service. Until a few years ago, Indians went to European doctors only when convinced that they were seriously ill. Poverty, penuriousness, and a continued reliance upon folk medicine lay behind this pattern. Recently, however, the response of Indians to the potentialities of modern medical care has changed drastically; they now apparently use the doctor's services and the hospitals about as much as do local Europeans at anything like a comparable economic level. Virtually all Indian babies, to cite that single but significant index, are currently born in hospitals.[7]

We tried not to neglect our fairly numerous opportunities to talk to doctors about their experiences with Indian patients and made it a point to visit Indian informants when they were ill or injured. One sensitive (and unusually verbal) physician is quoted extensively since his commentary sums up so nicely most of what was learned:

6. Another young accountant, fresh from England and perhaps unduly frightened at what he had heard locally of Indian business ethics, flatly refuses to do work for Indians: "I'm afraid to. You know, an accountant is legally responsible for any audit to which he puts his signature. I never accept a job unless I have absolute confidence in the books. And I don't have that degree of confidence in those Indian friends of yours."

7. During the federation period, hospitals were operated by the federal government as a basic public service. Fees were nominal, and even these were scaled according to income and race. Most Indian families paid less than a pound a day. The patient was required to pay the physician's fee himself unless he was under some insurance plan.

I wish I could take a different attitude toward my Indian patients. I have told myself that I must try to understand them. But the truth is I find them very difficult to deal with and very irritating.

An Indian patient comes in and asks for a consultation. So you examine him and write out a prescription if he needs it. But if there are, let us say, four doctors in town, you know without asking that he has already been to the other three, and he is coming to you just to see whether or not you agree with their diagnosis. He will probably begin by telling you that he has heard that you are a very fine doctor and that he is glad he can consult you for that reason. He does a good job on this piece of flattery; if you didn't know that he had said the same thing to all of the others in turn, it would be very flattering indeed.

Some of them are even naive enough to show you the prescription which the other doctor wrote out for them. If you then ask when they saw the other doctor they will say, "Oh, three or four days ago. But I haven't got any better so I'm coming to you." However, all you have to do is look at the date on the prescription to see that it was made out the same afternoon.

A common reason for trying a different doctor is the hope of getting an injection, if the first doctor has not given one: "If you don't give him an injection when he comes to you, then you can be sure that he's going to try some place else. He won't rest until he finally gets one."

Our informant goes on:

An Indian who is sick really wants you to come to his house to see him. If you won't do that, then he will come to you, but he wants to do it after hours so he won't have to close his shop. When you have been in your consulting room all day you want to go home and relax. But an Indian talks you into seeing him after shop hours. Now a very common thing happens. What he does is call up all of his

244

friends who have complained that they have something wrong with them and tells them that he has arranged an appointment with the doctor. And so when he comes in, he doesn't come alone, but in a pick-up truck with about twenty others. When the one who made the appointment comes in, he doesn't say that the rest are out there waiting to see you. He waits until you have finished with him, and then asks you whether or not you will see a friend of his, picking out the sickest of the lot. So, before you know it you have seen them all.

Interestingly enough, Indians do not quibble at or attempt to bargain over medical fees as they typically do over other professional payments. They pay what is asked and frequently offer the physician extra compensation for an especially good job.[8] The doctor quoted above finished his observations with the comment: "If one were unscrupulous enough, one could make a lot of money from Indian practice."

Some doctors, certainly, are much more popular with Indians than others, and the ones who are popular are those who make concessions—on consulting hours, for example—to Indian habits and expectations. An old and very easy-going American physician, retired from many years in African missionary practice, is immensely popular with the Indians of one community for this reason.

4. Indians and Europeans as colleagues in the public schools. Virtually all of the federally-supported schools created after 1953 for Indians had combined Indian and European staffs, and some of them also had Coloured teachers to round out the ethnic picture. Headmasters were either Indian or European, or very occasionally Coloured. Policy in recent years, however, has favored Indian headmasters for schools which are primarily Indian in enrollment, but in Southern Rhodesia

8. An injured informant reports: "When I went into the hospital I was still conscious. So I told the doctor, 'Don't spare any costs that are necessary.' When my father-in-law arrived, he said the same thing, 'As long as you do the best job you can, don't worry about the expense. We will pay for it.'"

especially this Indian headmaster was apt to be a South African and thus non-Gujarati in origin.

Involving as it does professional people with presumably common interests and orientation, one might suppose that the teacher-to-teacher relationship in such a situation would be one of the firmest bridges across the ethnic chasms of a plural society. Yet with some few exceptions, this seems not to be typically the case. A closer examination soon reveals some of the factors which help to account for this characteristic impersonality.

First of all, in the great majority of cases the ethnic difference is compounded by a difference in sex. Few Indian teachers are women, since few Indian women are as yet either educated or competent in English. Conversely, European teachers in Indian schools are rarely men, the only important exception being the few European headmasters. As in the case of the Indian shop owner and his European female assistant, the difference in sex guarantees not only a measure of reserve in interpersonal relations but also a fundamental difference in values and social orientation. The European teacher is typically the wife of a civil servant; she descends into the Indian community during working hours; and when she leaves, she returns to her family and a social life oriented around her husband's friends in the governmental bureaucracy. By contrast, teaching is the career of the Indian male teacher, and he works within a school which is physically and socially a part of his ethnic community.

The highly mobile character of the European staff reinforces the other tendencies working toward impersonality. In the two northern territories especially there has been (and still is) a chronic shortage of teachers. The major reservoir from which European teachers are drawn consists of the wives of civil servants: when their husbands go on leave, the wives naturally want to go with them. The European teacher is therefore not on the job long enough for very intimate relationships with her Indian colleagues to develop, even if other conditions were more favorable.

More important than these extrinsic factors are the socio-psychological barriers to intimacy created by the structure of the social situation. Indian teachers and European teachers typically (although certainly not invariably) hold each others' capacities and professional qualifications in low esteem. Indians believe that the European teachers who are assigned to the Asian and Coloured schools are marginal professionally. Europeans, on the other hand, question the capacity of most of the Indian teachers. Irrespective of the formal qualifications offered from Indian institutions (and many Indian teachers do not possess even these qualifications), European teachers and supervisors hold that their colleagues are poorly prepared in subject content and professional orientation.

Objectively speaking, we suspect that both of these respective charges are essentially true. In any case, it was perfectly clear that the gross discrepancy between Indian and European salaries greatly exacerbated these mutually derogatory evaluations. Under the so-called "branch system" which still prevailed when our fieldwork began, unqualified temporary Indian teachers were hired at about £25 a month, while equally unqualified temporary European teachers received about £45 a month.[9]

To morally justify a salary nearly twice the size of his In-

9. The so-called "branch system" seems to have been a personal creation of Lord Malvern (Godfrey Huggins), the first prime minister of the Federation. As such, it makes an interesting study in the meaning of "multiracialism" as this was understood in the European community during the period of federation.

The Federal Public Service, Lord Malvern explained in his request for legislation, would be open to all persons "irrespective of race or creed," but —he added significantly—it would be "unrealistic" to expect everyone to have the same conditions of service. Therefore, the civil service would be divided into four categories. Branch I was to be initially for Europeans only, and *all* Europeans appointed after the legislation came into effect (1957) were automatically to enter Branch I. Branch II was intended primarily for Asian and Coloured teachers and nurses. Branch III in effect was for African clerical and technical staff; Branch IV embraced African messengers, orderlies, and the like. An Asian or Coloured teacher would be initially appointed to Branch II, regardless of his formal qualifications. If in the course of a probationary period of service, he demonstrated "integrity, responsibility, efficiency and devotion to duty," he would be accorded "parity" with Europeans and be promoted from Branch II to Branch I. Cf. Federal *Hansard* (August 23, 1956), col. 1827–36.

dian colleague's, it would be logically necessary for the European teacher to devalue and denigrate the professional worth of his Indian colleague, and our empirical data suggest that this is exactly what happened. Conversation with European teachers and supervisors concerning Indian teachers consisted largely of illustrations of the Indians' inadequacies and ineptitude. Indian teachers, on the other hand, were so embittered and demoralized by this salary differential that conversation upon any other topic proved difficult with them, so engrossed were they in this discriminatory injustice.

Ceremonial Public Occasions

A certain amount of highly formal contact and interaction takes place between Indians and Europeans—as well as between these two ethnic groups and Africans and Coloureds—on ceremonial occasions made deliberately "multiracial" by policy and definition. A prime example is the annual Governor's Garden Party (or its terminological equivalent), which has a long history in British colonial areas.[10] Receptions for very important visiting dignitaries are less regular in occurrence but virtually identical in pattern. The host in these instances is the government (or one of its agencies); but, socially, very much the same sort of situation is created at the annual "fete" of the Red Cross—in Central Africa a quasi-voluntary, quasi-official association. The self-consciously integrative activities of certain more strictly voluntary associations (the Business and Professional Women's Club, for example) produce a very similar behavioral situation.

Whether its auspices are public or private, the multiracial ceremonial occasion has a remarkably fixed pattern. For the Governor's "Sundowner" (cocktail party) and similar receptions, participation is restricted to a formal guest list; invitations go to recognized community leaders, and the official list is firmly established and followed without much deviation. The same people thus appear on different occasions with a highly predictable regularity. Exactly the same people are also in-

10. Cf. Morris, p. 209.

vited to the private functions, since they are the ones known to the leadership of the European community.

The true role of the ceremonial occasion in the promotion of interaction across ethnic lines is difficult to assess with any pretense to accuracy. To deny it any significance would in our view certainly be an error. In however limited and formal a fashion, the ceremonial occasion offers an opportunity to the diverse leaders of the ethnic communities to make contact with each other and to do so in a deliberately defined atmosphere of "friendliness" and formal equality. In interviews, we noted that both Indian and European leaders typically refer to "friends" in the opposite ethnic group, despite the fact that their relationship is confined entirely to the periodic contacts of the ceremonial cycle.

It remains true, nonetheless, that most of the contacts made at the ceremonial occasion are grossly superficial. We had just arrived in Africa, and Mrs. Dotson was being introduced at one of these affairs to a prominent European who then held a ministry in the territorial government.

Mrs. Dotson: Who would you say the leaders of the Indian community are?

Minister: Well, I would say you have a pretty good cross-section of them right here. [No Muslims happened to be present, but he didn't seem to notice this fact.] I would say Mr. P, and Mr. D, and Mr. L.

Mrs. Dotson: By Mr. P, whom do you mean? I've been introduced to two. Do you mean P.C. or L.C.?

Minister: Oh, don't ask me what their first names or initials are! I never can keep them straight! I mean that little man over there [nodding his head in the direction of an Indian across the room who had long been a major leader in this particular community].

Interracial Athletics

Interracial athletics create a kind of ceremonial occasion but it is a very special one by virtue of the complex of values

249

which formal athletic activity has acquired in present-day cosmopolitan culture. The athletic contest is seen by a great many people throughout the modern world as the ideal meeting ground for people of different ethnic origins. This belief—or faith, really—is so pervasively and so fervently held that it virtually constitutes a secular cult.

It would therefore have been strange indeed if these notions—to which the British have contributed more than any other single national group—had not appeared prominently in Central Africa when multiracialism was being vigorously preached at the time of the establishment of federation. Indian athletic clubs formed in the early 1950s heavily stressed the theme in their organizational propaganda.[11] Prominent Europeans, as well as some middle-aged and very sedentary Indian patrons, were typically included as honorary members of the clubs, which sprang up all over the country in this period.

As might be expected, given this popular ideology, we were constantly assured upon our arrival in Africa that the athletic club was the most important link between the European and Indian communities. Little objective evidence, however, supported this widespread conviction. If substantially intimate and enduring ties between Indians and Europeans are (or ever were) formed within this context, they completely escaped our attention.

A prominent European player described for us the situational context of a typical game in a Northern Rhodesian town:

> You have to know the area where the X Sports Club field is located in order to appreciate what the situation is. There is nothing out there, really—nothing but bush and grass all around. Two minutes before the game the Asian team appears—seemingly out of nowhere. I've never been able to figure out where they park their cars. Then immediately after the game they just disappear into

11. "Interracial" athletics in this context means games between ethnic groups—not, as in the United States, teams composed of representatives from such groups.

the bush again. I don't know where they go. They must
go back to their houses or their little shops.

Then he added a somewhat guilty reflection: "I suppose it is
our fault. It's a shame, really. Cricket is such a friendly game."

Friendships, or Informal Voluntary Associations

"Friendship," let us recognize at the outset of this discussion, is a word with extraordinarily capacious connotations.
The essence of friendship presumably lies in its intrinsic qualities. It is in its purest form a relationship founded simply and
solely upon mutual congeniality.

Associations of this type are universal, or, perhaps more accurately, the imperative and profound needs which they serve
are universally present in the human condition. Yet in practice the associations which adult persons make with each other
are seldom in the first instance guided by pure congeniality,
and for a very simple reason. In Sumner's ringing phrase, "the
first task of life is to live." The world's work must be done,
and thus what happens in the usual case is that the functions
of friendship are served as a kind of incidental and fortuitous
bonus by relationships founded in the requirements of institutional organization or the accidents of spatial propinquity.
For this reason, more often than not, friends turn out to be
cousins, workmates, or next-door neighbors.

Since few of the relationships commonly described as friendship rest purely upon mutual congeniality, a distinction must
be made between those that approach this ideal and those that
are farthest from it. A simple four-point scale conceived as an
unbroken continuum may serve this purpose: (1) Most of the
persons whom I loosely call "friends" in the English vernacular might be more precisely described as acquaintances. These
are people whom I "know"; I can identify them readily by
name and social status and with them I chat informally upon
occasion. (2) People with whom I interact much more frequently than acquaintances are those "friends" met and known
on the basis of institutional organization and propinquity. With

these persons, I am on "friendly" terms in a circumscribed context of work or place, but I never deliberately seek their company outside of these contexts. (3) Beyond this degree of intimacy, I have somewhat more intimate friends, people with whom I interact fairly regularly within situations deliberately arranged as social occasions, at parties and formally appointed visits. (4) Finally, I have "clique-mates," persons whose company I value so highly that I seek them out spontaneously in order to enjoy it. Of all the relationships on our scale, this last of course is the only one based upon pure congeniality and thus, perhaps, deserves to be called "true" friendship.[12]

Applying this simple scale to our empirical materials, we quickly note that there are "friendly" contacts in fair abundance between Indians and Europeans, but that these are confined in the main to the first two types of association on the scale. When either Indians or Europeans speak of friends in the opposite ethnic group, it almost invariably turns out upon closer questioning that these relations are confined to contacts within formally organized roles.

An Indian, for example, finds it necessary to go to the immigration office so often that he and the inspector become "friends." Good customers become "friends" for the same reason. And so do professionals and clients. If it also happens that the participants in these relationships are leaders in their respective communities, then perhaps their contact will be extended to the ceremonial occasion. Interaction within these degrees of intimacy accounts for virtually all of the observable "friendships" between Indians and Europeans.

From time to time, it is true, there are experiments with contacts of the third order, such as mutual visiting or entertaining. Significantly, these are usually initiated by Indians and seldom develop into a regular exchange. Beyond this point

12. Friendship is best understood technically in terms of the social psychology of the self and the self-image. Fundamentally, it is and must be a relationship of moral equality, an interchange of mutual self-evaluation and acceptance. My "true" friend is that person with whom I can entrust my self-image at its least guarded level, safe in the assurance that he will accept it and enhance it in exchange for my acceptance and enhancement of his self-image at its least guarded level.

we can be categorical and simply report that we personally know of no Indian-European relationship which can be properly described as "true" or clique friendship, as it has been defined.[13]

These are the essential empirical facts. What then, we must ask, is their sociological significance? The answer must discriminate between factors which are, on the one hand, primarily cultural and, on the other, primarily organizational.

1. Cultural factors. Realistic sociological analysis must in the first place recognize that real intimacy and thus "true" friendship is quite impossible for most people across the barriers of any considerable cultural difference.[14] Such barriers to intimate intercourse are infinitely greater than the innocent tend to think: if this were not so, Forster's great novel, *A Passage to India,* would have no point. In any society composed of discernible ethnic groups there will inevitably be enough differences in culture to constitute important barriers to intimacy, since it is by such cultural variations that these groupings are defined.

The most obvious of these barriers is that of language; there can be no interchange of the kind which constitutes true friendship without adequate communication. Indian males in Zambia and Rhodesia (but not necessarily in Malawi) virtually all speak English. Nevertheless, a degree of language competency which is adequate for business purposes may not be adequate to sustain a friendship on a very intimate basis. Even if an Indian man speaks fluent English, his wife commonly does not. If he brings his wife when invited to a European friend's house (as convention among the Europeans demands) then the women can only stare "pleasantly" at each other through a gruesomely long evening.

Aside from the barriers of language, food and drink must be considered, for food and drink are everywhere a component

13. Two or three cases known to us are close enough to the clique type to be arguable. A well-educated and personable informant whom we knew to have extensive contacts in the European community once surprised us a bit by flatly announcing: "I have no European friends."
14. See below, pp. 273–74, n. 9.

of truly intimate social relations. Most Hindus are vegetarians in fact and principle. Muslims eat meat; but pork and pork derivatives are rigidly proscribed and, at least in theory, the meat should be butchered ritually. Neither Hindus nor Muslims commonly use alcohol, but among the Europeans of Central Africa the "sundowner" cocktail party is an all but universal form of entertainment.

If both meat and drink are taken freely by prospective Indian guests, then there is still a question of taste. Indian and British cooking styles are virtually antithetical. Some Europeans relish some Indian dishes occasionally if they are not too hot, but this observation applies only to the mildly adventurous and experimental. Indians, on the other hand, universally object to British food; they can eat it if they have to, but only under duress. To them European food is bland to the point of being positively disagreeable. "Whenever I am invited out to a European's house for dinner," a prominent Indian leader once told us, "I always eat at home first."

Beyond language and food lie sharp but less easily definable differences in manners, concepts of personal hygiene, and expected public behavior in sex roles. For example, all but rather thoroughly acculturated Indians find sitting on a European-style toilet highly disagreeable. They perceive the toilet seat as dirty, and the very idea of toilet paper is repulsive. On the other hand, the unsuspecting and unadventurous European is likely to find squatting over an open Indian-style toilet a fair test of his cultural tolerance—and to be left there without paper in an emergency a disaster.

At a less extreme level, there are small matters like table manners which are capable of causing mutual irritation. A thoroughly westernized Indian schoolteacher of South African origin made this observation with respect to his far less acculturated Gujarati neighbors:

Indians have a number of habits which greatly annoy Europeans. For example, many of them still eat with their fingers [virtually all do, in our observation]. This is very clean, actually, if it is done properly, but unless it is done properly, it strikes Europeans as being dirty and disgusting. Not only that, but Indians are noisy at the table. It is quite proper at an Indian table to belch; the host expects you to belch to show you are enjoying the food. And if they are eating a liquid—such as a soup with a spoon—Indians are apt to suck it, making a loud noise.

If entertainment includes social dancing, then it is quite impossible for Indians to participate, irrespective of whether they are Muslims or Hindus. Only two instances of social dancing by Indians came to our attention throughout our original fieldwork—and one of these hardly counts, since the man involved was a South African non-Gujarati Christian. To be unable to dance may signify nothing more than sheer ignorance among the very modern generation, but to the great majority of Indians, young and old alike, dancing is still thought of as highly promiscuous behavior.[15] The sole Indian member of a local country club, a young university-educated Muslim businessman, remarked on this point as follows:

I like to go there to play, and very often my European friends want me to drink with them at the bar. I always say "no," although I am willing to keep them company with a coca-cola. The one thing where I draw the line firmly, though, is the dancing. I never attend the dances which they hold at the club. We Muslims don't believe in dancing.

15. Lalloo indicates more experimentation in dating and dancing among the acculturated Southern Rhodesian youth than is certainly true in the two northern territories: "The quiet rebellion against parental pressure is witnessed by the frequency of attendance to cinemas, bars and dances. Patronizing these entertainment places, particularly the latter two, were considered a decade ago as shameless behaviour. Accordingly, rather heavy restrictions were imposed to prevent this activity. Traditional opinion even today does not appear to have changed much in this respect. In spite of these restrictive attitudes, the youth make clandestine arrangements and surreptitiously accede to the temptations and attractions these places offer." Lalloo, "The Hindu Family in S. Rhodesia," p. 48. Also, see below, p. 289, n. 20.

In theory and in hope, as their liberally optimistic founders saw them, the multiracial social clubs that sprang up over the country in the wake of federation were to build bridges between the ethnic components of the new state by providing the physical facilities within which friendly contacts could be formed and sustained. Most of these clubs were still in existence and functioning when we arrived in Africa. But by this time virtually all of the Indian members had ceased to participate actively in them, despite the fact that Indians had originally given the clubs their enthusiastic moral and financial support. Built mainly around drinking and dancing, the multiracial club possessed little intrinsic attraction to Indians beyond its abstract philosophy.[16] Comments upon them from Indians were monotonously similar to this one: "I used to belong to the X Club, but I dropped out and quit paying my dues. Now I never go there anymore. The last time I went, there was nobody at the Club but a bunch of drunks. I don't drink, so what is there in it for me?"

2. Organizational factors. An interpretation of ethnic relations which ignored the self-segregating cultural barriers to intimacy of the sort indicated above would be sociologically naive. But an interpretation cast solely or even primarily in these terms would be even more so. The fact is that the plural society is a socially organized hierarchy of power and prestige. Segregation does not simply exist because of cultural differences; it is actively and directly enforced by the dominant group.

Indians constantly complained to us that friendly overtures and hospitality extended to Europeans are not reciprocated. An affable, university-educated young Muslim businessman

16. Up to the period of our original fieldwork the multiracial club was still the only place in Northern Rhodesia where Africans could buy European beer at a bar, and the clubs attracted the small white-collared African elite for this reason. Many of their most active members were drawn from the Coloured community. It was rumored that certain middle-aged and well-to-do Indian Muslims used to come to the clubs fairly regularly in the hope of picking up Coloured girls. The few active European participants tended on the whole to be young, mildly Bohemian, and leftishly intellectual types.

who had tried hard to broaden his contacts into the European community commented bitterly:

> I used to give a lot of parties here at my house after I returned home from India [where he had been at school]. My European "friends" were glad to come and eat my *samosas* and drink my liquor. But they never reciprocated. In the thirteen years in which I have lived here, I have never been invited into a European's house.

This lack of reciprocation is noticeable enough to be remarked upon occasionally by Europeans themselves. One told us of a case which had come to his attention while he was employed in a smallish Northern Rhodesian line-of-rail town:

> Do you know old M [a well-to-do Muslim pioneer] down at X? Well, he donated an expensive trophy to the local rifle club down there. [The club referred to a subgroup organized within the more general European Club.] They shoot for it annually. But the blighters never invited him into the club. They don't even invite him to attend the annual dinner at which the trophy is awarded.

With respect to the processes of acculturation that lower the barriers created by cultural differences, the attitude of the dominant group always contains a fundamental ambivalence which has often been noted in the literature on ethnic relations. On the one hand, dominant groups expect subordinate ethnic groups to adopt their norms and values spontaneously and instantaneously, as it were, in recognition of their superiority. At the same time, those cultural traits characteristic of subordinate groups which can be devalued by the dominant group provide highly convenient symbolic justification for the social discrimination which supports the unequal distribution of power.

Rapid acculturation therefore is never welcomed by a dominant group, who inevitably (and correctly) perceive the process as threatening to their position. A remark made by a reasonably liberal civil servant illustrates this familiar phenomenon. He commented upon his reaction to the recent desegregation of his hitherto strictly segregated country club.

> There were a number of Indians present at this particular sundowner, and I must say they left a rather bad impression. As I have told you, I don't have any racial prejudice myself. I have had plenty of Indians to my house, and I have been on occasion to theirs. Still, I don't believe that we have yet reached the stage of evolution in this country where you can have an indiscriminate public mixing of the races. At this sundowner the Indians showed very clearly that they have a tendency to muscle in when they have a chance, and many people, myself included, don't like it.

ECOLOGICAL AND MORAL INTEGRATION

Set within a context of European dominance, Indian-European relations are markedly "ecological." But it should perhaps be noted once again that our usage of this term differs importantly from Park's original. In both instances, the polar opposite of "ecological integration" is appropriately "moral integration." To Park, the ecological was *amoral* since it was subsocial and biological, sociality being specifically equated in his mind with culture and communication.[17] To us, this amoral quality of the ecological relationship seems better interpreted as *a lack of moral equality*. In ecological integration, as we would have it understood, the dominant group possesses a system of moral values, and these are expressed in the social relationships which it imposes upon subordinate groups. The point to be emphasized is that these values (together with the concrete relationships with which they are always associated in practice) are imposed: there is no reciprocity. Morally, the dominant demands and the subordinate complies.

17. See in particular the paper "Human Ecology" in Robert E. Park, *Human Communities: The City and Human Ecology* (Glencoe, Ill., Free Press, 1952), pp. 145–58. Also see our extended discussion in Appendix, pp. 404–05.

Moral equality is not to be directly equated with equality in social status.[18] Nonetheless, it is difficult to achieve across any considerable gaps of socio-cultural differentiation; when great enough, the ample evidence of history suggests that moral equality is then impossible. In such a case, the only alternative is a social order put together upon the principles of ecological integration.

The plural society of the immediate past in Central Africa seems to provide a case in point. For the greater part of the lifetime of the older adult members who now compose it, the European-imposed system of social relations in this region met the only empirically applicable test of social possibility which we know. It worked. It was a grossly unequal system; *but no one expected it to be equal.* On this basis, while it lasted, it functioned reasonably well.

What we must note of relevance here is that the system worked because its abstract justice was never systematically brought up for moral evaluation and review. It could not be, given the enormous chasms of cultural difference and of the resulting distribution of social power. Progressive acculturation—unforeseen and certainly unwanted by the dominant group—has drastically altered this historical situation, and these internal processes have found powerful support from socio-political developments in the outside world.

The result has been an ever-increasing demand from the subordinate groups for precisely what had been hitherto lacking: greater moral equality with the dominant group. This demand is intimately associated in origin and character with the new and revolutionary egalitarianism which has arisen everywhere, now that the europeanization-of-the-world culturally nears completion. Nationalism is simply the political facet of this new moral norm.

Inevitably, normative convergence at a conscious moral level has brought increased social tension and conflict—inevitably, we say, since it underlies a ubiquitous psychological state, the social conditions for which did not previously exist.

18. See Appendix, p. 405.

This is the powerful sense of moral outrage now common to all non-Europeans in Africa at the "injustices" imposed upon them by European rule.

The average European in Central Africa during our period of fieldwork had no comprehension of the depth and intensity of this sense of moral indignation. A hint of it perhaps comes through in a remark once made by a mild-mannered Indian informant in a candid moment: "I know I shouldn't say this, Doctor. Our religion, like yours, says we shouldn't hate anyone. But the truth is I hate the European! I know it is wrong, but I can't help it. *He hates me, and I hate him in return.*"

Chapter Nine

INTERETHNIC RELATIONS:

INDIAN, AFRICAN, AND COLOURED

To a young Indian shop assistant whose previous knowledge of the great world had scarcely extended beyond the boundaries of his natal village, the greatest shock met upon his arrival in Africa was the African himself. No anthropologist, he had never quite realized before that people so different from himself existed.

> I'll tell you frankly, Doctor, when I first came out here, I didn't like the looks of these people. They were so dark and savage-looking; they were dirty and ragged, too, and they didn't seem at all civilized to me. After all, I had just come from the city of Bombay. I was not used to people like that.

These were people nonetheless whom he was to face across a shop counter every day for indefinite years to come. Once unbelievably exotic, the African was soon to become boringly familiar indeed. Upon the basis of this intensely perceived familiarity, the shop assistant rapidly acquired a profound conviction that he *knows* the African.

Nor can the sociologist dispute that he does know the African, although it must be noted that the range of what he knows firsthand is exceedingly narrow. Furthermore, the acquisition of even this small amount of solid empirical knowledge was guided by and interpreted through a set of culturally prescribed stereotypes already well established in the Indian community.

Some of the things the young Indian learned can be seen in representative statements from the interview protocols. Like all social stereotypes, these can be fairly easily separated and classified into a few predominant themes. For convenience in exposition the examples are grouped under a brief summary of the theme to be illustrated.

1. Africans lack culture. Indians, although they may be poor in India, are the products of an ancient civilization.

> You travel across India anywhere and you come, let us say, to a village on a hill by a river. Now if you were to stop and dig down underneath one of the houses in that village, you would find the remains of a house, and down beneath it, if you continued to dig, you would find the remains of another house, and so on, layer after layer, until you dug right down to the bottom of the hill. In other words, you would find that people had been living a civilized life in that village for centuries and centuries. Now suppose you went out and dug under a hut here in an African village. What would you find? All you would find would be sand and rocks! You wouldn't find a hint of civilization.

> The African has no roots in the land; he has no roots any place. When he farms, he scratches the soil for a few inches, and in two or three years he moves on. On moving day, his wife picks up his mat and his pot and his tools and walks off with everything that he has on her head. Finally, they come to a tree and he looks around and says, "I think this would be a good place to stop." And there he is in his new home. These Africans you see around town give a very distorted picture of what the real African is like. You might think by what you see here that they are pretty well civilized. You should see them out in the bush the way they really are.

262

2. The difference between Indians and Africans is not to be explained solely by education.

I don't mean by culture just education. You can acquire education without having culture. I don't use the word civilization either. If you want to, you can say that the Africans have a civilization which is just different from ours. That is what some people say. But I still would insist that they don't have a *culture* in the same sense that the Indians do. Indian culture is one of the oldest in the world. It goes back four thousand years. Indian culture is an instinct; that's what all culture is, an instinct. That's why I say you can't acquire culture just by becoming educated.

A lot of people can't read or write in India, and a lot of Indians in India are just as poor as any of these Africans are. Still, you have something in India which you don't have in Africa. Let me explain what I mean. Even the illiterate Indian peasant—a man who can't read or write —has a technical brain. If you show him a piece of machinery and how it works, he can go ahead and operate it himself. You can't do the same with an African. Africans don't have a technical brain.

These people, even the educated ones, don't have any culture. They get excited very easily, and when they get excited they might do anything. You or I wouldn't do the sort of things which they are apt to do when they get excited, because it would be against our culture to do it. But since they don't have the same kind of culture, then one can't trust them to behave themselves when they are in an excited mood.

3. Africans have a child-like mentality and cannot think logically.

If you ask them what they believe, they can't tell you. The African is a race in childhood. They themselves don't know what they believe, and so they can't explain it in words. . . . That's what makes these dances I was telling you about so interesting. They can express ideas in dances which they can't tell you about in words.

4. Africans are physically lazy and lack foresight.

In India there's no land; all of the land is already owned. But I'll tell you one thing; if these Africans were Indians, every one of them would be rich. I can't understand it. There are hundreds and hundreds of square miles of land in Northern Rhodesia upon which there is absolutely nothing but bush, and if any African wants to, he can clear off as much as he wants for a farm. But the Africans are a lazy people and are not interested in work. If they get four or five pounds a month, then they are satisfied. They never worry where the next meal is coming from.

[From a Goan electrician] I have had a lot of African apprentices in my time, and I have always tried to teach them the trade. But they won't learn. All they can see is that I earn a great deal more money than they do. That's all they can ever think of. But they have no conception of what it means to be an apprentice, to really learn something. They want to acquire everything all at once, and so after they have been with you awhile, they quit. I've tried to get them not to quit. I tell them, "You must learn, and to learn you must stay on the job and work. That's the only way you will ever learn." But they won't listen to me. They don't understand that if I scold them for doing something wrong it is for their own good. They just think I don't like them.

The Africans have an entirely different view of life than you or I. In spite of the fact that they don't have much, they are a happy people—a lot happier than you or I. What they don't have just doesn't bother them. They live for the day and never think about tomorrow. If they're happy today, then they're completely happy, and they think they will always be happy.

5. They are hopelessly self-indulgent, spend their money on things they could do without, and have no conception of sexual morality.

The trouble with the African is that he drinks too much. An African only gets four, six, or eight pounds a month, usually. If he gets six pounds a month, then he spends two pounds on beer. I ask you, at that rate what is going to happen to his wife and children?

[A tea-room assistant, disgustedly, after selling a dozen packages of cigarettes in as many minutes] These Africans don't mind going without food for a day or two. They're so poor they're used to that. But they can't do without smoking an hour!

How can Africans appreciate a woman's chastity? In their community chastity is only worth two-and-six! They would say, if you asked them, that it is because they are so poor. But in India people are very poor too; and yet even in the poorest family chastity is something which cannot be bought. It is a young girl's most precious possession.

They're a friendly people, a very friendly people. Yet I'll tell you one thing honestly: if the Europeans knew what Africans say when they walk behind European and Asian women, then there would be more trouble than there is! Fortunately, they [i.e. the Europeans] don't know what the Africans are saying. But I do. After all, I've been here thirty years. They're a crude, rough people —almost unbelievably rough and crude. Maybe they will eventually become civilized. I think myself they will. But it seems to me that it will take at least a hundred years.

Like virtually all outgroup stereotypes, these are true enough in terms of empirical content. But they lack perspective and depth and tend to be distorted through selective emphasis. Indians are universally convinced that they "know" Africans; but the facets of African behavior which they know are severely restricted and segmentalized by the nature of the role-situations within which the two groups interact. Before examining the most important of these roles as in the previous chapter, let us first consider the means of their communication, since it is so crucial to all else in Indian-African interaction.

PROBLEMS OF COMMUNICATION

The typical young Indian immigrant of recent years studied English for several years in school prior to coming to Africa. He was of course completely ignorant of any African language, and one of the most demanding tasks confronting him in his new job was the acquisition of enough of the locally used medium of communication to do his work and to get along with African servants. Constant example and practice in shop and household, however, soon rectified his initial ignorance; within six months to a year, he was able to communicate satisfactorily with Africans within these standard situations. From this point on, learning slackened off rapidly to a permanent plateau, beyond which there was little or no improvement. Few Indians ever acquire anything like complete competence in an African language for the simple reason that their social contact with Africans is too limited. To speak the language "like a native" would demand acquaintance with the full range of African institutions.

Ultimate ability to communicate with Africans also depends in the Indian case (as it does among Europeans, too) upon the local language learned. In Malawi, the language commonly used in trade and administration is Chinyanja. Although a *lingua franca* widely used by people whose mother tongue is a localized dialect, Chinyanja is a real language with close affinities to the other languages found in the area. The linguistic situation, however, is quite different on the Zambian Copper-belt, in the line-of-rail towns, and throughout Rhodesia. Here the trade language is called "Kitchen Kaffir," a pidgin Bantu heavily interlarded with Afrikaans and English words and phrases which arose in South Africa as a medium of trade, household service, and the supervision of native gang labor.[1] Within a given linguistic area, Kitchen Kaffir tends to reflect fairly strongly the predominant African language. In Bula-wayo, for example, it is described as a kind of "broken Sindebele." In Central Zambia, it is said to be a "mixture of Bemba and a half a dozen other local languages."

In every case, Kitchen Kaffir has one overriding sociological characteristic. It is the language of the master-servant relation-ship and reflects this fact in its vocabulary and structure. Except for the honorific "Bwana" and "Donna" (and these are applied only to non-African superiors), it is baldly free of all nuances of politeness and consideration. It is thus certain that sole dependence upon Kitchen Kaffir negatively colors the relationship Indians have to Africans in African eyes. Urban Africans who do not know each other's tribal language may themselves resort to Kitchen Kaffir, but Africans who know any English resent being spoken to in Kitchen Kaffir by a non-African. Yet, we soon observed that Europeans and Indians who know Kitchen Kaffir were apt to insist upon speaking it, even to Africans who spoke English. An African addressed initially in Kitchen Kaffir by an Indian shop as-sistant may respond in perfectly adequate English, only to be answered again in Kitchen Kaffir. Europeans (and a good many Indians) commonly insisted during the period of our fieldwork

1. Synonyms for Kitchen Kaffir widely used among Africans include Chila-palapa, Chilolo, Chikabanga, Chiboi, and Fanagolo. In one of the few published treatments, Epstein traces Kitchen Kaffir generally to Fanagolo, the South African "mine Kafir" which he says is about 70 percent Nguni (or Zulu), 24 percent English, and 6 percent Afrikaans. "Chilapalapa," the term ap-parently preferred by most Africans, is, according to Epstein, a reiterative (of "lapa") on the same pattern as "long" and "bilong" in Melanesian pidgin. A. L. Epstein, "Linguistic Innovation and Culture on the Copperbelt, Northern Rhodesia," *Southwestern Journal of Anthropology, 15* (1959), 235–53.

upon the honorific "Bwana" or "Donna" when being addressed by an African. Neglect of these titles, even when the conversation was otherwise entirely in English because the non-African knew no Kitchen Kaffir, was taken in the period of European dominance as a sign of insubordination.[2]

Hindus concede that Muslims as a group have on the average a somewhat higher level of competence in the native languages than they themselves have. Muslims often claim to know a native language, even in those areas in which the most common form of communication is Kitchen Kaffir. Not being linguists ourselves, we cannot vouch for the reality of this difference in language skills; but judging from what we were constantly told, it does seem to be a real one, traceable in good part, perhaps, to the previously mentioned rural-urban differences between Hindus and Muslims. Doubtlessly there are subtle differences of a subcultural character associated with this residence factor. As illustrated by the sexual relationships discussed below, Muslims do seem to find it easier to mingle freely with Africans than Hindus do—a difference that may be related ultimately to caste.

Yet if a difference between Hindus and Muslims exists in this respect, that difference is most assuredly a relative one. There is a general tendency among Indians (as well as among Europeans) to exaggerate competence in the African tongues. Our own linguistic deficiencies prevented a firsthand check, but we learned enough indirectly to make us suspicious of the claim constantly advanced by Indians—more often than not in *very* imperfect English—that they knew several native languages "perfectly." Only on occasion could such claims be checked with English-speaking Africans. When asked about the language facility of an Indian pioneer, an educated African informant laughed and replied:

> What African language are you talking about? Do you
> mean an African language, or do you mean Chilapalapa

2. Cf. the well known rules for racial etiquette in the United States. See, for example, Allison Davis, Burleigh B. Gardner, and Mary R. Gardner, *Deep South* (Chicago, University of Chicago Press, 1941).

[i.e. Kitchen Kaffir]? When you see old B standing out there in front of his shop talking to a crowd of women and children like he does, you might think he knows an African language well. But he is speaking nothing but Chilapalapa!

TYPICAL ROLES

Shopkeeper–Customer Relations

To the Indian shopkeeper and his assistant, the African is first and foremost a customer across the counter.[3] Hinged so directly upon the cash nexus, the buyer-seller relationship may be in the extreme or limiting case almost completely ecological.[4] Whatever this hypothetical minimum of normative consensus is, interaction across the counter of the Indian shop in the African trade must approach it, so little is the human exchange in addition to that of goods and money. A reflective shopkeeper once remarked in the course of an interview: "You ask me how well I know the African. Of course we know the African. He's around all the time. He's our business." And then, catching himself in his own contradiction, he significantly added: "But Africans are a very strange people. You never really get to know them very well. I think no Indian does."

By the minimum norms which do exist, bargaining is expected and accepted on both sides of the counter as the appropriate mode of procedure. Yet in effect this fact alone makes it almost impossible for either of the participants to have a very

---

3. Self-conscious liberals often object, sometimes in the strongest terms, to the phrase *"the* African" as used here. The objection, of course, is to the implicit stereotyping, to the replacement of the real individual with the abstract and impersonal verbal generalization. The sociologist may sympathize with the humane intent of this objection, and he of course is thoroughly aware of the distorting effects of social stereotypes. But he cannot ignore the social categories into which ordinary people put other ordinary people for the simple reason that these categories are, for the most part, what he is supposed to be studying. To the extent that social structure exists in the empirical world of reality, that structure is the system of symbolic categories which people carry around in their heads as guides to social action and interaction. From this perspective, social structure is little more than a complex of stereotypes.

4. See Appendix, pp. 405–06.

269

high regard for one another. Africans seem typically to leave an encounter with an Indian shopkeeper feeling cheated, an open question being left in their minds as to whether or not they paid more than they might have if they had held out a bit longer. One comments:

> Sometimes you can get them to take off as much as a pound on something which doesn't cost more than three or four pounds. Now I ask you: if they will take a pound off the price of something which doesn't cost more than three or four pounds anyway, doesn't that mean that all of their prices are too high? They *must* be dishonest!

Another informant, making the same point, reports a concrete case:

> I was looking at a watch the other day in L's shop. They don't mark their prices, so you never know what anything costs. When I first asked what the price of this watch was, they said ten pounds. When I didn't take it, they kept coming down and down. Finally, they came down to four pounds. Imagine! From ten to four pounds! I was so furious that I just walked out of the shop.

The conviction that Indians will cheat them whenever they can appears, by a wide margin, to be the most common single perception of Indians which Africans have. Yet objectively considered, it is difficult to see in a situation controlled by a mutual expectation of bargaining what meaning can be given to the term "cheat," other than in instances of gross deception, misrepresentation, or deliberate miscalculation. Blatantly dishonest practices could not be common for the simple reason that the African trade leaves so little scope for them. We have heard of time payments on bicycles which go on indefinitely, but shortchanging, to take what might be an obvious example, is no problem: Africans count their money.

It also became very clear, after some attention was given to the matter, that the African customer is far from being as gullible as he is sometimes made out to be by both Indians and Europeans.[5] Price norms for standard everyday items—and these, after all, constitute the great bulk of the trade—are inevitably established even without fixed prices, and these norms are well known to all concerned. An anthropologist who had worked for two years in a bush village a hundred miles from town assured us that the Africans in his village knew in detail the current prices of standard items in the city. Furthermore, he went on to point out, they refused to pay more than these prices to the local Indian trader, ignoring his perfectly sound argument that he must pay additional transportation costs to get his goods out there.[6]

When in town, the African becomes a relentless comparison shopper. He often amuses himself by going from shop to shop, asking the prices of items which he cannot buy because he has no money. The Indian trader cannot ignore these habits when quoting prices; he must make an estimate of the price quoted for the same item by his competitor next door. Nor can he count upon building up loyalty to his shop over others through special concessions. The "regular customer" pattern is rare to the point of virtual nonexistence in the urban African trade.

The behavior of the Indian on the other side of the counter shows accommodation to these basic realities. The amount of professional cordiality extended to prospective customers

5. During and immediately after the war, the merchant's problem in Central Africa as elsewhere in the world was merely to get goods, not to sell them, and it is clear from what Indians themselves have often told us that Africans were frequently charged plenty for what they got during this period. By the time we began our fieldwork, however, the relationship between supply and demand had changed completely. A great many former shop assistants had by that time completed their terms of service and had set themselves up in the African trade, with the result that competition in a generally slackening market was keen to the point of bitterness. Established shop owners now complained that the grossly under-capitalized little shops which had sprung up everywhere were cutting prices far below the economic margin. Such complaints—to which we listened patiently for many an hour—should not automatically be taken at their face value, but neither can they be completely discounted. It was plain enough that competition was in fact ruinous among the smaller, marginal shops, since so many of them were being forced out of business.

6. W. John Argyle, then a candidate for a D.Phil. in social anthropology at Oxford and Research Officer for the Rhodes-Livingstone Institute for Social Research.

differs somewhat from shop to shop, but on the whole the lack of aggressive salesmanship is striking. Sales depend more upon variety and price than upon any identifiable personal factor. Africans have not yet reached the stage where they can afford the luxury of being waited upon by obsequiously attentive sales personnel in shops of more than strictly utilitarian appointments.

When a customer enters the shop or, if several have been waiting, when the trader can at last give him his attention, he is addressed by the Indian with a peremptory "Yes!" The shopkeeper then listens closely while the customer tells him what he wants, close attention being necessary because of the difficulties of communication. Once the Indian is satisfied that he knows what is wanted, he gets the item down from the shelves—or perhaps the same thing in a choice of three or four samples—and slaps it down before the customer with a smart, characteristic gesture. Then he leans back, bored, and waits while the African looks at and fingers the goods to his heart's content. In the meantime, if necessary, he turns his attention to another customer. If it so happens that the customer wants several different items, each is treated as a single sale, the African handing over his money and receiving change for each separate transaction.[7]

In a good many shops, this pattern of interaction between shopkeeper and customer is short-circuited by an African shop assistant. This assistant meets the customers, shows them the goods, and collects the money if a sale is negotiated. The Indian interrupts only if he is asked to agree upon the final price. African shop assistants, however, are never allowed to make change or even deposit the money in the cash drawer if no change is necessary. If a European customer should appear in such a shop, then the Indian himself makes the approach, perhaps ignoring several waiting African customers in order to do so.

We observed very little informal chatting between African

7. In the short interval between 1961 and 1966, this pattern had already changed considerably, particularly in Zambia. See below, p. 362.

customers and Indian shopkeepers during the course of the fieldwork. Very high status Africans may be treated with professional cordiality if the shopkeeper knows who they are, but such people are statistically infrequent. The value of most sales, as indicated, is not sufficient to motivate the shopkeeper to put himself out in an attempt to be interesting and pleasant. But even if he were so motivated, the cultural barriers would make it difficult for him to do so effectively. The vocabulary of their mutually understandable medium of communication is in the first place simply not large enough to allow for pleasant exchanges of an informal nature.

Yet even if this language barrier did not exist, it is doubtful if much more informal exchange would actually take place. The fact is that Indians exhibit little curiosity about African beliefs, values, or personal problems; it is significant that with plenty of time and opportunity to practice and learn, they typically acquire so little of any African language beyond the necessities of the trade relationship. They assume—from their point of view they *know*—that there is nothing in what an African thinks or does which is of any intrinsic interest to them. In this respect, Indians are of course no different from Europeans, who typically react to Africans in exactly the same way. It need only be added that in the latter case Europeans also place Indians along with Africans in the same uninteresting category.[8] Can we not generalize from this observation, perhaps, and say that a social inferior is by definition a person in whom we have no intrinsic interest? [9]

8. Upon being told that we were making a study of the Indian community, a European woman laughed uproariously at the idea. She went on to explain: "But what is there to study about the Indians? What is there to find out? They run their little shops; they live in a room behind them, a half a dozen of them altogether. They eat their greasy food and they're not very clean, nor very honest. What else is there to know? I am sure I could tell you all you need to know about Indians in this country in fifteen minutes. They are just like I have told you."

9. A definition so cast takes care of the largest category of empirically observable interest in social inferiors: namely, that of professionals of various sorts, including social scientists. Professionals invariably have an extrinsic interest in inferiors which precedes and antedates any intrinsic interest in such people which they may in time develop. This is a point which these

Employer–Employee Relations

Since Indians make use of a good deal of African labor, the employer-employee relationship is a common one. African employees are of two main types: business employees and domestic servants. The first group is fairly heterogeneous; it includes such personnel as store-boys, shop assistants, tailors, drivers, and clerks.

1. Store-boys. Most of the African labor employed by Indians in their businesses fall into this category. In a large shop, these unskilled menials will at least equal in number, if they do not exceed, the Indian staff. A smallish grocery with a European clientele may employ half a dozen "boys" (whatever their age) to carry customers' purchases to their cars, to sweep up litter, and to fetch storeroom items upon demand.

To say that the status of these menials is one of little dignity borders upon understatement. At the beck and call of all the Indian staff, even the most lowly, the store-boy must answer promptly a continuous barrage of orders, issued sharply and peremptorily; his response is one of resigned sullenness. Between Indian and African in this situation the prevailing mood is one of constant mutual irritation. It is only fair to observe, however, that essentially the same mood also prevails in European establishments—shops, garages, hotels, and hospitals—where numerous African menials are used in much the same way.

An Indian shop assistant on the point of leaving a particularly harsh and mean-minded employer described the terms under which the store-boys work in his shop:

> They begin at two pounds, five shillings per month, plus their rations [another five shillings per week]. But they never see that money because they buy things at the shop. They are also charged for anything they break, and that

professionals—including, we are afraid, a great many sociologists and anthropologists—often ignore. They moralistically castigate the ethnocentrism which ordinary people always show in their relations to people different from themselves, without seeming to appreciate fully that their own detachment is a subsidized luxury which the ordinary person cannot afford.

too is subtracted from their wages. One of the boys who is working there now fell over a pyramid of drinking glasses the other day and broke the lot. He cut himself too, and should have gone to the clinic, but the boss wouldn't let him. Now he is being charged forty-eight shillings for those glasses, which means that he won't get paid for the next two months. Probably he will quit before the debt is paid. If one of these boys stays away from work one day, then he loses his ration money for that week. Even if he works the other five days, he still won't get his five shillings.

2. Shop assistants. In the smaller shops, store-boys and shop assistants are not differentiated. But in the larger ones that use African shop assistants in the manner described above, there is a clearer-cut division of labor. In the larger cities some shops employ an African assistant to stand out in the street and entice window-shoppers inside.[10]

3. Tailors. An African tailor, as pointed out in the economics chapter, is an essential part of virtually every establishment north of the Zambezi, and those with sufficient business to justify the expense have more than one. The tailor's main job is to make up into dresses the cotton material purchased by women customers.

In Northern Rhodesia, tailors were paid from £6 to £9 a month, about on par with a competent cook in a European household, during our original fieldwork. Indians complain that tailors ask for employment who barely know how to operate a sewing machine and leave to go elsewhere to bargain for better pay once they have acquired some competence. There does not seem to be anything like a formal apprenticeship to learn this trade; a man has to pick it up as best he can.

4. Drivers. In European-owned businesses, Africans do the driving of lorries and buses. When so employed, drivers do

10. Apparently, it used to be a fairly common practice for Indian shopkeepers (or their assistants) to grab onto passersby physically and attempt to pull them into the shop.

nothing but drive. Assistants do the loading and unloading, and drivers are not ordinarily expected to do mechanical or even maintenance work on their vehicles. Mechanics throughout Central Africa are (or more accurately were at the time of the fieldwork) either Europeans or Coloureds. Drivers, none-theless, were paid well by African standards, upward of £15 a month which placed them in the aristocracy of African labor.

Indians who are either in the transport business (as a few are) or who by the nature of their operations do a great deal of trucking follow the European pattern and employ African drivers. In the smaller Indian-owned businesses, vehicles are driven by Indian employees as an incidental part of their other duties.

5. Industrial workers. Some of the largest Indian employ-ers of African labor are the few small industrialists, most of whom, as has already been pointed out, process either food or clothing. These employers complain vociferously of all the familiar difficulties inherent in a labor force still not fully ac-customed to industrial discipline. An Indian manufacturer of clothing in Northern Rhodesia expanded on his labor prob-lems:

> We could get all of the labor we want if we paid on a monthly basis. But one can't pay these workers on a monthly basis. We tried that when we first set up our factory, but we found we couldn't do it. The natives around here are probably the laziest in Africa. If you pay them by the month, then they are in the toilet forty times a day. And when they are not in the toilet, then they tell you that they have to go out into the street and talk to some cousin or other. So now we pay them by the piece and let them work as much or as little as they like. That way what they make is up to them.

The best workers, according to the owner of this factory, were women; and of these the very best were wives of clerks brought up by the federal government from Southern Rhodesia:

The girls I just showed you come to the factory at 7:30 in the morning and they stay until 5:30 at night. The men on the other hand come here at 9:00 in the morning, and they leave about 2:00 to go to the beerhall. When the boycott was on at the beerhall [a brief, politically-inspired close-down] the men came at 8:00 o'clock and stayed until 5:00. During that time they averaged ten to twelve shillings a day.

These observations were followed by a long discourse on the evils of beer-drinking—a favorite theme among Indians, who view drinking as both a moral evil and a grossly frivolous economic waste:

The average native here never worries about what he is going to eat. It is not uncommon for them to starve themselves in order to have something to drink. We found that if we paid them their ration money on Saturday [the usual practice] then they wouldn't come to work on Monday because they were sick at the stomach from all the beer they drank on Sunday. So now we pay the ration money on Monday.

6. Clerks and bookkeepers.   Indians, as noted in the previous chapter, ordinarily do their own clerical work. In those relatively few instances in which anyone outside the immediate family is employed to do routine clerical work, an educated African is more apt to be employed than either an Indian or a European. Africans can be had more cheaply.

Domestic Servants

It is an exceedingly poor European household indeed in Central Africa which does not keep at least one African servant. And while the level of income among Indians is generally well below that of Europeans, the same observation may be made of them as well. Domestic servants are all but universal in Indian households; in large ones, several may be employed.

Servants are used rather differently, however, in Indian and European homes. In the typical European establishment, the single African servant is a combination cook-and-houseboy. If a second one is added, he is most apt to be a garden boy. In the Indian household, servants are employed in two main capacities: to do laundry and cleaning and to look after young children.

A houseboy in the Indian household typically does no cooking; the implication of this fact will be explored further below. Among Europeans, on the other hand, Africans are not typically required to look after children. Help with the burdens of child care is achieved among Europeans by relegating offspring at a very tender age to a "crèche" (or nursery school); there, in the usual case, they are under the care of a Coloured woman, who is supervised by the European owner or operator. This institution is not present among Indians; they employ instead a full-time "nanny boy." Males must be hired as African nursemaids are virtually impossible to obtain, and the few who are available are expensive by local standards. In most cases "nanny boys" are literally boys, but they may be adults of almost any age.

What information we have suggests that the wages of African servants working for Indians are usually well below those employed by Europeans. The rationale for the lower rate which Indians provide is based upon skill: since the servant is not expected to cook, it is argued, he can be paid at the minimum for laundry and garden boys, which is about half of that for competent cook-houseboys.[11]

In other respects, too, it is our impression that the lot of African servants working for Indians is somewhat harsher than it typically is for those who work for Europeans. The Indian-employed servant works seven days a week and is ex-

11. The *Central African Mail* (Lusaka), in a feature-story published August 6, 1965, reported African domestic servants working for Indians for wages as low as thirty shillings a month, with four shillings a week additional as ration money. The very best paid, according to this story, get six pounds a month. From our data, it seems likely that the normal range falls between two pounds and ten shillings to three pounds and ten shillings monthly.

pected to be always on call. In principle, servants are expected by Indians to earn their money by keeping busy.

In tone and quality, the relationship between the two groups in the master-and-servant role tends to be strictly impersonal and instrumental. We never observed an instance of unguarded familiarity between Indians and their servants. Indians are a serious-minded people, and there is nothing about which they are more serious-minded than social status.

As in the case of shopkeeper-customer relations, the operating assumption with respect to the African servant is that he is intrinsically uninteresting. When an informant was casually asked whether his houseboy and nanny boy (who looked somewhat alike to us) were related, he replied:

> I don't think so, but I don't know. I have never sat down and talked to them about such matters. I don't pay any attention to them as long as they do their work. I have to talk to enough Africans down at the shop all day. I'm not interested in talking with these servants when I get home.

When we then suggested that his wife might perhaps be able to tell us, we were assured that she could not do so either: "No, she lets them alone, too. She is satisfied if they just do their work. If they don't, then she has to speak to them. But she doesn't talk to them either unless she has to."

Support for these observations is found in an incidental remark made by a young Indian liberal politician, intent upon trying to line up his community behind an African nationalist party. Momentarily depressed by the resistance he was encountering, he commented with unwonted candor:

> The whole attitude of Indians toward Africans must change. Prejudice against Africans is not confined, I am sorry to say, to Europeans. We must do away with our prejudices, too. The Indian housewife, for example, has to begin to treat her African servant like a human being if we are going to stay in this country.

African servants seek work with Indians rather than with Europeans in part because they do not need to know English in order to work for Indians. To the Indian housewife, ability to speak English is no recommendation; she typically knows no English either. In this case, the medium of communication is Kitchen Kaffir or Chinyanja, which she probably speaks better than her husband since she is forced by circumstances to use the language in a greater variety of situations.[12]

Unfortunately, we had neither the time nor the linguistic equipment to explore the important relationship between African servants and Indian children. We do know from reports by school personnel that preschool children frequently use Kitchen Kaffir or Chinyanja among themselves rather than either Gujarati or English. Teachers view these linguistic habits as a serious problem educationally and thus commented upon them frequently.

SEXUAL RELATIONSHIPS

One is tempted to say without qualification that the most intimate relationship which Indians have with Africans is the sexual one.[13] Yet how much psycho-cultural intimacy is necessarily involved in even a prolonged and somewhat stabilized sexual arrangement? Unfortunately, we do not really know; the data upon these matters are neither abundant nor entirely clear. We did learn enough in this area, however, to be able to sketch out the broad organizational facts, and from these we can only conclude that whatever the degree of intimacy achieved in Indian-African sexual arrangements, it has not been sufficient to create an important bridge between the two groups.

Recent developments have radically changed the social or-

12. Not knowing English, Indian women are forced to resort to Kitchen Kaffir in communicating with European nurses and doctors while in the hospital.
13. Cf. Floyd Dotson and Lillian Dotson, "Indians and Coloureds in Rhodesia and Nyasaland," *Race* (Journal of the Institute of Race Relations, London), 5 (July 1963), 61–75.

ganization of sexual relations between Indians and Africans and have undoubtedly greatly reduced their proportionate frequency. Up until a decade or so ago, it will be remembered, it was usual for Indians to remain in Africa for years on end without their families. Under these circumstances, it would have been very strange indeed if contact had not taken place between the sexually deprived Indian male and the abundantly available African female. Of more pressing sociological interest is its social organization and symbolic significance.

The evidence points to a continuous and stabilized arrangement resembling marriage, particularly for the earliest period and in the more isolated rural areas. One of the few early (1905) descriptions of Indians in Southern Rhodesia contains a brief but relevant comment which indicates what was doubtlessly a very general situation. The report, provided by the civil commissioner of the Fort Victoria District,[14] discussed the some fifty to sixty Muslim Indians in the district who lived by a cattle-and-grain trade with the Africans. All but three were male.

> I have only to add that practically all the Indians in the Victoria District (there are no other coloured foreigners) are in the habit of keeping native women, whom, I believe, they obtain under the *lobola* [bride price] system, and there is gradually springing up a race of bastards, who, it is possible, may in the future be a source of trouble and inconvenience to the Government.[15]

Our interview accounts do not go back so far. Yet what was reported of the situation in Northern Rhodesia and Nyasaland thirty to forty years ago presents the same essentials. A Hindu informant, a shoemaker by caste and trade, considered settling in Nyasaland in the early 1930s. He decided not to, primarily it would seem, because the European population was too small to support much trade in shoes. Looking back on this experience now, however, he sees other reasons:

14. See above, pp. 37–38.
15. Central African Archives, Item T 2/2/18.

As you know, Nyasaland was originally settled mostly by Muslims. These people were very mean-minded. They thought in terms of pennies and tickeys—not even in shillings, let alone pounds. Their shops were mud-and-dagga affairs, with a piece of cloth hung over a pole for the trade. These Muslims didn't even employ a houseboy. What they did was to hire a young African girl instead. This girl was half houseboy and half wife. That way of living didn't appeal to me!

It is significant that the Indians referred to in both of these cases are Muslims. Leaving one's wife indefinitely in India was frowned upon by Hindus, particularly those of the upper castes. For this reason, most pioneer Indian women in Central Africa are Hindus. It does not necessarily follow from this observation that Hindus living in Africa without their wives never had sexual contacts with Africans; but it does seem to be clear that the kind of semi-permanent, openly acknowledged arrangement commonly prevailing among Muslims was never countenanced by Hindus.

To Europeans, the relationship which Muslims maintained with African women are always described as "marriages"— if not explicitly then implicitly, since the African woman in this context is called a "wife" by the Indian. If it turns out that the man in question had (or has) a wife in India, then Islamic law and custom is invoked as an explanation. For example, when asked about polygynous marriages in the local Muslim community (we had in mind only those involving Indian women), a young informant in Southern Rhodesia replied somewhat cagily: "There may be some, and there used to be a lot more. I mean, a man might have a wife in India and a non-Indian wife here. But of course our religion allows us more than one wife."

Yet clearly these arrangements were never quite respectable, even though openly acknowledged.[16] By the time of our

16. Since marriage among Muslims is governed by caste to a degree not essentially different from that of Hindus, a sociologically legitimate marriage would have to be with a woman of one's own caste. Yet even legalistically,

fieldwork, secondary "marriages" with an African woman had ceased to be a significant feature of local Indian society. What sexual contact continues between Indians and Africans is now on a strictly casual and mercenary basis. That there is still a fair amount of this appears certain, but it is not important enough to loom very large in the total picture of Indian-African relations. While not prudish in the Anglo-Saxon sense, both Hindus and Muslims are fundamentally ascetic in their basic attitude toward all sensual indulgence. Too obvious an interest in sex is viewed by others in the community as a woeful lack of foresight and self-control, both virtues which stand near the apex of the Indian scale of values. A caste-ingrained distaste for close physical contact with social inferiors probably must be added to this underlying predisposition toward asceticism.

An indication of the essentially ecological character of even the sexual relationship between Indians and Africans is found in the Indian attitude toward its most tangible result: the Indo-African offspring. To define this attitude presents the usual difficulty of making valid generalizations about variable social phenomena; there really is no *one* attitude. Still, the predominant tendency is clear enough: it is rejection—physically, psychologically, and socially.

There are degrees of rejection or, to put the matter positively rather than negatively, degrees of integration. Four families in the interview sample contained Indo-African children either currently or at some point in their history, and we were told about others whom we did not encounter directly. In two of these four families, the Indo-African sons had been sent to India for a part of their education. One of these was

most of these unions could not be considered legitimate; by Koranic law, a Muslim male must marry either a Muslim woman or a Christian. The fact that a good number of Africans in Central Africa are Muslims might in theory help to promote legitimate intermarriage between the two races. Up to the present this remains theoretical, since in practice marriage is controlled by customary regulations of Hindu origin. As Africans gain power and prestige and the temptation to intermarriage consequently becomes greater, this Koranic provision may in the future be invoked with greater and greater frequency.

already married to an Indian woman, and the father of the other told us he was actively seeking a wife for his son in India.

These children were publicly known as Indo-Africans. (If they had not been, then they probably would never have come to our attention.) It is possible—even likely—that there are cases in which a member of a family is Indo-African but successfully "passes" as Indian. A young Hindu professional, who by the nature of his position should know what he is talking about, claims that there are such cases in considerable numbers.

> As you know, there are a lot of African Muslims in this area [Nyasaland]. Perhaps for this reason, the [Indian] Muslims are often willing to absorb their Coloured children and take them into the community, unlike the Hindus who usually disown them. Some of these families try to protect their Coloured members and keep the fact that they are Coloured from the rest of the Indians.

Other evidence, however, suggests that this informant greatly exaggerates the number of such cases. Typically, children who might have been given some sort of recognition while the father was living with their mother were abandoned when that mother was "divorced" upon the arrival of the Indian wife from India. Rather than the Indian family closing ranks to protect the children, it is clear that more often than not the Indian community closed ranks to protect the father. On this point, a Coloured teacher had this to say:

> After his Indian wife arrived from India, he [the father] didn't want to have anything to do with his Coloured children. Often, too, the other Indians in the community helped him out in this. In a great many cases [of abandoned children cared for at the school] we have great difficulty in finding out who the Indian fathers of these children are because the Indian community itself protects the father's identity, although they know perfectly well what the facts are.

Another Coloured teacher provided us with a concrete case during the course of a casual conversation:

> I suppose you must know old B in X? When I was at the school there, we found that he had a Coloured son whom he wasn't paying any attention to, although as you know he is loaded with money. We got after him and made him put the child in school and support him while he was there.

INDIANS AND COLOUREDS

When we turn to the Indians' relationship to the Coloured community at large, we enter into a fascinating but little explored corner of Central African plural society. Indians and Coloureds objectively have nothing in common except the fact that *some* Coloureds have Indian parents or ancestry. But in the dominant European's eyes, they have historically seemed essentially alike, enough alike, in any case, to be equated in overall status. They were provided with a common Asian and Coloured school in most towns—and, in Southern Rhodesia, hospitals as well. Members of the two groups were typically admitted to or excluded from other public facilities such as municipal halls, theatres, and swimming baths on the same basis. Legally, they had the same status under federal defense legislation, and they received the same reduced pay, i.e. about two-thirds of the European rate, while serving in the armed forces. Similarly, they were entitled to the same benefits (again suitably adjusted to their status) under welfare legislation. When these were still in force, they were subject to the same legal restrictions with respect to alcohol and the possession of firearms. In keeping with these practices, they were (to our frustration) often categorized together without differentiation in official statistics.

Imposed by *fiat* by the dominant Europeans, these institutional arrangements resulted in a certain amount of forced association between Indians and Coloureds. Members from the two groups have often attended the same school, for example, or been instructed by a teacher belonging to the opposite group. Since they suffered from identical disabilities, their leaders have on occasion cooperated politically to fight discrimination. This enforced association, however, has not made relationships between the two very intimate. Typically there is little love lost between Indians and Coloureds. Indians dislike and (in an important sense to be elaborated upon shortly) fear Coloureds. Coloureds, on the other hand, have reacted predictably to their rejection by a group which in turn is generally downgraded. To appreciate the reasons for this mutual distaste, we must again look at both culture and society.

Insofar as there is a meaningful Coloured culture or subculture, that culture is almost entirely European in origin and content. But it cannot be assumed that all people of mixed blood participate in the Coloured "culture," however defined. The Coloured community consists only of those persons of mixed parentage who are *publicly labeled* as Coloureds. A good many persons of mixed blood live as Africans out in the villages. Some are presumably passing successfully as Europeans; it will be no news to those intimately familiar with southern Africa if it is suggested that a fair quantity of African genes have flowed into the European population.[17] A few may, as already pointed out, be passing as Indians.

The great majority of Coloureds in Rhodesia and Zambia are either Eurafricans or the second- or third-generation products (in a great variety of combinations) of a predominantly Eurafrican heritage. In Malawi, where the number of Europeans and Indians has historically been more nearly equal, the proportion of first-generation Indo-Africans is correspondingly higher.[18] Yet in Malawi as elsewhere, those Indo-Africans liv-

17. Cf. Sheila Patterson, *Colour and Culture in South Africa: A Study of the Cape Coloured People within the Social Structure of the Union of South Africa* (London, Routledge and Kegan Paul, 1953), especially pp. 18, 182–84.

18. The 1956 census statistics for the Federation as a whole report a European father and an African mother for 14.3 percent of the total Coloured population; a European father and a Coloured mother provided an additional 6.1 percent, making a subtotal of all those with European fathers of 20.4 percent. First generation Indo-Africans (those with an Indian father and an

ing in the recognized Coloured community are thoroughly europeanized culturally. They may have a Muslim name and a rather tenuous adherence to Islam as a religion, but fundamentally these labels mean very little. The young people have in all likelihood attended a school which is (and has been) organized on a strictly European pattern. These Indo-Africans speak English among themselves, although they may know both Gujarati and an African language as well. Rejected by the Indian community—often literally ejected as we have seen when they were children—they tend to dislike Indians, and in their self-conception they think of themselves as Coloured rather than Indo-African. Eurafricans, by contrast, play up as best they can the European side of their origin and try to identify with it.[19]

An informant now in his fifties provides a glimpse into the complicated social world of Central Africa as seen through an Indo-African's eyes. Unlike most Indo-Africans, this man was reared in the home of his Indian father and was sent to India for several years of education. But these experiences failed to give him an Indian identity. After observing that Africans "have a natural hatred for us," he went on to describe Europeans, Indians, and Coloureds in highly personal terms:

African mother) accounted for only 4.2 percent of the recognized Coloured population of the Federation, but the distribution of these by territory was very uneven. In both Southern Rhodesia and Northern Rhodesia, first-generation Indo-Africans were few in number and minute as a proportion of the total (2.2 and 3.4 percent respectively), but in Nyasaland they constituted no less than 18.0 percent as against 12.1 percent for first-generation Eurafricans. These territorial variations are of course to be explained for the most part by the great differences in the proportions between Europeans and Indians in these three territories. In 1956 there were nearly 180,000 Europeans in Southern Rhodesia as against only 5,000 Indians. In Nyasaland, there were 8,500 Indians and 6,700 Europeans. The basic difficulty with all official statistics for the Coloured population is the fact that only a fraction—and a completely unknown fraction at that—of the people of mixed parentage are recognized Coloureds. The official statistics are doubtlessly reasonably accurate for the recognized Coloured community. But they certainly seriously underestimate the actual numbers of first-generation Eurafricans and Indo-Africans in Central Africa. See Dotson and Dotson, "Indians and Coloureds in Rhodesia and Nyasaland," p. 63.

19. This point is elaborated upon in ibid., pp. 69–70.

This country owes everything to the Europeans. They are the ones who came out here and built up the country. Generally, I get along well enough with the Europeans, but if you invited me to your house I really wouldn't be anxious to go. If I went, I know I would be treated courteously enough while I was there, but I really wouldn't feel at home. As far as the Indians are concerned, I have already explained to you how I feel about them. [He had said in great detail that they were only interested in money, that they used to be exceedingly dirty, and that they were so dishonest that they couldn't be trusted under any circumstances.] Since I speak their language fluently, I can go to an Indian house and converse and get along well enough. But since they are, as I have said, completely unprincipled, I don't really like them. On the other hand, if I go to another Coloured person's house, then at last I feel at home.

When we asked a young Eurafrican, a man of some education from a socially stabilized family, what he remembered about the Indians as they were during his boyhood, all he could reply was: "When I was growing up here in X, we didn't have much to do with the Indians. My parents told me to stay away from them because they were dirty."

To define the Indian's attitude toward the Coloured, one must take into account several variables. Hindus tend to be more negative than Muslims; older people are more negative than younger people; the culturally and politically conservative are more negative than the more liberal and westernized. Yet in spite of these variations, it is safe to say that the prevailing attitude of all Indians towards Coloureds is negative, the difference being one of degree. The basic attitudes and values of Indians and of Coloureds are just not very compatible, and these differences are such that in the Indian mind the Coloured comes out defined as hopelessly inferior.

The unreconstructed Hindu finds a rationalization for his

prejudices in his religious philosophy, which helps to provide him with his view of the world. To him miscegenation is "unnatural" in the primary sense of the word, being against God and Nature. The following ideas, which come from an older Patidar, are unusual only in that they are so candidly expressed.

> I can't change my skin [pinching up the skin on the back of his hand demonstratively]. I was born with this skin; I have had it all my life, and I will die with it. But if God had not intended for me to have this skin, then He would have given me something different. He made the different races as they are, and if He had wanted them to be anything else, then He would have made them different. But He didn't. So that must be the way He wanted them to be. If you mix milk with water, you get something that may look like milk, but it really isn't milk. Nor is it water.

A more rational ground for the Indians' negative view of Coloureds—and, for this reason, one which is more freely expressed to Europeans—is the dangers of moral contamination of the young if the two groups are too intimate.[20] Confused and disorganized as they typically are, moral standards among Coloureds are notoriously low. Few parents with middle-class pretensions (Coloured parents included) care to have their children consistently exposed to the kind of behavior which constitutes the statistical norm within the Coloured community.

An unequivocal statement of this widespread fear appears in our interview protocols from what on the face of it might

20. Cf. Lalloo, "The Hindu Family in S. Rhodesia," p. 49: "At school, the younger Hindu generation comes into direct daily face-to-face contact with the youth of the Coloured community, which has values and a way of living more akin to that of the Europeans. Mutual interaction and close association with them has enabled the Hindu children to contrast their own values and customs with those of the Coloured community. This has acted to influence not only the thinking of the Hindu youth, but has also led them to adopt some elements of a different culture. For example, they learn to dance and date— things that were not done a decade ago."

seem an improbable source. One of the few Muslim Indian pioneers who has retained his African wife told us with a rising inflection in his voice:

> I am married to an African woman, and my children are Coloured. But I won't have a Coloured person within half a mile of this house. That is one thing I have told my children time and time again. No Coloureds in this house! The local Coloured population here completely lacks character —utterly. They might just as well be animals, because they act like animals.
>
> We have a saying—it's a kind of joke—that such people worship *ing*. We say that because the bad things which people do who don't have any character end in *ing* in English. There is, for example, smok*ing*. And drink*ing*. And danc*ing*. And then [just a bit hesitatingly] there is that bad word which begins with *f* and ends with *ing*. All these things people do who don't have any character, and the Coloured people do them all!

In the interests of accuracy, it should be pointed out that this informant is unusually pious. He is also extremely conservative politically and is certainly old-fashioned and rigid generally in his views. Nonetheless, it is safe to say that the great majority of younger people share negative evaluations of Coloureds that differ only in intensity and not in kind from his, despite the fact that most of them would never dream of saying anything so openly "reactionary" to a European.

The truth is, as we have said, that Indians and Coloureds are simply too different in behavior and values to be very compatible. To the extent that one can speak meaningfully of a Coloured culture, it is European in origin and content. But socially with few exceptions, Coloureds are from a European perspective lower class—or, as W. Lloyd Warner would say, lower-lower class. As such they share the value characteristics of severely depressed bottom-rung strata everywhere in the modern western world. They are individualistic, hedonistic, and present-oriented; they tend to live for the day and typically they have only a minimal sense of individual and communal responsibility. Sociologically, these characteristics are at one and the same time a product and an index of weak group controls and goals.

In these respects, Indians are everything that Coloureds are not. They are puritanical in principle and practice: abstemious, parsimonious, hardworking, future-oriented, and groupminded. It is no wonder then that Indians in a very meaningful sense *fear* Coloureds. Coloureds represent all to concretely to Indians the social and cultural abyss awaiting them if they fail to maintain their ethnic virtues in Central African plural society.

Quite clearly these realistically perceived dangers are associated in the minds of at least some Indians with concepts of caste. When we pointed out to the Patidar informant quoted above that not all Coloured children (as he had implied) were the responsibility of Europeans, he answered:

> Yes, that is true. But in that case those children have Muslim fathers. They're all Muslims. You will never find a Hindu behaving in that fashion. You see, when the Muslims came to India, the only people they could convert were those of the lower castes. They are the kind of people from whom you can expect such behavior.

Apparently, as the data on sexual relations suggest, Muslims do find it easier to mix more freely with Africans and Coloureds than Hindus do. But to conclude that Muslims are entirely free from ideas and values concerning miscegenation which have their origin in the caste-structured society of India would be seriously misleading. Muslim Indians, after all, *are* Indians. Any difference between the two groups in this respect is surely a matter of degree rather than kind.

INTERETHNIC RELATIONS AND CASTE

What role, we inevitably must ask, do caste-derived concepts play in Indians' relationships to and attitudes toward

Africans? The question seems inescapable, given the Indians' cultural heritage and the peculiar social situation in Central Africa.

Central African society as a whole might very well be described as organized in terms of "caste," if the word is understood in the sense given it by the popular "caste-class" school of race relations in the United States.[21] And in fact the rather obvious parallel between plural society and the Indian caste system is not lost upon the Indians themselves. To quote one informant:

> What we really have in this country is a caste system like the one we used to have [note the usual past tense] at home in India. You know the Indian system: there were Brahmans and Kshatriyas at the top, Vaishyas in the middle, and then down at the bottom the Sudras and the outcastes. Well, you have the same thing in this country. The Europeans are at the top, the Indians are in the middle, and the Africans are the Sudras.

When such parallels were explicitly drawn, however, a point of great significance was noted. The intention in the speaker's mind almost invariably was to illustrate the application of caste-like discrimination *to Indians by Europeans*. Indians will not ordinarily admit that their relations with Africans are influenced in any way by caste considerations.

Let us compare by juxtaposition two anecdotes touching upon commensality from the interview protocols. The first is representative of the illustrations of European discrimination related to us almost daily. The second, significantly, was told by a non-Gujarati South African schoolteacher:

> About three years ago I went to the agricultural show that they have here every year. Now at that time the

21. Within the extensive literature, the classic statement is W. Lloyd Warner's introduction to Davis, Gardner, and Gardner, *Deep South*. Also John Dollard, *Caste and Class in a Southern Town* (2nd ed. New York, Harper, 1949). For a recent critical comparison with India, see Gerald D. Berreman, "Caste in India and the United States," *American Journal of Sociology, 66* (1960), 120–27.

government had just made a big hullabaloo that the agricultural show would be completely nonracial. Nevertheless, when I went up to one of the stands which was serving milk, I was told by the European lady, "We can serve you only if you bring your own glass." I said, "This is ridiculous! I want a glass of milk!" But the woman wouldn't give it to me. All she would say when I reminded her that things were supposed to have changed was, "I'm sorry. It's against the rules."

Things have changed a lot recently—everyone has gotten more broadminded about such matters. But even now there is still a good deal of prejudice among Indians toward Africans. Three or four years ago I had an African advocate here at my house overnight. Afterwards, an Indian woman who is one of our next door neighbors said to me, "How can you possibly eat out of the same plates that man used?" Of course this African advocate was actually a better man than she or her husband, and I could have pointed that out to her. But I didn't.

Attitudes and values clustered about the preparation and serving of food provide us with the clearest indication that Indians do tend to perceive Africans as a lower caste, although not necessarily consciously. As we have pointed out, an African cook or a cook-houseboy is universal in European households. By contrast, it is a rare Indian household in which one finds an African cook, and virtually all of the few exceptions are Muslim. Africans rarely serve food at the table.

Various innocuous explanations are offered to the European who shows any interest in this obvious difference in the use of servants. Most commonly he is told by Indians that their food is so complicated that it is not worthwhile to try to teach Africans to prepare it. If the questioner then brings up the matter of serving, he is reminded that by Indian custom it is the wife's duty to serve her husband before she herself eats. If neither of these arguments are resorted to, then it is simply stated that Africans are "dirty."

These explanations are reasonable. But they do not explain why the very idea of an African handling food should on occasion bring so strong an emotional reaction from Indian informants. As might be expected, those who stress the "dirty" aspect of African cooking showed this revulsion most clearly. When asked if African servants ever helped with the cooking in his household, a wealthy Hindu replied with unguarded heat: "Never! In my house we would never think of having an African do the cooking. They are too dirty; I wouldn't trust them. I know Europeans all use them, but I wouldn't have one in the house."

An Anavil visibly shudders at his own graphic example:

> Some people allow their African houseboy to help out with the cooking, but personally I wouldn't. These people are much too dirty. For instance, when they are making something which requires sugar, they don't hesitate to put a spoonful of sugar in their mouths first and then dip the spoon back into the can without washing it.

The offering or withholding of food within a social situation ordinarily demanding hospitality has always been a prime symbol of social distance in Indian culture. In Central Africa when a Mochi or a Khumbhar stops at the house of a person of a higher caste than himself, he watches closely for clues of his host's real attitude in this nontraditional situation. If he is not immediately offered tea upon arrival, no matter what the circumstances or what the hour, he judges this as a deliberate slight. Higher caste persons often complained of the lower castes' sensitivity upon these matters—while loudly denying, we need hardly add, that they ever dreamed of trying to subordinate their guests in such a manner.

As an integral part of this established hospitality pattern, a European calling at an Indian shop in any other role than that of the most casual customer is invariably offered tea or a soft drink. Within this context, the following remark made by an African businessman is very instructive: "Before I sold it, I used to have a rather extensive [retail] business and I bought most of my goods from Indian wholesalers. But I have never been given a cup of tea in an Indian shop."

It is easier to see the application of caste norms and values in food behavior than it is in any other aspect of Indian-African relations since food occupies such a central place in caste symbolism. Still, hints of caste-derived attitudes are apparent elsewhere. The possible role of caste in sex relations has already been mentioned. Another hint can be seen in the interesting ambivalence which Indians show toward the nanny boy who takes care of their children.

The employment of nanny boys is very widespread. What came to impress us, however, about this particular relationship was the degree of discomfiture which the subject aroused whenever it was brought up for discussion in interviews. Many Indians deny that they themselves use nanny boys, and such informants tend to be extremely critical of those who do—a sure indication that this custom, like so many in all societies, is one which is tolerated in practice but not morally approved.

On our first visit to his house, a Brahman informant successfully avoided answering a tactfully worded question concerning the duties of his two servants. On a second visit, however, the nanny boy and his charges were physically present. When we then again brought up the subject of his duties, the only reply was: "He sees to it that the children don't get out into the street and get run over. That's all he has to do."

Most of those saying they do not use (or never have used) the services of a nanny boy in their families put their disapproval on hygienic grounds.

I don't believe in the color bar. But I wouldn't want an African taking care of my child. I know that some of the older Indians allow Africans to take care of their children, but that's because they don't know any better. The fact is the Africans aren't a very clean people. If they take care of the child, they might kiss it or allow it to play in dirty places, just because they don't know any better.

Others explain that the children might be abused or neglected: "I never allow Africans to take care of my children. Sometimes they are rather rough with little children. You can't trust them. I'm not saying that they hit them or anything like that. But when they cry, they don't pay any attention to them."

More analytical than most, one informant pointed to the cross-pressures which tempt people into behavior that is all but universally disapproved:

Usually, when you find a nanny boy taking care of children in an Indian family, you have this kind of situation. You will find that in those families the wife has four or five other children to take care of, and her husband works in the shop all day. So, now, I ask you, what can she do with all those kids? She turns them over to an African boy so that she can have a bit more time to do her other work.

Evidence of the kind just cited shows that Indians do perceive Africans to some extent within a framework of caste attitudes and values. Considering the importance of caste in the culture to which all Indian immigrants were originally socialized, it would be very strange sociologically if they did not. Now we must ask the really crucial question: what is the significance of this fact within the broader context of Indian-African relations? Has it made a critical difference? Posed in this way, we think the answer must be that it has not. Some difference, yes, an additional negative shading in tone and quality perhaps to an inherently impersonal relationship, but not a truly critical difference.

Following a normative interpretation of social behavior, it makes some sense to say that caste norms and values structure social relations in the Indian village. In Central Africa, it makes no sense at all. Obviously, the meaning which caste has is confined to the Indian group; it is not shared by the Africans. There is no consensus, no reciprocity, no system. The evaluation which the Indian makes is thus a private matter, without force or substance in an established institutional order.

But there is a second, more fundamental reason why judgments Indians make of Africans in caste terms are essentially irrelevant, given the circumstances under which they are applied. The inferiority which the ordinary Indian perceives in the ordinary African is no illusion: it is an objective socio-cultural reality quite independent of the Indian's perception of it. The behavioral characteristics of Africans, like those of other people, are a product not of an attitude but of history and evolution, set at a given level of development in point of time. It is these characteristics that the Indian sees and knows from direct experience, whatever his interpretation of them: the poor and irritatingly slow customer agonizing over a petty purchase, a seemingly shiftless and stupid menial sullenly performing dull and routine tasks, an inept and none-too-trustworthy servant blissfully ignorant of the niceties of civilized living and capable therefore of licking the sugar spoon. But the African is poor not because the Indian or anyone else *perceives* him as such. He is poor because his economy is primitive and under-developed. He is unlettered because he has not been to school; and he is unskilled in some of the simplest tasks set by modern cosmopolitan culture because he has not had an opportunity to learn them.

In all these respects, the African stands before the Indian's eyes as a person patently inferior to himself. To make this judgment, the Indian does not need the peculiar criteria of his caste culture. Europeans and the westernized African elite themselves arrive at essentially the same evaluation of the ordinary African's behavior without such criteria.

Chapter Ten

PRE-INDEPENDENCE POLITICS

With some exaggeration—for such complicated matters cannot easily be reduced to a sentence—the British Isles may be called the original home of modern representative political institutions. In any case, perhaps nowhere else has the conception of democracy as moral equality flourished more vigorously.[1] Every British settler and official coming to Africa therefore carried with him certain well-defined notions of political rights, political freedom, and political equality. Acting upon these institutional norms, British settlers demanded from the very first sufficient political power to control local affairs. In 1912, for example, when there were a mere 1,500 Europeans in Northern Rhodesia, these Europeans were agitating for legislative representation.[2]

But society, we have argued, cannot be seen simply and solely as a projection of any given set of cultural norms, no matter how old or how firmly established. An African colony was not—and could not be by the nature of the *social* situation which it presented—the equivalent of an English town. Within such a context, the legitimate demands for political freedom and equality which British people might make upon each other were one thing. When demanded by non-Europeans they were another.

1. Kohn does not use our teminology, but he, among others, provides essential material for the argument. See Hans Kohn, *The Idea of Nationalism: A Study in Its Origins and Background* (New York, Macmillan, 1961), pp. 166–83. On moral equality, see Appendix, p. 405.

2. Gann, *Birth of a Plural Society,* pp. 163–68.

If a white settler in any part of British-occupied Africa had been asked during the period of European dominance why non-Europeans could not be given equal political rights, he would have given the stereotyped reply: "Because they do not measure up to European (or civilized) standards." And sociologists can hardly even begin to understand his behavior in Africa unless we immediately concede the empirical basis for the European's perception and definition of the situation. Here, as elsewhere, we must be able to see the truth behind the stereotype, however distorted it may be. Real social inequality, apart from any normative conception of it, has always been inherent in the evolutionary gap which separates Europeans from non-Europeans. These differences, it is true, have been progressively obscured by the extensive acculturation which has taken place. But in the first years of occupation when the enduring definitions of who-was-who-and-why were laid down, the gap was indeed so wide that insofar as the ordinary European was capable of perceiving them, the objective facts presented by his day-to-day experience conformed fairly well with his conviction that *any* European was superior to *any* non-European.[3]

To recognize the empirical foundation for the European's *perception* of his social situation in Africa is nonetheless insufficient for an understanding of his behavior. Belief and evaluation must be manifested in action if they are to be turned into concrete social reality. Instrumentally, the perceived differences

---

3. This reading of the European-standards rule in terms of what might be called sociological realism may be usefully compared with the popular psychological interpretation. Surrounded by crude savagery and barbarous practice, this argument runs, the European felt threatened—physically, socially, and morally—and overreacted accordingly. The moral threat, in particular, has fascinated the literary psychologist from Conrad on: the temptation to "go native," to give up the rigors of "civilized standards" and to revert to a presumably less demanding primitive level of behavior. Supporting evidence for this kind of psychological reaction can be found abundantly anywhere in the histories of the colonial world. To deny its reality would therefore be foolish indeed. But to erect a theory of ethnic relations upon such psychological phenomena is to confuse cause with effect, the fundamental with the incidental. The error seems to us characteristic of culture-and-personality approaches to socio-cultural change.

separating European from non-European were turned to the European's advantage, becoming in the process a highly convenient moral justification for privilege. The argument, endlessly repeated in stereotyped phrases wherever settlers gathered, went something like this:

> We Europeans "built up this country" and have "made it what it is." When we arrived in Africa, we found a population of "savages barely out of the trees," who "didn't even have the wheel." The fact that they are as civilized as they are now is due entirely to our precept and example. For this priceless gift of civilization, the present-day African shows little gratitude. True we enjoy a higher standard of living, but that is solely because we have contributed proportionately more. If we insist upon a monopoly of political power, that is because only we have the necessary knowledge and experience to employ power wisely in the interests of all. If we insist upon what in the shortsighted view seems like a provincial and small-minded snobbish seclusion in our intimate social relations, that too is only because European standards must be protected at all costs. In any fair perspective which would give adequate weight to our sacrifices and labors, it would be seen that we have acted justly and on the whole unselfishly.

Implicit in the European-standards rule was a promise that non-Europeans will enjoy the privileges which Europeans now enjoy, once they have earned them by becoming the cultural equal of the European. That there *was* a promise, it should be emphasized, is significant: it reflects the basically equalitarian norms of modern cosmopolitan culture. But we note that the timetable for the completion of the equalization process is made comfortably long. Up to and during the period of fieldwork for this study, Europeans characteristically spoke of the "two thousand years" which it took to create European civilization. The unspoken implication was that it would also take the African about that long.

300

INDIANS VERSUS EUROPEANS IN AFRICA

The rise of African nationalism has obscured the historical fact that it was Indians, not Africans, who first challenged the European-standards rule in British-occupied Africa. Until the most recent adult generation put in its appearance, Africans were so far removed from any seemingly valid claim to socio-cultural equality that a really serious political challenge from them would have seemed fantastic to most Europeans.

Indians, however, as pointed out in the historical chapter, were placed by the Europeans in an entirely different category. Given the opportunity, they were known to possess the capacity to acquire wealth and education rapidly; and from experience in India and South Africa, it was concluded that they would not hesitate to press for political rights whenever and wherever they felt strong enough to do so. As early as the 1920s they had made a bid for the franchise and for rights-of-entry into the exclusive White Highlands of East Africa. Not accidentally, this move coincided with Gandhi's successful agitation of nationalist sentiment in India.

The juxtaposition of these events reveals an additional and highly realistic facet of the European settlers' fear of Indians in Africa. Seriously pressed as it was in India, the British government refused to complicate matters there by giving a few thousand settlers in Kenya the restrictive powers over Indians which they demanded. It was thus shown that Indians in Africa could exert considerable leverage upon the Colonial Office through India.[4]

4. This East African affair of the 1920s is obviously somewhat tangential to our interests here, but there are two additional aspects of it which are worth noting. The first is the relationship between Indians and Africans during this period. Gandhi had fought the Indian cause in South Africa virtually without mentioning the African population. (Cf. M. K. Gandhi, *Gandhi's Autobiography: The Story of My Experiments with Truth,* translated by Mahadev Desai, Washington, D.C., Public Affairs Press, 1948. It contains very few references to Africans.) In East Africa, too, Indians demanded political equality with Europeans with no suggestion whatsoever that these same rights should be extended to Africans. Clearly, as perceived by both Indian and European settlers at this time, Africans were a part of the natural landscape, hardly conceivable as human beings with any claim to political rights.

In Central Africa, Indians have always been a very small minority compared to the European population, with the exception of Nyasaland. A test of power between Indian and European of the kind which occurred in East Africa was therefore numerically impossible and never came about. Still, as we have seen, the very rapid increase in the Indian population of the two northern territories during the prosperous postwar years immediately preceding federation brought the always latent fear of Indians among Europeans to the surface, and the achievement of independence in India gave this fear an added edge. Imaginative politicians again hauled up before rapt audiences the old bugaboo of an Africa overrun by the "teeming millions of Asia." A prominent Southern Rhodesian political figure of the period, N. H. Wilson, elaborated the theme:

> For 2,500 years the Asiatic hordes have been pressing against Europe and the peoples of Europe have been just holding them off. . . . And now through the agency of Indian imperialism, Asia is making an attempt that may be far more deadly than any of [those] preceding attempts. . . . The population of India is increasing at the

Yet, as it turned out, Africans did enter decisively into the settlement of this quarrel between Indians and Europeans. When laying down the guiding principle to be followed by the Crown in any future dispute of this sort, the British government declared in a famous White Paper (1923) that considerations for the interests of the African population must be "paramount" over those of the immigrant groups. Within the context of the immediate situation, the declaration might be interpreted somewhat cynically as a clever tactical maneuver. By making African rather than Indian or European interests paramount, the colonial officials extricated themselves from a potentially dangerous conflict because of the possibility of creating trouble in India, which in the British government's view was always more important than Africa.

Actually, from the standpoint of content, there was little which was radically new or different in the doctrine of paramountcy; it was in essence a reiteration of the concept of "trusteeship" which had long been established in British colonial policy. See Kenneth Robinson, *The Dilemmas of Trusteeship: Aspects of British Colonial Policy between the Wars* (London, Oxford University Press, 1965), particularly pp. 19–26. But once made explicit, especially as it was amplified and elaborated seven years later in the Passfield Memorandum of 1930, paramountcy became a kind of charter for African nationalist demands and a red flag to settler groups throughout East and Central Africa. See, among other sources, Edward Clegg, *Race and Politics: Partnership in the Federation of Rhodesia and Nyasaland* (London, Oxford University Press, 1960), pp. 60–70.

rate of some five million a year. To transfer two million people a year from India to Africa would not be by any means difficult. The voyage from Bombay to Dar-es-Salaam is much shorter and much easier than from Hamburg to New York, and in the 'nineties of the last century and the 1900s of this, a million immigrants a year crossed the North Atlantic. . . . If the Afro-Asiatic plan to eliminate the white man from East Africa succeeds, as it has in Asia, there is little doubt but that [if free entry is allowed] by the end of this century there will be two hundred million Indians in Africa, perhaps twice as many. It will be completely impossible to keep them from flowing over into the Rhodesias, the Congo, Angola, Mozambique, French Equatorial Africa, West Africa, and North Africa.[5]

People like Wilson saw in the ancient Coolie Question a dependable demagogic issue, but more responsible leaders took a calmer view. It would thus be a gross exaggeration to claim that Indian immigration per se played a very important role in the formation of the Federation of Rhodesia and Nyasaland. It does not stretch the historical facts, however, to observe that a great many European settlers—many of whom were less than enthusiastic about federation on other grounds—saw in it a welcome means to end the Indian threat once and for all. Exclusion of the Indians, it will be remembered, was one of the very first acts of this new government when it came into power. Federation came into effect September 3, 1953, and further immigration by Indians was closed off by executive order on November 20, 1953. Actual passage of an immigration bill awaited the formation of the Federal Assembly the following year.[6]

5. N. H. Wilson, *The Central African Dilemma: A Preliminary Study in the Survival of Western Civilization in Central Africa* (pamphlet, publisher not indicated, 1954).

6. Speaking to the press in Lusaka, the retiring South African Commissioner in London congratulated the new federal government upon its decisive action. Indians, he said, had already managed to gain a "stranglehold in East Africa," and without the measures provided so expeditiously by the federal government the same could have been expected in Central Africa. "Nehru is the champion

FEDERATION: THE IDEAL AND THE REALITY

It is only one of its abundant ironies that the Federation of
Rhodesia and Nyasaland, billed so enthusiastically upon its
launching as a great experiment in "racial partnership," should
have begun its short career in history by an attempt to eliminate
one of its presumed partners. The Federation was full of such
paradoxes. An ambitious undertaking, it combined in an unusual measure some highly idealistic intentions with a good
many cynically calculated judgments of expediency and self-
interest.

The Federation was born under a cloud of suspicion and
ill-will which never lifted and, like most failures, it continues
to be held in low repute. The *idea* of federation, however, had
a perfectly respectable internal logic and a strong moral appeal to men of good will, and it is quite impossible to comprehend the recent history of Central Africa without fully ap-
preciating this fact. The only difficulty was that the ideal which
federation embodied and the realities of life in Central Africa
were entirely different things. The case provides a particularly
instructive lesson for those who believe and hope that rationality should rule human affairs.[7]

---

of the Coloured races this side of the Iron Curtain," he went on. "If he can
weaken the European influence in Africa, then it will mean Africa for the
Indians." *Central African Post* (Lusaka, July 21, 1954).

7. As we have tried to point out elsewhere, the "ideal" federation offers an
exceedingly interesting study in the relationship between abstract theoretical
rationality and social conflict. F. Dotson, "Rationality and Conflict," paper
presented to the XVI Congreso Nacional de Sociologia, Veracruz, Mexico,
November 22–26, 1965. Fundamental conflicts of interest can always be rec-
onciled in the world of logical abstraction by the assumption that people
should act according to reason: reason dictates that they mutually give up
shortsighted, selfish advantages in the interests of compromise and cooperation. In abstract logic, conflict invariably has a bad name: being destructive and
wasteful, it is against everyone's "true," "real," or "ultimate" interests. The
rationalist's solution to the problems of social organization is thus always to
try to get people to see and do what "reason" dictates. But conflict is not so
easily exorcised in the real social world. It is questionable whether it is
possible for real people either to perceive or to act upon the "true" or
"ultimate" interests of a whole society. *People can only act upon what they
perceive,* and perception, we take it, is irrevocably limited by the boundaries
of group experience.

What we for convenience here designate—and the term is ours—as the "ideal" federation was in origin an essentially collective and anonymous brainchild of Colonial Office bureaucrats and their intellectual advisers; in time it came to be the accepted policy of the British government for dealing with Central African affairs.[8] Logically, its starting point was the thoroughly valid assumption that colonialism in its historic form was a thing of the past: the large portions of the world previously administered under colonial rule would be and must be reorganized upon some other basis. The only substantive question, therefore, was how this goal was to be obtained.

Provided with the wonderful wisdom of hindsight, we now know the answer. Reorganization would be accomplished through an extension everywhere of the nation-state, founded upon the legitimating principle of self-determination. But we must remember that this answer was by no means so obvious a short twenty years ago when federation in Central Africa was being considered. Steps in this direction, however, were already being taken. Keeping a wartime promise to the Philippines, the Americans set an example in colonial disengagement by granting these islands their independence in 1946. Independence for India quickly followed (1947), and, with considerably less grace upon the part of the occupying powers, for Indonesia and Indochina. By the early 1950s, farsighted British officials were even conceding that much of West Africa would soon be ready for independence.

Yet granting a liberal optimism about the possible success of these ventures into self-rule—and not everyone was optimistic—the problem of what to do with such areas as East and Central Africa remained seriously troublesome to those authorities responsible for thinking about their future. The native

8. On the background and development of the Federation, see Clegg, *Race and Politics*; Harry Franklin, *Unholy Wedlock: The Failure of the Central African Federation* (London, George Allen and Unwin, 1963); Gray, *The Two Nations;* Colin Leys, *European Politics in Southern Rhodesia* (Oxford, Clarendon Press, 1959); Philip Mason, *Year of Decision: Rhodesia and Nyasaland in 1960* (London, Oxford University Press, 1960); Richard Hall, *Zambia* (New York, Praeger, 1965), pp. 145–90.

peoples of these areas were extremely backward culturally, far more so than those of the relatively advanced populations of West Africa, to say nothing of the civilized peoples of colonial Asia to whom self-government had just been granted. That these Africans could rule themselves within anything like the foreseeable future was an idea which simply did not occur to Europeans intimately acquainted with the facts of their development.[9]

To look backward, however, was impossible. Older administrative policies such as Lord Lugard's "indirect rule" had clearly served their day.[10] Indirect rule had eased the strains of adjustment to a European-dominated world but tended to perpetuate primitive institutions. Under its aegis, little or no provision could be made for economic and social development out of tribal society into the modern world, although in fact tribalism was everywhere breaking up under the impact of the white contact that had already taken place. Larger and better integrated socio-political units than the tribe were obviously necessary to accommodate even the existing pace of change.

To complicate matters further, East and Central Africa had been colonized by "immigrant races." This was now seen by most colonial experts as unfortunate; but for moral and practical reasons the interests of these people could not be ignored.[11] Furthermore, the largest single block of these set-

---

9. As late as 1948, the Governor of Kenya described the idea of a self-governing state in his territory as "fantastic." His model for the future was a Dominion for Kenya, with some non-European unofficial representation but with Europeans in firm control. *Annual Register: A Review of Public Events at Home and Abroad for the Year 1948* (London, Longmans, Green, 1949), p. 148.

10. For a good recent discussion, see Robinson, *The Dilemmas of Trusteeship*, particularly pp. 20–26.

11. Ibid., pp. 73–74: "Many a harassed Colonial Secretary might have agreed that it would have been more convenient, as well as possibly more virtuous, if Indian or Chinese labour had never been brought to territories like Malaya, Fiji, Trinidad, or British Guiana, or if European settlement had not been officially encouraged in Kenya in 1903 or in Palestine after the first world war, or if Britain had not in Ceylon or Cyprus found herself in control of territories where, in a far more remote past, earlier colonizations had produced sizeable minorities, like the Ceylon Tamils or the Cypriot Turks, wholly distinct in language and culture from the majority of people."

tlers, those of Southern Rhodesia, had already been given a very considerable degree of self-government in an earlier period when this seemed entirely just and moral. The best way to safeguard the rights of Africans in Southern Rhodesia, it could be plausibly argued, would be to establish some kind of larger and more inclusive arrangement with the built-in guarantees of continued paternalistic interest which those of the two northern territories enjoyed.

Given these fundamental problems, what could be more logical than a compromise solution which would resolve all of them within one tidy package? Rational men in the twentieth century should be capable of rational solutions! Central Africa would be neither a stagnant and unprogressive purely African state (Uganda, perhaps?), nor would it be a cruel, outright white-dominated oligarchy like the Union. Instead, it would be something new under the sun: a *racial partnership* within which the capital and skills of the immigrant races would direct the exploitation of the abundant natural and labor resources. Rapid economic development—hardly conceivable under other auspices—would provide the solid material base for equally rapid cultural progress for the African population.

Europeans would inevitably have to be given a near monopoly of political power in the new state at the beginning. Africans could not be expected to participate much at first, although a few could do so. However, the door would be left open for them to enter into an active political role just as fast as they could be brought up to a suitable "standard." In the meantime, their rights would be protected by firm constitutional guarantees, backed by reserve powers retained by the British government. Educated prosperous Africans, it was rather casually taken for granted, would necessarily see the logic of a government founded upon so rational a basis; seeing the light, they would not jeopardize its continued existence by lining up with the undeveloped African masses in opposition to their European benefactors.[12]

12. This assumption, which seems so preposterous in the light of recent events, was actually well grounded in European experience prior to the period

Briefly, this was the ideal federation in its most disinterested form. Nor were earnest and intelligent persons wanting in Central Africa who accepted the ideal and worked hard to see it put into practice. But these were relatively few, and for the most part they were expatriates: highly placed civil servants within the Colonial Office, intellectuals, journalists, professionals, and executives in the corporate bureaucracy. Except for the temporary advantages of maneuver that it might offer, neither the Africans nor the European settlers could wholeheartedly accept the basic premises of the ideal federation.

Africans educated to the point of political awareness wanted no part of any arrangement that would put settlers in control of their destinies, despite the promise that this control would be temporary. To them, the ideal federation was a hypocritical ploy to put the settlers in power. Particularly in Nyasaland, where the level of education and political sophistication tended to be somewhat higher than in Northern Rhodesia, Africans managed from the first to express their opposition emphatically and effectively. In an effort to placate them (and their liberal European supporters), a provision for a constitutional review after an interim trial period was written into the Federal Constitution. But African opposition remained implacable and gained impetus with each success of the nationalist movement elsewhere on the continent.

The settler population, on the other hand, could take neither the philosophy nor the practice of multiracialism seriously, although all but the most conservative were willing to go along with federation as the expedient course of action under the circumstances. What the settlers really wanted was what they had always wanted and had continuously pressed for: namely, autonomy sufficient to arrange once and for all the social and political order within, as they said, "their own country." Most

---

in question. Before the coming of nationalism, acculturated Africans had as a demonstrable fact identified with the Europeans. For this reason, it did not occur to knowledgeable people familiar with Africa at firsthand that such Africans would not continue to do so indefinitely. Theoretically speaking, this illustrates once more the fallacy of simple linear projections in the prediction of social behavior.

were realistic enough to realize, however, that under existing circumstances complete control was impossible. Therefore, if federation was the closest approximation to full autonomy which they could get, then it would have to be accepted on that basis.

What appeal federation possessed for the settlers lay in the promise of immediate and effective local control. For the future, they saw ample grounds for hope. Rapidly increased European immigration would indefinitely offset the vote of a few non-Europeans, and once the European population was more properly balanced with the non-European, a renewed drive for independent dominion status could be launched that would be hard for the British government to resist. If in the meantime a certain amount of verbal nonsense about racial partnership was necessary to soothe the sensibilities of fuzzy liberals in Britain and the United States who were ignorant of the real facts of life in Africa, then this would be a small price to pay for the substance of European control. They themselves need not be fooled. Partnership within Central Africa would be understood as *that which exists between horse and rider*— to use a sardonic cliché of wide currency. Or, to put the matter more politely, it would be a partnership between the junior and senior members of the firm.[13]

THE INDIAN AND THE FEDERATION

Indian reaction to federation underwent a cycle of: (1) passionate (but futile) opposition; (2) a period of fairly comfortable accommodation; and finally (3) reluctant rejection under the pressures of African nationalism.

Like Africans, Indians feared the loss of Colonial Office protection under any arrangement that would provide for white settler rule. As an object lesson of what such a shift in

13. The "horse and rider" phrase is usually, but perhaps apocryphally, attributed to the Southern Rhodesian politician who became the Federation's first Prime Minister, Sir Godfrey Huggins (later Lord Malvern). See T. R. M. Creighton, *Southern Rhodesia and the Central African Federation: The Anatomy of Partnership* (New York, Praeger, 1960), pp. 101–02.

power might ultimately mean, South Africa was always at hand. But more immediately and concretely, Indians were concerned with the restrictions upon immigration certain to come with local autonomy for the Europeans. As far back as 1939, Indian witnesses told the Bledisloe Commission, which had been appointed to consider the feasibility of a closer association of the three territories, that they feared such a union might adversely affect their entry rights as it would probably be dominated by Southern Rhodesia.[14]

When federation gradually moved closer to reality, Indians did what little they could to oppose it. They held meetings, issued resolutions, and appealed to those few European politicians who for one reason or another had ever expressed any interest in their problems. A special body which called itself the Central African Asian Conference was formed to carry on these activities. On the eve of federation in 1953, the Conference formally declared that Indians should have "complete equality in the political, economic, and social functions of the [new] Federal State."[15] As a final futile gesture, the Conference declared the day the federal immigration law came into effect to be one of public mourning. Indian shops were closed throughout the two northern territories, and the adult male population, wearing black armbands, paraded the streets and attended mass protest meetings, ostensibly for "prayer and meditation."[16]

What Indians had in mind by their demand for complete equality must be assessed against inequalities existing both before and during federation. Since many of these disabilities were embodied in legislative enactments and administrative policies they constituted the issues of most direct political interest to Indians. A somewhat more systematic listing and review than hitherto set forth therefore seems in order.

14. Rhodesia-Nyasaland Royal Commission, *Report* [Bledisloe Commission Report], Cmnd. 5949 (London, His Majesty's Stationery Office, 1939), pp. 238–39.

15. *Northern News* (Ndola, August 29, 1953).

16. *Central African Post* (October 18, 1954); *Northern News* (November 1, 1954).

1. Immigration. Of all the specifically legal disabilities imposed upon them, Indians, as we have seen, probably felt most strongly about immigration. In a resolution adopted just before it came into power, the Federal Party had made quite explicit the patently discriminatory policy which it intended to follow:

[It will be our policy . . .] to encourage *planned and selective* immigration at the greatest rate at which the Federation can absorb immigrants, in the belief that *a large European population* is essential to the progress, prosperity, and happiness of all races. [And] to take such steps as may be necessary to prevent the entry into the Federation of *peoples or individuals* whose presence might be inimical to the economic, racial, or political stability of the Federation.[17]

Nowhere, needless to say, do the words Indian or Asian appear in the legislation written to achieve these goals. The law did specify criminals, prostitutes, and homosexuals in the course of illustrating what it meant by undesirable individuals—with whom, by implication, those peoples undesirable because of their "economic" and "racial" attributes were to be equated.

Practically, the bar to future entry imposed more hardships upon some Indians than upon others. Some of these effects have been previously discussed as they pertain concretely to economic organization, religion, and the family.[18] But more important generally than any one of its concrete applications was the symbolic affront this legislation presented to all Indians. An immigration policy which specifically invited all Europeans (including, as Indians never tired of pointing out, enemy nationals of the late war) while slamming the door in their faces was resented with a bitterness few Europeans ever appreciated.

2. Schools. Public schools up to the University College at Salisbury were thoroughly segregated until the end of federa-

---

17. From the policy adopted by the first Federal Party Congress, quoted in *Northern News* (September 22, 1953). Emphasis added.
18. See Chapters 3, 4, and 6.

tion. Construction of schools in adequate numbers for Indians and Coloureds always lagged behind those built for Europeans, whose schools were given deliberate priority. This was true despite the fact that an extensive school-building program for all races was one of the impressive achievements of European government during this period.[19]

By 1959, schools for Indians were available everywhere at the primary level. But the lack of secondary schools was still acute. In 1959, there were thirty-eight government secondary schools for Europeans in the Federation, in effect, one or more in every sizable town. There were, however, only two government secondary schools for Indians and Coloureds, and both of these were in Southern Rhodesia. Elsewhere Indians with children of secondary school age (and the number in the relevant demographic cohorts rose very rapidly between 1950 and 1960) had no choice but to send them to India or England, if they could not obtain a place for them in the increasingly overcrowded schools in Southern Rhodesia. Yet in this period, the fathers of these Indian children perhaps drove daily past a spanking new school for Europeans, completely free and considerably overbuilt in anticipation of future demand.

The irony of this situation was especially felt in some of the smaller towns. Here there might only be half a dozen Indian children of secondary school age. Their exclusion under such circumstances stood out as crudely and cruelly discriminatory in Indian eyes, especially when it is remembered that the fathers of some of these children regularly paid taxes far in excess of most of the European families.

3. Military service and social welfare. Under federal defense legislation, European, Coloured, and Indian youths were subject to compulsory military training. (Africans were exempted.) Service units were segregated and Indian draftees were automatically assigned to transportation and quartermaster duties. No Indian ever rose above the enlisted ranks, and pay for Indians and Coloureds was arbitrarily set at two-

19. Schools for Europeans, Indians, and Coloureds were federal. Those for Africans were a territorial responsibility.

thirds of that for Europeans at equivalent rank. Similarly, Indians and Coloureds were entitled to only two-thirds of the European rate for welfare benefits, chief of which were old-age allowances.

4. Civil service. With a few exceptions, the only Indians in the civil service during the federation period were teachers in the segregated schools. These teachers were employed under the discriminatory 'branch" system already described.[20]

5. Spatial segregation. Until the postwar period, most Indians lived in behind-the-shop quarters, and many still do so. They were thus concentrated residentially wherever their businesses were located, meaning in most towns in a segregated secondary trading area devoted exclusively to the African trade. Following the war, separate residential areas for Indians began to be set aside as a matter of planning policy. Urban growth in Central Africa is subject to fairly close control, and effective segregation by racial blocs was easily accomplished informally through powers over land use exercised by the municipal councils.[21]

6. Public services. Public transportation is so little developed in Central Africa that its use has never assumed the role in race relations which it has in the United States and elsewhere. What exists has been subject to segregation. Indians brave or foolish enough to purchase a first-class rail ticket, for example, always discovered upon boarding the train that there was "no room" in the first-class cars and were required

---

20. See above, p. 247 and n. 9.

21. Driving up a main road leading into the best European residential district of one Northern Rhodesian town, an Indian informant pointed out that the Indian houses along the way were all set back several hundred feet from the road, with a still undeveloped area for a park between the houses and the road. Once the European area is reached, the houses are set near the street in the usual fashion. "When this area was built, we wanted our houses and the mosque over there placed up here near the main street like the European houses and that church are. We didn't object to the idea of a park; but why does it have to be where it is? There is no park between the street and the European houses, and you'll notice that they haven't done anything with it anyway. What the Europeans really wanted was to put a China Wall around the Indians so that nobody coming up this fancy new street would know that we live over there."

by the conductor to sit in the second-class accommodations. The brothers of a Catholic school for Indians and Coloureds in Southern Rhodesia told us that they had given up trying to make reservations for their pupils to go home for holidays, when the trains are crowded with European children making the same journey.

Public toilet facilities are not provided for Indians in Salisbury, and Indians are not allowed to use European ones. In the downtown area of the new capital city of Lusaka, segregated facilities were provided in a single building. Each of the separate entrances has a conspicuous sign over the door designating its particular racial type—European, Asian, or African.

Hospitals are operated by the government in Central Africa and thus properly belong under the rubric of public services. Entirely segregated units for Asians and Coloureds are the rule in Southern Rhodesia, these being generally attached as a wing to the European hospital. In the northern territories, Indians were always admitted to the European hospital. Indian patients, however, were often placed in a separate room out of deference to the European patients.

7. Cinemas, cafes, hotels, and public swimming baths. Until the late 1950's, Indians were rigidly excluded (along with the Africans and the Coloureds) from virtually all transient, recreational, and cultural facilities of this character. Older Indians of the immigrant generation resented these barriers primarily on principle. Commonly, they had no particular desire to attend European films or eat in European cafes or drink in European bars. Not to be allowed to do so was an insult, but no hardship. Younger people, particularly the African-born, were already acculturated enough to feel genuinely deprived by these restrictions.

8. Liquor and firearms. Indians were categorized with Coloureds in legislation and customary practice covering the purchase and use of these items. The ban on liquor was lifted shortly before our arrival in Africa, but the long-standing administrative policy of denying permits to Indians for the pur-

314

chase of firearms was generally followed throughout the federation period.

Exasperated by the inequities imposed upon them, Indians repeated to us again and again a version of the following stereotype:

> The situation here is really worse than it is in South Africa. At least in the Union, you know what to expect. The Europeans here are just as prejudiced as they are in the Union, but being British they are more hypocritical than the Dutch people are, and they like to pretend that they aren't. Underneath, if anything, they are worse.

To Americans, this kind of comment has an exceedingly familiar ring. And just as the American homologue—that race prejudice is as real in the North as it is in the South but is hidden and implicit rather than open and explicit—has a large element of truth in it, so does this one. After making necessary allowances for the very considerable differences which exist between British South Africans and Afrikaners, there is certainly a recognizable European subculture for southern Africa as a whole. Prominent in this subculture is its complex of stereotypes by which non-Europeans are socially defined and evaluated. In this respect, indeed, the difference between South and Central Africa is strictly relative, and insofar as this is what Indians mean by the kind of remark just quoted, they are essentially correct.

But as we have so often sought to underline in this volume, culture does not automatically translate itself into social organization and here again is a case in point. In spite of their great similarities in respect to basic sentiment upon racial matters, the Union of South Africa and the Federation of Rhodesia and Nyasaland were very different states, a difference ultimately traceable to the fact that in the Union, Europeans enjoyed the political autonomy which those of Central Africa would have liked to have had but did not possess.

Nowhere, perhaps, was this fundamental difference between the Federation and the Union more marked than in their respective statuses of the Indian population, legally and socially. Briefly stated, some of the most important of these differences were as follows:

1. Indians have always possessed the franchise in Central Africa, insofar as they have been able to meet the stated qualifications. Indians have been disenfranchised in the Union since 1896.[22]

2. Although effectively lacking certain employment opportunities, notably in the civil service, Indians in Central Africa have always had the same rights to own property (including land) and to do business that Europeans have. In South Africa, Indians are rigidly excluded from all profitable employment, both public and private; and they are, in addition, subject to the cruel and arbitrary infringements of property rights written into the Group Areas Act.[23]

3. After 1959, with the repeal of the Interterritorial Movement of Persons Act which barred the settlement in Southern Rhodesia of Indians from the two northern territories, Indians enjoyed complete freedom of movement within the Federation. In South Africa, an Indian resident of Natal who wishes to visit the neighboring Transvaal must obtain a permit and go through a bureaucratic rigamarole comparable to that involved in a trip to a foreign country, and a transfer of permanent residence is out of the question.

4. Aside from certain specific disabilities (such as immigration), Indians have enjoyed essentially equal justice with Europeans in the courts of Central Africa. This statement cannot be made with the same confidence for South African courts.

5. In spite of the inequities which have been mentioned,

22. This is the date when the Indians of Natal, where the great majority have always lived, lost the parliamentary franchise; they lost the municipal franchise in 1924. In the former Boer republics, Indians never had political rights.

23. On the application of the Group Areas Act to the Indians of Natal, see Leo Kuper, Hilstan Watts, and Ronald Davies, *Durban: A Study in Racial Ecology* (New York, Columbia University Press, 1958). The law itself has not been appreciably modified since this detailed work was published, but time has shown what Kuper and others had found difficult to believe: namely, that an Afrikaner government would actually take the progression of steps necessary for its implementation.

Indians in Central Africa have, in comparison to those of South Africa, shared far more equitably in the legally provided public services. Education, the most important of these by far, provides a telling example. Indians in South Africa not only pay taxes like other people, but they must also provide out of their own meager resources a good part of the funds spent for the education of their children.[24] The free public schools which the Federation built for Indians were not comparable in number or quality to those provided for Europeans, but their very existence stood as a marked contrast to the situation in South Africa.

6. Finally, the right to legitimate citizenship for Indians actually resident in the Federation was always taken for granted, despite the barriers created to further immigration. In South Africa, the very right of Indians whose fathers and grandfathers were born there to remain in the country has been openly and officially disputed, and schemes to ship the entire Indian population back to India have been constantly discussed.

Taken together, these add up to a tremendous difference in the effective legal status of Indians in the two countries. Nonetheless, the notable lack of gratitude on the part of Indians for the difference is understandable. The Indian position has always been that they were entitled not only to the rights which they in fact enjoyed but full equality with the Europeans. Moreover, they are well aware that the differences which mark them off from their brethren in the Union were in no sense a free gift from the local Europeans. Indians know that if the white settlers of Central Africa had their way, the differences would have been smaller. That Indian rights and privileges under federation were in fact a kind of ecological accident, unpremeditated and unwanted by the dominant group, can be illustrated by taking the franchise as an example.

The ideal federation based its bid for moral recognition in the outside world upon its claim to have solved constitutionally the dilemma posed between the alternatives of white or

24. Van den Berghe, *Caneville*, pp. 40–42, 144–46.

317

black domination. By its inherent logic, each component group had to be given meaningful political rights; none could be categorically excluded if the charge of racialism was to be avoided. Yet by the same inherent logic, the great mass of the population had to be excluded. Otherwise, the inevitable result would be black domination. In simple numerical terms, all non-African groups were tiny minorities whose votes in any system approaching universal suffrage would become utterly insignificant.

Balancing these necessities imposed a tremendous burden upon the ingenuity of the constitution makers and accounts for the incredibly complicated constitutional law of the federation period. In essence, however, the problem can be simply stated: Africans had to be given some access to the franchise in order to make "partnership" at all plausible to the outside world. But they could not be given much if control were to be kept firmly in European hands.

A solution to this fundamental dilemma was continually sought in a franchise set upon some suitable combination of education and property. Such a franchise could be defended morally in cosmopolitan world culture: the restrictions, it could be plausibly maintained, were nonracial since anyone who could meet the qualifications could vote, no matter what the color of his skin. That very few persons except Europeans could meet the qualifications the constitution makers always had in mind was a highly convenient but not entirely accidental result of their calculations.

The real contest in the franchise issue was of course between Africans and Europeans. Indians, quite literally, did not figure in these calculations for the simple reason that they were too few in number to make much difference one way or another.[25]

25. The fact that there are more Indians in Nyasaland than Europeans was not overlooked at the time the Federal Constitution was written, but it did not arouse undue concern. For one thing, Nyasaland was never considered really critical to the federal experiment. Furthermore, the Europeans in Nyasaland were not immediately threatened as fewer Indians in Nyasaland could meet the franchise requirements than in the Rhodesias. With immigration firmly cut off by federation, the confident expectation was that Nyasaland's Europeans would increase rapidly enough to offset any potential

If Indians had been somewhat more numerous than they in fact were, we can be very sure that no franchise based solely upon education and property would have been adopted, since the whole point of these intricate calculations was to keep power—for the time being at least—securely in European hands.[26]

Nonetheless, by ecological accident Indians found themselves the recipients of a small but welcome measure of real political power. The record shows that they exploited the franchise fully and intelligently. Those who could qualify registered for both the federal and the local elections, and it appears that with few exceptions those who registered actually voted.

In most districts, there were either no Indians at all or so few that they did not matter. Where Indians were concentrated in appreciable numbers, however, they could not with impunity be ignored. One prominent liberal Northern Rhodesian politician of the federation period stated:

Asians should be given every opportunity to get into the civil service and other professions such as medicine and engineering. I would like to give every encouragement to Asians. It is a blot on our reputation that we have these people here and do so little for them. I would like to give Asians every opportunity to get into our civil service not only for the lower levels but the higher levels as well.[27]

The speaker is Dr. Alexander Scott, candidate for reelection to the Federal Assembly in 1958 for the Lusaka East constituency, a district in which registered Indian voters accounted for some 10 percent of the total electorate. No candidate from that district who lost the Indian vote could hope to be elected —a reality which was impressed upon Dr. Scott himself in the

dangers inherent in this temporary imbalance between the Indian and European populations.

26. Empirical support for this generalization is supplied in the discussion of the "liberal" Macleod constitution on pp. 337–39.

27. *Central African Post* (October 24, 1958).

ensuing election, when the Indians were successfully wooed into the United Federal Party camp.

In defeat, Dr. Scott lashed out bitterly at the Indians for their ingratitude, pointing out that he had always been conspicuous in their defense. This was true. But the Indians were more interested in substance than in kind words. As a member of a minority party, Scott was unable to deliver; and for this particular election, the ruling United Federal Party had made a "deal" with the Indians. In exchange for their support, the government would push the construction of the secondary school in Northern Rhodesia which had long been promised them but also long delayed. Shortly after the election, the school began to materialize.[28]

THE INDIAN AND AFRICAN NATIONALISM

Because it offered a measure of real political power as well as an efficient administration under which they prospered economically, Indians managed on the whole a fairly comfortable accommodation to federation, despite the inequalities which they so deeply resented. Whatever advantages federation provided, however, were to be short-lived. The great experiment in multiracialism lasted barely a decade before it succumbed to African nationalism.

As demonstrated in Chapter 9, the ordinary Indian knows the ordinary African as an illiterate and essentially incomprehensible savage. Most Indians, therefore, found it difficult, when first presented with the idea, to believe that Africans were capable of governing the country. In this respect their basic attitude differed very little from that of most Europeans. Variants of the following themes appear with fair frequency, particularly in the early interview protocols:

I don't know what people in Britain and the United States are thinking about when they insist upon giving these

28. It was generally acknowledged to us by European politicians themselves that the fact that the Indians had any schools at all was due in large part to their political influence. In short, while Indian political weight did not amount to much, it was still worth a school or two.

320

Africans independence. They're not ready for it and won't be for a hundred years. I tell you, Doctor, giving these people the government would be like giving fire to a monkey.

If the Europeans leave this country, it will be set back a hundred years. You can't achieve anything by giving the poor man what the rich man has. [The informant is a wealthy man.]

About five percent of the Africans in this country are all right. But the other ninety-five percent are very bad. If they were given the government today, then tomorrow all the Indians in this town would be killed.

If the Africans get into power, then we will have no choice. We will have to leave. Even now, every day, I hear them out in the street saying to each other, "When we get into power, I am going to set fire to this place [i.e. an Indian-owned factory and warehouse]."

Africans come in here and say, "Why do you work so hard? In four or five years all of this [i.e. the shop and its goods] will be ours!" That kind of attitude is discouraging.

Yet despite this highly negative assessment of the African's capacity for self-government, relatively few Indians drew the simple and unambivalent conclusion stated by one prominent patron who openly aligned himself with the ruling United Federal Party: "I don't see how the Indians can do anything except side with the Europeans. They have too much of a stake in this country."

Sheer expediency dictated a large part of the Indians' determination to remain unaligned with one side or the other as long as possible. Many had come to believe by the time we arrived in Africa that Africans had an excellent chance of ultimately coming into power and in that case a record of support for the Europeans could do the Indians little good. But behind these highly rational considerations for hedging their support of the European cause were others to which an interpretation of outright and simple expediency does less than justice.

The expediency interpretation overlooks, for one thing, the very large reservoir of ill-will which Indians had accumulated against the Europeans. Indians would only have been human if they derived a fair measure of perverse satisfaction from seeing the tables turned on the Europeans for a change, even at some expense to their own interests. When it became apparent from constitutional talks then going on in London that an African majority in the next Northern Rhodesian Legislative Council would be assured, an Indian pioneer gleefully exclaimed: "The wheel [i.e. the steering wheel] is no longer in their hands. When the Africans get into power, they will cut the Europeans off just like the Europeans cut us off!"

Furthermore, our data make it clear that a good many Indians had come to accept the necessity of an African government as a moral right, irrespective of how short-range Indian interests would be served. Obviously, this principled position was much more palatable if one believed that African government was inevitable anyway. For example:

> The Africans constitute well over ninety-five percent of the population of Northern Rhodesia. It's only natural under these circumstances that they want their own government—any people would. The only realistic thing for the Europeans and Asians to do is to recognize this as a fact and help them to achieve self-government in the best possible way so that our own interests can be protected.
>
> But you will say the African has no sense. I know he has no sense. All right, so we agree that the African is no more than a child—a very rough child, indeed. But he has a brain and he is capable of learning, and our task is to teach him.

Indian willingness to accept the African's *right* to self-government—even in the face of marked doubt concerning his *ca-*

pacity for it—was helped along by a tendency to equate Indian and African nationalism and thus to identify emotionally with the African cause:

> These people are oppressed, just like we were in India before we got our independence. You can't blame them for wanting their own government. And it is only a matter of time now until they get it. If the Europeans and Asians want to stay in this country, they have to recognize that as a fact.

The principled position on African nationalism was advocated as a matter of policy by the Indian government and actively propagated through the office of the Indian High Commissioner in Salisbury. Immediately upon our arrival in Africa, Europeans began hinting of mysterious, oriental connections between the African nationalists and the Indian High Commissioner. In fact, however, there was nothing mysterious whatsoever concerning the pro-nationalist policy of the Indian government, as anyone could have learned by a visit to the High Commissioner himself. In keeping with his attempt to capture the moral leadership of the neutralist world, Nehru had announced soon after Indian independence that India would support the legitimate national aspirations of any colonial people. Educating local Indians in this basic policy and its practical implications for them was a high priority task for the High Commissioner, who systematically toured the Federation, preaching this basic doctrine wherever he went.[29]

By taking this stand the Indian government inevitably created a problem for the local Indians. The more timid feared (with good reason) the animosity toward all Indians thus aroused among the still dominant, powerful, and dangerous Europeans. Others, particularly the African-born generation, resented the High Commissioner's interference in local affairs. It nevertheless seems safe to conclude that many Indians,

29. Shri Pant, the High Commissioner for East Africa, had earlier made this policy explicit for his area at the time of the Mau Mau crisis. Cf. John Gunther, *Inside Africa* (New York, Harper, 1955), pp. 326–28.

wavering between a temptation to support the Europeans on the grounds of expediency and a strong latent identification with African nationalism, were won over by the High Commissioner's arguments. His influence seems apparent, for example, in the following statement: "I think that our policy should be that of India's. Basically, I think most of our people are sympathetic to African nationalism. We too had to fight for our independence in India, and we are naturally sympathetic to the Africans' point of view."

The pro-nationalist stand of the Indian government lent a certain plausibility to the ubiquitous rumors of direct financial support to the African cause circulating within the European community when we arrived in Africa. Insofar as could ever be determined, nothing more substantial than the old myth of Indian imperialistic ambitions in Africa lay behind these widespread convictions of oriental subversion. The only material aid from India to the nationalist cause known to us was a modest scholarship program for African students which was initiated by the Indian government soon after their own independence. Several Africans now in the higher echelons of the governments of Zambia and Malawi owe what higher education they received to this program.[30]

Toward the end of our stay in Africa, we arranged interviews with two Northern Rhodesian leaders who had been in India under these auspices. Both expressed appreciation for the opportunity which India had thus provided them, but both clearly had returned to Africa with strongly negative attitudes toward the country and its people. They were shocked, they said, by the stark poverty of the Indian masses, which seemed to them more severe and degrading than African poverty. Poverty to this extent, it is clear, made it difficult for them to accept at face value the Indian claim to a great civilization. Predictably,

30. Federation officials frowned upon the idea of Africans going to study in Indian universities, as indeed they also did upon those going to the United States. "They [i.e. the Indians] are only taking the chance to teach them to be anti-British whenever they can lay their hands on them," was the way the Prime Minister put it. *Bulawayo Chronicle* (October 30, 1953). The program was virtually dormant throughout the period of our fieldwork.

both men reacted very strongly to caste: one gave a vivid description of the little boxlike cubicle in which a fellow student had been forced to sit while attending class because he was an untouchable. Both complained of the difficulty of making meaningful contacts with Indians at a personal level. Significantly, neither by their own admission learned more than a smattering of an Indian language.

Did color have anything to do with the Indians' reactions to African students? Looking back, one of the informants is sure that it was an important factor:

> There is a tendency for the lower-caste people to be dark, and consequently Indians tend to be suspicious about the social place dark-skinned people occupy in their own country. While I was in India, I used to see advertisements in the paper for marriage. A man would say that he was looking for a wife, and then he would add that she must not be too dark in color.

With respect to interpersonal relations in general, the same informant went on to say: "Indians are a very cold people. They're not very warm or enthusiastic. For that reason, most African students are very lonely in India. After classes, the only thing that you could do would be to go back to your room and read." When pressed, he admitted that some of his fellow students had been friendly, but he added:

> Even if an Indian student likes you, he hesitates to invite you to his home because he doesn't know how his parents will react. If they are high caste and you go to their house and eat something, then the dishes you have used will have to be broken because you have defiled them. Knowing that, he doesn't ask you.

Both men mentioned the petty corruption that they encountered everywhere in India, and one elaborated the point as follows:

> Let us say that you go to a government office to see about your passport. You are seated and then you wait for two

or three hours. Finally, you get restless and ask what is the matter. The clerk suggests that for a small consideration, your business might be taken care of more quickly.

The same informant later drew a moral from this experience. We had pointed out that Indians had always served in the East African civil service and that they were still doing so in the new African government. What would his own attitude be with respect to Indians in the civil service?

> Personally, I think that Nyerere is creating a problem for himself. I am sure that he thinks he can handle it, but if he isn't careful he is going to find himself in difficulties. The one thing which an African government has to have is absolute honesty and integrity. Unless Nyerere watches closely, he is going to find that he has a great deal of corruption among those Indian officials of his. Not that it is their fault, you understand. They've never known anything else.

Most significantly of all, neither of these men even pretended to have any intimate contacts within the local Indian community. On this point, one said:

> As far as I can tell, I can't see that my education in India makes the slightest difference in my relationship to these local people. The few Indians I see are those interested in politics, and I can't see that the fact that I was educated in India has anything to do with that whatsoever.

The other put his lack of contacts upon the basis of education and social class, repeating thereby the rather seriously distorted stereotype common among Europeans:

> You know of course that we only have the small trader-type of Indian here. Most of these people are handicapped by the fact that they don't have much education. Most of them are nearly illiterate. It's very rare that you have anyone here with any education at all.

The one thing which both of our informants found admirable in Indian culture was the principle and practice of nonviolence. Elaborating upon this theme a little, one said:

One of the things which most impressed me in India was the fact that all the time I was there I never saw Hindus fight each other. They would quarrel, but they would never hit each other. I think that Gandhi got his doctrine of nonviolence out of Hindu culture rather than implanting it there. This is certainly one of the things which I admire about the Indians.

These sentiments were delivered with every indication of sincerity and conviction. However, we were not surprised to hear them. The United National Independence Party, of which the speaker was (and is) a prominent member, had always made a great deal of its philosophy of nonviolence; his statement had for this reason a very familiar ring.[31]

TRANSITION POLITICS

To Europeans of Central Africa it must have seemed during the middle 1950s that all was going extraordinarily well. Federation provided an efficient administrative apparatus, and after its inaugural the economy boomed under the blessings of high prices for copper and tobacco. True, the Mau Mau affair in

31. "I was determined [at the beginning of my career]," UNIP's founder and president of Zambia tells us in his autobiography, "to combine Gandhi's policy of nonviolence with Nkrumah's positive action." Kenneth D. Kaunda, *Zambia Shall Be Free: An Autobiography* (New York, Praeger, 1963), p. 140. Kaunda himself was not however among the leaders of his party who went to India for their education, although he had been offered a scholarship. He did go to India briefly in 1958 at the invitation of the Indian Council for Cultural Relations, and while there he visited Nehru and other Indian leaders. Ibid., pp. 84–92.

That UNIP's philosophy of nonviolence was a transparent but effective window dressing was simply taken for granted by Europeans in the pre-independence period. These suspicions extended—unjustifiably, we think—to Kaunda himself. Leaving him aside, there is no reason whatsoever to believe that the philosophical subtleties of nonviolence ever permeated very far into the top membership of the United National Independence Party, to say nothing of the African masses which the Party led to victory.

Kenya stood like a black cloud on an otherwise bright horizon; the news from East Africa was always followed in Central Africa with intense interest. But fortunately these events were two thousand miles away, and in any case the outbreak had been brought under control.

By the fall of 1959, however, the situation had changed dramatically. Fear and uneasiness were now widespread through all segments of the population. In the immediate background lay the "Emergency" of the previous spring, the events of which had completely destroyed what complacency Europeans had hitherto enjoyed. Violence—not much, but violence nonetheless—had broken out in several parts of the Federation. Fearing that they faced a Mau Mau-type rebellion, the authorities had reacted swiftly and (in the view of liberals) harshly. Most of the important nationalist leaders were either imprisoned or "ruralized" into guarded isolated areas.[32] In Nyasaland emergency measures had resulted in virtual martial law.

Political instability during 1959 was due in the first instance to the approach of the promised constitutional review. Such a review, it will be recalled, had been provided for when the original constitution was written. Important changes which could permanently affect the balance of power between Africans and Europeans were certain, but there was no certainty as to what these changes would be. Hence, the uneasiness, the mood of excitement, anxiety, and expectancy.

Two eventualities were considered possible but unlikely. The least likely appeared to be what in fact occurred: namely, a breakup of the Federation and the emergence of African governments in the two northern territories. But it is safe to say that a grant of dominion status to the existing federal government in the name of the necessity to maintain law and order seemed more probable to most people of all races. Depending upon where one stood politically, one either strongly hoped or strongly feared that a Conservative government in Britain, if victorious in the upcoming elections of October 1959, would prove amenable to this solution.

32. Kaunda was released January 9, 1960; Banda, in early April 1960.

In our opinion, however, what most people really expected to happen, irrespective of their own political convictions, was the third contingency: namely, a continuation of federation with important constitutional modifications. African nationalists of course wanted complete independence in the abstract, and they continually talked loudly in these terms. Yet it is hard to believe that even they thought it likely that they would get it as soon as they did. In any case, their most immediate and pressing tasks were to fight off the threat of dominion status and to increase if they could their participation in the existing government.

Fearing the formation of a European-dominated independent state if they did not act forcefully and quickly, the African nationalists had organized for action as the time for the constitutional review approached. Given the situation, there was little they could do except verbally protest as loudly and as often as possible and sporadically reinforce words with destructive acts in order to call attention to themselves. This, then, was their strategy. If they could make enough noise and create enough headline-worthy trouble, they could attract attention and sympathy in Britain and the outside world. If they relaxed and acquiesced in the status quo, they were lost. If they should appear content with existing arrangements, then the demand for dominion status coming from the side of the white settlers would pick up momentum and achieve its goal. The pressures therefore had to be put on and kept on firmly until the constitutional issue—temporarily up for grabs—was again temporarily settled.

This assessment of the situation and the strategy which it dictated eventually proved itself in action. Practically, however, it was an extremely delicate operation for the nationalists to implement. On the one hand, the African masses must demonstrate in a dramatic way their dissatisfaction, and the only way to get them to do so was by provocative agitation. On the other, outright Mau Mau-style race war was both tactically and strategically impossible and had to be avoided. Tactically, it would be impossible to fight such a war in Central

329

Africa, where both geography and the strong military forces in the Europeans' hands ruled against it. Strategically, it would be disastrous in proportion to its tactical successes. If the European settlers were seriously threatened with physical violence, sympathy in Britain and the United States would quickly shift to them. Supported by cosmopolitan public opinion, they would then either be given or simply take whatever measures were necessary to subjugate the Africans, and from that position of power they would push on relentlessly to European-dominated independence.

Political action of the kind open to Africans spelled great danger to the Indians who were in a seriously exposed position, given real trouble. Disliked by both Europeans and Africans, they stood as an easy target for random aggression. Fortunately, as it happened, the transition from European to African rule in the two northern territories was achieved with remarkably little violence. But the fact that Indians suffered as little as they did must be rated as a happy accident: all the potentialities were present to make a very different story.

Organized withdrawal of economic cooperation is an obvious first step open to dissatisfied masses without other weapons. Thus when the African National Congress (the first nationalist organization in Northern Rhodesia) wished to impress its existence upon the Europeans, it did so by a boycott of retail shops in 1956. Both Europeans and Indians were affected. But since the African trade was mainly in Indian hands, it was the Indians who were especially hurt. A measure of the boycott's effectiveness is the fact that it was still a major reference point for discussion three years later when our fieldwork began. A prominent Indian leader related the following story:

At the time of the boycott, I had a visit from Harry Nkumbula [president of the ANC]. I asked him, "Why do you insist on boycotting Indian shops? We have never done anything to you." Do you know what he told me? He said, "I know it is hard on you, but we have to have some way of expressing our dissatisfaction with the state

330

of affairs in this country. Of course, we don't really have anything against *you;* but this is the only way we can call attention to our problems."

Never really complete, this particular boycott was still severe enough to bring into bankruptcy a number of Indian business-men.

A boycott, however, is not overt violence. This first ap-peared later, at the time of the Emergency of 1959, in the form of a spate of arson incidents, nearly all of which involved Indian shops. Indians in isolated areas in particular were help-lessly exposed to whatever violence might have been generated through political excitement. Police might not be immediately available; and even if there were police in the area, our data suggest that in most instances they would have hesitated to intervene in an attack upon Indians for fear of provoking a larger reaction than they could control.

While visiting a bush shop in Nyasaland during a politically tense period, we asked the young man behind the counter how things were:

> Things are very bad. The Africans, all the time, they come in here and talk nonsense. They say, "We don't want you here. Why do you stay? Why don't you go back to India where you belong?" If they ask you for credit and you refuse, then they say, "Soon, all these things will belong to us." And even in front of my brother's wife they say bad words.

With a rising tone of indignation in his voice, he became more specific:

> Yesterday afternoon there was an African who came in here and started talking nonsense, like I told you. He is always coming in here and making trouble. Well, yester-day afternoon he came in and asked for beer. I couldn't get it for him right away, since I was taking care of another customer. And so I said, "Just wait a minute." But he said, "I want my beer now." Then he started

331

shouting all kinds of nonsense [i.e. obscenities and threats]. I told him, "Wait a minute." But he wouldn't listen and kept on shouting.

Finally, I told him if he didn't shut up, I would call the police. When I reached for the telephone, he jumped over the counter and grabbed on to me to keep me from calling. My brother's wife was with me here at the time. She was standing right here holding the baby [a six-month old child]. This African, he grabbed ahold of her; before that, he had said a lot of bad things to her. I picked this up [brandishing a heavy bronze yardstick] and I hit him as hard as I could across the back. There were a lot of Africans standing around watching, but they didn't do a thing to help me. One of these was an African policeman.

After I hit him, he let go my brother's wife, and I cleared out the store and locked it up for the rest of the day. Then I went down to the *Boma* and talked to the European assistant inspector there [the sole European policeman in the area]. All he said was that I would have to pay a fine of ten shillings for hitting that man.

Why is it always Indians these Africans attack? Why don't they go after the Europeans? Why don't the police do something to help us? If an African comes in here and makes trouble and you go down to the police, they just laugh at you and say, "Don't worry!" But they don't do anything to help you. It would be a lot different if an African attacked a European lady in the same way.

Still, these Indians were fortunate to live at a district head-quarters near police. Police anywhere in the more isolated rural districts could have been easily overpowered in any general uprising. But to their credit they did manage to exert a restraining influence during tense periods, keeping minor incidents like the one just described from growing into massacres. Some Indians, however, kept shops in areas where there were no nearby police. An owner of one of these even more isolated shops told us nervously:

Everything is fortunately very quiet around here. And it is just as well that it is, because there is no police or any other protection for us. Consequently, when we deal with the Africans, we speak very sweetly to them. We try not to hurt their feelings in any way.

An easy target for African aggression, Indians predictably also provided a convenient scapegoat for European irritations and frustrations during the transitional period to African government. One informant put it to us in a vivid simile: "We Indians here in Central Africa are just like a drum. The Africans beat on one side until they get tired. And when they have finished, the Europeans beat on the other."

Indians, we have pointed out, were the first non-Europeans to challenge European political dominance in British-occupied Africa. Europeans therefore easily came to the conclusion that Indians were responsible for African nationalism when it first appeared. Anything so complicated as an organized political movement, the reasoning went, was clearly beyond the African's capabilities; Indians, who were known to possess the capacity, must consequently be behind it. This assumption was given an added measure of plausibility by the open moral support of the African nationalists by the Indian government.[33]

In 1953, when the African nationalist movement was barely getting under way, the *Central African Post* ran an editorial entitled "Disturbers of the Peace." Two villains were discussed under this rubric: "misguided English liberals" and the local Indians.

Another agency [i.e. in addition to the misguided English liberals] which would fain to create African discontent is an Indian one. We do not for one moment suggest that all Indians are engaged in such activities. We are sure they are not, but there is a certain number who by dis-

33. Cf. Gunther, pp. 326–28. As late as 1961, a Northern Rhodesian lawyer and would-be politician told a large and excited European audience that he had "proof" that large sums of Russian money were being distributed to the African nationalists through a leader in the local Indian community.

tributing buttons and publishing certain kinds of booklets [e.g. a life of Gandhi] try to make Africans believe that their best line of action is to oppose British rule by what is termed "nonviolence." . . . The British people will stand a good deal from those who subvert their rule, but they will only tolerate so much. Indians may have a few social disabilities in this country, but they have a pretty good run for their money in industry and commerce and they have nothing to gain by setting one people against another.[34]

As the political contest between Europeans and Africans sharpened in intensity, so too did the demand that Indians stand up and be counted. Indians were thus put on the horns of a dilemma often posed in the interviews:

If we identify ourselves too strongly with the Europeans, then the Africans are angry with us. If we try to get along with the Africans, then the Europeans think that we are ganging up with the Africans against them. What are we supposed to do?

The obvious answer as most Indians construed it was provided by another informant in a candid moment:

Indians in Africa are orphans. Nobody likes us. The only thing we can do if we want to survive in this country is to look out for ourselves.

No universal consensus existed on the best tactic for survival. But most Indians believed that the solution was to do nothing for as long as possible. This tactic, however, was interpreted by Europeans as at best cowardice and at its worst disloyalty. When at the eleventh hour the Indian leaders of Nyasaland openly announced that they would support the Malawi Congress at the constitutional talks then going on in London, the editor of the *Nyasaland Times* wrote under the title "They Show Their Colours":

34. *Central African Post* (May 22, 1953).

I cannot believe that the Asian people of Nyasaland have given a mandate to the London delegation to bend the knee, on their behalf, to thuggery. I cannot believe they are such cravens as to knuckle under to intimidation or to desert the people who gave them the opportunity to make their homes in Nyasaland.

The British Raj opened wider horizons for them. It has protected them, fed them, clothed them, taught them and healed them. And I refuse to believe that they are all of the type who basely set aside their principles of honour and gratitude in favour of expediency. Those who have now taken that step and declared their allegiance to a terror organization have nailed their colours to the mast. Come what may they have branded themselves and we will not forget it.

Everything they have and are they owe to the Europeans who settled a savage country and made it safe for them to live in. Their acceptance of a regime that has tried to upset the peace of the country and undo all that has been done puts them to one side. They can achieve nothing through this alliance but the contempt of those whom they hope to appease.

This group having shown its colours, it is now up to the other Asians in Nyasaland to declare themselves publicly.[35]

Obsessed as they were with the dimensions of their own defeat, few Europeans showed any appreciation whatsoever for the Indians' true predicament politically. Nor did any European, apparently, question the reasonableness of expecting gratitude from a group which they traditionally despised and rejected.[36]

35. *Nyasaland Times* (Blantyre, July 19, 1960).

36. A curious and highly significant aspect of the European reaction in Nyasaland was commented upon by a perceptive Indian informant. He pointed out, quite correctly, that prominent local European liberals had announced their support for the Malawi Congress well ahead of the Indians without creating any stir whatsoever: "Of course nobody criticizes them for their opinions. You can't criticize respectable European corporation executives. They are gentlemen. But when you are cross, you can always blast out at the Asians. They can't defend themselves and they make a fine target."

Politically, the most important result of the Emergency disturbances of 1959 was the Devlin Report, a detailed work of the commission of inquiry appointed by the British government to look into the causes and meaning of African unrest in the Federation.[37] Hailed at the time as a masterpiece of energetic investigation and judicious interpretation, there is little in the ideological content of this document which is exceptional, given the circumstances and the period. Ideologically, it exemplifies the basic philosophy of the ideal federation, moved forward a few years to accommodate the arrival of African nationalism as a political force that could not now be ignored. Without remotely suggesting that immediate independence was in order, the Devlin Report was nonetheless very sympathetic to frustrated African political aspirations and highly critical of the treatment which Africans had received at the hands of the European settlers. As the major factual source for current politics in Central Africa circa 1960, it had great influence upon the thinking of the members of the Monckton Commission, which was appointed to collect evidence and make recommendations for constitutional revision.

The arrival of the Monckton Commission in Central Africa in February 1960 created great dramatic interest and tension. Everyone who wished to express a political opinion was encouraged to appear before the Commission as they toured the Federation, making themselves available to the public. The Commission particularly welcomed statements from leaders capable of speaking authoritatively for organized bodies of opinion.

Several Indians appeared before the Commission, but they spoke as individuals rather than as official representatives of recognized associations. No important Indian organization in either of the two northern territories presented evidence before the Commission, although there was much discussion and debate in the community upon the advisability of doing so. Thus

37. Nyasaland Commission of Inquiry, *Report* [Devlin Commission Report], Cmnd. 814 (London, Her Majesty's Stationery Office, 1959).

tacitly, but not yet openly, the Indians moved to the nationalists' side.[38] All African parties in the northern territories had dramatized their demand for complete independence by boycotting the Commission's proceedings.

The Monckton Commission's report, released in October 1960, provided in turn much of the basic thinking incorporated into the Macleod proposals for constitutional change.[39] Technically, these were confined to revisions in the constitution of Northern Rhodesia. In fact, as everyone knew, these negotiations were critical to the continued existence of multiracial government in Central Africa.

Fundamentally, the Macleod Constitution again represented the established liberal position. It was, in short, simply a newer version of the old ideal federation, the rationalistic and official British solution to the problems of interracial relations in modern Africa. As always, the crucial problem was conceived as the distribution of the franchise, and the Macleod proposals presented a particularly complicated and ingenious formula.

Without beginning to do this formula justice, it is sufficient for our purposes to say that the proposals envisaged a tripartite legislative council. A third of the seats would be provided by a "lower" roll for which Africans in large numbers could qualify. Another third would be filled from an "upper" roll for which, by virtue of education and income, Europeans could qualify but few Africans. Africans and Europeans would thus each be guaranteed representation: these seats were in effect reserved. The ingenious heart of the Macleod plan, however, lay in its provision for so-called "national" seats, to be filled by votes from *both* the upper and the lower rolls, weighted by a set

38. A highly vocal minority of "progressive" Indian leaders took the position that it was time—even past time—that Indians openly declare themselves on the side of the Africans. The soundness of this argument was widely appreciated; but most Indians feared the easily predictable European reaction. When a major liberal leader rose before a community meeting in Northern Rhodesia and advocated open alignment, he was shouted down from the audience with cries of: "What! Do you want us all kicked out of the country?"

39. Iain Macleod, Secretary of State for the Colonies.

formula. To be elected to this third of the legislative council, a candidate would have to appeal to both the African and the non-African electorate.

Indians under this scheme would have voted almost entirely on the upper roll, since most Indians could meet the qualifications set for it. Insofar as these seats were concerned, they would thus help elect European candidates. But Indians would also vote, like everyone else, for the national seats for which both Africans and Europeans would be standing. Here, under certain circumstances, their vote would weigh fairly heavily in the chances of an African or a European candidate respectively.

Neither the Africans nor the Europeans were pleased at the Macleod proposals. Both feared for their advantage under the rather ambiguous terms defining the procedures for filling the national seats. Angrily, the United Federal Party ministers in Northern Rhodesia's Executive Council resigned en masse in protest. A revision to meet the settlers' objections was shortly announced. Among other changes intended to strengthen the European position, a *single separate national seat* was created for Asians and Coloureds combined, and they would now have no right to vote for other national candidates. From a position of power beyond their numerical deserts, the Indians now found themselves virtually disenfranchised![40]

Naturally enough, the Indians were furious at this sudden and radical change in their paper fortunes. The president of the Northern Rhodesian Indian Association put it this way in a press statement:

> The [British] Government has tried to please the United Federal Party and other reactionary elements at the cost of most of the democratic and fundamental rights of Asians as Rhodesian citizens. The Asian community has never asked for any reservation of special seats. . . . We are sure that under the present scheme, the African aspira-

40. For a summary of Macleod's proposals of February 1961 and of the June proposals, see David C. Mulford, *The Northern Rhodesia General Election 1962* (Nairobi, Oxford University Press, 1964), pp. 20-28.

tions of having a majority in the Legislative Council will never be fulfilled.[41]

The single Indian member of the territorial Legislative Council spoke in even more bitter terms:

This has really shaken our faith in British justice and fair play. . . . Our position has been made more precarious by picking out only the Asians while all the various alien communities of non-British stock [Italians, Greeks, etc.] have been accorded full rights and the only reason that could be conceived for this is nothing else but because we non-Europeans are of darker skins. This . . . is therefore really discriminatory.[42]

We can be sure that the "democratic and fundamental rights of Asians" concerned the Africans as little as they did the Europeans. But since the new revisions strengthened the European position, Africans were also incensed. Their reaction was even sharper than the European one had been. A wave of disturbances reminiscent of the Emergency of 1959 swept the country. Schools were burned, bridges were destroyed, European cars were stoned, and there were many sporadic cases of arson—arson and gasoline bombs being the standard weapons of the African terrorist.

Weary of the interminable search for a rational constitution for Central Africa along the lines of the ideal federation, the British government suddenly gave in. It announced in September 1961 that further representations with respect to the proposed constitution would be considered if the disturbances ceased. And they did.

Thereafter the trend toward African government in Northern Rhodesia moved rapidly forward. Elections held in October

41. *Northern News* (June 28, 1961).
42. Northern Rhodesia *Hansard* (July 5, 1961), col. 258. The speaker (V.D. Mistry) was appointed in March of 1959 as a nominated unofficial member of the Legislative Council by Sir Arthur Benson, then Governor of Northern Rhodesia. Although the nomination of an Asian to such a post had precedents elsewhere in British Africa, Mistry was the first to serve in this capacity in Northern Rhodesia.

1962 under a new constitution, worked out after the collapse of the Macleod plan, provided an African majority in the Legislative Council. In December, elections in Southern Rhodesia produced defeat for Sir Edgar Whitehead, the last United Federal Party territorial prime minister. A few days later, the new Colonial Secretary in London, R. A. Butler, formally announced that the British would accept Nyasaland's demands for secession from the federal state. These developments effectively sealed the fate of political multiracialism in Central Africa. Officially, the Federation ended December 31, 1963.

Chapter Eleven

FOREIGNERS IN THE NEW NATIONS

Realized or not, the hope of the sociologist is to enlarge in some perceptible measure the adequacy of theoretical generalizations. Most fundamentally, from the standpoint of theory, we have argued for a shift in emphasis in studies of this kind from the normatively defined structures of ethnic relations toward a more dynamic approach that stresses interaction in history, group conflict, power, and change. Giving interactional factors their proper weight would seem desirable in any study of race relations; it appears absolutely essential to a comprehension of the peculiarly fluid and potentially explosive plural societies of modern southern Africa.

Ethnic groups emerge in this perspective as products of an ongoing evolutionary process, products in the particular instance of a specific historical past. In interaction, they confront each other primarily as interest groups in active competition and conflict, each equipped from its past with the cultural means for the struggle. Analytically, it is thus the instrumental character of culture which needs to be stressed sociologically. Cultural means provide the foundation to power and hence the key to an understanding of social dominance and subordination. It must be appreciated, however, that the means which such groups possess to further their interests are inherently both different and unequal. Inequality of position and status is the inevitable result in the new order which comes into being out of their interaction. Economically, differences

341

in development are reflected in a well marked ethnic division of labor. Socially and politically, they are expressed in a hierarchy of power and prestige.

Through a modernized version of Park's original concepts, we show that ethnic dominance has two facets: one "ecological," the other "moral." Dominance may remain largely unconscious when first imposed—as it typically is—through coercion or impersonal exchange. Or to be somewhat more precise, its characteristics and effects may—and demonstrably often do—lie beyond the level of "moral" awareness and control. When brought to the level of conscious awareness through sustained interaction, elements of the ongoing socio-cultural process cease to be ecological and acquire a normative moral definition. At this stage, these elements tend to become issues of group interest, and moral suasion is applied to their promotion. Seen in this perspective, society appears not as a static structure of norms but as a dynamic "emergent"—partly conscious and partly unconscious, partly normative and partly nonnormative. A product of continuous interaction, its future forms are never fully prefigured in the normative content of any one of its constituent groups at any given historical present.

The balance struck between the normative and the ecological elements in given social orders is subject to great variation. Comparatively stable and homogeneous societies may be expected to manifest more of the former, plural societies caught up in the throes of rapid socio-cultural change more of the latter. But among plural societies themselves an extremely important difference in this respect appears when viewed down the time dimension. As our material suggests and as comparative studies would surely show, ethnic interaction is always far more ecological in the earliest phases of group contact. Continued interaction, however, widens the basis of moral order through progressive acculturation of subordinate groups to the dominant group's institutional norms and values.

Ethnic group phenomena present anywhere in the world today cannot be understood apart from the socio-cultural

342

processes initiated by European imperialism. Out of European imperialism as a phase of world history, a cosmopolitan world culture has been created, within which there is now near universal consensus upon an ever widening range of moral values, particularly with respect to those centered in the egalitarian complex and in nationalism. In recent years, this "europeanization-of-the-world" has been immeasurably accelerated by technological progress in means of communication.

Narrowing consensus, however, does not necessarily lessen ethnic conflict. On the contrary, given great historically created disparities of wealth and status of the sort characteristic of southern Africa, consensus upon the new cosmopolitan moral norms may simply provide underprivileged groups with effective weapons in their struggle with privileged ones. In a sociological context, this is the inherent meaning of the nationalist movement in Africa and elsewhere throughout the former colonial world.

Applying these notions to Central Africa, we acquire a certain amount of intellectual leverage in understanding what has been happening there. By means of their superior culture, Europeans have been dominant in Central Africa, as they have been over most of the world for five hundred years. But in interaction with subordinate groups, they (as dominants invariably do) created situations and initiated processes which they neither fully comprehended nor fully controlled. Through contact with Europeans, non-Europeans in Africa have acquired both the technical and the moral means to challenge successfully the Europeans *in their own terms*. Now, seventy years later, the older imperialistic form of European sociopolitical dominance has passed from the scene, although the powerful influence of European culture remains.

This fissure in the historic relationship between social and cultural dominance has created in Central Africa, as in the plural societies of the former colonial areas everywhere, a radically emergent situation without close historical parallel. The fissure, it is true, is more apparent than real: the African masses are nearly as backward as before, but they are now led

343

by an acculturated elite equal in all essential respects to the advanced groups of immigrant origin. In terms of group identity, however, the reversal of roles is real. Culturally advanced minorities (Europeans and Indians) now find themselves subordinated politically to the hitherto submerged Africans, and to remain in Africa they have no choice but to adjust accordingly.

THE NEW STATES

A return to Central Africa during the summer of 1966 revealed how painfully challenging some of these adjustments may be, although generalization is made difficult for the region as a whole by the emergence of three sovereign states where there had been but one before. In the very brief period of time which has elapsed since the breakup of federation, each of these political neonates has established a sharply distinctive "personality," rooted in its respective history, population, resources, and geographic position with respect to neighboring countries. The effect of these national differences upon ethnic relations looms so large that even the most cursory treatment must take them into account. Each country, therefore, will be given an impressionistic overview prior to an analysis of social, cultural, economic, and political facets of the Indians' position in the region as a whole.

Zambia

Zambia achieved independence on October 24, 1964 under the leadership of Kenneth Kaunda and his United National Independence Party. The carefully promoted image of the President is that of a modest, "democratic," friendly man, rigorously ascetic in his personal habits, high minded, hard working, and wholeheartedly devoted to the true interests of all his people.[1] The last qualification is of critical importance

1. As experience elsewhere in Africa shows, the successful nationalist leader must establish an appealing *persona,* the distinctive features of which symbolize supposedly unique charismatic qualities. Comparing Zambia's President to a potential rival, a knowledgeable European observer commented: "[Blank]

in Zambia where tribal divisions of the kind which have caused so much trouble elsewhere in Africa lie just below the facade of newly created national sentiment.

Clearly, however, the true source of the country's extraordinary dynamism and buoyancy is not its President's benign smile but its copper. This rich natural inheritance puts Zambia in that select company of developing nations (Saudi Arabia, Libya, Venezuela, etc.) whose problems are not money, but are instead social and political. Zambia's good fortune in this respect is directly traceable to independence. The copper has always been physically where it now is; but with the end of federation, the wealth flowing from its exploitation is distributed differently. Tax revenues no longer go south to Salisbury for redistribution over three territories. They now stay entirely within the country—to Zambia's benefit and the others' loss.[2] Moreover, the present government has greatly extended the base upon which these revenues are collected and rising prices in recent years have greatly increased their value.[3]

---

is probably more intelligent. As an administrator, he could do just as good a job as Kaunda, if not better. What he doesn't have is the personality."

2. Comparison of Zambia with Katanga is very instructive. Threatened independence for Katanga was widely viewed in the world press as immoral and uneconomic; without Katanga, it was said, the rest of the Congo could not survive. But significantly, the same issue was not raised with respect to Zambia's independence—or, more accurately, it was not raised by anyone except supporters of federation who had stressed the advantages of economic unity over as large an area as possible. The arbitrary, "ecological" nature of "national" boundaries in Africa could scarcely be better illustrated. Ultimately, of course, Zambia owes its national existence to the fact that Northern Rhodesia had been treated as a distinct administrative unit by the British while Katanga had been considered by the Belgians as an integral part of their Congolese empire.

3. Soon after coming into power, Kaunda's government announced that it would no longer continue to recognize the mineral rights granted in perpetuity to the British South Africa Company, and royalties, recently amounting to £60 a ton, were thereby redirected into the government's instead of the company's coffers. In 1966, a 40 percent surtax upon the value of all copper sold in excess of £300 a ton was imposed. (On the surtax, see *New York Times*, April 25, 1966.) At the beginning of 1964, the price of copper on the London Metal Exchange was £238, and by December of that year it had risen to £459. By the end of 1965 it was £550. (Bank of Zambia, *Report and Statement of Accounts for the Period August 7th 1964 to December 31, 1965*, 1965, p. 28.) By early April 1966 it momentarily passed the £700 mark. (*Zambia Mail*, April 29, 1966.) Thereafter, it dropped to around £450 at the end of the year.

The overt manifestations of this new affluence appear slightly fantastic to an observer whose last view of the local scene was during the pre-independence period. Streets of the larger towns are packed with well-dressed Africans.[4] Downtown shops—not so many years ago exclusively European—are filled with the same types, as are also bars and restaurants. African private cars are seemingly as numerous as European ones. Completely new are those driven, often with manifest amateurishness, by African women, black matrons from the hitherto European suburbs.

But the revolution thus portrayed from the center of the largest towns must be kept in perspective. This startling new Zambia is almost entirely an urban phenomenon. And even in the cities its most conspicuous beneficiaries are the new elite of high officials and an entirely new middle class composed in large part of government employees. Given the resources which it has at its disposal, the government can be generous with its own workers, who constitute a very large proportion of the employed labor force.[5] For work previously performed by a European, salaries after Africanization have generally been kept at or close to the European scale. For example, an African clerk with a few years' primary education and a

4. Strikingly noticeable is the replacement of rubber-and-canvas shoes by leather ones for men; once all but universal (see p. 56), now rubber-and-canvas footgear is rapidly disappearing among urban Africans in Zambia. Inexpensive molded plastic shoes are current among women. Jacket, shirt, tie, and long trousers have long been usual for urban white-collar workers, but these are now of notably better quality. The old standard "uniform" of khaki shirts and shorts seems to be on its way out for manual workers, who now wear dress shirts, long trousers, and leather shoes. Africans, like people in other developing countries, spend a large proportion of any increase in income upon clothing, hence the vividness with which this index of the changing standard of living is objectively reflected.

5. Available statistics do not identify government workers as such. It is commonly estimated, however, that about 85 percent of those counted under non-domestic service are government employees; on this basis, the proportion of government employees to the total paid labor force would have been nearly 20 percent during 1964. There were 52,400 Africans in non-domestic service employment and a total of 237,000 African employees in 1964, the latest annual figures available in Zambia, *Monthly Digest of Statistics* (August 1966). The number of government employees has certainly increased since independence.

modicum of typing ability is paid around £60 a month since this is what European secretaries formerly got; prior to independence, he would have been fortunate to have received £15. Similar guidelines have been used by the government in setting minimum wages for private employment.

Wages for unskilled and semiskilled labor employed in government, commerce, and industry have risen less spectacularly than those of white-collar personnel. They have nonetheless increased greatly; for example, the store-boys described in Chapter 9 must now be paid about £16 when the compulsory allowance for housing is added. A typical industrial worker gets a little under £20 a month. Wages for semiskilled work long done by Africans, such as tailoring and driving, have more than doubled since the original fieldwork.[6]

What has to be remembered when quoting these figures, however, is that in a country like Zambia regular employment in government, commerce, or industry is itself a privilege of no mean order. One of the largest categories of paid employees is still that of domestic servants, some of whom are paid as little as £5 a month.[7] But at least servants have jobs, which the ubiquitous and unnumbered unemployed who have flocked to the cities from the countryside do not.[8]

A drive from the bright bustle of downtown through the still largely European suburbs to one of the outlying unauthorized "high density" residential areas[9] brings a returning visitor to

6. As elsewhere, there has been considerable inflation in Zambia between 1961 and 1966. This, however, has not been excessive: the official consumer price index (January 1962 = 100) rose from 99.3 in 1961 to 117.8 for the first quarter of 1966. Ibid.

7. In 1964 domestic servants constituted 15 percent of the total paid labor force; the proportion, of course, is larger in the towns where the servants are concentrated. Ibid. Virtually all domestic servants work for Europeans or Indians. Paid servants are just appearing in the homes of the African elite.

8. Out of a total African population of 3,500,000, only 237,000 were in paid employment during 1964. Ibid. Even this figure considerably exaggerates those in the modern sector of the economy; it includes many in the rural areas who are employed at very low and irregular wages by fellow Africans, often little better off than themselves.

9. An attempt was always made under European administration to control migration into the towns. "Authorized" housing for African employees and their families was consequently built to some minimum standard in a "loca-

something much closer to what he remembers—except that these slums of haphazardly constructed shacks and huts have spread enormously. Beyond their boundaries, out into the seemingly endless bush which begins where the city ends lie the villages of subsistence farmers, hundreds of thousands of them, almost completely out of the modernized sector of the new Zambia and its economy.

How these rural people, in particular, are to be brought into the mainstream of modern life constitutes a major preoccupation of government. Its announced intention, for example, is that every child of suitable age in Zambia will be in primary school by 1970, and it is building schools as rapidly as the exceedingly short supply of materials and skilled labor will allow. In a country where there were exactly two academic preparatory schools for Africans in 1960, there is now one in every administrative district. Compared to similarly new schools elsewhere in Africa, these secondary schools are luxuriously staffed with fully qualified expatriate teachers, recruited from all over the English-speaking world.[10]

---

tion" set carefully apart from the European quarter and operated by the government. As in nearly everything else throughout southern Africa, South Africa set the original pattern. See, among other numerous sources, D. H. Reader, *The Black Man's Portion: History, Demography, and Living Conditions in the Native Locations of East London, Cape Province* (Cape Town, Oxford University Press, 1961). Control, however, was never fully successful; inevitably, the Africans themselves built "unauthorized" housing on private land adjacent to, but outside the jurisdiction of, the official locations. Africans still live in the original locations, but the terminology has changed with independence. They are now called "suburbs." To differentiate between them and the formerly European areas, the terms "high density" and "low density" are used.

10. Most of these teachers are Europeans from Britain. But more than a hundred (as of 1966) are Indians, many of whom are from South Africa. Teachers were at first recruited from India, but their English proved to be so poor that only applications from Indian nationals who have taught elsewhere in an English-speaking territory (usually East Africa) are now considered. These teachers constitute the largest bloc of a minor post-independence influx of Indians into both Zambia and Malawi. In addition, there are a fair number of doctors, as well as a few engineers and other technical personnel. All of these persons are on contract; none have immigrant visas. Some will undoubtedly manage to remain more or less permanently—particularly, we would guess, the doctors. But the government offers them no encouragement to think in these terms, the assumption being that they will be replaced by Africans as rapidly as possible.

Within this new Zambia, so bright and hopeful in most respects, Indians prosper economically to a degree never approached before. Physically, too, they have been undisturbed. But spiritually they live in an uncomfortable state of anxiety, fearing with substantial reasons that their present lot is too good to last. Political revolutions which deserve the name are not carried through for the benefit of a country's former rulers —or of the marginal minorities attached to them by the accidents of history. Zambia is truly revolutionary in this fundamental sense. Malawi and Rhodesia are not.

Rhodesia

The emergence of African governments in the two northern territories toward the end of federation created the inevitable reaction south of the Zambezi.

Sir Edgar Whitehead was the last United Federal Party territorial Prime Minister. With the victory of the Rhodesia Front in December 1962, the country moved "right"—if this standard terminology can be meaningfully applied in a situation where politics are racial, not ideological. On November 11, 1965, Ian Smith announced his Unilateral Declaration of Independence.[11] The British government countered this move with a series of hopefully back-breaking economic sanctions. Within Rhodesia itself security measures were strengthened, including censorship of all telltale statistical indicators of the effects of sanctions upon economic life and emigration.

Whatever these effects are, they were not very apparent to the unassisted eye of a casual observer during the summer of 1966. The planes from Lusaka to Salisbury are crowded with Rhodesians doing business in Zambia and Malawi. Immigration and customs formalities are no more rigorous than in Britain. Once in the country, we found the social atmosphere somewhat frosty; but with patience, we discovered plenty of settlers anxious to explain their side of the story.

---

11. Ian Smith replaced Winston J. Field as Prime Minister in April 1964. This change was intra-party; it resulted from a feeling that Field was too "moderate."

In particular, they wanted to confirm our impression that sanctions had failed thus far to cut very deeply into the average person's normal life. Rhodesians (meaning the white population) point with pride to the fact that streets are full of cars; this to their minds is a potent symbol of their success, since the petrol ban was supposed to be the key to their downfall. Shops are filled with ordinary commodities in seemingly ample supply. Food is abundant and cheap; it is in Zambia, where the government's token cuts in the hated Rhodesian trade have restricted normal supplies of Rhodesian-grown beef and vegetables, that shortages appear—not in the Salisbury markets.

Indian merchants report that retail trade is now at more or less normal levels after a severe post-independence dip when factories cut production. But production was soon resumed to something like previous levels in most instances, and the remaining slack in industrial employment was partly offset by the quick emergence of completely new small industries, anxious to exploit the gaps created by import difficulties. Wages for ordinary workers are as high in Rhodesia as they are in Zambia; and since by any measure Rhodesia is a far more developed country economically, the employment base is more than twice as wide.[12] Judged impressionistically by the standard of dress and appearance, Rhodesia's urban Africans, like those of Zambia, are much better off than we remembered them.

Surprises of a social as well as of an economic character are in store for the visitor. For example, Meikles Hotel, once an

12. With a total African population roughly similar in size, the latest Rhodesian statistics available (1964) show 621,000 Africans in paid employment, compared to 237,000 at the same time in Zambia. It should be pointed out, however, that a great many more Africans are employed in commercial agriculture in Rhodesia than in Zambia, 44 percent as against 15 percent. Comparing non-agricultural employment, the figure for Rhodesia is 348,000; for Zambia, 202,500. Rhodesia, *Monthly Digest of Statistics* (February 1966); Zambia, *Monthly Digest of Statistics* (August 1966). Wage levels for ordinary Africans are essentially the same in Rhodesia and Zambia, and in both countries they have risen considerably since our original study. See Tables 5 and 6 in Chapter 3 above, which provide statistics from 1954 to 1964.

entrenched preserve of European exclusiveness, has a well-patronized public bar for Africans. The fact is that since our original fieldwork great inroads have been made upon the traditional pattern of racial segregation. Officially, parks, hotels, cafes, and cinemas are now open in Rhodesia to anyone who cares to use them. The Land Apportionment Act still restricts Africans residentially to the locations; but Indians may open businesses freely anywhere, and a few have bought houses in the hitherto exclusively European suburbs. No gift of the present government, this considerable liberalization with respect to public segregation is the cumulative result of progress made in the final years of federation.

Rhodesia's Indians complained bitterly of the discrimination imposed upon them by the Europeans under federation, and they are well aware of the near-desperate plight of many Indians in South Africa, now that the Group Areas Act is beginning to be seriously enforced. But all things are relative. Rhodesia under Ian Smith is not South Africa; and rightly or wrongly, the Indians in Rhodesia see African nationalism as the far more dangerous threat.

Along with the hundreds of Africans rounded up and sent off to detention camps when Smith came into power were two Indians, the most outspoken of the young liberals who identified themselves with the nationalists during the federation period. These martyrs to the African cause have received little sympathy in the Indian community. Persons who more or less agreed with them in principle believe that they acted rashly and therefore could only expect to pay the price for their folly. But not everyone by any means supported them even in principle. To some the troublemakers got what they deserved.

Like their counterparts in Zambia and Malawi, the Indians of Rhodesia listen to the news coming out of East Africa, and they congratulate themselves upon living in a "civilized" country. As one of them commented, making the same point which Europeans are fond of making:

351

It's not at all like what you read in the newspapers before coming to Rhodesia, is it? There are Africans all
around and no police in sight; yet we are perfectly safe.
It's the same everywhere—even out in the bush. That's
because we have law and order in this country. Anyone
of any race can do what he likes as long as he doesn't
mix in politics and obeys the law. It's the troublemakers
who get into trouble.

Another—an old friend not much given to political comment
—startled us momentarily by saying:

Our Prime Minister doesn't make a very good impression
on television—he is not what you would call a "television
personality." His face, you know, was badly hurt during
the war. So he never smiles and he speaks in a very monotonous voice. But that doesn't matter. We Indians and
Europeans have every confidence in Mr. Smith.

Malawi

From the time of Johnston, Nyasaland was always conceded by Europeans to be an inherently African territory
where few of them could hope to have more than a temporary
place. Yet today Malawi is in certain respects the least African of any of the new African states. Having gained independence on July 6, 1964, the country continues to be administered largely by Europeans. Its Indian minority feels
secure in a way which their more prosperous counterparts in
Zambia envy. Economics, politics, and geography helps to
explain this paradoxical state of affairs.

Malawi shares in the prosperity now characteristic of the
Central African region as a whole. There has been a steady increase in peasant-grown commercial crops. And on the basis
of a dozen or so new industries—some of them quite substantial—one recent observer has gone so far as to speak of a
"miniature industrial revolution" in Malawi.[13] But set in the

13. A feature article on Malawi in the *Financial Mail* (May 1966) discusses
these developments. Among the new industries are several textile and clothing

midst of a population of four million subsistence farmers, the contribution of these new developments is necessarily small. The fact is that Malawi remains what it always has been—a very poor country. The familiar ragged crowds seen in the streets of the larger towns proclaim it, and stand in sharp contrast to the urban Africans in Zambia and Rhodesia. Indian shops—many are very small affairs in ramshackle buildings—do not bulge with stock; to all appearances they look exactly as they did half a dozen years ago. Their owners report that business is brisk but in no way extraordinary.

These economic realities underlie and help to account for the somewhat peculiar politics of Malawi. Yet in the immediate foreground stands the colorful figure of Dr. Kamuzu (Hastings until independence) Banda—the Ngwazi, meaning "The Great One" with supernatural overtones. Since his summary dismissal of three cabinet ministers and the subsequent resignation of three others barely two months after independence, Banda has been running the country by himself insofar as basic political decisions are concerned.

Administrative matters are handled in the main by British expatriates, as before independence. Banda's brush with his obstreperous young ministers apparently left him with a poor opinion of African intellectuals; consequently he has not been in any great hurry to Africanize the higher civil service posts. As one of his expatriate officials told us, with obvious relish:

> Dr. Banda has said time and time again that there will be no Africanization in this country just for the sake of Africanization. It will come eventually; there is an African understudy for every important post in the government. But he will not take over until he is ready for it. He will have to prove first that he can do the job.

Generally speaking, it is agreed that Banda has proved to be a shrewdly realistic leader who thoroughly comprehends both the internal and external conditions of his country's national

---

factories, a large new brewery, a small but ultramodern electronics plant which makes transistor radios, and a sugar refinery.

existence. For example, he has gone out of his way not to antagonize the Portuguese through whose territory Malawi's only railroad enters. He has kept good relations with Rhodesia, which remains a source of manufactured goods, skilled labor, and jobs for unskilled Malawians. Little is heard nowadays—although much was before independence—of the conditions under which some 200,000 Malawians work in Rhodesia and in the mines of South Africa.[14] Perhaps more indicative than anything else of Malawi's continued dependence in independence is her cooperative attitude toward the British who, in one form or another, still underwrite approximately a third of the country's annual budget.[15]

In sharp contrast to Northern Rhodesia, where Kaunda consistently preached racial brotherhood as he rose to power, the nationalist movement in Nyasaland before independence was marked by a strongly anti-Indian flavor. Nevertheless, Indians feel more secure in Malawi than they do in Zambia, and the reason is not far to seek: in Malawi they see a government firmly kept in "civilized" hands. Banda's personal anti-Indian attitude is unfortunate but does not really matter. As long as he remains in power, Indians are confident that the country will stay stable, that "law and order" will prevail, and that nationalist demands made elsewhere in Africa for a redistribution of the available wealth and an end to "foreign" control will not be raised. Thus what they fear is not the Ngwazi but rather that "something" will happen to him—a fear which they share with the Europeans. "We pray every day," an Indian told us with meaningful emphasis, "that Dr. Banda will have a *very* long life!"

14. The number of Malawians working in Rhodesia and South Africa is greater than the number (130,000) in paid employment inside the country. Malawi, *Budget 1966: Background Information*, Treasury Document No. 5 (Zomba, Government Press), p. 13.

15. In other words, something more than £5 million out of a total budget which in recent years has been in the neighborhood of £16 million. Ibid., pp. 81–85.

ASPECTS OF MINORITY RELATIONS

As sketched in broad strokes, these distinctive features of the now sovereign states of Central Africa condition ethnic relations within them. The social, cultural, economic, and political facets of these relations contain many elements common to the entire region but national contexts cannot be avoided.

Social Relations

Generally speaking, public segregation of the kind discussed in Chapter 10 had almost entirely disappeared in the two northern territories by the end of federation and great inroads upon the traditional color bar had been made even in the European stronghold south of the Zambezi.[16]

Nonetheless, a great deal of de facto segregation remains everywhere; and naturally enough, de facto segregation is particularly marked in Rhodesia, where non-whites hesitate to assert their legal rights in the face of powerful white opposition. Nor can it be forgotten that in Rhodesia some very

16. Perhaps the high point in desegregation was reached when the High Court of Southern Rhodesia announced in October 1961 that the municipal swimming baths of that country must be opened to all races. For the record, it can be noted that it was an Indian who brought the action before the court. (See *Central African Examiner,* September 1961, p. 7 and November 1961, pp. 10–11.) To what extent segregation will be reimposed in Rhodesia if the present government retains its power seems at this writing to be an open question. A tightening up on so-called "excesses" in racial mixing would appear to be a certainty; already, for example, the government has informally warned the Indians that it frowns upon their moving into European residential areas although legally they have a right to do so.

In our opinion, nonetheless, the trend toward more segregation will be limited; apartheid South African style seems most unlikely for Rhodesia. In the first place, the government would be foolish to deliberately exacerbate African antagonism. Nor—and this is the really significant factor—will there be any irresistible demand for such measures from the Europeans. In cultural origin, apartheid is a peculiarly Afrikaner notion. The Rhodesians are predominantly British, many of them of recent origin. According to Rogers and Frantz, Afrikaners constitute well under 20 percent of the total European population in Rhodesia. These authors show statistically that recent British immigrants are more liberal in racial attitudes than the British-born of longer residence. Afrikaners, on the other hand, tend to be more conservative than either. Cyril A. Rogers and C. Frantz, *Racial Themes in Southern Rhodesia: The Attitudes and Behavior of the White Population* (New Haven and London, Yale University Press, 1962), pp. 60, 120–24.

important legal measures are still defined in racial terms. Chief of these are the Land Apportionment Act which restricts Africans residentially and the segregated school system up to the level of the University College.[17]

In Malawi, Banda has quietly allowed the Europeans to keep their schools more or less intact. Otherwise, it is tacitly understood, Europeans will not live in Malawi—and Malawi cannot get along without its Europeans. Indians and Coloureds, on the other hand, must see their children integrated with Africans in schools that are currently in a chaotic state. As in most countries at a comparable economic level, facilities are minimal and seriously overcrowded. Teachers are ill-paid and ill-prepared, and competent supervision scarcely exists.[18]

In Zambia, an important measure of both quality and de facto segregation has been maintained by putting the former non-African schools on a fee-paying basis.[19] But the government views this arrangement as a temporary expedient; its ultimate and not distant goal is free, non-segregated schools throughout the country. Unlike Malawi, Zambia will not much longer tolerate essentially European schools for that portion

17. The future of the University College was thrown into serious doubt in July 1966, when nine liberal faculty members were "detained" by the police and then deported. In the wake of this action, the institution was temporarily closed. In September, it reopened and up to the present writing remains multiracial. As of 1966 there were 42 Indians enrolled, 469 Europeans, and 191 Africans. *Zambia Mail* (August 19, 1966). As in East Africa, Indians are over-represented in the "hard" sciences in contrast to the Africans, who are predominantly in the humanities and social sciences. In some departments and schools—chemistry and engineering, for example—Indians currently constitute from a third to a half of the enrollment at the University College, according to an informal estimate given us by one faculty member.

18. One of the not-so-minor tragedies of Malawian independence was the closing of the Chichere Coloured School at Blantyre, a federally-supported institution of very high quality. More than a school, Chichere had been home to many of its pupils who had no other. Of course a financially hard-pressed African government could not be expected to maintain an expensive institution of this kind for a small minority, no matter how deserving.

19. Fees are £12 a year at the primary level and £18 at the secondary level. Given incomes prevailing at the time we collected our original data, a good many families with several children would have had great difficulty in meeting such payments. Recent prosperity has solved this problem; to our knowledge, no Indian child in Zambia is being kept from school because his parents cannot afford the fees.

of her population. But it must be recognized that Zambia can take this attitude because of the wealth that allows her to bid for teachers upon the world market and thus to maintain her integrated schools at a relatively high level. Quite simply, Malawi cannot afford to do so.

It is difficult to generalize with confidence about the more informal areas of social relations in the absence of systematic data. There is undoubtedly freer racial mixing in work and in public places than there used to be, even in Rhodesia. Where the social situation demands it, second-generation Indians in all three countries have no difficulty whatsoever in interacting adequately with either Europeans or educated Africans. Broadly speaking, of course, the reason for this fact is a cultural convergence toward common cosmopolitan norms.

Yet even in Zambia the racial groups typically do not mix much at the strictly voluntary level of association. A visit to the Lusaka Theatre Club, which presents amateur productions open to the public, helped to establish the point. From the faces in the crowd, one might have been back in the colonial era; not a single non-European was in the audience. By the same token, neither Africans nor Europeans attend the Indian films shown in the local Hindu Hall.

Lack of "integration" is one of the more serious charges which African governments level against their Indian minorities. Yet in one notable respect it appears quite clear that de facto segregation is unintentionally promoted by these governments themselves. Now that racial categories are no longer officially recognized in the African state, no systematic attempt is made, as there used to be, at racial representation for "the ceremonial public occasion." Both Europeans and Indians who do not have close personal ties with important African officials have found themselves dropped from the established guest lists. One gains the impression, too, that these affairs have become less numerous and more informal than they used to be, with active participation confined to the ruling elite and their favorites. The result is a small added measure of isolation for the already seriously isolated Indian community.

Of infinitely greater practical significance is a change so revolutionary that at first it is difficult to quite believe. In the pre-independence period, face-to-face interaction between Africans and non-Africans was often characterized by gross rudeness, sometimes unintentional but often enough very deliberate. Loud shouting, name-calling, and cursing were commonplace, particularly among working-class Europeans. Indians were much less given to these cruder forms of impoliteness, but the difference was strictly one of degree. Their technique of subordination through cold and superior disdain was perhaps more resented than the Afrikaner's curses and blows.[20]

With African governments in power, the cruder forms of abuse have "miraculously" disappeared, despite the fact that irritating encounters with Africans have multiplied rather than lessened. Non-Africans now have to deal not only with subordinates in menial positions but with a great variety of clerks and officials, many of whom are as yet much less than ideally efficient.[21] The frustrated non-African, however, can only seethe in silence. To give open vent to his anger is, in the present political context, exceedingly dangerous.

One can sympathize without qualification with the official position on this issue: independence has no meaning so long as citizens can be gratuitously abused in their own country. Yet at the same time, the objective report can only be that no "foreigner" can feel secure in a country where an indiscretion of this kind—an indiscretion perhaps long conditioned by cultural habit—can lead to instantaneous deportation.[22]

20. It is one of the paradoxes of race relations in southern Africa that Afrikaners are on the whole much better liked as persons by Africans than are the British. Gruff and on occasion brutal, Afrikaners do not hold themselves aloof from Africans in interpersonal relations the way English people do. Indians tend to be even more aloof than the British and are more disliked accordingly.

21. Buying a stamp at the Lusaka post office during the end-of-the-month rush period, for example, can turn into a four-hour task. Indian merchants, who necessarily rely upon the post, find themselves constantly frustrated with the service.

22. The number of European farmers in Zambia dropped from a total of about 1,100 in 1964 to something like 600 in 1966. *Rhodesia Herald* (July 29,

Cultural Trends

As predicted in the body of our text, europeanization of both the Indian and the African populations continues apace on all fronts—and at nearly incredible speed. A precise measure of change in the area of caste, for example, would surely reveal marked differences between now and the brief five to seven years ago when the original data were collected. Two new cases of intercaste marriage and two cases of outgroup marriage came to our attention, and it is only reasonable to assume that several more have occurred of which we did not hear.

It is clear that these institutional changes among Indians are considerably more advanced in Rhodesia than elsewhere. A section of the late adolescent population in Rhodesia is in open rebellion against the restrictions imposed by the traditional culture and its surrogates. A group of young men in Salisbury have formed a semi-clandestine storefront club to which they attempt, with some success, to entice girls for beer drinking and jukebox dancing—a development less surprising than the fatalism with which the parental generation seems to accept it. Drinking generally has either increased or become more open; and one gathers the same applies to eating meat as well.[23] The patron-client system, which had already considerably withered by the time of the original fieldwork, seems now to have all but disappeared. With it unquestionably have gone further severe inroads into the joint family institution, although kinship still plays, and will continue to play indefinitely, a larger role among Indians than it does among Europeans. It

---

1966). It is difficult to account for this exodus except as a reflection of the difficulties in dealing with African labor, traditionally an ill-used and heavily exploited group. European farmers in Zambia have been discontented with some of the government's agricultural policies, but on the other hand farm prices and profits have never been higher.

23. Agehananda Bharati reports rather heavy drinking among the Indians of East Africa, where acculturation is in many respects more advanced than it is in Central Africa. Agehananda Bharati, "The Indians in East Africa: A Survey of Problems of Transition and Adaptation," *Sociologus, 14* (1964), 176.

is obvious that the unusual economic prosperity of recent years has greatly accelerated these trends.[24]

With these institutional changes have come very marked shifts in styles of life, the trend being predictably away from the old Indian simplicity and asceticism toward greater emphasis upon the material luxuries and pleasures characteristic of Europeans. In the absence of more precise measures, our experience in Rhodesia on successive evenings may illustrate this trend, although the instances of behavior cited are admittedly extremes.

The first evening was spent in a behind-the-shop home of an old friend. Housing everywhere in Central Africa today is short and expensive, and the small but seriously dilapidated quarters in which he and his family live are therefore still being used. Until some dozen years ago, however, they were occupied not by a single family as now but by the wealthy Indian who still owns them, by his partner and his family, and by a third family of tenants. All had numerous offspring.

Before the landlord moved away to his present single-family home, the partner died. His body, we were told, was laid out and carried to the cremation grounds in a discarded soap box from their warehouse—an example of penuriousness severe enough to be remarked upon at the time since their business was already worth several hundred thousand pounds.

The father of our host for the next evening must have lived with his family in a similar behind-the-shop style. His university-educated son, however, has become a successful industrialist on the foundation of the family-accumulated fortune. To do so, as the son himself pointed out, a drastic reorientation was necessary in his thinking, away from the old "bazaar mentality" of his father's generation to a modern conception of life and economics. Accordingly, as his guests we were picked up at our hotel in a black Mercedes, the prime

24. While not entirely neglected by sociologists, the sheerly economic *cost* factor in socio-cultural change could receive more attention than it has. In comparing 1966 with 1959–61, we were impressed again and again by the fact that many of the changes which we noted would have been difficult or impossible without the increased income that supports them.

status symbol in Central Africa. We were then driven out to the young man's recently acquired house in a hitherto pristinely European suburb—a house completely equipped and furnished in upper-middle class European style. Here, we were provided with drinks and a catered Chinese dinner by our hostess, a bright and slender young woman who engaged in lively small talk in perfect English. Throughout the evening, only three items of behavior indicated unmistakably that we were in an Indian's home: the hostess and the second guest's wife wore saris; the men ate in solitary masculine splendor, being served in the proper manner by the wife; and the Indian guest (but not the host himself) carefully picked the meat out of the excellent dinner.

Economic Organization

A good deal of space has already been devoted to the economic context of post-independence ethnic relations in Central Africa in the conviction that nothing else is more important. In this section the emphasis will be confined mainly to developments in the social organization of Indian economic activity.

From our original data, we anticipated a progressive reduction in the number of small Indian shops, partly through a gradual displacement by Africans and partly through a consolidation of small businesses into larger units. Indian shops have instead proliferated, particularly in Zambia. And while the absolute number of African-owned businesses has undoubtedly increased, in neither Zambia nor Malawi has their growth yet displaced Indians, discounting a few marginal shops in the rural areas.

In Zambia, it is the Indian shop assistant rather than the small shopkeeper who is threatening to disappear. Traditionally, the assistant has always been a shop owner in his heart, waiting impatiently for the day he could launch out upon his own. The extraordinary expansion of economic activity during the last few years has allowed this dream to come true by guaranteeing at least a modicum of success in such ventures, and a great number of former shop assistants have taken this step. Those who remain work for the very largest firms at salaries more than double those prevailing for experienced help five years ago.

The virtual disappearance of the Indian shop assistant (particularly in Zambia, but the trend can be observed in the other countries as well) has made room for a new class of African assistants and, with them, a rather different pattern of trade than that described in Chapters 3 and 9. The newly affluent African customer places more emphasis upon quality and variety and less upon price than he used to. Bargaining has by no means disappeared, but of necessity fixed prices which can be quoted by an African assistant are now the rule in the larger shops. In these shops, however, the Indian owner or a member of his family still makes change, and Indians take the initiative and responsibility for stock maintenance and display.

The absolute increase in the number of Indian-owned businesses is directly correlated with the growth of the larger towns. No one knows how many people the capital city of Lusaka now has; the Director of Central Statistics estimates a current annual rate of increase of something like ten percent. The Blantyre-Limbe metropolitan complex in Malawi is probably growing at a roughly comparable rate and for similar reasons.[25]

The larger towns, where both buying power and population are increasingly being concentrated, have attracted Indians from the rural areas and the smaller settlements. If the size of the school population provides a valid basis for judgment, Lusaka now has at least twice as many Indians as it did in 1961 and roughly a third of the total number in Zambia. In this process, a good many bush shops have been either deserted or turned over to Africans.

Adequate data on the number of African-owned businesses

25. The estimate for Lusaka was given to us by Director of Census and Statistics, Mr. D. H. Bhate, an Indian national on loan to the Zambian government from UNESCO. While not the capital of Malawi, Blantyre-Limbe performs many of the administrative functions of a capital city.

are not readily available. That such businesses have increased seems certain, but it is also certain that their share of the total retail trade is still very small. Impeding African advance into this economic area are not only the socio-cultural obstacles discussed toward the end of Chapter 3 but also the abundance of less demanding yet very rewarding opportunities, particularly in government employment. Indians still assume that Africans will eventually absorb the small retail trade. But it is obvious that many of them (as well as ourselves) have overestimated the speed with which this will occur.[26]

In keeping with our original expectations, a number of Indians have moved into manufacturing. Existing plants have expanded their operations and a fair number of new ones are being built. Lusaka alone now boasts two Indian-owned knitting mills, where none existed before. Clothing factories have mushroomed in both Zambia and Malawi. Import-substitute growth of this character had already occurred during federation in Rhodesia. Everywhere, Indians are highly conscious of the potentialities in industry and constantly discuss them. Given a modicum of encouragement, a very rapid movement of Indians into industry could confidently be predicted.

Unfortunately for everyone concerned, this modicum of encouragement cannot be taken for granted, given the political realities inherent in the African state. The truth is that Indian investment in industry, in real estate, or even in the expansion of wholesale and retail trade falls well short of its theoretical potential. The reasons are entirely political.

Political Relations

In turning to a discussion of the politics of Indo-African relations, one overriding fact needs to be made unambiguously clear lest there be misunderstanding. Indian fears in Central Africa today are appropriately labeled anxieties: they are

---

26. Cf. our original summary upon this point, pp. 80–85 above. Having lost £25,000 in uncollected credits, a large Indian wholesaler in Zambia told us that he will no longer try to do business with African retailers.

forebodings of what *might* happen rather than what *has* happened. Putting aside a few isolated incidents of extortion, robbery, and intimidation in the rural areas immediately following independence, Indians have yet to be seriously molested in either Zambia or Malawi. But that they and their compatriots in Rhodesia are anxious concerning the future could not escape even the most superficial investigation.

As a general factor underlying everything else and crosscutting the entire region, there is the question of the stability of these infant states, so recently born that they have not yet had an opportunity to prove that they can stand, let alone walk. Indians consequently fear that even favorable circumstances may not long remain as they are.

Zambia, for example, is a plausible model of what many would consider the ideal African state. Within Zambia, "nonracialism" (note, not "multiracialism") is both officially preached and practiced. Its leaders are on the whole a remarkably able, even-tempered set of men who are guided by an exceedingly stringent ideal of probity and energetic performance. Nor are Indians in Zambia blind to their good fortune in this respect. They simply remember that Ghana at one time and Nigeria more recently were also hailed as model African states. And they see (or think they see) the as yet safely defused powder kegs lying underneath the placid surface of Zambian politics.

It is precisely because Dr. Banda and Ian Smith, in their very different ways, represent "stability" that they receive the moral support of their Indian minorities. Quite patently, neither Malawi nor Rhodesia is an Indian paradise; nonetheless, they are regimes in which, with the notable exception of politics, the tested rules of Anglo-Saxon justice and equity apply to life and property. Yet neither Malawi nor Rhodesia provides Indians with real security, as they themselves very well know. This is particularly true of Malawi, where all seems to hang precipitously upon the slender thread of one aging man's mortality.

More concretely, Indians know that the potentialities for

trouble which they fear but have not yet experienced have been manifested often enough elsewhere to confirm that they are not illusory. Outside of Africa, Indian experience in Burma stands as a particularly gruesome lesson of what can happen to a hated foreign minority when the government decides to move against the "stranglehold" that it exercises upon the economy. A fair number of families in Central Africa had relatives in Burma, where an estimated 125,000 Indians were compelled to leave the country penniless after their property was confiscated through a nationalization program that reached down to the smallest retail shop.[27] More remote to the people of Central Africa but still familiar in a general way is the situation in Ceylon, where Indians resident from time out of mind are being forced to leave.[28] They are also aware of the continued

27. The plight of the Indians of Burma has received little attention in a world press, inured in this twentieth century to far more spectacular horrors. The fullest account known to us in the American press is a short article, "Asians v. Asians," *Time* (July 17, 1964), p. 29, and another in the *New York Times* (July 24, 1964) which appeared under the by-line of Jacques Nevard. Cf. incidental references in Richard Butwell, "Burma Doesn't Want Aid," *New Republic* (September 3, 1966) and Louis J. Walinsky, "Unhappy Burma," a letter to the editors, ibid. (September 17, 1966); also *Keesing's Contemporary Archives, 14* (1963–64), 20315–16. The background of the nationalization program, however, is clear enough. As another *Times* newspaperman noted, "there is a deeply rooted distrust of foreigners" in Burma, where the memory of British colonialism "still rankles," accompanied by an intense desire "to eliminate the vestiges of the old dominant foreign cultural and economic influences." Seymour Topping in *New York Times* (December 30, 1963).

There is nothing uniquely Burmese in these attitudes. In Burma, as elsewhere, they arise out of the structure of a plural society, the inherent conflicts of which are free to manifest themselves once European rule is replaced by a nationalist government. To former colonial subjects, political power has little meaning unless it can be translated into economics—in other words, the redistribution of available wealth and jobs. With respect to this point, the East and Central African countries differ from Burma only in that the former are still too dependent upon hated "foreigners" economically and socially to allow freer expression of xenophobia. Far more developed internally, Burma can at least contemplate a "go-it-alone" policy. Egypt provides still another example of the precariousness of minorities in the newer nations. Tens of thousands of Greeks, Jews, and Italians have left the country under the pressures of Nasser's Egyptianization policies. Cf. Jay Walz in *New York Times* (May 21, 1962).

28. How many of Ceylon's 970,000 Indians will ultimately be repatriated to India has been a subject of intense and bitter negotiations between the two governments. Cf. *New York Times* (October 29, 1964) and *Keesing's Contemporary Archives, 14* (1963–64), 20405.

and precariously balanced conflict between Indians and Negroes in Guyana.[29]

It is to events in East Africa, however, that Indians in Central Africa are most closely attuned. Both the people and their situations are quite similar; and in the processes of decolonization and Africanization, East Africa has been just a step ahead of Central Africa. This region therefore stands in their minds as a barometer of what they too might expect.

Indians accordingly shivered in horror as reports poured in from Zanzibar, where an unknown (and thus easily exaggerated) number of Indians lost their lives and property in the revolution of January 1964. The Zanzibar events give a sharp point to the otherwise seemingly vague and anchorless fears Indians have of instability.

At a less dramatic but much better documented level, the Indians of Central Africa know that thousands of Indian civil servants in East Africa either have been deprived of their jobs through Africanization or live in daily dread that they will lose them. They know too that the Kenya government has continually and publicly demanded a greater African share in commerce and that it has on more than one occasion broadly hinted that political power will be used if necessary to get that share—presumably at Indian expense.[30] While thus econom-

29. Such a wealth of widely-spaced conflict situations contributes to a common Indian conviction: namely, that all Indians outside of India are fated to remain pariahs, everywhere disliked and persecuted. When we remarked to a not very cooperative informant that Indians did not seem very popular in East Africa, he replied with a hard edge to his voice: "Since you are an expert on Indians, *you* tell me where Indians are popular!"

30. Two examples: "The Asian community maintains . . . a virtual stranglehold on commerce, and no Africans have been promoted to high posts in Asian firms. Even the moderate Mayor of Nairobi, Alderman Rubia, was moved to say that Africans would not rest until they saw more African names above shops in the main streets of Nairobi. At the present there are two." *Central African Mail* (July 17, 1964). "A new bill, aimed at speeding up the Africanisation of jobs in private business will soon be introduced in Kenya. . . . Work permits for all non-Kenyans, including the hitherto 'privileged' permanent residents, and the compulsory introduction of 'understudies' for jobs held by them, are the main provisions of a draft bill now nearing completion. . . . The Minister of Labour, Dr. Julius Kiano, said: 'There is no reason why permanent residents should not be treated the way all other foreigners are treated. After all, they were brought in by the colonial government, not us.'" *Zambia Mail* (October 7, 1966).

ically harassed, the East African Indians' loyalty has been continually brought into question. The charges are typically vague but terribly inclusive: Indians fail to "identify" themselves socially and culturally with the African people. Political disloyalty is inferred in short from the social aloofness so characteristic of Indians in their relations to others.

Anti-Indian sentiment in Zambia has remained for the most part submerged. Explicit expression of it, particularly by members of the government, is inconsistent with the official nonracial policy. On occasion, however, it manages to rise to the surface; and when it does, the stereotyped definition of Indo-African conflict in Central Africa contains exactly the same elements as it does in East Africa. A feature article elaborating the familiar themes appeared in the country's only Sunday newspaper during our 1966 visit. Prominently titled "Zambia's Indian Community Comes under Heavy Fire," this story leads off as follows:

> The tightly-knit Indian community in Zambia is facing heavy criticism from the Government. Since Independence this vulnerable community has remained isolated and introvert, finding difficulty in integrating more closely with other sections of society.

Having made this seemingly innocent and almost sympathetic observation, the reporter's heavy guns are lowered:

> "If the Indians want to survive in Zambia," said one Government official, "they must put their house in order."
> . . . There is an obvious resentment among Zambians that the wealth of the country is mainly concentrated in the hands of foreigners. . . . The public image is low and until the reasons which give rise to the prejudice and criticism are removed, it is likely to remain so.

Reasons for "prejudice and criticism" are in the main echoes of the established stereotypes found everywhere in East, Central, and South Africa. Indians "overcharge" and "cheat" their customers. They employ no one but relatives "to keep the wages bill low." They seriously exploit their domestic servants. Finally, they are dirty; but in this particular statement, the familiar charge is made to hinge upon a specific incident. The reporter reminds his readers that since Indians "spend no money on maintaining their shops," the government had recently been "forced" to issue an "ultimatum" to clean them up.[31]

This newspaper story did not mention the most serious charge pending against the Indian community: that its members are the chief violators of the currency control regulations with which Zambia (like virtually every other developing country in the world) tries to dam the outflow of capital. Perhaps the author did not feel that it was necessary since the local news at this time had been dominated for weeks by releases on the progress of the investigation which the government was making. Or perhaps he was trying to be fair; Europeans as well as Indians violate this legislation, and at the moment he was discussing Indians.

Penalties for currency violations are theoretically severe but substantiation is difficult. There is little doubt, therefore, that through its well-publicized investigations the government hoped to frighten potential violators as much as to catch actual ones. Nonetheless, Indians as a group could not help but suffer from the publicity, whatever the sins of individual members. As we know, the belief that Indians "send everything they

31. *Zambia News* (July 24, 1966). A very similar article appeared in the *Zambia Mail* (July 29, 1966). Upon arriving in Lusaka, we noticed that the old secondary trading district, where most of the African trade is still conducted, had an unwonted clean, sharp look. One of our first informants explained: "Last month, the President got up and made a speech in which he said he wanted the capital of Zambia to look nice. He gave us three weeks in which to paint our shops, inside and out. Otherwise, he said, we would lose our licenses. I'll tell you, we really had to scurry around here for a while. You couldn't hire any painters—they were all too busy. And there were scarcely enough paint and brushes in town to do the job." Other informants told us that in those cases where there was a delay for a few days in getting started with the paint job, ordinary Africans from the street who had heard the President's speech came in and "ordered" them to get busy. Indians also report that Africans have "ordered" them to display the President's picture or, in some cases, to display it more prominently and with more "respect." Currently, the President's picture is a conspicuous part of the furnishings of even the simplest shop.

make out of the country" is an old stereotype in southern Africa; it is thus inevitable that suspicion falls most heavily upon Indians when it is reported that huge sums are regularly leaving the country.[32] Furthermore, it must be appreciated that such charges have ramifications far beyond the merely economic: within a context where nearly every act which a "foreigner" commits can acquire political significance, "lack of faith in the country" as indicated by unwillingness to invest is taken as positive proof of real or incipient disloyalty.

The ultimate sanction which the African state dangles over the heads of all "foreigners" who for whatever reason cannot "adjust" to the new order (the favorite official terminology in Zambia) is deportation. No Indians have yet been deported from Zambia; generally speaking, its officials have acted with great restraint in this as in other delicate matters of race relations, considering the objective situation and the history which gave rise to it. The sanction, however, has been used frequently enough against Europeans for both Europeans and Indians to get the message unambiguously.[33]

Here again East Africa provides the handwriting upon the

32. It will be remembered that when this matter was discussed in Chapter 3, we concluded that the stereotype was almost entirely mythical. Applied to conditions as they then existed, we are still confident that we were essentially correct. But situations change. Given present circumstances, it should not surprise us that Indians who are in a position to do so are sorely tempted to try to build up a cash reserve abroad—although, naturally, these are matters which are not discussed very candidly. Some of our informants discussed techniques that unnamed others—never, of course, themselves—use to accomplish this purpose. For example, you can ask a trusted supplier abroad to inflate invoices sent to you, with the understanding that he will bank for you the difference between the real price and the price which appears on your invoices.

33. We did not attempt a count of the number of Europeans deported; while not *in toto* large, it has nonetheless been considerable. To date the largest single number at one time was in October 1966 when twenty-three (mostly miners from the Copperbelt) were deported. *Zambia Mail* (October 28, 1966). An African member of the National Assembly commented: "The hon. Members who used to go to the drive-in and to other cinemas saw at the beginning how our white friends were resisting the idea of standing to attention when the National Anthem was being played. Surprisingly they now stand as if *God Save the Queen* is being sung. Some people say that perhaps Mr. Chona's [the Minister of Home Affairs] deportations helped but whatever the reason is I do not know." Dr. K. D. Konoso, Member for the Sesheke Constituency in Zambia *Hansard* (July 28, 1965), col. 435.

wall for the Indians of Central Africa to interpret as best they can. Toward the end of the summer of 1966, six Indians were summarily deported from Kenya under charges no more specific (at least publicly)than "disloyalty." [34] Following the original story, the local newspaper carried an ominous comment under a Nairobi dateline:

> The Government-run Voice of Kenya radio accused Asians in the country of paying lip service to integration in the new Kenya. In a commentary on the deportation of six Asians yesterday, Voice of Kenya said *the entire 180,000-strong Asian community stood indicted by the actions of its members.*[35]

Nor did Zambia's own government-supported radio neglect the news, according to the testimony of one of our informants:

> I first heard about the deportations over the six o'clock morning news which I always listen to just after I get up. The same story was repeated on every newscast made that day [a total of eight]; I know because I checked just to be sure. Then it was broadcast twice the next day. The government didn't take all that trouble for nothing. They wanted to be sure that all of us [i.e. the Indians] heard it.

One thing which the Indians in Central Africa particularly noted regarding the Kenya deportations was that two of the six persons involved held Kenyan citizenship. Yet Kenyan citizenship did not save them from deportation; these men were treated exactly as if they too had been foreigners.[36] The

34. As quoted in the local newspaper, the official phrasing was: "They have shown themselves by act and speech to be disloyal and disaffected towards Kenya." The statement went on to say: "Loyalty to the State and the President is absolutely essential for anyone who wishes to continue living and working peacefully in Kenya." *Times of Zambia* (August 15, 1966).

35. Emphasis added. Ibid. (August 16, 1966).

36. The Kenya government's statement on this point, as reported in ibid. (August 15, 1966), is worth reproducing: "Whereas the constitution of Kenya provides for non-Kenyans to take citizenship, it must be expected that those who choose to become Kenya citizens *will identify themselves fully with the country in all aspects* and will not in any manner engage themselves in sub-

Indians of Zambia paid close attention to this implicit lesson, since at the time this story appeared they were in the process of trying to make up their minds as to what to do about the all-important question of citizenship.

Zambia's provisions for citizenship are in all essentials similar to those of the East African countries. Concerned over the fate of British subjects and their colonial-born descendants, the British government wrote provisions for their protection into the acts of independence of all these countries. They and all other "British-protected persons" of foreign origin who might otherwise unwillingly find themselves citizens of a newly independent country by default were given the option of applying for a British passport before independence. Indians throughout East and Central Africa seized this opportunity to acquire in effect United Kingdom citizenship. The passport division of the British High Commission in Nairobi was literally swamped with applications from Indians and had to close down for a while in order to catch up on the work.[37]

After independence, Zambia followed the East African precedent and allowed a two-year grace period from the date of independence for filing applications for local citizenship. All adults were required to file; but it was understood that within

---

versive activities against the State or any other activities calculated to cause discord among the peace-loving citizens of this country." Emphasis added.

37. Inevitably, there were fears (expressed in public charges) that closure of the passport office was an attempt by the British to force Indians either to stay in Kenya or go back to India. Cf. *Central African Mail* (November 22, 1963). There appears to have been virtually no options for an Indian passport; even recent immigrants on Indian passports turned them in for British ones. With very few exceptions the only Indians in East and Central Africa who hold Indian passports are Indian nationals who entered these countries on contract after independence (see note 10 above). According to the Indian High Commissioner in Lusaka these total no more than about 150 in Zambia.

The Indian government has consistently encouraged immigrants to take out citizenship in the country where they reside. Nonetheless, the haste with which Indians in Africa seized the opportunity to acquire British passports sorely miffed the Indian diplomatic corps in the new African countries. Indians, they point out, still come to them with their problems. "But we tell them," snapped one official, "that they have come to the wrong place! Let them go to the British High Commission—that is where they belong!" Technically, of course, the Indian government can do nothing for nonnationals, but these officials always emphasize that Indians with no place else to go will be accepted back in India.

the grace period approval would be virtually automatic for those born in the country or who possessed the old federal or other Commonwealth citizenship. Thereafter, all applications would be treated individually, with a final decision to be made upon "merit."

In East Africa, the two-year grace period had already elapsed by 1966. Few Indians there, and virtually none of the immigrant generation, had acquired local citizenship, preferring instead to retain their British passports.[38] In Zambia, people were making up their minds as the deadline of October 24, 1966 approached. Within the community the pros and cons of local citizenship were constantly and anxiously discussed. When informants allowed themselves to speak freely, it was generally agreed that Zambia's Indians would, on October 25, 1966, find themselves exactly in the same position as the great majority of Indians in Kenya: foreigners in a country where they have every intention of remaining as long as they are allowed to do so.

Of all people, Indians are among the least to be charged with indifference to the future, and they have not come to this pass without a careful searching of all possible alternatives. They know that by hedging as long as they have on the question of citizenship they have exposed themselves to the charge of a lack of faith in the country and its leaders. But they know too that their citizenship status, whatever it is, in no way changes their sociological status as Indians and "foreigners" in the eyes of the African majority.[39] One informant put it this way, before the Kenya incident occurred:

38. We were unable to obtain dependable official statistics on the number of Indians in Kenya who are now citizens. Estimates from Indian consular officials and others who should know range from 40,000 to 60,000 (of all ages) out of a total population of 180,000. It was emphasized that those who did apply for citizenship had in most cases been born in Kenya.

39. No one can argue that legal status does not count, but comparative evidence shows that in serious conflict situations sociological status generally assumes precedence in the contestants' minds. The fact that they were technically citizens has not saved Chinese from slaughter in Indonesia (see pp. 374–76 below). Americans, too, might remember the incarceration of the Japanese—citizens and noncitizens alike—during World War II.

What am I going to do about citizenship? Well, to tell the truth, I haven't made up my mind yet. I'm still thinking [the typical response]. But whatever we Indians do, I don't think it will change anything really. We will always be considered foreigners in this country, no matter what we do. A piece of paper which says that you are a citizen of Zambia won't make you into an African, will it? All you have to do is to have a quarrel with an African, and you will be deported just like that [snapping his fingers]. And before they put you on that plane, they won't bother to ask whether you are a citizen or not.

It is a telling comment upon the way in which matters of political significance are handled in Malawi that the question of citizenship for either Europeans or Indians has scarcely arisen. Apparently, very few non-Africans have been granted citizenship; and, in sharp contrast to Zambia and Kenya, no automatic citizenship within a grace period was ever offered in Malawi. In any case, the conviction seems to prevail among Indians that the Ngwazi believes that Malawian citizenship is primarily for Africans. To our knowledge, no Indians have bothered to apply. Like those elsewhere, however, they were careful to acquire British passports when given the opportunity prior to independence.

Neither has the issue of citizenship arisen in Rhodesia—for very different reasons. The Unilateral Declaration of Independence was directed outward and it did not in and of itself affect the internal constitution. Under the federation, Rhodesia's Indians became for the most part federal citizens, as did the European population. So far, their right to Rhodesian citizenship has not been questioned and there is no reason to suppose that it will be; Indians, for example, get Rhodesian passports without difficulty. Until the more fundamental issue of the constitution has been settled, all such matters await in abeyance in Rhodesia.

THE FUTURE

You have traveled around and studied this country from every angle, Doctor. What would you do if you were in our place? What is going to happen here?

This question was often and insistently put to us during our 1966 visit. The optimistic answer, of course, is that nothing disastrous has yet happened to the Indians of Central Africa, nor are there infallible indications that any gross catastrophe will. Still, as they themselves are well aware, their situation is precarious and will remain so indefinitely.

With luck, there is a fair chance that Indo-African conflict will be muted into a livable pattern of accommodation, which is the most common resolution of conflict everywhere. Reason points in this direction, for whether they recognize it or not, Africans need the Indians. Yet we scarcely have to point out that neither reason nor need is always served in human affairs. Without luck, the Indians' fortunes could easily take a dangerous turn. Zanzibar, Burma, and most recently, Indonesia provide suggestive prototypes of how ethnic conflict comparable to that of Central Africa can erupt into an apocalyptic form.

Except for the fact that the Chinese in Indonesia have suffered heavily from overt violence and the Indians of Africa have not as yet, the parallels between these two minority situations are indeed striking. There are important differences, of course, since Indonesia is much more highly developed and has been independent longer than any East or Central African state. Furthermore, the ideological association of all Chinese with the Peking regime and the local Communist Party—irrespective of actual affiliation—is a unique feature of the Indonesian situation not duplicated in Africa. This association, however, has clearly provided the excuse for the savage attacks upon the Chinese—not the root motivation.[40]

40. "The massacre of Chinese in Indonesia this year had Communism as a pretext, but most of the victims were probably doomed for being (a) wealthy

The root motivation for the overt violence arises out of a social situation, as described by Donald Kirk,[41] that is basically very similar to that of the Indian minority in Africa. Both the Chinese of Indonesia and the Indians of Africa occupy middleman trader roles in a former colonial plural society; both are perceived by the indigenous population as "dominating," or as exercising a "stranglehold" upon, the distributive sector of the economy. Yet in neither case is the indigenous population developed enough to perform this function. Within these contexts, the immigrant minority in each instance has risen economically far above the base population by dint of hard and persistent effort, sharp wits, the ability to cooperate within tightly organized kinship units, and rigorous controls over consumption.

Like the Indians of Africa, the Chinese of Indonesia entered the area under the umbrella of European rule; they were thus identified in the minds of the local people with the "imperialists," although the minorities themselves are strongly anti-European. Trying hard to shift this identification, the leaders of both groups have made strenuous efforts to submerge themselves politically into the indigenous population.[42] In neither case have these efforts been successful, although the Chinese have tried harder than the Indians of Africa. Noting that a good many Chinese have sought anonymity in Indonesian citizenship and that some have gone so far as to adopt Indonesian names, Kirk adds that "the Indonesians hate them all the more." The difficulties of integration in both instances are well summed up in a comment quoted from a young Chinese university lecturer: "It is not easy to integrate into the style

and (b) alien." Alex Campbell, "Who's Afraid of China? Many Americans, No So Many Asians," *New Republic* (April 9, 1966), p. 16. See also the series of articles by Seymour Topping, *New York Times* (August 22–25, 1966), and shorter notices in *New York Times* (October 16, 1965, and February 14, April 16, May 5, September 23, December 15, 1966).

41. The account below is drawn from Donald Kirk's excellent article, "Indonesia's Chinese Are People Without a Country," *New York Times Magazine* (October 23, 1966), pp. 32 ff.

42. " 'We must show our undying love for Indonesia,' yelled Kwee Eng Oen, leader of the rally." Ibid., p. 149.

of a society whose social and working standards are inferior to yours." Kirk concludes with an observation which, if it is true of Indonesia, is all the more true for less developed Africa. The Indonesians, he points out, can "ill afford" to lose the Chinese; if they go, "the impoverished Indonesian economy would only deteriorate further." [43]

Despite the remarkably close parallel with Indonesia, it would of course be most premature to predict similar developments in Central Africa. The quite extraordinary economic prosperity prevailing throughout the region at the moment of writing augurs favorably for successful accommodation. Fortunately for the Indians, prosperity is particularly marked in Zambia, where owing to political factors the potentialities for serious overt trouble are also the greatest. If economic and political development continues at its present pace in Zambia, opportunities may be created fast enough for the mobile part of the African population so that the relatively privileged niches occupied by the small Indian minority may go unnoticed and unenvied—not absolutely, of course, but for all practical purposes. This is the best explanation for the relative quiescence up to the moment, and historically it describes fairly well the evolution of Indo-European relations in Rhodesia.

The fact that Indo-African relations are currently more acute in East Africa than they are in Central Africa is in part simply a matter of time, the East African territories having achieved independence earlier. But relative prosperity and the size of the minority population are also very important factors. With the exception of Malawi, East Africa is on the whole much poorer than Central Africa, both actually and in prospects. At the same time, Indians in East Africa are far more conspicuous by their greater numbers; it is easier to believe (as it commonly is) that they literally stand in the position which Africans must have if they are to advance socially and economically. But these favorable factors in their

43. Ibid., pp. 154, 156. And also: "A question of vital importance to Indonesia's future is whether the Indonesians can learn to accept the Chinese as fully as they insist the Chinese should adjust to Indonesia."

situation do not guarantee the Indians of Central Africa security. A sharp and prolonged fall in copper prices, for example, would soon put Zambia economically in the company of other African states.[44] And precisely because African aspirations have for some time been raised on the foundations of copper, such a development could create a situation of great danger for the Indians.[45]

Outside of these considerations, the prosperity which Indians currently enjoy is a highly favorable factor in their situation. Money allows them choices or alternatives which would simply not exist for poorer people. This helps to explain why some Indians take it for granted that sooner or later they will have to leave Africa and are also surprisingly complacent in the face of the prospect.

Wealth, for example, allows families to invest in education for their children, and Indians strive to obtain as much of it as they can. Constantly in the back of their minds is the thought that well-educated people with marketable skills are in short supply the world over; such people, they know, are welcome in a way in which the unskilled—overnumerous everywhere—are not. So, too, are people with capital. If one were forced in the last extremity to seek refuge in overcrowded India, it would make a tremendous difference whether one were to go there with or without capital.

Few of the young and vigorous, however, have any intention of going to India if they are driven out of Africa. Nor by a stroke of great good fortune will they have to. As an inherit-

44. One of the nightmares in Zambia is technological substitution for copper, aluminum being the major candidate. Aside from this fear, copper prices are subject to very wide fluctuations. Finally, there is the possibility of exhaustion; at the current rate of exploitation, known reserves will not much more than outlast the present century. Economic advisers to the Zambian government therefore emphasize the need to diversify the country's economy as quickly as possible. Bank of Zambia, *Report,* pp. 8–9.

45. The concept of "relative deprivation," originally introduced into the literature of the behavioral sciences by Samuel A. Stouffer and others, *The American Soldier: Studies in Social Psychology in World War II* (Princeton, Princeton University Press, 1949), *1*, is by now so widely accepted that it needs no elaboration. The "revolution of rising expectations," now a cliché in the pronouncements of every politician in Africa, directly derives from this notion. So much for diffusion in cosmopolitan world culture!

ance from a past which they have been taught to decry comes a gift which to many is their most precious single possession: their British passport. With it, if necessary, they can go to Britain or possibly to Canada or some other British-settled country. If they go with education and money, their prospects are by no means dismal.[46]

Short of sheer catastrophe, we see no mass exodus of Indians from either East or Central Africa. What is much more likely is selective emigration, variable in volume according to the circumstances. Both "push" and "pull" factors will operate, as in most instances of human migration. The "push" will come with mounting pressures from the African population, the "pull" from perceived alternatives elsewhere. Lured by the lingering dreams of their childhood, a good many of the immigrant generation will return to India for their retirement —and, predictably, some of these in disillusionment will try to get back to Africa.[47] The younger people do not carry these illusions; commonly, those with firsthand experience in the land of their fathers view India with something akin to horror.[48]

46. Like most blessings, this one is double-edged. A British passport makes one in Africa—where most Indians really want to stay—legally as well as sociologically a foreigner, and foreigners will presumably be increasingly treated like foreigners. Consider the implications for education, for example. In East Africa, hints are already being made that scarce school space should go to citizens, not foreigners. There is thus a very strong possibility that Indians in East Africa will be unable to send their children to the schools which they themselves built.

47. The precedent upon which this prediction is based comes from East Africa, where many who went to India soon after independence have already returned.

48. Upon first arrival in India, the African-born are appalled by the crowding and poverty of its people. This initial impression is often accompanied, in their experience, by physical discomfitures from weather far warmer than that to which they are accustomed, and from diarrhea and other ills brought on by exposure to contaminated food and water against which they have no acquired resistance. Culturally, they become disoriented—and disappointed or even disgusted—when the Indian values which they had been taught in Africa to esteem are exemplified before them in concrete practice (naked, dirty holy men, for example). Socially, they are punished by their relatives who ridicule their dress, mannerisms, awkwardness in speaking Gujarati, and general ignorance of the niceties of Indian culture. Sometimes, they are called "Africans." At the same time, these relatives resent what they interpret as the superior airs of the visitors; they are nonetheless openly envious of their wealth—real or presumed—and try to exploit them through the traditional

Of the African-born generation, those who acquire professional or entrepreneurial skills of a high order are the most likely to emigrate, and after them those who have sufficient capital to establish themselves comfortably elsewhere. Ordinary people not in these privileged categories will resist emigration as long as possible, preferring instead to stay where they are and make what adjustments they can to do so.

If the theoretical stance taken in this volume has validity, Indians like the rest of us face a future unknown because it has yet to be created. Or, to speak somewhat more precisely, the forms of this future have yet to emerge clearly from the ecological processes even now at work in the complex of social and cultural elements which constitute society in Central Africa.

What is certain is the continuation of conflict. What is uncertain is the form of its resolution. But fortunately for them —as is surely substantiated in this study—Indians are not weaponless in their struggle for survival. Intelligent and tenacious, they are not to be easily written off in any contest involving wit and endurance.

---

ties of kinship. In all of these matters, the relatives are aided and abetted by fellow villagers, making the visitors feel alien and excluded.

APPENDIX

PLURAL SOCIETY: A CRITIQUE

AND AN ALTERNATIVE

Arthur Vidich has observed that community studies typically provide both stimulus and framework for personal and intellectual self-revelation. The reasons for this fact, he points out, supply a cogent rationale for the community study as a method in social science.[1]

In more formalized research, of which the sample-survey is the prime example, the outcome is set in large measure by the original design. The design of the project therefore constitutes the creative element; the data, collected by hired assistants, fill prearranged slots, the cumulative totals of which statistically confirm or deny a priori hypotheses. Presumably, such studies concern human behavior; but the only behavior the director sees is that of his subordinates, who report processed results through the channels of what is often an elaborate hierarchy.[2] He himself is very effectively insulated from the shocks and hazards of fieldwork.

The social scientist engaged in a community study has no such luxury. He must daily confront the complexities of real behavior of real people, and he must constantly try to square what he sees with the theoretical model that he brought to the task. If what he sees does not fit this conception, he is forced to rethink his theory, in short, to change his mind on some fundamental matters.

As pointed out in the Preface, we began work in Africa with the intention of using plural society as the chief organizing concept. At that time, Furnivall's analysis seemed to almost everyone working

1. This is the major theme of his *Reflections on Community Studies*.
2. For an incisive commentary upon the inevitable results of bureaucratization in research, see Vidich and Joseph Bensman, "The Springdale Case: Academic Bureaucrats and Sensitive Townspeople," in ibid., pp. 313–49.

in the former colonies to suggest the obvious sociological answer to the complexities of their structure. But, as we have explained, we became increasingly dissatisfied with this approach: its implicit assumptions simply did not fit the social reality unfolding day by day before our eyes as the colonial past, represented by the moribund Federation of Rhodesia and Nyasaland, disintegrated to make room for the independent African state.

It must be remembered, however, that the mentality of social scientists is, like that of other people, inherently and irrevocably cultural. It is thus no accident that our second thoughts on the subject of plural society should coincide with a recent and very radical shift in elementary sociological theory. Ultimately, the concept of plural society reduces to the question of the nature and character of societal unity and integration—to nothing less than our basic ideas on what society existentially is, how it is put together, and how it works or functions. These ancient and vexatious matters have been a central concern in recent years during an intensive search in sociology for something better than what current theory offers. Reviewing these developments in light of our experience in Africa, we gradually became convinced that the whole question of social integration has been seriously confused at certain critical junctures, particularly as it applies to the situation that Furnivall described as "plural society."

THE CONCEPT OF CULTURE IN NORMATIVE-FUNCTIONALIST THEORY

Departing only slightly from well-established usage, we will designate the most common current conception of what society is as the "normative-functionalist" model.[3] M. G. Smith, a British social

3. Many—perhaps most—American sociologists would expect "structural-functionalism" in this context rather than "normative-functionalism," since the theoretical issue in point has been most often presented in the recent literature as either an attack upon or a defense of the work of Talcott Parsons. In our opinion, this heavy stress upon Parsons in discussions of the theoretical issues contained in modern sociological functionalism is most unfortunate. The real question, as we see it, is the validity of a cultural definition of society, not Parsons' particular version of it. (For Parsons' use of "structural-functionalism," see *The Social System* (Glencoe, Ill., Free Press, 1951), pp. 19–22.) In fairness to Parsons, it should be added that of course his theory does not logically *demand* the normative emphasis which he gives it in practice, and this fact constitutes another excellent reason for attempting to dissociate him as much as possible from the problem.

anthropologist about whom a good deal more will be said shortly, calls it straightforwardly "the modern view." [4] Certainly it has been the dominant view for the majority of the previous generation both in American anthropology and sociology and in British social anthropology. Despite serious shortcomings, normative-functionalist theory represents an enormous advance over premodern sociology in certain fundamental respects that we must appreciate in order to appraise it adequately.

Before the twentieth century, theories of societal unity and integration floundered between two unsatisfactory poles. One pole was represented by what might be called the atomistic model. Here society appears in essence as a voluntary association: an aggregate of uniquely discrete individuals, each with a "mind" and, perhaps, a God-given immortal soul. These individuals, collectively and more or less deliberately, create their society much as a group of people organize a private club. They are, therefore, capable of altering it at will.

The assumptions of this model are most explicitly developed in classical Anglo-Saxon political theory and economics, but the ideas which it embodies have deep historical roots in Christian religious conceptions of the nature of man and his relation to God, and, somewhat farther back in time, in Stoic philosophy and Roman law. It is, perhaps we need hardly add, the fundamental conception of society which laymen to this day possess in most Western countries.

The atomistic model of society is philosophically nominalistic in character and inspiration. The second and contrasting model, on the other hand, rests upon an idealistic construction of reality. Here society is seen as primary to the individual in both a moral and a substantive sense: it is identified with a larger "mind," "spirit," or "soul" which transcends the individual and within which he has his being. German social philosophy from Fichte to Spengler provides abundant examples, but the philosophical idealism upon which social realism rests is anciently rooted in a long and highly respectable tradition.

It is easy enough from a modern perspective to see that each of these great traditions seized upon one facet of social reality and ignored the other. The atomistic model stressed what we would now call functional interdependence. From this point of view, the bond

4. See pp. 391–93.

holding men together in groups is no great mystery. It is nothing more nor less than stark necessity. Like it or not, and irrespective of whether they fully appreciate what they are doing, men must cooperate in order to achieve a human life. But social unity is obviously rather more complicated than cooperation in terms of sheer self-interest. And it is upon this truth that the social realists seized—somewhat clumsily, to be sure. They knew intuitively that "mind" is not to be grasped as isolated individual experience, although in the absence of an adequate social psychology they were unable to express this insight in other than mystical terms.

What is lacking in both of these classical conceptions of social unity and integration is an adequate grasp of human nature and human mentality in both its individual and social forms. A solution to this problem—the combined fruit of modern anthropology, social psychology, and sociology—was not available until well into the twentieth century.

The key came with the *modern* conception of culture.[5] By showing how individual mind and behavior may be understood in terms of a historically evolved tradition, carried and maintained collectively in the group through the mechanism of symbolic communication, the concept of culture provided for the first time a reasonably adequate explanation of how man can be a unique individual in both the biological and psychological senses and at the same time a profoundly social animal utterly dependent spiritually upon the group. In effect, therefore, the concept of culture thus transcended the dilemma posed by the classical theories of human nature and social order.

The normative-functionalist conception of society is built directly upon this radically new perspective of human nature. Linton provides us with the simplest and most straightforward definition in these terms: a society is the largest aggregate of people who organize their daily lives according to the patterns of a distinctive culture,[6] "patterns" and "distinctive" being the key terms. Culture cannot

5. Like all ideas of comparable complexity, the concept of culture has a long developmental history. In its present technical form, however, it clearly does not antedate the first decades of the twentieth century. See A. L. Kroeber and Clyde Kluckhohn, *Culture: A Critical Review of Concepts and Definitions* (New York, Vintage Books, 1963), particularly pp. 81–154.

6. Ralph Linton, *The Cultural Background of Personality* (New York, Appleton-Century, 1945). Ralph Linton, *The Study of Man: An Introduction* (New York, Appleton-Century, 1936).

exist as a mass of unrelated bits and pieces; by the nature of its own internal dynamics, it can only exist in units with some degree of internal consistency and integration. Existentially, in the last analysis, nothing more than a set of mental patterns, culture can only exist if it is carried and maintained by an organized group, sufficient in size and internal diversity to perform all the patterns present and to transmit them to the next generation. This inclusive group, wherein relationships between individuals are organized and defined by participation in a common, integrated culture, is *society* in the modern view.

It is especially important in the present context to recognize that the normative-functionalist model of society was developed primarily by the first generation of scientific field ethnologists, and within the context of a particular set of problems and working conditions. The conception of culture held by the previous generation of classical anthropologists—Bachhofen, Morgan, Tylor, Maine, Lippert, et al—was more or less traditional. They saw culture as a single (but not necessarily "integrated") unit, as the collective experiential heritage of mankind in its totality, and they studied it in the library by the classical comparative method.

When firsthand investigation became the approved method of ethnological study in the following generation, attention was necessarily focused intensively upon one cultural group at a time. The ethnologist thus became expert in that culture and could more easily appreciate its distinctive features vis-à-vis others which non-experts commonly assumed were either similar or identical. He was helped in this way to the conclusion that what in fact he was dealing with was not "culture" in the older unitary sense—the heritage-of-mankind idea—but isolates of historical phenomena that were in an important way true "wholes" in and of themselves.[7] When Radcliffe-Brown and Malinowski began insisting that these isolates were not merely descriptive and classificatory conveniences but integrated entities with a historical and existential autonomy of their own, the transition from the older unitary to the newer pluralistic functionalist view of culture was completed.

Principally a product of the new twentieth-century scientific

7. Of the several available reviews of this development, perhaps none is superior to that of Robert Redfield in his *Peasant Society and Culture: An Anthropological Approach to Civilization* (Chicago, University of Chicago Press, 1956), pp. 1–34.

ethnology, the normative-functionalist model of society was adopted eagerly and enthusiastically by sociologists once they were exposed to it.[8] The model has great virtues. With it the sociologist could do what he could not do so satisfactorily before: namely, specify in plausible detail what society existentially is, how it is put together and maintained, and how it shapes and motivates its individual members. Furthermore, the normative-functionalist model can be applied empirically with relative ease. With a bit of diligent effort, the basic values constituting the underlying institutional structure of any reasonably homogeneous cultural group can be uncovered, described in outline form, and the interconnections between and among these values indicated. By making the large but inherently plausible assumption *that values determine social relationships in concrete groups,* a convincing picture of the overall structure of a society can be sketched—a picture, incidentally, which cannot otherwise be so easily achieved, considering that any large social system is in detail almost incredibly complicated. Concentrating upon basic institutional norms rather than upon social relationships provides the high level of abstraction and generalization necessary to describe a whole society. With these impressive virtues in its favor, it is small wonder that the normative-functionalist model came to dominate sociological thought and effort for a generation.

Dissent from and dissatisfaction with certain of the implicit and explicit assumptions of normative-functionalist theory are nonetheless being heard in an ever-rising crescendo from sociologists and particularly from those engaged firsthand in the study of concrete

---

8. Sumner clearly offered a precursor to normative-functionalist social theory in his now classic *Folkways* (Boston, Ginn, 1906), a fact recognized by Malinowski—a man not in the habit of lightly acknowledging intellectual equals. However, Sumner did not himself use the term "culture," preferring instead "folkways" and "mores." The first American sociologist to use the culture concept self-consciously for theoretical analysis seems to have been W. F. Ogburn in *Social Change: With Respect to Culture and Original Nature* (New York, Huebsch, 1922). On this assessment, cf. Kroeber and Kluckhohn, p. 24. The first important empirical study in American sociology to use a normative interpretation of society is by Robert S. Lynd and Helen M. Lynd, *Middletown: A Study in American Culture* (New York, Harcourt, Brace, 1929). Data for this famous work were collected by social survey techniques; but what saved it from becoming simply one more social survey report among the hundreds already in existence was its application of the culture concept, for which the Lynds were indebted directly and personally to Clark Wissler. On Wissler's importance in establishing a modern, analytical concept of culture among anthropologists, see Kroeber and Kluckhohn, pp. 291–310.

social organizations. The normative-functionalist model of what a society is like, it is constantly pointed out, makes no adequate provision for conflict (in either the social or cultural sense), for change (or, perhaps more accurately, for certain kinds of change), or for the role of power and coercion in societal integration.[9]

Looking backward into the developmental history of sociology, however, we see something of great significance. All of these missing elements served in one form or another as the cornerstone of classical sociological systems. The sociologists of the nineteenth and early twentieth centuries worked prior to the development of the concept of culture, and for this reason their conceptions of society are vitiated without exception by obsolete notions of human nature. Yet, paradoxically, the best of them are more congruent in certain fundamental respects with social reality as we know it than are

9. Of the theoretical critiques, perhaps none is more incisive than that of Ralf Dahrendorf; see his *Class and Class Conflict in Industrial Society* (Stanford, Stanford University Press, 1959), particularly pp. 157–240, and his widely cited paper, "Out of Utopia: Toward a Reorientation of Sociological Analysis," *American Journal of Sociology, 64* (1958), 115–27. Dahrendorf acknowledges the influence of David Lockwood, who made many of the same points in an earlier review article on Parsons, "Some Remarks on 'The Social System,'" *British Journal of Sociology, 7* (1956), 134–46. Pierre L. van den Berghe attempts a reconciliation of "conflict theory" and "functionalism" in an important paper, "Dialectic and Functionalism: Toward a Theoretical Synthesis," *American Sociological Review, 28* (1963), 695–705.

It would be a mistake, however, to conclude that all criticism of normative-functionalist theory and methodological procedure is confined to the last few years, important as recent comment has been in sharpening the issues. Of special interest to us are the older criticisms that stem from firsthand acquaintance with modern southern Africa. See Max Gluckman, particularly *Analysis of a Social Situation in Modern Zululand,* Rhodes-Livingstone Paper No. 28 (Manchester, 1958), first published in *Bantu Studies, 14* (1940), and "Malinowski's 'Functional' Analysis of Social Change," *Africa, 17* (1947), 103–21. Gluckman's "situational" alternative to functionalism is reflected in the work of his students and associates, e.g. J. C. Mitchell, *The Kalela Dance,* Rhodes-Livingstone Paper No. 27 (Manchester, 1956), and A. L. Epstein, *Politics in an Urban African Community* (Manchester, Manchester University Press, 1958). While less polemically antifunctionalist, an interesting and valiant effort to create a viable alternative framework for the interpretation of modern African society was also produced (in collaboration with his wife) by the first director of the Rhodes-Livingstone Institute: Godfrey and Monica Wilson, *The Analysis of Social Change* (London, Cambridge University Press, 1945).

Ideas certainly have histories to a large extent independent of geographic locale. Yet we tend to see something of broader significance in this concentration of antifunctionalists among scholars with field experience in southern Africa. Society in this region, we take it, is just not very amenable to functional analysis.

normative-functionalist concepts. The reason seems to lie in good part in the circumstances under which the basic postulates of classical sociology were developed. Unlike the anthropologists of a generation or so later, pioneer sociologists were intensely interested in the modern world, and it was this world that they had in mind, rather than the tiny primitive isolate, when they sat down and attempted a statement of what society is like.

The normative-functionalist model fits nicely (we are told) the small isolated primitive group where it was first systematically worked out and applied. Such societies are homogeneous in both the social and cultural senses: there is one society and one culture, and the two fit tightly together, as Radcliffe-Brown and Malinowski insisted. Unless traumatically affected from the outside, neither ideas nor social forms change perceptibly from one generation to another. There is little conflict at the institutional level since there are few alternative patterns of behavior and none acceptable for really important matters. What internal conflict exists is personal; being socially as well as culturally homogeneous, the primitive isolate has no strata or interest groups in the modern sense. In short, the institutional norms are firmly and clearly established: they have that appearance of solidity and permanence inevitably suggested by the term "structure," a favorite of the social anthropologist.

In any modern society the observer gets a very different impression. Here he sees behavior that is easily recognizable as cultural in nature and origin. But he does not see (unless he wears a particularly efficient pair of functionalist blinders) *a* culture in a unitary sense. Variability in response and conflict in norms and values constantly appear. Above all, there is the fact of *group* (as opposed to strictly individual) conflict. And there is the overriding fact of relatively rapid change through time. Whatever structure a modern society has at any given moment, it is certain not to be that of the next generation.

In all these respects, the best of the classical sociologies represent modern society better than normative-functionalist theory does. A basic reason for this superiority in handling conflict and change lies in the fact that they stress process rather than form. Society has structure; but structure is achieved and maintained dynamically by a set of forces operating through time. In Adam Smith's thought, for example, social unity and integration is seen as an outgrowth of the division of labor. Men create society by acts of rational choice and decision; but the rationality of human action is limited and functionally specific. Individual acts, rationally guided to limits of human capability, coalesce at an unplanned, unpremeditated, and largely unconscious level to produce the social order, which functions like a well-oiled machine if only it is let alone. According to Marx, social order appears as a product not of the benevolent unseen hand of individual competition in self-interest but of tension and conflict between opposing interest groups—the historically created social classes, which represent phases of universal sociocultural evolution. In the writings of Simmel, the old notion that unity grows out of conflict and competition is given a more modern and more strictly sociological treatment. Thus the present day sociologist turns to Simmel for the prototypical statement of the role of conflict in the creation of social order.[10]

Dynamic conceptions of society such as those of Marx and Adam Smith have in common the fact that they stress the role of functional interdependence in the creation and maintenance of unity, rather than consensus based upon common norms and values in the manner of modern normative-functionalist theory. Both consensus and functional interdependence are recognized in another classical approach to the problem of social integration, but these are seen as phases of an evolutionary sequence. The work of Toennies provides the representative example. Consensus is seen as the dominant integrative factor in primitive and peasant societies: here social unity rests upon *Gemeinschaft* principles. In industrial, urban society, however, social unity depends upon rationally calculated self-interest, expressed and guaranteed impersonally by contract. The social relations between the ethnic groups of Furnivall's "plural society," based solely as they are upon the marketplace, represent a virtually pure case of *Gesellschaft* in Toennies' terminology.

A variant of Toennies-type theory developed by Robert E. Park to account for the organization and integration of the modern urban community is of particular interest, since it parallels so directly the unity problem of a plural society. The Chicago of 1910 that Park described was, in Furnivall's terms, a "medley of peoples" drawn from the four corners of the earth and they manifested in their daily lives a crazy-quilt patchwork of dress, language, and custom.

10. Cf. Lewis Coser, *The Functions of Social Conflict* (Glencoe, Ill., Free Press, 1956).

Yet it was not the diversity of Chicago which fascinated Park when he considered this scene: rather it was the *unity in diversity*.[11]

The astonishing fact to Park was that this great heterogeneous mass of more than two million people organized itself somehow into a living community. Obviously, the organizing principle could not be consensus; insofar as Park could see, there was no overall consensus. This did not mean that consensus did not exist. If one looked within any of the numerous ethnic communities which in the aggregate made up Chicago—the "ghettoes," the "Bohemias," the "little Italies," or the "little Polands"—he found a system of social order that could be understood only in terms of consensus. In these ethnic enclaves, order was based upon moral norms shared by the community and enforced by its members, and these norms clearly had their origin in the traditional culture of the group. But if one sought the unity lying beyond and among these little moral communities, how was it to be accounted for? Superficial impressions to the contrary, all was not chaos. Obviously, there was a larger impersonal order by which the city lived and worked and grew.

Adam Smith would have explained this larger unity in terms of the division of labor, that is, in terms of functional interdependence. Toennies would have added his *Gesellschaft* principles of rationality and contract. Park, however, had been reading in the new science of plant ecology. When he looked at Chicago, he saw a parallel between the biotic community described by the ecologists and the human community of Chicago that seemed to give this whole matter of integration through functional interdependence a deeper, more organic significance. The ecologists had convincingly shown that all living things, and not simply human beings alone, live in intricate systems of mutual interdependence, in short, in what ecologists themselves described as "communities" or "societies." Could it not then be, perhaps, that those functional relationships within the human community which lie beyond consensus (and thus the boundaries of conscious awareness and control) are simply projections of this universal, biologically determined order?

If this were true, then sociologists need to recognize two fundamentally different foundations for social organization and structure:

11. Park's papers on human ecology have recently been collected in a single volume: Robert E. Park, *Human Communities: The City and Human Ecology* (Glencoe, Ill., Free Press, 1952).

(1) a strictly and uniquely human level of *moral order* based upon communication and normative consensus, and (2) a largely unconscious, unrecognized substratum of *ecological order* shared with the non-human species. To this ecological order, founded in the fundamentally biological principles of competition and blind cooperation, Park attributed most of the overall unity which he saw in the diversity of the modern urban community.

Our understanding of human nature and behavior has changed—hopefully, it has advanced—since Park's day. Modern students reject as completely outdated the notion that a large proportion of human social behavior is to be understood in primarily biological terms. Yet the theoretical issue Park raised and so forcefully stated in his ecological theory—namely, the basis, character, and mechanisms of that portion of societal integration which lies beyond normative control—remains curiously neglected in current sociological conceptions. The issue was bypassed rather than solved by the adoption of the normative-functionalist model of society, which interprets social integration almost entirely in terms of consensus.

NORMATIVE-FUNCTIONALIST THEORY AND THE CONCEPT OF PLURAL SOCIETY

This in fact is the theoretical problem posed by Furnivall's plural society. A plural society built upon consensus is a contradiction in terms. What then is its mode of integration? When we ask this question, we are left with exactly the same problem as that with which Park struggled. Despite the widely voiced dissatisfaction with normative-functionalist theory, no comprehensive alternative theory of social order of comparable simplicity and clarity, which is applicable to whole societies, has arisen to take its place.[12]

12. Significantly, much of the current dissatisfaction with normative-functionalist theory stems from what, for the lack of a better term, may be called "organizational" studies; by its nature, this work is limited and concrete rather than comprehensively theoretical. The empirical research of such varied sociologists as William F. Whyte, Peter M. Blau, and Erving Goffman provides examples: detailed analyses of "corner" boys, work groups, hospital wards, etc. A systematic review of these studies would show, we believe, that the best of them developed more or less independently of—but not in the first instance in self-conscious opposition to—normative-functionalist theory. But such a review would also show how the evidence from this type of research has cumulatively helped to reveal the serious limitations of a strictly normative, consensual interpretation of group structure and processes. See,

The most elaborate and successful attempt at a theoretical formulation of plural society since Furnivall has been contributed by M. G. Smith.[13] While retaining a normative-functionalist orientation, Smith's analysis nonetheless begins with a radical departure from the usual assumptions. "The modern view of society," he points out, "implies that a culture and a society are always coterminous and interdependent." Yet even the most cursory review of the modern world reveals that this cannot literally be true. By this measure all societies should be unitary in culture, while patently they are not. All modern social systems are socially and culturally heterogeneous to some degree; the range is from relatively slight demarcations by class to the deep and fundamental ethnic divisions characteristic of the "medley of peoples." Social theory, if it is to apply to the modern world, must account for this wide variation in structure. Smith's answer is a typology that distinguishes between homogeneous, heterogeneous, and plural societies, showing how society and culture are related in each of these basic types.

This task is accomplished by drawing a distinction between "core" ("basic" or "compulsory") institutions and "exclusive" ("alternative" or "specialist") patterns. The original idea goes back to Linton; but the particular formulation which Smith adopts is that of Nadel, who synthesized Linton's analysis of differential participation in culture with a Malinowskian conception of institutions that has long been more or less standard in British social anthropology.[14] As both Linton and Nadel point out, a distinction of this sort is needed to account for differential cultural participation in even the simplest society; in no society does everyone participate in the total

for example, Whyte's biting comments upon Parsons' contributions to organizational theory, "Parsons' Theory Applied to Organizations" in Max Black, ed., *The Social Theories of Talcott Parsons: A Critical Examination* (Englewood Cliffs, N. J., Prentice-Hall, 1961), pp. 250–67.

The evolution of the thinking of George C. Homans, who has repeatedly synthesized and interpreted organizational studies, is instructive. In *The Human Group* (New York, Harcourt, Brace, 1950), Homans tried hard to be a fairly orthodox functionalist. In *Social Behavior: Its Elementary Forms,* he completely abandons the effort and embraces an "exchange" theory of social relations which he shares with Blau.

13. M. G. Smith, "Social and Cultural Pluralism," *Annals of the New York Academy of Sciences, 83* (1960), 763–77; reprinted in Pierre L. van den Berghe, ed., *Africa: Social Problems of Change and Conflict* (San Francisco, Chandler, 1965), pp. 58–76.

14. S. F. Nadel, *The Foundations of Social Anthropology* (London, Cohen and West, 1951), pp. 118–23.

culture in the same way or to the same degree. The term "common culture" is therefore always a misnomer if applied literally to what people actually do. If nothing else, differences in sex and age guarantee some diversity of pattern. Furthermore, there are alternative means for satisfying the same general needs in all societies. Thus the phrase "common culture" must mean, if it means anything, only the "universal" or "core" patterns understood (and to some extent practiced) by fully socialized members of the entire group. It cannot literally mean that everyone either thinks or acts in exactly the same way.

Smith is thus able to show that a society need not be culturally homogeneous in order to constitute a single social unit. A homogeneous society is defined as one in which members share a single set of institutions. A heterogeneous society is one in which the "core" institutions are shared by a variety of class and ethnic groups, each of which maintains at the same time distinctive "exclusive" (or "alternative") institutions of its own. *A plural society is one united politically under the aegis of a single national government, but which contains substantially important groups who differ from one another not only in their alternative but also in their core institutions.*

Obviously, the concept of "core" institution is the key to the entire typology; fundamentally, therefore, Smith's conception of plural society remains an institutional or normative one. As examples of what he means by core (or basic) institutions, Smith lists "kinship, education, religion, property and economy, recreation, and certain sodalities." Government, however, is pointedly excluded from this list: "The continuity of such societies as units is incompatible with an internal diversity of governmental institutions." In the pure case, a common government is therefore the only unity which a plural society has. Without this crucial dimension of integration, the plural society would dissolve into its culturally component groups.

The same logic drives Smith to virtually identify "society" with the national state or its equivalent in dependent areas. "In my view," he writes, "only territorially distinct units having their own governmental institutions can be regarded as societies, or are in fact so regarded." This is indeed a radical and highly arbitrary solution to the problem of deciding what a society is, apart from its culture. Yet it serves Smith well since it allows him to do what he otherwise could not do: namely, to apply institutional theory originally devel-

392

oped to describe and interpret primitive social systems where culture and group coincide to modern ones where they do not.

The paradox of plural society is that which fascinated Park in the modern urban community: its unity in diversity. Smith's approach provides clear and concise guideposts in the search for both unity and diversity, and his typology establishes some benchmarks to measure the results. His analysis therefore constitutes a clear-cut advance over all previous attempts to make sense out of this particular form of social structure.[15] In particular, his distinction between heterogeneous and plural societies appears to be a fruitful one, granting the assumption that it is wise to talk about plural societies at all. Consistently applied, it provides a solution to a quandary into which nearly all of his predecessors floundered: the interpretation to be made of class, race, and ethnic group phenomena in this context. A fundamental confusion on this point has caused many commentators to call the United States a plural society, and one has gone so far as to suggest that the concept might even be applied to Great Britain, by any reasonable standard one of the most thoroughly integrated large countries in the world.[16]

But good as it is in these respects, Smith's conception of plural society still does not escape the serious flaws and limitations inherent in normative-functionalist theory. He sees something of the basic problem and even hints at its solution in his insistence that society

15. Important contributions to the theory of plural society, with direct applications to southern Africa, have appeared since this appendix was originally drafted. See, in particular, two papers by Pierre L. van den Berghe, "Dialectic and Functionalism," and also "Toward a Sociology of Africa," *Social Forces,* *43* (1964), 11–18; and one by Leo Kuper, "Some Aspects of Urban Plural Societies in Africa," in *The African World: A Survey of Social Research,* Robert A. Lystad, ed. (New York, Frederick A. Praeger, 1965), pp. 107–30. Kuper further elaborates the concept of pluralism in an attempt to make it more useful analytically; he, like Smith and ourselves, stresses the necessity of carefully separating social and cultural components in such situations. Van den Berghe parallels in good part our own critique of functionalism; he, however, attacks the problem in a rather different way and arrives at somewhat different conclusions. Both of these scholars, it seems fair to say, see more diversity and less unity in the structure of southern African society than we do.

16. Cf. John Rex, "The Plural Society in Sociological Theory," *British Journal of Sociology, 10* (1959), 114–24. In fairness to Rex, it should be added that the main point of his article is the error of overemphasis upon consensus at the expense of conflict. "The study of plural societies . . . draws attention to the fact that social systems do exist in which conflict is more obvious than consensus" (p. 124).

and culture are not necessarily coterminous as they are usually made out to be. Yet he never comes to grips with the theoretical implications inherent in the separation that he proposes, apparently because the institutional theory to which he remains wedded makes no provision for this separation. On the contrary, it insists that culture and society, if not quite the same thing, are tightly and irrevocably interrelated. The separation that Smith makes between society and culture is a superficial and arbitrary one; it forces him to identify society with one of its own institutions—the national state. His position, therefore, remains "the modern view," as he himself states clearly enough. "To define the social structure we must . . . analyze the institutional system . . . [and] to define a system of social value or action, we must identify and analyze the institutional framework." Thus in the end we are left to go round and round on this issue as in all normative-functionalist theory.

More fundamentally, Smith's conception of plural society shares another common characteristic of the normative approach to social phenomena: it is static and lifeless, a descriptive categorization rather than an analysis of process. We are not told how or why plural society comes into existence, how it is maintained, why it changes into heterogeneous society, or by what steps. To break out of this box, a more dynamic, less abstract, and more realistic conception of society is clearly needed.

Where, for example, are the homogeneous societies postulated in Smith's typology as empirical entities? To ask the question is to answer it: there are in fact *no* unitary societies in the modern world as defined by the one-culture-one-society formula. There are no homogeneous societies for one good and sufficient reason: all non-European societies have been either overrun socially by Europeans or had their cultures heavily influenced by that of the Europeans. Homogeneous society is thus a strictly historical phenomenon, a fact not made clear in Smith's presentation.

More directly to the point, where indeed are the plural societies, those distinguishable from heterogeneous societies in the manner which Smith suggests? On the basis of his own list of core institutions (kinship, education, religion, property, etc.), an examination of the existing culture of almost any non-European group reveals that these institutions, one and all, are permeated to a greater or lesser degree by norms and values of specifically European origin.[17]

17. Few sociologists and anthropologists are likely to question the enormous

Again, the lesson is noted: as in the case of unitary society, plural society makes a certain amount of sense if placed within a historical perspective. Truly distinctive core institutions, as Smith uses the term, are thus past, not present, reality. Even in such a remote corner of the world as modern Central Africa, there is no evidence that pristine core institutions still exist. It necessarily follows, if this is true, that Smith's conception of plural society becomes vitiated, *except as a stage or phase in evolutionary history.*

AN EVOLUTIONARY ALTERNATIVE TO PLURAL SOCIETY

In briefest outline, the essentials of a broadly evolutionary perspective upon ethnic group phenomena were sketched in the first chapter of this volume.[18] The discussion which follows spells out in greater detail some of the theoretical assumptions implicit in this point of view. The issues are unavoidably complex; even an extended statement therefore must remain elliptical and dogmatic.

---

diffusion of European traits into non-European cultures as an empirical observation. Many, however, will insist that non-European cultures may remain very different in pattern and value emphasis—and for this reason highly distinctive units—despite extensive but superficial europeanization. "Core" institutions, it will therefore be argued, may remain essentially what they always have been, profoundly non-European. As former students of Ralph Linton, we can hardly be charged with ignorance concerning the important distinction to be drawn between form and content in cultural analysis. Furthermore, our study makes a good deal of use of a closely related (and now widely recognized) principle: that ethnic group *identity* may remain a powerful determinant in social organization after virtually complete acculturation. Cf. Patrick Moynihan and Nathan Glazer, *Beyond the Melting Pot: The Negroes, Puerto Ricans, Jews, Italians, and Irish of New York City* (Cambridge, M. I. T. and Harvard University Presses, 1963); and Milton M. Gordon, *Assimilation in American Life: The Role of Race, Religion and National Origins* (New York, Oxford University Press, 1964). We nonetheless believe that both the extent and functional significance of europeanization has been both underestimated and misinterpreted by social scientists who have, in a sense, overlearned their normative-functionalist theory. Those who discount the amount of europeanization which has taken place commonly (and mistakenly) think of it as something that occurs mainly at the material or technological level—a curious position, incidentally, if one is a committed functionalist. As demonstrated from our own material, the most significant borrowing is in fact moral. Those who believe that cultural content can be replaced by foreign traits without affecting original institutional forms have a unitary, asocial view of culture which, as we have tried to show, is very different from our own.

18. See above, pp. 5–10.

Both to sharpen the issues and to point the discussion in the desired direction, the argument will be presented in terms of a series of interrelated propositions concerning the nature of society, culture, the socio-cultural process, power, ethnic group conflict, and the national state.[19] Listed, these are:

1. Society is prior to culture.
2. Culture is adaptive and instrumental.
3. All cultures are adaptive, but not all cultures are equally adaptive. This is the cultural base for differential social power among ethnic groups and societies.
4. Cultural superiority has historically expressed itself socially in interethnic relations as dominance.
5. European imperialism has led to a europeanization-of-the-world culturally.
6. Nationalism represents an emergent form of societal integration at the world political level.
7. The new national state creates new majority-minority relations and establishes the basis for continued ethnic conflict.

1. Society is prior to culture. An accurate statement of the relationship between the social and the cultural components of human behavior has proved a vexatious problem for sociological theory. Yet it cannot be avoided if we are to understand with any degree of theoretical sophistication the phenomenon of plural society. Here we agree with Smith: analysis of ethnic relations in such contexts must proceed from a recognition that society and culture are not coterminous. We find it necessary, however, to take a step beyond Smith and baldly assert for its heuristic value the evolutionary and historical precedence of social processes over cultural ones.[20]

19. Purists would restrict the term "theory" to mean in social science what it means in natural science: that is, a body of interrelated propositions, hierarchically ordered with respect to generality, logically tight throughout, and supported empirically by data controlled to some approximation of laboratory standards. See George C. Homans, "Contemporary Theory in Sociology," in *Handbook of Modern Sociology,* ed. Robert E. L. Faris, pp. 951–77, for a rigorous presentation of this point of view. There is, needless to say, very little such theory in sociology or the other social sciences. Most social scientists necessarily use "theory" in a much looser sense, as we do here, to refer to the body of descriptive and interpretive concepts historically developed within their disciplines, together with the more or less accepted empirical generalizations made in terms of these concepts. Cf. S. F. Nadel, *The Theory of Social Structure* (Glencoe, Ill., Free Press, 1957), pp. 1–2.

20. No one questions that in human evolution the protohuman was a social

Obviously, such a proposition is nonsense if "society" is reduced, as it tends to be in normative theory, to its cultural definition. The distinction between the social and cultural must be made at the analytical, not the concrete, level. In concrete behavior they are locked together in inextricable union. Both are in fact conceptual abstractions from a common empirical phenomenon: the acts in thought and deed of men. In short, they are two dimensions of the same thing. One dimension points to the active, interactional *process* of communication and response through which human individuals are related to other individuals in organized groups. The other dimension is reduced ultimately to the mental *content* consciously and unconsciously present in the "minds" of these individuals.

It is quite true that human social processes always involve cultural content. Such content is indeed the stuff of interaction. Its forms and character thereby set irrevocable limitations and conditions upon the potentialities for action. Furthermore, it is also true that, under all but the most unusual circumstances, "ego" and "alter" (in Parsonian terms) approach each other through normatively defined channels and appraise each other in the ensuing confrontation by previously established values.

It is nonetheless becoming increasingly clearer to social scientists who reflect seriously upon what they empirically know about defining norms on the one hand and behavioral acts on the other that the relationship between the two *is never rigidly determined,* as it would be in a straightforwardly consistent normative theory of behavior.[21] Otherwise, there would be no such thing as conflict and change; and conflict and change are ubiquitous features of the human scene. Clearly, the locus of conflict and change must be sought

---

animal before he was a cultural one. Ontogenetically too, the human infant is a social animal before he is a cultural one; he interacts with others socially before he acquires culture. Furthermore, the historical evidence unambiguously shows that peoples of the most diverse cultures interacted upon first contact with one another; they did not wait until they had acquired a body of shared norms.

21. Goode, for example, has recently and cogently argued that the individual *cannot* follow the norms of his society in anything like a literal sense, being prevented from doing so by inherent role conflict. William J. Goode, "A Theory of Role Strains," *American Sociological Review, 25* (1960), 483–96. See also the highly significant article (considering who the authors are by their previous theoretical predilections) by Judith Blake and Kingsley Davis, "Norms, Values, and Sanctions," in Faris, ed., *Handbook of Modern Sociology,* pp. 456–84.

in the active social process. It cannot be found in cultural content per se, which is unable by its very nature, to change itself.[22] This point has often been insisted upon recently, but for emphasis and clarity let us insist upon it once more: "cultures" and "social systems" cannot actually *do* anything. To talk loosely as if they can is to court the ever present and serious danger of reification.[23] Only biological organisms in the form of human individuals have either the physical equipment or the requisite energy to act and think.

The basic model of society which is most consistent with these realities of behavior appears to be the older, prenormative one of *any aggregate of interacting individuals:* human individuals in their biologically concrete forms, brought together by fate and history to live out their lives in cooperation, conflict, and competition. However molded, limited, directed, and controlled these individuals are by preexisting cultural content, their behavior patently cannot be reduced to its forms. Society conceived as an interactive process is thus clearly more elementary and fundamental than culture conceived as form. It is in this sense, and in this sense only, that society is prior to culture; but the proposition is nonetheless necessary if we are to understand conflict and change.

22. This is the logical trap set by normative-functionalist theory. "Culture" and culturally-derived conceptions of "societies" or "social systems" are very high order abstractions, indispensable for many analytical purposes, but constantly subject to the temptation of reification—even by those fully cognizant of the danger. Cf. Kroeber and Kluckhohn, *Culture*, p. 267. Since "whole societies" are most easily described by singling out major normative structures and their value anchorages for emphasis, the temptation to hypostatize the resulting scheme becomes all but irresistible.

To the degree that functionalist analysis is equated with systemic analysis at this high level of abstraction, we for this reason remain unimpressed with recent attempts to state a functionalist theory of change. The qualification is important, for "functionalism" is a slippery term at best. As Kingsley Davis has demonstrated in a now famous paper, there is a sense in which we are all functionalists: "The Myth of Functional Analysis as a Special Method in Sociology and Anthropology," *American Sociological Review, 24* (1959), 757–72. See also Neil Smelser, *Social Change in the Industrial Revolution: An Application of Theory to the British Cotton Industry* (Chicago, University of Chicago Press, 1959); Francesca Cancian, "Functional Analysis of Change," *American Sociological Review, 25* (1960), 818–27; and van den Berghe, "Dialectic and Functionalism."

23. Is it not perhaps significant of the renewed interest in this problem that the presidential addresses of both the American Anthropological Association and the American Sociological Association, in 1963 and 1964 respectively, should deal with this theme? Morris E. Opler, "The Human Being in Culture Theory," *American Anthropologist, 66* (1964), 507–28; and George C. Homans, "Bringing Men Back In," *American Sociological Review, 29* (1964), 809–18.

2. Culture is adaptive and instrumental. Some critics of normative theory and the methodological procedures based upon it have
dealt harshly with the concept of culture. Gerth and Mills, for example, charge that culture telescopes all explanation of human nature and behavior into a single concept, producing a spongy, all-
enveloping determinism. Since culture explains everything, in fact it
explains nothing; therefore, they argue, it should be dropped from
the vocabulary of serious theoretical dialogue.[24] Certainly "culture"
is a highly general term, but there is nothing wrong with general
terms per se; they are an indispensable part of all scientific theories.
The real difficulty, we believe, is not that the idea of culture is hopelessly spongy. Rather, as we have seen in our first proposition above,
the difficulty lies in the tendency to ascribe to culture an autonomy
which it does not possess.

Here as elsewhere an evolutionary perspective is helpful, indeed
necessary. Seen in the light of general evolution, culture is above all
instrumental; it is man's peculiar mechanism for survival. As such,
it comes to any concretely given group or individual from the past
in the form of mental content—a precipitant, as it has been called,
of history. It is determining in the negative and limiting sense that
known culture constitutes the only guide to action that either groups
or individuals have. Where no known alternative exists, the force
of custom may thus appear to have the kind of coercive irresistibility
attributed to it in Sumner's classic *Folkways.* But modern cultures
are all heterogeneous in content and thus pose many potential alternatives.

Through the exigencies of life in the modern world, both groups
and individuals constantly find themselves torn from familiar traditions and forced to survive in new social relationships with strangers
and foreigners who manifest in their daily lives different cultural
traditions. White settler, immigrant Indian shopkeeper, and tribal
African all found themselves in such inherently new social situations
in modern Central Africa. Yet the peculiar drama of their circumstances should not lead to an exaggeration of the uniqueness of their
situations. The German peasant moving from his ancestral village to
the Ruhr steel town of the last century, or the Polish immigrant

24. Cf. Hans Gerth and C. Wright Mills, *Character and Social Structure:
The Psychology of Social Institutions* (New York, Harcourt, Brace, 1953),
pp. xxii–xxiii.

taking passage to America, made a confrontation with the strange and the unfamiliar almost as violent.

What the observer sees under these circumstances is not a people being pressed willy-nilly into a cultural mold that has come down in unbroken continuity and wholeness from the past. What he sees is people constantly trying—almost desperately at times—to *use* their culture, the old and the newly acquired, to meet the problems which they face in their daily lives. They do not thereby escape the influence of the culture into which they were originally socialized, and of course that influence can be seen constantly. But neither do they passively accept their cultural heritage as an irresistible given, to be accommodated to at all costs. Placed in new social situations where the old does not fit, they search actively for the new that does.

Sifting and sorting, selecting the usable and discarding the outworn, the Indians of Central Africa as we have met them in this book continuously review what they have inherited from the past and are learning in the present, in a constant effort to meet the ever pressing needs presented by their life-conditions. Much of this adaptive effort is rational and highly self-conscious; much of it is also unconscious and non-rational—an almost random searching as of a rat in a maze.

To the extent that adaptive effort rises to the level of conscious awareness, it acquires a social definition as a "problem" to be solved through collective action. At this point the problem is transformed into a more or less rational "interest"; and the association organized around its focus becomes an interest group, actively promoting its "solution" in competition with other interest groups. In other words, culture becomes in this instrumental view *group policy* as opposed to the older, unitary notion of a "super-organic thing sui generis" governing the destinies of people from the past.[25]

By emphasizing the adaptive nature of culture, we should not leave the impression that all culture is necessarily adaptive or that this description adequately encompasses all that culture phenomenologically is. Quite clearly, for example, cultures *create* problems as well as solve them; and we are aware of the other long-standing critiques to which the concept of adaptation has been subjected.[26]

25. Cf. Anthony F. C. Wallace, *Culture and Personality* (New York, Random House, 1961), p. 28.
26. See the excellent critique of this particular way of looking at culture by Kroeber and Kluckhohn, pp. 108–11.

We still insist, nonetheless, that the main thrust of human life-striving can be usefully described as adaptive, as long as we keep firmly in mind what is meant by the word. In any case, it has been our contention that the observed behavior of ethnic groups in modern Central Africa makes a certain amount of sense in these terms. Alternative interpretations—systemic equilibrium theory, for example, or perhaps Moore's notion of "tension management"—might hypothetically be better. But if so, this remains to be demonstrated.[27]

3. *Cultures are adaptive, but not all cultures are equally adaptive. This is the cultural base for differential social power among ethnic groups and societies.* Culture is power in two senses. First, it is power in a more or less technical sense: the power to act, to do things, to achieve technically defined goals. Knowledge is power; without it man cannot do what he can with it. But, second, there is power in the narrowly sociological sense: power over men rather than things through skills of organization.[28] It is not as widely recognized as it might be that concrete social behavior inevitably involves both elements—the technical means to act and the socially organized power at the institutional level to direct and control action.

Yet it is a simple truth that superior means provides superior power in both senses, everything else being equal. An empirical social result, amply demonstrated by history, is that groups with superior cultures tend to assume dominant positions over groups with inferior cultures when they are brought together in interactive situations. Here hackles are certain to rise among some of our readers. We can almost hear the angry shouts: What do you mean by "superior" and "inferior" cultures? We mean exactly what we have said. In our opinion it is impossible to talk intelligently about the relations of ethnic groups to one another without explicitly recognizing the facts of cultural superiority and inferiority. Admittedly, such judgments are complicated matters demanding great care in their statement if serious distortion is to be avoided. Superior and inferior in what respects, precisely? That is the inevitable question.

In response, it can be said that the judgments of "superior" and "inferior" must of course always be made in terms of quite specific

27. Wilbert E. Moore, *Social Change* (Englewood Cliffs, N. J., Prentice-Hall, 1963), particularly pp. 10–11.
28. Romans and Zulus exemplify the principle: for the most part they were superior to their opponents organizationally, not technically. But the *pattern* for such organization is nonetheless cultural.

criteria. They cannot be made absolutely. According to the criteria and the standards chosen for judgment, perhaps all (or most) cultures are both superior and inferior in some respects to others. But if we are talking about power, as we are here, then argument over the relevant criteria and the applicable standard of judgment is greatly simplified. Whether and in what sense one group exercises power over another is an empirical fact fairly easily subjected to verification. If at the same time we remember that the exercise of power requires cultural *means*—that it is not just something which happens *in vacuo*—then we have encompassed all we intend in the third proposition.

Indisputably, societies and groups are (and have been) unequal in the means at their disposal to exercise power effectively, vis-à-vis one another. This we take to be bedrock reality, not to be obscured by argument over abstract questions of moral equity or comparative spiritual worth. Nor is it relevant when we are concerned solely with the cultural bases of social power to shift the argument to the biological level by pointing to the essential equality of all normal human beings in their *capacity* to acquire culture. With respect to existing cultural differences, abstract capacity in the biological sense is irrelevant.

The confusion between the empirical facts of behavior and their moral evaluation that muddies so much of social science thinking has long distorted thought upon problems involving differential power among societies and groups. Evolutionists of the Victorian period accepted our proposition explicitly; in this, as in other respects, the stance taken here resembles theirs. But they also equated—as we have no intention of doing—scientific, technological, and economic development with moral progress, and they unblushingly used these criteria as moral justification for imperialistic expansion.

Twentieth-century man has had plenty of reason to question this implicit equation; and, in particular, the generation of social scientists who immediately followed the Victorians were morally revolted by the wreckage wrought upon weaker peoples by European imperialism. In reaction they sought to substitute cultural relativism for the doctrine of superior and inferior cultures inherent in the older evolutionism. To this end they ceaselessly preached the dignity and worth of all ways of life, including the most primitive. This moral stance was considerably reinforced theoretically by the post-evolutionary doctrine of functionalism. Polygyny and headhunting, it could now be pointed out, make ethical sense when they are seen in their full cultural and social setting and can even be viewed with sympathy and understanding.

The strengths and weaknesses of cultural relativism as an ethic are irrelevant to our present argument. What is relevant is its effect upon a reading of history and consequent sociological generalization. What cultural relativism has done is to help obscure and misdirect analysis of ethnic conflict. "Whatever happens, we have got/The Maxim gun, and they have not . . ." may indeed be morally repugnant, as Chesterton intended to show it to be. But empirically and historically, the Maxim gun proved its superiority when tested against the spears and rawhide shields of Lobengula's warriors on the veld of Southern Rhodesia.[29] This proven superiority allowed a handful of Europeans to establish themselves in Central Africa, just as the same superiority had previously allowed them to establish themselves at will everywhere in the world of culturally weaker peoples since the time of Cortés.

There is no need to quarrel unduly over words. If it is objected that this is not cultural superiority but crude, raw power immorally or amorally directed, then we will not protest too much. The relevant point here is that plural society was thus created in Central Africa as elsewhere, and to ignore its true origins is to seriously prejudice its correct interpretation.

4. Cultural superiority has historically expressed itself socially in interethnic relations as dominance. Raw power, deliberately applied and directed, is an obvious and essential element in social life. But a good deal of power, and particularly that power expressed in ethnic relations, tends to be misunderstood and misinterpreted sociologically when conceived of in these terms. The error is to think of power primarily in terms of a conscious and rational manipulation of others toward predetermined ends of group- or self-interest. Power, however, is not necessarily as conscious and rational as this. It is often exercised not as a carefully weighed instrument wielded to a clearly envisaged end but as a kind of unconscious and unrecognized by-product of superiority in a field of common action. Following Park, we may call this kind of power "dominance."

Park derived both term and concept directly from his studies in biological ecology, in which the term dominant is applied to that

29. On the Matabele Wars of the 1890s in which automatic weapons played a prominent part, see Gann, *A History of Southern Rhodesia,* pp. 108–39.

species of plant or animal that by its presence within a common habitat structures the interdependent relations of the entire community of associated species.[30] Within the biotic community one species is dependent upon another in a variety of complex ways, but the relationships of mutual interdependence are inherently unequal and the dominant occupies a very special position within the total system. As its demands are primary, it takes freely the space, light, and food which it needs for survival without making important adjustments to the needs of other species. They, in contrast, must adjust not only to the common physical environment which all share but also as best they can to the dominant's presence, which in itself becomes the major factor in the subordinate species' life situation.

Now of course the biotic community is not the human community, and experience has abundantly proved that the analogy can be very misleading. Yet granting the uniqueness of the specifically human relationship, founded as it is upon symbolic communication and culture, the parallel between the forms of the biotic and human community is still often a striking one indeed. The analogy constantly forced itself upon our attention as we worked in Africa. The historical role of the European particularly seemed to fit the picture of ecological dominance drawn above, virtually without modification. The European arrived in Central Africa, took what land and resources he needed, and lived a life dictated by the original sociocultural norms he brought with him, virtually unrestrained by the other groups who shared the region with him. His life was not without struggle to be sure, but the opposition was obdurate nature—physical, biological, and human—not a socially organized will opposed to his. By contrast, all other groups were constrained not only by the physical and biological character of their common habitat but, above all, by the overriding presence of the dominant European whose will prevailed over theirs in any contest of interests.

Park, it will be recalled, drew a distinction between the moral and ecological orders in his discussion of social integration: it was precisely the amoral character of the latter which seemed to him subhuman and biological. But the same distinction can be made without this objectionable and unnecessary inference, if one approaches the ecological relationships typical of the plural society through the concept of dominance, defined as we seek to do here in terms of cul-

30. Cf. Frederic E. Clements and Victor E. Shelford, *Bio-Ecology* (New York, J. Wiley, 1939), pp. 238–39.

tural superiority and its results in social power. Insofar as it has the power to do so, one group can extend its control over another and incorporate this subordinate group into its system of social organization without incorporating it *morally*. Within the new social unit so created, two principles of integration now prevail that directly parallel Park's moral and ecological orders: the principle of moral integration through normative consensus within each of the two original communities, and the ecological principle based upon coercive force which now binds the two groups together into one functionally interdependent unit.

Relationships founded in moral consensus rest in the last analysis upon a special kind of equality, an equality that may be designated as *citizenship* in a moral community.[31] This equality is not of status in the ordinary sense, i.e. of wealth or class or prestige; it is in the mutually recognized right to judge the behavior of others by the moral standard common to the community and to get voluntary compliance in accordance with these judgments. The test is mutuality: moral integration by its very nature *cannot* be a one-way street with claims and compliances going all in one direction. For the essential element that defines coercion in sociologically relevant terms is that coercion *is* a one-way street with respect to claims and compliances. In the ultimate limiting case, the dominant claims and the subordinate complies.

It has long been recognized that there is one other possibility for social integration which may be largely if not quite completely amoral and thus ecological by our reckoning, namely, that of exchange. This is where Furnivall placed the emphasis in his plural society. People of the most diverse cultures will normally trade physical goods eagerly upon contact. Sociologically considered, such exchange is by definition mutual; if it is not, it is to that degree coercion, although often the two cannot be neatly separated empirically. Logically, in the limiting case, exchange does not demand a broader basis of moral consensus among the participants than the immediately perceivable situation, mutually defined entirely in terms of respective self-interest. "Alters" may or may not perceive each other as moral beings to whom obligation is owed outside of

31. Our use of "citizenship" in these terms derives primarily from Max Weber, *General Economic History*, pp. 233–49. See also Talcott Parsons, "Full Citizenship for the Negro American? A Sociological Problem," *Daedalus, 94* (1965), 1009–54.

the exchange relationship. They may of course, but the point is that they need not—and in the extreme case do not—for contact and interaction to take place.[32]

5. European imperialism has led to a europeanization-of-the-world culturally. The ethnic group and plural society appear in history as results of the imperialistic expansion of strong cultural groups over weaker ones. Upon this point the historical record is indisputably clear: at a certain stage in their development—a stage coinciding roughly with a sufficient degree of cultural and societal complexity to be called "civilization"—advanced societies have typically over-run their weaker neighbors.[33] Repeated within seemingly endless cycles, is it not perhaps too much to say that these processes of imperialistic expansion *are* history, sociologically, from Sargon the First through Queen Victoria?

This generalization should not be taken to imply that the imperialistic process is necessarily the same in all periods. Socio-cultural evolution, like other evolutionary processes, is irreversible and continuously "emergent." Each phase is historically specific and unique in detail and scale and is not to be compared without this fact in mind to any preceding one. Because of this emergent character it is a gross error to see relations between ethnic groups solely (or even primarily) in terms of the past—even the immediate past. At the same time the past cannot be forgotten.

The expansion of European peoples over the entire world during the past five hundred years is now complete and is a part of history which will not be repeated. From this point on, socio-cultural evolution can only take a very different direction. Yet in cultural terms, the imperialist phase of history dominated by Europeans takes on an enormous, incalculable significance. It has led to what can be called

32. Anthony F. C. Wallace has brilliantly attacked this classical problem of the relationship between social unity and consensus from a fresh perspective. Applying symbolic logic, he discusses it as a matter of culture and personality organization. At the minimal level, he concludes, the "cognitive maps" of participants in socio-cultural interaction demand "complementarity," not "conformity." "Cognitive sharing . . . [is not necessary] . . . for stable interaction. . . . The two parties . . . need not know what the 'motives' of their partners . . . are. Indeed, they need not even correctly know *who* their partners are." *Culture and Personality,* pp. 29–41.

33. See Ralph Turner, *The Great Cultural Traditions: The Foundations of Civilization* (New York, McGraw-Hill, 1941), for an elaborated theory of "urban imperialism" cast in terms of a sociologically sophisticated conception of culture, society, and the nature of the interrelationship between the two.

without fear of exaggeration a europeanization-of-the-world: the emergence of a new cosmopolitan world culture that is largely European in content and origin.[34]

When speaking of the europeanization-of-the-world, we do not wish to imply that cultural differences among societies have ceased to exist. Quite patently they have not. Nor, indeed, have these cultures necessarily lost their integrity as distinctive units, profoundly different in many respects from European ones. Concretely, the europeanization-of-the-world means that other cultures have been permeated with elements of European origin. Put in Smith's terms, the core institutions of every important cultural group in the world have been affected not only by European technology and its associated values but by an intrusion of specifically European *moral* values as well. Nationalism is the prime example.

6. Nationalism represents an emergent form of societal integration at the world political level. Nationalism is so radically new and so overwhelmingly important sociologically that it is indeed remarkable how it tends to be taken for granted—and, like all things taken for granted, ignored. In origin, it is strictly European but even in Europe it is a very recent phenomenon. Much of Europe, it will be remembered, was still organized on the basis of the prenational dynastic state up to World War I. A great many people still had little or no comprehension of the degree to which nationalism had penetrated East and Central Africa in the 1950s. Until the close of that decade, most of Africa was still formally under the control of the colonial powers; now virtually all of it is independent. The world's peoples, it is clear, have decided that the national state, organized at least in terms of lip-service to the principle of self-determination, is to be the political form of world order.

The new nationalism is of supreme importance to sociologists because it provides a now all but universal moral consensus for the legitimation of political institutions throughout the world. As a

34. Sociological generalizations as broad as these are apt to sound at best like pompous truisms. But truism or not, the point here is a basic one for the understanding of ethnic and race relations, much too often neglected. On the concept of "cosmopolitan world culture," we call to our support no less an authority than A. L. Kroeber: "What is of interest in this connection is the contemporary trend of other cultures to assimilate themselves to Occidental civilization, of Turks, Arabs, Indians, Chinese, and Japanese to 'Westernize' their ways of life and standards. Mankind has never before been essentially unitary in culture. It is not yet unitary; but at the moment, it is traveling fast that way." *Anthropology* (New York, Harcourt, Brace, 1948), p. 385.

socio-political principle, national self-determination is closely associated with other radically modern moral concepts, the general tendency of which may perhaps be best described as egalitarianism. Inherited status differences of all kinds are challenged as being unjust, whether these be the remaining privileges of the European nobility, the traditional rights and property of landlords in the Middle East or Latin America, caste in India, race in the United States, or hereditary chieftainships in Africa. Since the defeat of Nazi Germany, "democracy" has become a heavily laden value term carrying this notion of "equality," and nowhere more so than in the Communist countries. But this worldwide demand for social and cultural equality is no longer tied, as it was in the European countries of its origin, with the institutions of representative democracy. On the contrary, more often than not, the demand for greater equality and more national "freedom" is made by a highly authoritarian ruling elite with scant respect for civil liberties as these are understood in the advanced countries.

7. *The new national state creates new majority-minority relations and establishes the basis for continued ethnic conflict.* National self-determination, freedom, and democracy are exceedingly popular everywhere; they are, in short, the dominant moral values of the new worldwide cosmopolitan culture. Americans, in particular, support them enthusiastically; after all, they are in a special sense *our* values since Americans led the world in first putting them into practice.[35] And certainly it is fair to add that nowhere among Americans generally are these values more firmly held than among academic people.

These moral commitments probably explain better than anything else why the plight of minorities caught up in the cross fire of national liberation movements throughout the old colonial world has received little empirical attention and less sympathy from social scientists. That political freedom might not have the same meaning for all groups in an ethnically complicated society—and particularly one in the throes of extraordinarily difficult political and economic adjustments to the modern world—is a thought easily brushed aside in the onrush of enthusiastic moral approval of the new nationalism.

The ethnic minority appeared in history as a distinct social phe-

---

35. Cf. Seymour M. Lipset, *The First New Nation: The United States in Historical and Comparative Perspective* (New York, Basic Books, 1963).

nomenon only with the state.[36] The recent creation of a great many more states can scarcely have any other result than the concurrent creation of a great many more minority problems, although it is also true that relationships between dominant and subordinate groups in the new states will inevitably take a different form than in the advanced industrial countries since the total context is radically different. Sociologists concerned with minorities need have no fear that this area of human social life is about to disappear.

36. Cf. Charles Wagley and Marvin Harris, *Minorities in the New World: Six Case Studies* (New York, Columbia University Press, 1958), pp. 240–44.

BIBLIOGRAPHY

OFFICIAL PUBLICATIONS AND DOCUMENTS

Advisory Commission on the Review of the Constitution of Rhodesia and Nyasaland, *Report* [Monckton Commission Report, including Appendices I through V], Cmnd. 1148, London, Her Majesty's Stationery Office, 1960.
——, *Report: Appendix VI, Survey of Developments since 1953* (*Report by Committee of Officials*), Cmnd. 1149, London, Her Majesty's Stationery Office, 1960.
——, *Report: Appendix VII, Possible Constitutional Changes* (*Report by Committee of Officials*), Cmnd. 1150, London, Her Majesty's Stationery Office, 1960.
——, *Report: Appendix VIII, Evidence*, Cmnd. 1151, 1151-I-IV, 5 vols. London, Her Majesty's Stationery Office, 1960.
Bank of Zambia, *Report and Statement of Accounts for the Period August 7th 1964 to December 31st 1965*, 1965.
British South Africa Company, *Reports on the Administration of Rhodesia, 1897–1898*, Printed for the Information of Shareholders, [London] 1899.
——, *Reports on the Administration of Rhodesia, 1898–1900*, Printed for the Information of Shareholders, [London] no date.
——, *Reports on the Administration of Rhodesia (with Appendix)*, *1900–1902*, Printed for the Information of Shareholders, [London] 1903.
Central African Archives (later as National Archives), Salisbury, various documents.
Central African Statistical Office, *Economic and Statistical Bulletin for Northern Rhodesia, 5, 6* (1953–54), Salisbury.
——, *Statistical Handbook of Nyasaland, 1949*, Salisbury, Rhodesian Printing and Publishing Co.
Colonial Office, *Northern Rhodesia, Proposals for Constitutional Change; Presented to Parliament by the Secretary of State for the Colonies by Command of Her Majesty, February 1961*, Cmnd. 1295, London, Her Majesty's Stationery Office, 1961.

————, *Northern Rhodesia, Statement by the Secretary of State for the Colonies on Proposals for Constitutional Change; Presented by the Secretary of State for the Colonies by Command of Her Majesty, February 1961*, Cmnd. 1301, London, Her Majesty's Stationery Office, 1961.

————, *Nyasaland* [Annual Report, title varies], London, Her Majesty's Stationery Office.

————, *Report on Northern Rhodesia* [Annual Report], Lusaka, Government Printer.

Federation of Rhodesia and Nyasaland, *The Constitution of the Federation of Rhodesia and Nyasaland, Being the Federation of Rhodesia and Nyasaland (Constitution) Order in Council, 1953, as Amended by Acts of the Federal Legislature at the 1st September, 1959, Incorporating Relevant Papers and Indices, Reprinted for Information on the Authority of the Minister of Law*, Salisbury, Government Printer, 1959.

————, *Federal Roll of General Voters Entitled to Vote at Elections of Elected Members and Elected African Members of the Federal Assembly, 1958, Lusaka West, Lusaka East, Lusaka Rural*, Lusaka, Government Printer, 1958.

————, *Report on an Economic Survey of Nyasaland, 1958–1959* [Jack Report], C. Fed. 132, [Salisbury, 1959].

Federation of Rhodesia and Nyasaland, Central Statistical Office, *Census of Population, 1956*, Salisbury, 1960.

————, *Monthly Digest of Statistics*, Salisbury.

————, *National Accounts of the Federation of Rhodesia and Nyasaland, 1954–1959*, Salisbury, 1960.

————, *Preliminary Results of the Federal Census of Population and of Employees: (1) Industrial and Racial Distribution of Employees*, Salisbury, 1962.

————, *Preliminary Results of the Federal Census of Population and of Employees: (2) Detailed Geographical Distribution of the Non-African Population*, Salisbury, 1962.

————, *Preliminary Results of the Federal Census of Population and of Employees: (3) Results of a Ten Per Cent Sample of the Non-African Census Forms*, Salisbury, 1962.

Federation of Rhodesia and Nyasaland, Commission of Inquiry into the Health and Medical Services of the Federation, *Report*, C. Fed. 139, Salisbury, Government Printer, 1960.

Federation of Rhodesia and Nyasaland, Department of the Federal Prime Minister, Economic Section, *Economic Survey of Livingstone*, Salisbury, Government Printer, 1957.

Federation of Rhodesia and Nyasaland, Department of the Prime

Minister and Cabinet Office, Economic Section, *Economic Survey of Broken Hill,* Salisbury, Government Printer, 1958.

Federation of Rhodesia and Nyasaland, Federal Assembly, *Debates* [Federal Hansard], Salisbury, Parliamentary Printers.

Federation of Rhodesia and Nyasaland, Ministry of Economic Affairs, *Economic Report* [Annual], Salisbury.

Federation of Rhodesia and Nyasaland, Ministry of Education, *Annual Report,* Salisbury.

Fox, Wilson, *Memorandum on Problems of Development and Policy,* Printed for the Use of the Directors, British South Africa Company, London, 1910. Copy in Central African Archives library, Salisbury.

Library of Congress, Reference Department, General Reference and Bibliography Division, *The Rhodesias and Nyasaland: A Guide to Official Publications,* comp. Audrey A. Walker, African Section, Washington, D.C., Government Printing Office, 1965.

Lusaka, Medical Officer of Health, *Annual Report, 1960,* Lusaka, 1961.

————, *Annual Report, Years 1957–1958–1959,* Lusaka, 1960.

Lusaka, Municipal Council, *Minute of His Worship the Mayor for the Year ended 31st March, 1959,* Lusaka, 1959.

————, *Minute of His Worship the Mayor for the Year ended 31st March, 1960,* Lusaka, 1960.

————, *Valuation Roll,* December 1958.

Malawi, *Budget 1966: Background Information,* Treasury Document No. 5, Zomba, Government Press.

Malawi, Ministry of Finance, *Quarterly Digest of Statistics,* Zomba.

Northern Rhodesia, *African Affairs: Annual Report, 1959,* Lusaka, Government Printer, 1960.

————, *Census of Population,* 1911, 1921, 1931, 1946, 1951.

————, *Election Roll of Ordinary and Special Voters Entitled to Vote at Elections of Elected Members of the Legislative Council of Northern Rhodesia, 1959,* Lusaka, Government Printer, 1959.

————, *Government Gazette,* Lusaka.

Northern Rhodesia, Central Race Relations Advisory and Conciliation Committee, *Annual Report* (for 1957 through 1960), Lusaka, Government Printer.

Northern Rhodesia, Commission of Enquiry into the Closed Townships, *Report,* 1948.

Northern Rhodesia, Commission of Inquiry into the Cost of Living (Harry R. Burrows, Chairman), *Final Report,* Lusaka, Government Printer, 1950.

Northern Rhodesia, Committee Appointed to Inquire into the Businesses Ordinance, *Report,* Lusaka, Government Printer, 1959.

Northern Rhodesia, Committee Appointed to Investigate the Extent to Which Racial Discrimination is Practiced in Shops and in Other Similar Business Premises (B. P. de O'Byrne, Chairman), *Report*, Lusaka, Government Printer, 1956.

Northern Rhodesia, Department of Labour, *Annual Report*, Lusaka.

Northern Rhodesia, High Court, *Law Reports of Northern Rhodesia, in the Exercise of its Original, Revisional, and Appellate Jurisdiction, 1949–1954*, J. G. Fearnley Scarr, ed., *5*, Lusaka, Government Printer, 1958.

Northern Rhodesia, Legislative Council, *Official Verbatim Report of the Debates* [Northern Rhodesia Hansard], Lusaka, Government Printer.

Northern Rhodesia, Ministry of African Education, *Triennial Survey, 1958 to 1960 Inclusive, Including Statistics for 1960*, Lusaka, Government Printer, 1961.

Northern Rhodesia, Ministry of Local Government and Social Welfare, *Annual Report of the Commissioner for Local Government*, Lusaka, Government Printer.

———, *Annual Report of the Director of Social Welfare*, Lusaka, Government Printer.

———, *Report on the Preliminary Investigation into the Complaints as to the Conduct and Management of the Affairs of the Municipal Council of Luanshya*, Lusaka, 1959.

Northern Rhodesia, Trades Licensing Committee, *Report*, Lusaka, Government Printer, 1946.

Nyasaland, *Report on the Census*, 1901, 1911, 1921, 1926, 1931, 1946.

Nyasaland Commission of Inquiry, *Report* [Devlin Commission Report], Cmnd. 814, London, Her Majesty's Stationery Office, 1959.

Rhodesia, Central Statistical Office, *1961 Census of the European, Asian, and Coloured Population*, Salisbury, [1965?].

———, *Final Report of the September, 1961 Census of Employees*, Salisbury, 1965.

———, *Monthly Digest of Statistics*, Salisbury.

Rhodesia-Nyasaland Royal Commission, *Report* [Bledisloe Commission Report], Cmnd. 5949, London, His Majesty's Stationery Office, 1939.

Southern Rhodesia, *Census of Population*, 1901, 1911, 1921, 1926, 1931, 1936, 1941, 1946, 1951.

Southern Rhodesia, Central Statistical Office, *National Accounts and Balance of Payments of Northern Rhodesia, Nyasaland and Southern Rhodesia, 1954–1963*, Salisbury, 1964.

Southern Rhodesia, Department of Statistics, *Statistical Year Book of Southern Rhodesia, 1938; The Official Annual of the Social and Economic Conditions of the Colony,* Salisbury, Government Stationery Office, 1938.

Southern Rhodesia, Legislative Assembly, Select Committee on Disabilities of Eurafrican, Coloured and Asian Communities, *First Report, Second Report, Third Report,* Salisbury, Government Printer, 1959–60.

Southern Rhodesia, Native Production and Trade Commission, *Report, 1944,* Salisbury, 1945.

Union of South Africa, Bureau of Census and Statistics, *Union Statistics for Fifty Years: Jubilee Issue, 1919–1960,* Pretoria, Government Printer, 1960.

United States Department of Commerce, Bureau of Foreign Commerce, *Investment in Federation of Rhodesia and Nyasaland; Basic Information for United States Businessmen,* Washington, D.C., Government Printing Office, 1956.

United States Department of Labor, Bureau of Labor Statistics, *Bibliography on Labor in Africa, 1960–64,* Bulletin 1473, Washington, D.C., Government Printing Office, 1965.

Zambia, *Preliminary Report of the May/June 1963 Census of Africans in Northern Rhodesia,* Lusaka, 1964.

——, *Second Report of the May/June 1963 Census of Africans in Northern Rhodesia,* Lusaka, 1964.

Zambia, Central Statistical Office, *Final Report of the 1961 Census of Non-Africans and Employees,* Lusaka, 1965.

——, *Monthly Digest of Statistics,* Lusaka.

Zambia, National Assembly, *Official Verbatim Report of the Debates* [Zambia Hansard], Lusaka, Government Printer.

WORKS ON INDIA AND INDIANS

Asian Civil Rights League, "Memorandum Submitted by the Asian Civil Rights League to the Select Committee on Disabilities of the Asian Community," Bulawayo, 1959 [mimeographed].

"Asians v. Asians," *Time* (July 17, 1964), p. 29.

Benedict, Burton, "Factions in Indian and Overseas Indian Societies: V. Factionalism in Mauritian Villages," *British Journal of Sociology, 8* (1957), 328–42.

——, *Indians in a Plural Society: A Report on Mauritius,* Colonial Office: Colonial Research Studies, 34, London, Her Majesty's Stationery Office, 1961.

Berreman, Gerald D., "Caste in India and the United States," *American Journal of Sociology, 66* (1960), 120–27.

Bharati, Agehananda, "Patterns of Identification among the East African Asians," *Sociologus, 15* (1965), 128–42.

————, "The Indians in East Africa: A Survey of Problems of Transition and Adaptation," *Sociologus, 14* (1964), 169–77.

————, "The Unwanted Elite of East Africa: An Indian Minority's Wealth and Sense of Superiority Stir African Resentment in Kenya, Uganda, Tanzania," *Trans-Action* (July–August 1966), pp. 37–41.

Boute, Joseph, *La Démographie de la branche indo-pakistanaise d'Afrique,* Louvain-Paris, Editions Nauwelaerts, 1965.

Calpin, G. H., *Indians in South Africa,* Pietermaritzburg, Shuter and Shooter, 1949.

Crowley, Daniel J., "Cultural Assimilation in a Multiracial Society," *Annals of the New York Academy of Sciences, 83* (1960), 850–54.

Cumpston, I. M., "A Survey of Indian Immigration to British Tropical Colonies to 1910," *Population Studies, 10* (1956), 158–65.

Davis, Kingsley, *The Population of India and Pakistan,* Princeton, Princeton University Press, 1951.

Delf, George, *Asians in East Africa,* London, Oxford University Press, 1963.

Desai, Rashmi, *Indian Immigrants in Britain,* London, Oxford University Press, 1963.

Dotson, Floyd and Lillian Dotson, "Cultural Values and Housing Needs," in Raymond Apthorpe, ed., *Social Research and Community Development, Based on the Fifteenth Conference of the Rhodes-Livingstone Institute for Social Research,* Lusaka, Rhodes-Livingstone Institute, 1961.

————, "Indians and Coloureds in Rhodesia and Nyasaland," *Race* (Journal of the Institute of Race Relations, London), *5* (July 1963), 61–75; also in Pierre L. van den Berghe, ed., *Africa: Social Problems of Change and Conflict,* San Francisco, Chandler, 1965, pp. 267–82; and in Milton L. Barron, ed., *Minorities in a Changing World,* New York, Alfred A. Knopf, 1967, pp. 77–95.

Dubois, Abbé J. A., *Hindu Manners, Customs and Ceremonies, Translated from the Author's Later French Ms. and Edited with Notes, Corrections, and Biography,* by Henry K. Beauchamp, Oxford, Clarendon Press, 1906.

Eglar, Zekiye, *A Punjabi Village in Pakistan,* New York, Columbia University Press, 1960.

Firth, Raymond, "Factions in Indian and Overseas Indian Societies: I. Introduction," *British Journal of Sociology, 8* (1957), 291–95.

Fischer, Louis, *Life of Mahatma Gandhi,* New York, Harper, 1950.

Gandhi, M. K., *Gandhi's Autobiography: The Story of My Experi-*

ments with Truth, trans. Mahadev Desai, Washington, D.C., Public Affairs Press, 1948.

Ghai, Dharam P., ed., *Portrait of a Minority: Asians in East Africa,* Nairobi, Oxford University Press, 1965.

——— and Yash P. Ghai, "Asians in East Africa: Problems and Prospects," *Journal of Modern African Studies, 3* (1965), 35–51.

Gillion, K. L., "The Sources of Indian Emigration to Fiji," *Population Studies, 10* (1956), 139–57.

Hazareesingh, K., "The Religion and Culture of Indian Immigrants in Mauritius and the Effect of Social Change," *Comparative Studies in Society and History, 8* (1966), 241–57.

Hollingsworth, L. W., *The Asians of East Africa,* London, Macmillan, 1960.

Huttenback, Robert A., "Indians in South Africa, 1860–1914: The British Imperial Philosophy on Trial," *English Historical Review, 81* (1966), 273–91.

Hutton, John Henry, *Caste in India: Its Nature, Function, and Origins,* Bombay, Oxford University Press, 1961.

Jayawardena, Chandra, "Religious Belief and Social Change: Aspects of the Development of Hinduism in British Guiana," *Comparative Studies in Society and History, 8* (1966), 211–40.

Klass, Morton, "East and West Indian: Cultural Complexity in Trinidad," *Annals of the New York Academy of Sciences, 83* (1960), 855–61.

———, *East Indians in Trinidad: A Study of Cultural Persistence,* New York, Columbia University Press, 1961.

Kondapi, C., *Indians Overseas 1838–1949,* New Delhi, Indian Council of World Affairs, 1951.

Kuper, Hilda, *Indian People in Natal,* Natal, University Press, 1960.

Lalloo, Chagan, "The Hindu Family in S. Rhodesia—Traditional versus Modern," mimeographed paper, Lund, Sweden, University of Lund, Department of Sociology, December 1963.

Lamb, Helen B., "The Indian Merchant," *Journal of American Folklore, 71* (1958), 231–40.

Mahajani, Usha, *The Role of Indian Minorities in Burma and Malaya,* Ph.D. dissertation, Johns Hopkins University, 1957, issued by Institute of Pacific Relations, New York, Bombay, Vora, 1960.

Marriott, McKim, "Caste and Ranking and Community Structure in Five Regions of India and Pakistan," *Bulletin of the Deccan College Research Institute, 19* (1958), 29–105.

———, "Little Communities in an Indigenous Civilization," in McKim Marriott, ed., *Village India: Studies in the Little Com-*

munity, American Anthropological Association Memoir No. 83, Menasha, Wisconsin, 1955, pp. 171–222.

Martin, C. J., "A Demographic Study of an Immigrant Community: The Indian Population of British East Africa," *Population Studies, 6* (1953), 233–47.

Mayer, Adrian C., *Caste and Kinship in Central India: A Village and Its Region,* Berkeley, University of California Press, 1960.

———, "Factions in Indian and Overseas Indian Societies: IV. Factions in Fiji Indian Rural Settlements," *British Journal of Sociology, 8* (1957), 317–28.

———, *Peasants in the Pacific: A Study of Fiji Indian Rural Society,* Berkeley, University of California Press, 1961.

Meer, Fatima, "African and Indian in Durban," *Africa South, 4* (July–September 1960), 30–41.

Morris, H. S., "Factions in Indian and Overseas Indian Societies: III. Communal Rivalry among Indians in Uganda," *British Journal of Sociology, 8* (1957), 306–17.

———, "Indians in East Africa: A Study in a Plural Society," *British Journal of Sociology, 7* (1956), 194–211.

———, "The Divine Kingship of the Aga Khan: A Study of Theocracy in East Africa," *Southwestern Journal of Anthropology, 14* (1958), 454–72.

———, "The Indian Family in Uganda," *American Anthropologist, 61* (1959), 779–89.

Naik, T. B., "Religion of the Anavils of Surat," *Journal of American Folklore, 71* (1958), 389–96.

O'Malley, L. S. S., *Modern India and the West: A Study of the Interaction of Their Civilizations,* London, Oxford University Press, 1941.

Palmer, Mabel, *The History of the Indians in Natal,* Natal Regional Survey 10, Cape Town, Oxford University Press, 1957.

———, Hilda Kuper, B. A. Naidoo, J. Naidoo, A. D. Lazarus, and S. Cooppan, *The Indian as a South African: A Symposium,* Johannesburg, South African Institute of Race Relations, 1956.

Parmar, L. G., "Memorandum to the [Monckton] Commission on Constitutional Changes," mimeographed, Luanshya, 1960.

Patel, Hasu, "Changing Asian Politics," *Central African Examiner* (August 27, 1960), pp. 14–15.

Pocock, David F., "Difference in East Africa: A Study of Caste and Religion in Modern Indian Society," *Southwestern Journal of Anthropology, 13* (1957), 289–300.

———, "Factions in Indian and Overseas Indian Societies: II. The Basis of Faction in Gujerat," *British Journal of Sociology, 8* (1957), 295–306.

————, "Inclusion and Exclusion: A Process in the Caste System of Gujerat," *Southwestern Journal of Anthropology, 13* (1957), 19–31.

Schwartz, Barton M., "Caste and Endogamy in Trinidad," *Southwestern Journal of Anthropology, 20* (1964), 58–66.

Sheean, Vincent, *Mahatma Gandhi: A Great Life in Brief*, New York, Alfred A. Knopf, 1955.

Smythe, Hugh H., "The Indian in Africa: A Problem for Sociological Research," *Sociology and Social Research, 39* (1954), 32–35.

Southern Rhodesia Asian Organisation, "Memorandum—January, 1960, Submitted to the Monckton Commission—1960," mimeographed, Bulawayo, 1960.

Srinivas, M. N., *Religion and Society among the Coorgs of South India*, Oxford, Clarendon Press, 1952.

————, "The Social System of a Mysore Village," in McKim Marriott, ed., *Village India: Studies in the Little Community*, American Anthropological Association Memoir No. 83, Menasha, Wisconsin, 1955, pp. 1–35.

Tandberg, Olof G., "The Duka-wallah: The Backbone of East Africa's Early Economy," in *Asians in East and Central Africa, A Directory*, by Shanti Pandit, Nairobi, Panco Publications, 1961.

Weber, Max, *Religion of India: The Sociology of Hinduism and Buddhism*, trans. and ed. Hans H. Gerth and Don Martindale, Glencoe, Ill., Free Press, 1958.

OTHER SOURCES

African Mail (later as *Central African Mail, Zambia Mail*), Lusaka.

Annual Register: A Review of Public Events at Home and Abroad for the Year 1948, London, Longmans, Green, 1949.

Arensberg, Conrad, "The Community Study Method," *American Journal of Sociology, 60* (1954), 109–24; reprinted in C. M. Arensberg and S. T. Kimball, *Culture and Community*, New York, Harcourt, Brace, and World, 1965.

Barber, William J., "Economic Rationality and Behavior Patterns in an Underdeveloped Area: A Case Study of African Economic Behavior in the Rhodesias," *Economic Development and Cultural Change, 8* (1960), 237–51.

————, *The Economy of British Central Africa: A Case Study of Economic Development in a Dualistic Society*, Stanford, Stanford University Press, 1961.

Barnes, J. A., *Politics in a Changing Society: The Political History of the Fort Jameson Ngoni*, London, Oxford University Press, 1954.

Becker, Howard, *Man in Reciprocity: Introductory Lectures on Culture, Society, and Personality*, New York, Praeger, 1956.

Blake, Judith and Kingsley Davis, "Norms, Values, and Sanctions," in *Handbook of Modern Sociology*, ed. Robert E. L. Faris, Chicago, Rand McNally, 1964, pp. 456–84.

Braithwaite, Lloyd, "Social Stratification and Cultural Pluralism," *Annals of the New York Academy of Sciences, 83* (1960), 816–31.

Bulawayo Chronicle, Bulawayo.

Bullock, Charles, *The Mashona and the Matabele* (1st ed., 1927), Cape Town, Juta, 1950.

Campbell, Alex, "Who's Afraid of China? Many Americans, Not So Many Asians," *New Republic* (April 9, 1966), pp. 12–16.

Cancian, Francesca, "Functional Analysis of Change," *American Sociological Review, 25* (1960), 818–27.

Central African Examiner, Salisbury.

Central African Post, Lusaka.

Churchill, Winston S., *My African Journey*, London, Hodder and Stoughton, 1908.

Clark, Percy M., *The Autobiography of an Old Drifter; The Life Story of Percy M. Clark of Victoria Falls*, London, George C. Harrap, 1936.

Clegg, Edward, *Race and Politics: Partnership in the Federation of Rhodesia and Nyasaland*, London, Oxford University Press, 1960.

Clements, Frederic E. and Victor E. Shelford, *Bio-Ecology*, New York, J. Wiley, 1939.

Clutton-Brock, Guy, *Dawn in Nyasaland*, London, Hodder and Stoughton, 1959.

Colson, Elizabeth and Max Gluckman, eds., *Seven Tribes of British Central Africa*, Manchester, Manchester University Press, 1951.

Coon, Carleton S., *Caravan: The Story of the Middle East*, New York, Henry Holt, 1951.

Coser, Lewis, *The Functions of Social Conflict*, Glencoe, Ill., Free Press, 1956.

Creighton, T. R. M., *Southern Rhodesia and the Central African Federation: The Anatomy of Partnership*, New York, Praeger, 1960.

Crowley, Daniel J., "Plural and Differential Acculturation in Trinidad," *American Anthropologist, 59* (1957), 817–24.

Dahrendorf, Ralf, *Class and Class Conflict in Industrial Society*, Stanford, Stanford University Press, 1959.

———, "Out of Utopia: Toward a Reorientation of Sociological Analysis," *American Journal of Sociology, 64* (1958), 115–27.

Davis, Allison, Burleigh B. Gardner, and Mary R. Gardner, *Deep South*, Chicago, University of Chicago Press, 1941.

Davis, Kingsley, "The Myth of Functional Analysis as a Special Method in Sociology and Anthropology," *American Sociological Review, 24* (1959), 757–72.

Dollard, John, *Caste and Class in a Southern Town,* 2nd ed. New York, Harper, 1949.

Dotson, Floyd, "Los Modelos de sociedad y la realidad social de los nuevos estados de Africa," *Revista Mexicana de Sociología, 25* (1963), 573–90.

———, "Rationality and Conflict," paper presented to the XVI Congreso Nacional de Sociología, Veracruz, Mexico, November 22–26, 1965.

"Enlightened Educators: Edwin Townsend-Coles Reviews the De Kiewiet Report," *Central African Examiner* (February 1963), pp. 18–19.

Epstein, A. L., "Linguistic Innovation and Culture on the Copperbelt, Northern Rhodesia," *Southwestern Journal of Anthropology, 15* (1959), 235–53.

———, *Politics in an Urban African Community,* Manchester, Manchester University Press, 1958.

Franck, Thomas M., *Race and Nationalism: The Struggle for Power in Rhodesia-Nyasaland,* London, George Allen and Unwin, 1960.

Franklin, Harry, *Unholy Wedlock: The Failure of the Central African Federation,* London, George Allen and Unwin, 1963.

Furnivall, J. S., *Colonial Policy and Practice: A Comparative Study of Burma and Netherlands India,* New York, New York University Press, 1956.

Gann, Lewis H., *A History of Northern Rhodesia: Early Days to 1953,* London, Chatto and Windus, 1964.

———, *A History of Southern Rhodesia: Early Days to 1934,* London, Chatto and Windus, 1965.

———, "Liberal Interpretations of South African History," *Human Problems in British Central Africa, Rhodes-Livingstone Journal, 25* (1959), 40–58.

———, *The Birth of a Plural Society: The Development of Northern Rhodesia under the British South Africa Company 1894–1914,* Manchester, Manchester University Press, 1958.

——— and Peter Duignan, *White Settlers in Tropical Africa,* Penguin African Series, WA 13, Baltimore, Penguin Books, 1962.

Gelfand, Michael, *Northern Rhodesia in the Days of the Charter: A Medical and Social Study, 1878–1924,* Oxford, Blackwell, 1961.

Gerth, Hans and C. Wright Mills, *Character and Social Structure: The Psychology of Social Institutions,* New York, Harcourt, Brace, 1953.

Gluckman, Max, *Analysis of a Social Situation in Modern Zululand,*

Rhodes-Livingstone Paper No. 28, Manchester, Manchester University Press, 1958; first appeared in *Bantu Studies, 14* (1940).

————, "From Tribe to Town," *Nation,* Sydney, Australia (September 24, 1960), pp. 7–12.

————, "Malinowski's 'Functional' Analysis of Social Change," *Africa, 17* (1947), 103–21.

————, *The Judicial Process among the Barotse of Northern Rhodesia,* Manchester, Manchester University Press, 1955.

Goffman, Erving, *The Presentation of the Self in Everyday Life,* New York, Doubleday Anchor, 1959.

Goode, William J., "A Theory of Role Strains," *American Sociological Review, 25* (1960), 483–96.

Gordon, Milton M., *Assimilation in American Life: The Role of Race, Religion, and National Origins,* New York, Oxford University Press, 1964.

Gray, Richard, *The Two Nations: Aspects of the Development of Race Relations in the Rhodesias and Nyasaland,* London, Oxford University Press, 1960.

Gunther, John, *Inside Africa,* New York, Harper, 1955.

Gussman, Boris, *Out in the Mid-day Sun,* New York, Oxford University Press, 1963.

Hall, Richard, *Kaunda: Founder of Zambia,* Lusaka, Longmans of Zambia, 1964.

————, *Zambia,* New York, Praeger, 1965.

Hanna, A. J., *The Beginnings of Nyasaland and North-eastern Rhodesia, 1859–95,* Oxford, Clarendon Press, 1956.

————, *The Story of the Rhodesias and Nyasaland,* London, Faber and Faber, 1960.

Herberg, Will, *Protestant-Catholic-Jew,* Garden City, N. Y., Doubleday, 1955.

Holleman, J. F., *Shona Customary Law,* London, Oxford University Press, 1952.

Homans, George C., "Bringing Men Back In," *American Sociological Review, 29* (1964), 809–18.

————, "Contemporary Theory in Sociology," in *Handbook of Modern Sociology,* ed. Robert E. L. Faris, Chicago, Rand McNally, 1964, pp. 951–77.

————, *The Human Group,* New York, Harcourt, Brace, 1950.

————, *Social Behavior: Its Elementary Forms,* New York, Harcourt, Brace, and World, 1961.

————, "The Strategy of Industrial Sociology," *American Journal of Sociology, 54* (1949), 330–38.

Huxley, Elspeth, *White Man's Country: Lord Delamere and the Making of Kenya,* 2 vols. London, Macmillan, 1935.

Johnston, Harry H., *British Central Africa: An Attempt to Give Some Account of a Portion of the Territories under British Influence North of the Zambezi*, London, Methuen, 1897.

Kaunda, Kenneth D., *Zambia Shall Be Free: An Autobiography*, New York, Praeger, 1963.

Kirk, Donald, "Indonesia's Chinese Are People Without a Country," *New York Times Magazine* (October 23, 1966), pp. 32 ff.

Kohn, Hans, *The Idea of Nationalism: A Study in Its Origins and Background*, New York, Macmillan, 1961.

Kroeber, A. L., *Anthropology*, New York, Harcourt, Brace, 1948.

—— and Clyde Kluckhohn, *Culture: A Critical Review of Concepts and Definitions*, New York, Vintage Books, 1963.

Kuper, H., A. J. B. Hughes, J. van Velsen, *The Shona and Ndebele of Southern Rhodesia*, London, Oxford University Press, 1954.

Kuper, Leo, *Passive Resistance in South Africa*, New Haven, Yale University Press, 1957.

——, "Some Aspects of Urban Plural Societies in Africa," in Robert A. Lystad, ed., *The African World: A Survey of Social Research*, New York, Frederick A. Praeger, 1965, pp. 107–30.

—— Hilstan Watts, and Ronald Davies, *Durban: A Study in Racial Ecology*, New York, Columbia University Press, 1958.

Lasker, Bruno, *Asia on the Move: Population Pressure, Migration, and Resettlement in Eastern Asia under the Influence of Want and War*, New York, H. Holt, 1945.

Levin, L. S., ed., *Central African Airways Guide to the Federation of Rhodesia and Nyasaland*, Salisbury, A. J. Levin, 1960.

Lewin, Kurt, *Resolving Social Conflicts: Selected Papers on Group Dynamics*, New York, Harper, 1948.

Leys, Colin, *European Politics in Southern Rhodesia*, Oxford, Clarendon Press, 1959.

Linton, Ralph, *The Cultural Background of Personality*, New York, Appleton-Century, 1945.

——, *The Study of Man: An Introduction*, New York, Appleton-Century, 1936.

Lipscomb, J. F., *White Africans*, London, Faber and Faber, 1955.

Lipset, Seymour M., *The First New Nation: The United States in Historical and Comparative Perspective*, New York, Basic Books, 1963.

"Literate Masses or Educated Few: How the Territories Differ in Policy," *Central African Examiner* (January 1962), pp. 14–15.

Lockwood, David, "Some Remarks on 'The Social System'," *British Journal of Sociology*, 7 (1956), 134–46.

Lowie, Robert H., *Social Organization*, New York, Rinehart, 1948.

Lynd, Robert S. and Helen M. Lynd, *Middletown: A Study in American Culture*, New York, Harcourt, Brace, 1929.

McKay, Vernon, *Africa in World Politics*, New York, Harper and Row, 1963.

Mason, Philip, *Birth of a Dilemma: The Conquest and Settlement of Rhodesia*, London, Oxford University Press, 1958.

———, *Year of Decision: Rhodesia and Nyasaland in 1960*, London, Oxford University Press, 1960.

Mead, George Herbert, *Mind, Self and Society from the Standpoint of a Social Behaviorist*, Chicago, University of Chicago Press, 1934.

Mead, Margaret, "National Character," in *Anthropology Today*, under A. L. Kroeber, Chicago, University of Chicago Press, 1953, pp. 642–67.

Mills, C. Wright, *The Sociological Imagination*, New York, Grove Press, 1961.

Mitchell, J. C., *The Kalela Dance*, Rhodes-Livingstone Paper No. 27, Manchester, Manchester University Press, 1956.

———, *The Yao Village: A Study in the Social Structure of a Nyasaland Tribe*, Manchester, Manchester University Press, 1956.

Moore, Wilbert E., *Social Change*, Englewood Cliffs, N. J., Prentice-Hall, 1963.

Moynihan, Patrick and Nathan Glazer, *Beyond the Melting Pot: The Negroes, Puerto Ricans, Jews, Italians, and Irish of New York City*, Cambridge, Mass., M. I. T. and Harvard University Presses, 1963.

Mulford, David C., *The Northern Rhodesia General Election 1962*, Nairobi, Oxford University Press, 1964.

Murphy, Gardner, *Personality: A Biosocial Approach to Origins and Structure*, New York, Harper, 1947.

Nadel, S. F., *The Foundations of Social Anthropology*, London, Cohen and West, 1951.

———, *The Theory of Social Structure*, Glencoe, Ill., Free Press, 1957.

New York Times, New York.

Northern News, Ndola.

Nyasaland Times, Blantyre.

Ogburn, W. F., *Social Change: With Respect to Culture and Original Nature*, New York, Huebsch, 1922.

Oliver, Roland, *Sir Harry Johnston and the Scramble for Africa*, London, Chatto and Windus, 1957.

Opler, Morris E., "The Human Being in Culture Theory," *American Anthropologist, 66* (1964), 507–28.

Park, Robert E., *Human Communities: The City and Human Ecology*, Glencoe, Ill., Free Press, 1952.

Parsons, Talcott, "Full Citizenship for the Negro American? A Sociological Problem," *Daedalus, 94* (1965), 1009–54.

———, *The Social System,* Glencoe, Ill., Free Press, 1951.

Patterson, Sheila, *Colour and Culture in South Africa: A Study of the Cape Coloured People within the Social Structure of the Union of South Africa,* London, Routledge and Kegan Paul, 1953.

Powdermaker, Hortense, *Copper Town: Changing Africa, the Human Situation on the Rhodesian Copperbelt,* New York, Harper and Row, 1962.

Rayner, William, *The Tribe and Its Successors: An Account of African Traditional Life and European Settlement in Southern Rhodesia,* New York, Praeger, 1962.

Read, Margaret, *Children of Their Fathers: Growing up among the Ngoni of Nyasaland,* New Haven, Yale University Press, 1960.

Reader, D. H., *The Black Man's Portion: History, Demography, and Living Conditions in the Native Locations of East London, Cape Province,* Cape Town, Oxford University Press, 1961.

Redfield, Robert, *Peasant Society and Culture: An Anthropological Approach to Civilization,* Chicago, University of Chicago Press, 1956.

Rex, John, "The Plural Society in Sociological Theory," *British Journal of Sociology, 10* (1959), 114–24.

Richards, Audrey I., *Land, Labour, and Diet in Northern Rhodesia,* London, Oxford University Press, 1939.

Robinson, Kenneth, *The Dilemmas of Trusteeship: Aspects of British Colonial Policy between the Wars,* London, Oxford University Press, 1965.

Rogers, Cyril A. and C. Frantz, *Racial Themes in Southern Rhodesia: The Attitudes and Behavior of the White Population,* New Haven and London, Yale University Press, 1962.

Rotberg, Robert I., *The Rise of Nationalism in Central Africa: The Making of Malawi and Zambia, 1873–1964,* Cambridge, Mass., Harvard University Press, 1965.

Ryder, Norman B., "The Cohort as a Concept in the Study of Social Change," *American Sociological Review, 30* (1965), 843–61.

St. John Wood, Anthony, *Northern Rhodesia: The Human Background,* London, Pall Mall Press, 1961.

Sampson, Richard, *So This Was Lusaakas: The Story of the Capital of Northern Rhodesia to 1936,* Lusaka, Lusaka Publicity Association, 1959.

Smelser, Neil, *Social Change in the Industrial Revolution: An Application of Theory to the British Cotton Industry,* Chicago, University of Chicago Press, 1959.

Smith, M. G., "Social and Cultural Pluralism," *Annals of the New*

York Academy of Sciences, 83 (1960), 763–77; also in Pierre L. van den Berghe, ed., *Africa: Social Problems of Change and Conflict,* San Francisco, Chandler, 1965, pp. 58–76.

———, *The Plural Society in the British West Indies,* Berkeley, University of California Press, 1965.

Sofer, Cyril, "Working Groups in a Plural Society," *Industrial and Labor Relations Review, 8* (1954), 68–78.

Spiro, Herbert J., "The Rhodesias and Nyasaland," in Gwendolen M. Carter, ed., *Five African States: Responses to Diversity,* Ithaca, Cornell University Press, 1963, pp. 361–470.

Stouffer, Samuel A. et al. *The American Soldier: Studies in Social Psychology in World War II,* vols. 1–2 Princeton, Princeton University Press, 1949.

Sumner, William Graham, *Folkways,* Boston, Ginn, 1906.

Taft, Donald R. and Richard Robbins, *International Migrations: The Immigrant in the Modern World,* New York, Ronald Press, 1955.

Turner, Ralph, *The Great Cultural Traditions: The Foundations of Civilization,* 2 vols. New York, McGraw-Hill, 1941.

Van den Berghe, Pierre L., *Caneville: The Social Structure of a South African Town,* Middletown, Conn., Wesleyan University Press, 1964.

———, "Dialectic and Functionalism: Toward a Theoretical Synthesis," *American Sociological Review, 28* (1963), 695–705.

———, *South Africa, A Study in Conflict,* Middletown, Conn., Wesleyan University Press, 1965.

———, "Toward a Sociology of Africa," *Social Forces, 43* (1964), 11–18.

Van Velsen, J., *The Politics of Kinship: A Study in Social Manipulation among the Lakeside Tonga,* Manchester, Manchester University Press, 1964.

Vidich, Arthur J., Joseph Bensman, and Maurice R. Stein, *Reflections on Community Studies,* New York, John Wiley, 1964.

Wagley, Charles and Marvin Harris, *Minorities in the New World: Six Case Studies,* New York, Columbia University Press, 1958.

Walker, Eric A., *A History of Southern Africa,* London, Longmans, 1959.

Wallace, Anthony F. C., *Culture and Personality,* New York, Random House, 1961.

Weber, Max, *Ancient Judaism,* Glencoe, Ill., Free Press, 1952.

———, *General Economic History,* New York, Collier Books, 1961.

Westie, Frank R., "Race and Ethnic Relations," in *Handbook of Modern Sociology,* ed. Robert E. L. Faris, Chicago, Rand McNally, 1964, pp. 576–618.

Whyte, William F., "Parsons' Theory Applied to Organizations," in Max Black, ed., *The Social Theories of Talcott Parsons: A Critical Examination,* Englewood Cliffs, N. J., Prentice-Hall, 1961, pp. 250–67.

Wills, A. J., *An Introduction to the History of Central Africa,* London, Oxford University Press, 1964.

Wilson, Godfrey and Monica Wilson, *The Analysis of Social Change,* London, Cambridge University Press, 1945.

Wilson, N. H., *The Central African Dilemma: A Preliminary Study in the Survival of Western Civilization in Central Africa,* pamphlet, publisher not indicated, 1954.

Winder, R. Bayly, "The Lebanese in West Africa," *Comparative Studies in Society and History, 4* (1962), 296–333.

INDEX

Acculturation: territorial and religious differences in, 53–54, 119; male ambivalence toward, 186; of African-born, 211–12; generational differences in, among Indian-born, 212; European customers and, 232–33; of subordinate groups in plural societies, 257–58, 259, 342–43; and European-standards rule, 300; of African elite, 343–44

Adaptiveness: of socio-cultural characteristics for trade, 66–67; of religious culture and organization among Muslims, 121–24; of culture, 400–01

African Lakes Company: establishment of, 21; in Northeastern Rhodesia, 50

African National Congress, boycott of *1956*, 330–31

Afrikaners: as early trader-adventurers, 22–23, 79; compared with British, 315, 355n., 358n.

Aga Khan, sacred lineage of, 110n.

Agriculture, African, in Nyasaland, 46n., 47, 60, 352–53

Agriculture, European: and mining in Rhodesias, 20, 21; in Nyasaland, 21, 46–47; exodus from Zambia, 358–59n.

Ahimsa, rule of, in diet, 102–03

Alcohol: sale of, by Indians, 64, 118; and social relations with Europeans, 253–54; at multiracial clubs, 256 and n., racial discrimination in sale of, 256n., 285, 314; Indians on, among

Africans, 265, 277; increase in open use of, 359

Amba Mata, vow to, for hair-cutting ceremony, 91–92, 100

Anavils: position of, on caste, 127–28, 149 and n., 194, 195; representation of, 131, 135, 136; in India, 135; as community leaders, 135, 149, 150

Apartheid, likelihood of, in Rhodesia, 355n.

Arabic, prayers and Koran in, 122 and n.

Arensberg, Conrad, on community-study method, 11n.

Argyle, W. John, on Africans and prices, 271

Artisans, European perception of Indians as, 85–86

Arya Samaj, among overseas Indians, 104n.

Asceticism: ideals of, among Patidars, 132, 143–44; and sexual relations with Africans, 283; trend away from, 360–61

Asian, Asiatic, terminological reference of, 40n.

Athletic clubs. *See* Clubs, athletic

Aum: God in formless state, 93; symbol for, in temple, 97–98

Automobiles: as status symbol, 216–17, 360–61; with petrol in Rhodesia, 350

Banda, Kamuzu Hastings, Dr.: political decisions by, 353–54; mutual attitudes of, and Indians,

427